AF552597

LORD HASTINGS AND HIS ADMINISTRATIVE MEASURES

Encyclopaedic History of Indian Freedom Movement Series

LORD HASTINGS AND HIS ADMINISTRATIVE MEASURES

Edited by

OM PRAKASH

ANMOL PUBLICATIONS PVT. LTD.

NEW DELHI - 110 002 (INDIA)

ANMOL PUBLICATIONS PVT. LTD.
4374/4B, Ansari Road, Daryaganj
New Delhi - 110 002
Ph.: 23261597, 23278000
Visit us at: www.anmolpublications.com

Lord Hastings and His Administrative Measures

First Edition, 2004

ISBN 81-261-1513-0

PRINTED IN INDIA

Published by J.L. Kumar for Anmol Publications Pvt. Ltd., New Delhi - 110 002 and Printed at Mehra Offset Press, Delhi.

Contents

Preface

'Golden bird' as India was known in yore days, rich in natural resources and well-developed cottage industries it was considered an affluent country. Indian spices, fabrics and other handicrafts were in great demand the world over. In the lure of having these goods and riches, many European powers made adventurous voyages to locate India.

The story of European expansions in Asia forms one of the great epics of modern times. India was the cornerstone of European imperialism in Asia. It was the lure of the lucrative 'Indian trade' which incited European adventurers to seek a new route to India, thus inaugurating a new era of contact between these two distant lands. Among the European empires in Asia, the British empire was the most enduring and prosperous one. And India was the finest jewel of the British dominion. It is worthwhile to remember that European exploration and adventure in the east were encouraged by the great demand in Europe for the products from Malabar like spices and calicoe cloth. Symbolically, the European age in Indian and indeed Asian history began with the landing of Vasco-de-Gama at Calicut on the 27th of May 1498. During this period, there was a continuous struggle between European traders and their native rivals and among the Europeans themselves. By the end of the eighteenth century this struggle for supremacy had been resolved in favour of the English.

The European traders were originally in the position of supplicants before the native rulers in India. For example, when William Hawkins arrived at the court of Jehangir with a letter from King James I asking for trade facilities, he had brought with him, a gift of 25,000 Gold pieces. As Lane Poole observes,

"There was nothing to suggest the most distant dream that in two centuries and a half the slight introduction Hawkins was then effecting between England and India would culminate in the sovereignty of a British Queen over the whole empire."

But unlike their European rivals like the Portuguese and the Dutch, the English made their bid for power in India only when the powerful Mughal empire had begun to decline. In any case the Portuguese and the Dutch had only small coastal settlements in India even at the height of their power and influence in this country.

By the end of the seventh Century, the Portuguese had been displaced by their Dutch rivals in Malabar and in the islands, of the East Indies. As for the Dutch, they were compelled by force of circumstances to regard the factories "which they established on the main land merely as marketing points for the products of an Empire which had its capital at Batavia in the East Indies."

Moreover, the Dutch power in India was largely jeopardised on European battle fields.

The wars with England and France drained the resources of this nation. Thus, it was left to the French to provide real opposition to the English in India.

The same pattern can be detected in the story of European activity in Malabar. Here the intensity of their rivalry was greater because of three main reasons. Malabar with its many fine harbours and backwaters was more accessible from the sea, increasing the scope for European interference.

Thus, European powers who came to India with the intention of trade snatched the political power and sovereignty from the local states, principalities and feudal lords. And established complete control over India. After over hundred years colonial rule, the feeling of national integration and freedom from the clutches of foreign power developed among the Indians. Thus, began the saga of freedom movement.

This encyclopaedic study is phased into two most significant and historic diversions having deep bearing on varied kinds of events which moulded the destiny of millions of people of Indian sub-continent. These events having complete political overtones, became a glaring phenomenon with the downfall of the Mughal Empire almost with the commencement of the 18th century. The ambitious piercing eyes of four European powers — the British, the French, the Portuguese and the Dutch—did cast upon several gainful economic successes in India.

Of these powers, the East India Company's government, with well organised force, bureaucracy and diplomats achieved phenomenal successes against their adversaries. The first phase,—therefore has been marked from Plassey to the Mutiny of 1857 (The First War of Independence) when the Company's role came to an end.

The second phase, naturally, came very much in the hands of the British Government functioning under the Whitehall and ended with the dawn of Swaraj on 15 August 1947.

This multi-volumes study would take up several themes, viz. political, socio-economic, religious, constitutional, educational, press, revolutionaries, local pioneers, legislation, revenues and judicial policy, on-going process of reaction — violent and non-violent, moderates and extremists, local and all India movements, reaction of the British Raj, efforts for conciliation, significant Acts passed by the Central Legislature, the impact of two global wars, 1914-1919 and 1939-1945; Congress, Muslim League, Hindu Mahasabha and the British Policy, a significant change in Britain soon after 1945, the Labour Government of Clement Attlee and Partition of India in August 1947.

In the first lot eleven volumes have appeared while in the present second lot ten volumes are being brought out namely the Marathas and their administration; Lord William Bentinck and Metcalf era of reforms; Raja Rammohun Roy: the reformer; Mutiny and its aftermath; History of Anglo-Sikh wars;

Emergence of Maharaja Ranjit Singh; Lord Hastings and his administrative measures; Ranjit Singh administration and British policy; British policy of intervention and expansion; and Lord Wellesley and policy of expansion.

This prestigious project is arranged, managed and looked after by a team of most dedicated and long experienced scholars of modern Indian history.

In gathering the authentic information, we have taken liberty to draw the material from the learned works of many great scholars in the field. We are deeply beholden to all those whose works are partially cited or substantially made use of in the project. I am indebted to Mr. J.L. Kumar, Managing Director, Anmol Publications Pvt. Ltd., New Delhi for his constant inspiration and moral support and finally to bring out this work. Last but not the least I am thankful to all those who have assisted me one way or other while preparing the manuscript.

—Om Prakash

1

Condition of Central India

Some attempt has already been made to explain the views and circumstances under which, after Lord Wellesley's departure, the British government determined to retire within its own administrative borders, to transact in future its political affairs upon the principle of limited liability, and to maintain, outside its actual obligations, the attitude of a placid spectator, unconcerned with the quarrels or misfortunes of his neighbours. It is a policy which from time immemorial a strong European State, placed in the midst of uncivilized rulers or races, has vainly endeavoured to uphold. It appears at first to be simple and prudent, to be dictated by enlightened self-interest, and by public morality. Unfortunately it has hitherto invariably failed to do more than check or postpone for an interval the really inevitable tendency of an organized power to override, if not to absorb, loose tribal rulerships and ephemeral despotisms, which spring up and survive merely because more durable institutions are wanting and until they are supplied. Not only, indeed, is the check temporary, the reaction is apt to produce a rebound; a halt is followed by a great stride forward, a few steps taken backward look like preparation for a longer leap; so that masterly inactivity is attributed to astute calculation, and we are often unjustly accused in India of allowing the pear to rot that it may drop the easier into our hands. It is usual to lay the blame of this invariable expansion upon those who direct imperial affairs on the frontier or in the outlying provinces, but the true impulse comes quite as often from the metropolis, where the accumulation of capital, or the impulse of national interests—of war or diplomatic complications in Europe—drives forward war and enterprise along the line of least resistance. This onward movement may be temporarily arrested by such physical obstacles as mountains or deserts, but it comes to a standstill only when the way is at last blocked by a rival power of equal calibre, or when the central forces begin to decline. The truth is that in the art of political engineering solid construction depends on the material available and on the proper adaptation of resistance to natural pressure. It is as impossible to lay down a frontier on an untenable line as to throw a dam across a river on bad foundations. The dam is carried away at the next flood; nor will the strictest prudence long maintain a frontier or a system that does not run upon the natural lines of political or territorial permanency.

When, therefore, at the beginning of this century we drew back from what seemed to Lord Cornwallis a network of embarrassing ties and compromising guarantees, we retained, as has been said, certain great States within the sphere of our surveillance; but we left almost all central India, including Rajputana, to take care of itself. All round our own territories we drew a cordon of rigid irresistible order; while outside this ring-fence, in the great interior region that contained the principalities of the Maratha families and of the ancient Rajput chief, we allowed a free hand to Sindhia, Holkar, and the predatory leaders. Scattered among the Maratha territories were a crowd of tribal chiefships and petty feudatories in various stages of dependence. Beyond the Maratha border, toward the great western desert, lay the Rajput States, too weak and disunited to oppose the exactions and dilapidations of great predatory armies. This group of primitive tribal chiefships, the last surviving relics of mediaeval India, had outlasted the Afghan and the Moghul empires, and had weathered the tumultuous anarchy of the eighteenth century. But they were rent by intestine feuds, and the militia of the Rajput clans was quite in capable of resisting the trained bands of the Marathas or the Afghan mercenaries of Amir Khan. Some of these States were now remonstrating earnestly with the British government for refusing to admit them within its protectorate, which they claimed as a matter of right. 'They said that some power in India had always existed to which peaceable States submitted, and in return obtained its protection against the invasions of upstart chiefs and the armies of lawless banditti; that the British government now occupied the place of that protecting power, and was the natural guardian of weak States which were continually exposed to the cruelties and oppression of robbers and plunderers, owing to the refusal of the British Government to protect them.[1]

Lord Minto, who had gone out to India with the intention of maintaining what was called the defensive policy, changed his views materially before he made over charge of the Governor-Generalship, in 1813, to Lord Moira, afterwards Marquis of Hastings. He had found himself compelled to interpose with an armed force for the protection of Holkar's government against a captain of banditti, and to place an army in the field to overawe the freebooter Amir Khan, who was about to overrun the Nagpore country. From 1811 to 1813 the Pindarees increased rapidly in numbers. The origin of these famous bands is to be found in the scouts and foragers who had always formed the loose fringe, so to speak, of every Indian army, receiving no pay, subsisting by pillage, but submitting generally to the orders of the commander of the whole force. As the regular armies of the native States were reduced, and the governments lost strength, these bands detached themselves from all military or civil subordination, and set up as hordes of free lances under their own leaders. By this time they had invaded, plundered, and ransomed the territories of the Nizam and the Peshwa, our allies, and they were now threatening with fire and sword our own rich province of Behar. The principle of non-interference seems to have been defended upon the ground that all these jarring and complicated elements of disorder would gradually settle down and become fused into strong and solidly constituted states. But it soon became manifest that an attempt to confine epidemic disease within fixed areas in the midst of some populous country would be not much more unreasonable than the plan of allowing political disorders to breed and multiply in the centre of India. For in the first place the Maratha chiefs were sullen, discontented, naturally ill-disposed towards the government which had recently overthrown their predominance, and seeking by all means to repair and augment their military forces. Secondly, the enforcement of systematic order all round them, and of restriction within fixed boundaries, was irreconcilable with the conditions that had engendered their power and that were still necessary to its existence; for the Maratha princes could maintain large armies only by levying exactions from their neighbours and by constantly taking the field upon marauding excursions. And, thirdly, it was evident that the cessation of irregular warfare and the establishment of a steady protectorate over the greater portion of India must inevitably aggravate the sufferings and intensify the confusion in those parts where the supreme pacifying authority disclaimed jurisdiction, and formally abdicated every right of interference. Large bodies of troops were disbanded by the British government and by its allies. But as all this multitude of men who lived by the sword and the free lance found their occupation gone within the pale of orderly government, they poured out of the pacified districts into the kingdoms of misrule like water draining from a cultivated upland into the low-lying marshes.

It was indeed impossible that a kind of political Alsatia, full of brigands and rovin banditti, could be long tolerated in the midst of a country just settling down into the peaceful and industrious stage. Such a situation, nevertheless, followed necessarily upon the introduction, by a sharp turn of policy, of the new principle. The British government could not now stay at home and stand apart without stopping half-way in the pacification of India, and leaving one great homogeneous population under two different and entirely incompatible political systems. For although the Indian people are broken up into diversities of race and language, they are as a whole not less distinctly marked off from the rest of Asia by certain material and moral characteristics than their country is by the mountains and the sea. The component parts of that great country hang together, physically and politically; there is no more room for two irreconcilable systems of government than in Persia, China, or Asiatic Turkey. The attitude of insulation might not have been inconsistent in the infancy of the English dominion, when the forces of the native States were better divided and more equally balanced, and when we might have confined our enterprise to the establishment of a great maritime and commercial power on the shores of the Indian and Arabian seas, like the Phoenicians or the Venetians in the Mediterranean. But it has been seen that during the second half of the eighteenth century we penetrated inland, striking in among the local wars and seizing territory, in order to protect ourselves and forestall the French. Then before the last apprehensions of French rivalry had vanished we had been confronted by the Marathas and the Mysore rulers, whose natural jealousy of our rising power was abetted by the French, and whose well-appointed armies directly threatened our position. To meet this danger Lord Wellesley had organized subsidiary forces on a large scale, undertaking on the part of the British government the general defence of all States that submitted to our political influence, and confining within fixed boundaries all those that held aloof. Lastly, when Mysore and the Maratha confederacy—the two powers that made head against us—had been the one destroyed and the other disabled, our own ascendancy had so overshadowed all India that it was too late to descend from the height we had attained, or to stand still abruptly on the road to universal dictatorship. We had now become a conquering power, we had assumed a continental sovereignty; and upon us the duty of providing the police of India had manifestly fallen. When we attempted to disclaim it no one else could undertake the business; and the smaller chiefships, who saw themselves spoiled and devoured, protested against a government that had pre-occupied the imperial place but evaded the imperial obligation. It was already manifest that British supremacy was the keystone of the arch that supported the great political edifice set up by Lord Wellesley, and that unless this keystone were firmly driven home the whole fabric would be unstable and insecure. For we had now gone so far on the road toward empire that it had become impossible to stand still. About this time Mountstuart Elphinstone wrote: 'We have long since abandoned the policy which might perhaps have averted the jealousy of other Indian States; and we have stopped short in the midst of the only other line that was either safe or consistent—that of establishing our ascendency over the whole of India. In consequence we have still the odium without the energy of a conquering people, and all the responsibility of an extensive empire, without its resources or military advantages. There would be some reason in remaining in this dangerous position if we were strengthened by peace, but so far are we from that, our provinces and the dominions of our allies are much more exposed to invasion and plunder than they would be in the time of war.

In the meantime the condition of the whole central region was sinking from bad to worse. It has been seen that in the eighteenth century India was crowded with mercenary soldiers who followed the trade of war; and an incredibly large proportion of the population subsisted by freebooting, a flourishing profession that had now been openly practised in India for several generations. The annexations and conquests of Lord Wellesley's era, the enlargement of our borders and of our protectorate, had led to an extensive disbandment of troops. It was reckoned by a competent authority that, at a moderate computation, this wide pacification of the country had turned loose half a million professional soldiers. Many of these men, with most of the freebooting class, whose occupation was disappearing with the contraction of that field of private enterprise, had collected in central India, where, instead of diminishing and settling down as had been expected, they increased to an alarming degree. Some of the native rulers encouraged them secretly, they intimidated the rest, and no power was strong enough to suppress them. The swarming of these predatory bands, which had been a comparatively transient and occasional evil when they could range over the whole Indian continent, became a mortal plague when it was hemmed in within set bounds, for the inland countries were exhausted by endemic brigandage. While the lesser principalities were thus being systematically bled to death, the great military chiefs were recruiting their forces, replenishing their treasuries, and enlarging the range of their operations, not without some prospect of recovering the formidable military footing which they had lost in the previous war.

The subsidiary system, moreover had other consequences besides those of causing the disbanding of the loose mercenary militia and the condensation of the freebooting plague. As the military power of the States which contracted these treaties was conveyed into British hands, the result was to weaken the internal authority of their rulers, by diminishing their feeling of responsibility for governing well and moderately, because they were sure of our protection in the event of attack of revolt. Undoubtedly the sense of dependence upon a higher power relaxed the energies of a native prince, who knew that in the last resort he could always call in the British government to save him from utter destruction. Against these disadvantages of the subsidiary alliances must, however, be set the consideration that without British protection most of the allied States would certainly have been dismembered in the incessant warfare that prevailed wherever they were left to themselves. The effect of our alliances upon the majority of these States was, therefore, to arrest the natural process of their disruption but not to strengthen the internal authority of their rulers. In this manner the burden of repressing disorder within the territory of our allies followed the transfer of the duty of external defence, and became gradually shifted on to the shoulders of the British government. Our policy might vary, backward or forward; we still found ourselves mounting step by step up to the high office of ultimate arbiter in every dispute and supreme custodian of the peace of all India.

Under the circumstances that have just been described, the marauding bands of central India, like the Free Companies of mediaeval Europe, had prosper and multiplied; until in 1814 Amir Khan, a notable military adventurer, was living upon Rajputana with a compact army of at least 30,000 men and a strong artillery. That a regular army of this calibre should have been moving at large about central India, entirely unconnected with any recognizable government or fixed territory acknowledging no political or civil responsibility, is decisive evidence of the prevailing disorganization. But Amir Khan's troops were under some kind of discipline: they were employed upon a system in some degree resembling regular warfare, their commander's aim being to carve out a dominion for himself. The true Pindari hordes had no other object but general rapine; they were immense bands of mounted robbers; their most popular leader, Cheetoo, could number no less than 10,000 horsemen; they could only subsist by irruptions into rich and fertile districts, and they were a perpetual menace to the country possessed or protected by the British Power. It can not be doubted that they maintained a secret understanding with the independent Maratha rulers at Poona, Nagpore, and Gwalior, who were not particularly anxious to join in the suppression of armed bodies that spared Maratha districts while they harried British lands and the Nizam's country, and who probably remembered that in any future attempt to make head against British domination the Pindaris might prove very serviceable auxiliaries.

REFERENCE

1. Letter from Sir Charles Metcalfe, Resident for Rajputana, June, 1816.

2

Revision of our Political Alliances

Lord Moira's early—opinions on Indian wars and government—Pindaris—their place in political study of the time—Moiras's outlook—the defective state of political relations—revision needed—a league proposed—discussion—Edmonstone's dissent—criticised Moira's scheme as impracticable and unsuitable—Moira's tour of upper India, 1814-15—Meets Metcalfe—agreement in views—the latter's influence—a minute prepared for council—forward action urged suppression of Pindaris—ascendency over independent princes—protection of smaller states—reflections on Moira's general policy. Particularly his attitude towards Sindhia—disagreement in council—disapproval from the authorities in England—his own ideal unchanged.

The Board of Control and the Court of Directors, in appointing Lord Moira as their Governor-General in India must have expected that he would carry out the instructions laid down for and observed by his predecessors in office, Barlow and Minto.

Speaking in a debate in the House of Lords on the 11th April 1791, when the question of the war against Tipu Sultan was discussed, he had denounced that war in unmeasured terms, declaring that "A scheme of conquest, for the extension of territory, was not only held generally as an improvident act, but particularly so in India." Referring to the Government of India, he said:- "That Government was founded in injustice and had orginally been established by force." He exclaimed further: "The war which now subsisted was a serious calamity, whether favourable or adverse it was no less the subject of deprecation and regret."[1]

Although he expressed these views on the Mysore War of the days of Cornwallis, he was essentially different in temperament from men like Barlow in his general outlook on political affairs. It is not, therefore, surprising, that his opinions on Indian matters underwent a complete change soon after his arrival in India. And he became the advocate of that very policy that he had condemned in his earlier days.

As is well known, the Minto Government had begun to take action against the Pindari danger. These freebooters directed their attack against the territories of the allies of the British, the Rajas of Bundelkhand, the Nizam; the Peshwa, and also the Raja of Nagpur. The British were bound to protect those territories (with the exception of Berar) and were obliged to adopt precautionary measures for the safety of their own. With that end in view they organised a close watch on the activities and movements of the different Pindari leaders, and also undertook military measures to check their inroads into the British or allied areas.[2]

In a study of the political relations between the British government and the Indian States, the Pindaris have obviously no proper place. They were a class of "free Companies" whose profession was plunder. They never became an organised political community in the sense of a territorial State. Therefore any space devoted to them here requires an explanation. It must be recognised that the very lawless, uncontrolled position which they came to occupy in the country, gave them a political significance. Although not a State themselves, they were the scourge of all the other States of Central India. Nominally residing in the jurisdiction of some Prince or other, they respected neither their government, nor their laws, nor their territorial frontiers.

As has already been remarked, the dominions of the Peshwa, the Nizam, Holkar, Sindhia and Bhonsla, suffered alike from their depredations. As they grew in strength and numbers, and as they extended their activity and organised their forces, they became the cause of serious concern to all the States. Some of them, as previously stated, were too weak to overpower them, and others (such as Sindhia) were too proud to admit that weakness, more especially to their rivals, the British.[3] It is obvious, therefore, that the Pindari problem must have assumed a political complexion of considerable perplexity, and provoked in the minds of the rulers of that time, political speculation of far-reaching consequence. The military measures initiated by the Minto Government, and continued after Moira's arrival, naturally attracted the latter's early attention. Then again, the peculiar methods for Pindari warfare, and the consequent difficulty and disadvantage of carrying on operations against them, led the Governor-General to examine the whole question of political relations. He saw that Central India was plunged into a state of serious disorder and in security. And the Pindaris were ravaging these areas without any systematic check on the part of their rulers. In the last Maratha war, the British had considerably broken the power of Sindhia, Holkar, and the Raja of Nagpur. This was, however, followed by the policy of withdrawal on the part of the British. Thus, the Pindaris found a free field in which to grow and spread. They became a peril to public peace and private property.

The consideration and the proper estimate of his Pindari danger led Lord Moira to form his own views as to how to meet the situation. It was thus that his former opinions underwent revision and transformation.

He was naturally eager to destroy the Pindaris and establish peace in the country. So far as the question of ridding the country of the Pindar evil was concerned, there was unanimity of opinion amongst the members of the Governor-General's Council. There was a genuine desire to extirpate them by all legitimate means.

But the means of achieving that purpose became a question of considerable controversy and discussion. The Governor-General maintained that the question of the extermination of the predatory bodies was intimately bound up with the larger problem of the relations subsisting between the States of India and the East India Company. He thought that the destruction of the Pindaris could be effected without much difficulty But that would not do. "Having achieved your object, you cannot sit down without establishing such arrangements as would be necessary towards drawing a permanent benefit from the success, and if we once set forth on that ground we shall find that we have opened a field of questions of immense extent."[4] It was not sufficient to suppress the Pindaris. Their re-organisation must be prevented. Their support must be cut off. Similarly, it was necessary to break Amir Khan's power, and reduce his army. The Governor General believed that Amir Khan's interests were identified with those of Holkar. He asked whether the destruction of Amir Khan, which would mean the dissolution of Holkar's Government, would not raise such issues as would excite the jealousy of the Peshwa and Sindhia. To him, the Pindari eruption was only the symptom, whereas he aimed at the destruction of the disease itself. The Pindari hordes must be extirpated, in order to confer peace and security on the country. He argued that no peace could be permanent, without one supreme Power to maintain it, a Power which would be acknowledged supreme by all the States, and to whom all questions of peace and war would be submitted for arbitration.

Since he considered the annihilation of the Pindaris inseparable from the revision of existing relations with the Indian States, he reviewed those relations in a minute, which he wrote on the 3rd April 1814.[5] He felt convince that they were in a state of confusion, and that most of the embarrassments which faced the Government were the result of that confusion. There was resentment, friction and general restlessness on the part of those States. Neither side was satisfied. The British did not reap the full advantages of their position and the States were keenly dissatisfied at the interference which the British Government exercised in their affairs often in violation of solemn engagements. He complained in the same minute: "We do not, in the connections we establish with them, either [allow] to the native princes spontaneity of action as independent rulers or exact from them obedience as feudatories."

After serious reflection on the situation, he came to the conclusion that the case demanded a most speedy treatment. With the view of removing those serious disadvantages and difficulties, the Governor-General recommended that all the principal Sates should be invited to join a league which he proposed to form, with the British Government as its head. The members of the proposed confederacy would have to surrender the right of making war on one another, and would have to submit their differences to the arbitration of the British Power, as the acknowledged head of the League. He suggested that the proposal should be tactfully put before the Indian Princes, in a way that should not hurt their pride. According to his scheme, the States would enjoy real independence in their internal Government, and would also be free to regulate the succession to their sovereignties according to their own custom or desire. It would be a genuine federation of States, internally free, but deprived of the functions of external sovereigntly.

The subsidiary States would remain almost unaffected by the formation of the League. He anticipated that they would welcome it on the ground that they would regain that freedom in their domestic concerns which had been promised to them in their treaties. The Raja of Nagpur would be forced by circumstances to join it, and Lord Moira was determined to impose on him the condition of a subsidiary alliance before admitting him into the Confederacy. "None but Sindhia and Holkar, to whose mode of existence it could not be reconcilable would have the foly to remain out of the pale of security."[6] And the Governor-General's proposals involved the severance of all relations with those States which declined to "improve their connection with us in the terms of the League."[7]

These were the views which in the early days of his office Moira formulated for his government. They display his powers of imagination and his earnestness of purpose. At the same time, a closer examination of those proposals reveals a lack of Indian experience, leading him to propound theories both impracticable and inapplicable to the situation he was attempting to remedy. Considered in the abstract, his ideas appeared sound, and it looked as if they might successfully remove the various inconsistencies which had arisen in the held of Indian politics. But they lost their charm and value when applied to the conditions for which they were intended.

As Moira himself admitted, the subsidiary States would have found their position practically unaffected by his proposals. It might be expected that they would rejoice at the proposed restoration of their internal freedom. The fulfilment of that expectation, as Moira lived to learn, could not be attained, even under his own regime. In spite of his strong disapproval of this method of interference, Moira himself was forced to admit its necessity. Once a State was deprived of its independence, the loss of its military strength was a necessary consequence. The ruler was relieved of the primary responsibility of protecting his State against foreign aggression. Through that weakness, he almost invariably fell into a repose which was degenerating and demoralising in the extreme. Internal administration very generally suffered also, and trouble followed. Then the British Government sooner or later had to interfere to set matters right, often by force of arms.[8]

But at that time the chief embarrassment of the British Government was not due to the Subsidiary States. The three independent Maratha rulers were the chief cause of anxiety, since they would not acknowledge the British supermacy or agree to be bound by subsidiary ties and reduced to a condition of political impotence like the Nizam and the Gaekwar. Sindhia and Holkar would not have found any advantage to attract them in Moira's League. As Edmonstone remarked, referring to Sindhia:— "It is not apparent in what way he could be in the slightest degree benefited by the arrangement. I perceive no basis of negotiation."[9]

Lord Moira was either unduly optimistic or else he failed to understand with whom he had to deal. He imagined that the full significance and meaning of his Scheme, namely, the acknowledgement of the British as the feudal overlord, with other States as vassals, would be agreed to, if only the States were approached in a tactful manner. "Were we to tell them," he wrote in his minute, "that they must become vassals, their pride would revolt, their apprehensions would take alarm." He was far from correct in his judgment, that only the form in which the plan was presented to the Princes mattered, and that they would readily assent to the arrangement, if the meaning of the proposed confederacy were suitably explained. He must have soon learned that his imagination had not helped him to a correct conclusion. The negotiations with the Raja of Nagpur and the Nawab of Bhopal, showed that even those Chiefs, in the days of their declining prosperity, were zealous to retain their independence

None of the rival States, which were jealous of British ascendency, would have willingly supported the League. Therefore, for all practical purposes, it could not be brought into being without an appeal to arms, or, once formed, it would have remained no more than a name.

The Council of the Governor-General did not support him in his plan for a federation of States founded on feudal notions. The senior member of the Council, Edmonstone, a highly experienced civil servant of the Company, who had received his political training under Wellesley, vehemently opposed Lord Moira's proposals. He disputed Moira's contention that the subsisting relations were ill-defined and conducive of frequent irritation. From his long experience and local knowledge, he urged that the proposed scheme was unsuitable and impracticable, and declared that the suggested change in the existing relations would lead to anarchy, confusion and warfare.[10]

The controversy that began in the early months of 1814 between Moira and his colleagues continued for close on two years. The opposition were strengthened in their attitude by the consciousness that they were acting in accordance with the declared wishes of the authorities in England, who had enjoined a policy of strict economy, and forbidden any steps likely to lead to hostilities with Sindhia and Holkar.

Lord Moira, although he was thwarted and opposed in Council, still remained firm in his views. In the summer of 1814 he decided to make a tour of Upper India. His extensive travel throughout the winter of 1814-15, afforded him an invaluable opportunity of making personal acquaintance with the various nobles, Rajas and Nawabs, and of understanding the customs and institutions prevailing in the country.[11] Amongst other things, this tour also brought him into contact with a person whose help he sorely needed at that time, and he was not slow to avail himself of this service.

Amongst many of his other notable deeds, the masterful and aggressive genius of Wellesley had, during his term of office, trained a few distinguished officers, who played a very important part in the annals of Anglo-Indian administration. Malcolm, Metcalfe, Elphinstone and Jenkins are famous figures on the pages of British history in India. Although Wellesley had been recalled, and his policy censured, yet, what one might term "the Wellesley School," survived in India long after his departure. And it is very interesting to note how this school influenced events in Moira's time.

In his journey through Hindustan, he learned to value and admire the services he received from one member of that talented group. Charles (later Lord) Metcalfe was, at that time, Resident at Delhi. Moira's first impressions of Metcalfe were derived from a persual of the private letters which the latter wrote to the political secretary, John Adam, another disciple of the same school.[12] Ever since 1806, in the freedom of private correspondence, Metcalfe had, on many occasions, strongly condemned the policy laid down by the directors, and so faithfully professed by Cornwallis and Barlow.[13] Such a person would be a tower of strength to the Governor-General in his disputes with his colleagues. Being obstructed by his Council, Moira threw himself into the arms of the Delhi Resident, whose political principles were so agreeable to him.

News of the British reverses in the Gurkha War distressed Metcalfe, and in November 1814, he wrote a note to the Governor-General on the proper mode of conducting operations.[14] This was followed by another paper in January 1815, on the situation in India and his views on its treatment. His papers were very favourably received at the Governor-General's camp. A number of points were put down for discussion with him, and he was invited to the camp, where he spent several weeks of the winter of 1814-15.[15]

While Moira and Metcalfe agreed in their general outlook, it is clearly visible that the latter was largely responsible for giving further and final shape to Moira's views on the problem of political relationship. As the estrangement between himself and his Council, more particularly the vice-president, Edmonstone, grew deeper, his confidence in Metcalfe increased day by day. When, in the autumn of 1815, Moira returned to Calcutta, he took with him a lengthy minute prepared for him by his private secretary. Ricketts, based on the notes and opinions furnished by Metcalfe.[16] The Governor-General put that minute before his Council on his return.[17] It surveyed the whole situation exhaustively, from military and political standpoints, with regard to the Indian Princes and the Pindaris, and also contained an elaborate exposition of the creed which Moira had, but that time, embraced for his political conduct in India. "The policy it inculcated was indeed emphatically Metcalfe's policy."[18] Not only were the arguments and the plan his, but in many parts his own words were reproduced, as admitted by Ricketts in a letter to Metcalfe.[19] In the opinion of Lord Moira, as expressed in that very interesting document, in order to avert the impending evil, strong and urgent measures were desirable in the interest of the British Government in India. The Marathas and the Pindaris constituted two great dangers. The former were disunited as a result of the Treaty of Bassein, but could and would, at any time, combine against the British by the impulse of their common hatred. "What in rivalship between themselves, could exist so strong as their dread and hatred of our power? What in the memory of wrongs could affect any one of them with such bitterness of animosity as the recollection of narrowed dominion, curtailed revenue, diminished reputation and extinguished preponderance suffered from us?"[20]

The Pindaris were strong and growing; they could command 20,000 fine horse, or even more. Amir Khan was able, clever and courageous, and had under his command a very efficient and well-equipped force[21] which he was using to harass and oppress the defenceless States of Rajasthan. He was convinced that both Sindhia and Holkar were interested in maintaining the Pindaris and would in the long run be driven to go to war against the British, "as a relief from the still greater ills of poverty, hunger and despair" from which they were suffering.[22]

He complained that his Government did not enjoy the advantages which they had a right to expect. The evil could not be remedied by the Powers whose duty it was to remove it, for they were too weak for the task. The British should apply the remedy which would lead to the settlement of the Maratha Powers and the destruction of their irregular forces, and object which could not be accomplished under the existing relations. In its pursuit, a war with the Marathas was extremely probable. But the Governor-General had no hesitation in preferring the option of an immediate war, to that of a prolonged and expensive system of defence against the predatory bodies.[23] Then there were the Rajput States in the west, whom he called, "our natural allies and the natural enemies of the Mahrattas."[24] The British would increase their military resources and gain a valuable strategic advantage by establishing their influence over them. Both policy and humanity united to require that those States should be brought under protection.[25] But by the treaties with Sindhia and Holkar, the British were forbidden from entering into an alliance with these States." It would be a fundamental part of this plan, that we should be liberated from those restrictions which now prevent our interference with some of the petty states."[26]

The plan was to effect a complete change in the political conditions of the country, making the British the unquestioned arbiters of its destinies. This purpose was to be achieved by military power, and he therefore advocated the maintenance of a strong army. "Our power depends, "declared Metcalfe, "solely on our military superiority."[27] Moira did not foresee a long war, for he estimated that the Indian Powers, (in which he included the Pindaris), could only muster a total force of 80,000 horse,[28] and that their infantry was inefficient. He was quite hopeful of destroying it without much difficulty, in a possible contest, with his available resources. But he was earnestly of opinion that a reduction of military strength would be unwise.[29] "It is necessary to keep afoot in peace, a force suited to a state of universal war."[30]

The whole of his policy could be summed up in his aim at the establishment of peace in India through the protection and guarantee of one supreme Power, which must be the British. "We should thus have a complete control over the politics of the Confederacy."[31] This plan was to be achieved by effecting three things:—the complete suppression of the predatory system, the acquisition of ascendency over the military chiefs, which should preserve public tranquillity and restrict them within their own territories, and lastly, "the protection of all harmless states under our superintendence."[32]

This long minute was a document with a military outlook and an anti-Maratha spirit. In tone, it was frankly aggressive, and both in the interests of the British Power in the East, and the public peace of India, it pleaded for early and decisive action, even war, if necessary.

It is difficult to withhold a tribute of appreciation for that able and masterly sate paper. It displayed a clear perspective of the conflicting political factors which complicated the situation, and a bold and vigorous spirit in grappling with them. Nor is it wholly necessary to agree entirely with the justness of its sentiments or the soundness of all its arguments in order to admire its sagacity and skilful draftsmanship.

It was undoubtedly true that the Pindari menace was growing worse every day, and that to keep up a defensive attitude against their light horsemen by guarding the passes on the frontier, was an extremely expensive and trying method.

The only Power which could succeed in extirpating them was the British Government. And if, as the strongest Power in the country, it desired to attain a paramount position over all other States, this was an excusable ambition, according to the prevailing political notions of inter-state relationship. There were three States left outside the pale of the British Confederacy, which were weak, impoverished and mutually antagonistic. Their own territories were the scene of depredations. The Pindaris oppressed their subjects and levied contributions from their tributaries. Their armies were disorganised. The Raja of Berar was in an almost defenceless state. Holkar's court was under the sway of the unscrupulous adventurer, Amir Khan. Sindhia was only comparatively better situated than the other two. However unwilling they might have been to surrender their independence, their pretended jealousy of the British Power was inconsistent with their actual military strength. Lord Moira rightly thought that the British were not reaping the full advantage of their superior position. He saw before him clearly, the opportunity of raising the position of his Government by breaking the independent power of the Maratha Princes. In other words, he simply wished to complete the work left unfinished by

Wellesley. He had no scruples against achieving that end by warfare, if necessary, as he thought might be likely. As Metcalf put it in his usual bold manner, "With regard to all the great military states, and all the predatory powers, it is clearly our interest to annihilate them, or to reduce them to a state of weakness, subjection and dependence.[33] On the grounds of self-interest, the Governor-General urged a forward policy.

At the same time, it would not be correct to say that this policy was demanded by the need of preserving the British Power. There was no serious rival to the British in the field. Moreover, the scheme for the extermination of the Pindaris was not so indissolubly connected with the subjugation of the independent Princes.

Holkar's Government, under its regent. Tulsi Bai, was far from cordial towards Amir Khan and his party at her Court, and would have been glad to get rid of the Pathan adventurer.[34] Many times their differences were openly avowed,[35] and they led to constant intrigue and assassinations.[36]

It was well-known that the Raja of Nagpur was too weak, and his country in too impoverished a condition to permit of any aggressive designs on his part against the British. Moreover, amongst them all, he was, perhaps, the worst sufferer from Pindari outrages,[32] and could have no desire or interest in being their well-wisher.

Daulat Rao Sindhia was considered the nominal sovereign of the Pindari freebooters. But Lord Moira knew that Sindhia himself was engaging his arms against them.[38] Close, the British Resident at his Court, considered that he was genuine in his anxiety at the rumoured release of Karim,[39] and in the steps he took at the British Government's suggestion, to obstruct the passage of the Pindaris to the Deccan. Close reported the despatch of a letter (dated 17th Nov. 1816) from Sindhia to Chitu, in which the latter was forbidden to molest any country. In that letter, Sindhia also made professions of friendship for the Company. The Resident observed that this communication gave "a true and correct insight into his Highness' feelings."[40]

Moira was also afraid that their common distrust of the British might drive them into a confederacy for the purpose of overthrowing the British.[41] On a little examination, one finds that his fears were unduly exaggerated.

He knew, that Sindhia and Amir Khan had always hated each other.[42] Amir Khan was all powerful at the Court of Holkar, and naturally exerted his energies to exclude Sindhia's influence from that State.[43] The traditional jealousy of the two houses of Sindhia and Holkar, must have been well-known to Moira. It was extremely improbable that they would unite for a common purpose.[44]

Moira attached rather undue importance to another attempted combination between Sindhia and Raghuji Bhonsla with the object of crushing the Nawab of Bhopal.[45] Sindhia and Bhonsla both had an old grudge against Bhopal.[46] Their alliance did not appear to have an anti-British design, although it would be true that if they had succeeded in reducing Bhopal, their strategic position would incidentally have improved considerably.

There is fairly reliable evidence that Sindhia had no desire to ally himself permanently with the Bhonsla Raja of Nagpur. Gokul Parekh, the minister whose advice carried great authority in Maharaja Sindhia's Councils, was opposed to any proceeding which might interrupt the existing amity with the British Government. A friendly communication received from Nagpur met with no response. The Resident wrote:—" I understand Sindhia to have declared that from experience he could place no confidence in the alliance and support of the Rajah."[47] This declaration of Sindhia's is all the more remarkable, since it was made subsequently to his annoyance in the previous November over the Bhopal affair, when he might have been expected to be especially unfriendly towards the British.[48]

Even if we suppose the improbable, that the independent Powers could combine their forces in a common cause, Moira was confident that they had not much chance of success. "Our means are ample against any combination," wrote the Governor -General.[49]

As Lord Moira was drifting fast into the Wellesley School of Indian Politics, it would not be altogether in appropriate to notice that concurrently with that evolution in his opinions, the possibility of a revival of the Maratha Confederacy, with Daulat Rao Sindhia as its effective leader, occupied the same position in his mind, as did the French in that of Wellesley. Just as the later aimed at destroying the French, so Moira could not rest content without reducing Sindhia.

It is not to be wondered at that he should have developed that feeling against Daulat Rao. The latter must have appeared to him, more by his free position than by his actions, to be the chief obstacle to the establishment of British paramountcy. In addition to this, was the galling article of the Treaty of 1805,[50] by which the British were bound not to enter into treaty relations with his so-called tributaries in Malwa, Mewar, and Marwar. It seriously conflicted with the realisation of Moira's plans, and so the desire grew within him to break Sindhia's independent power. He must have felt with Metcalfe, that "India contains no more than two great powers, the British and the Marathas, and every other state acknowledges the influence of one or the other.[51] The independent status of Sindhia, who was apparently the most powerful representative of the Marathas, was inconsistent with British aim.

This naturally led Moira to become excessively suspicious of Sindhia. It is a matter of melancholy interest to compare his attitude towards Baji Rao with his dealings with Sindhia. It is not difficult to detect an unusual and undeserved confidence in the former, of whose treacherous nature he must have heard, as compared with his exaggerated distrust of the latter. Of course, there is an obvious explanation for this attitude of mind. Baji Rao was bound by ties of subsidiary alliance, and a British force was stationed in his territories. He could not, therefore, be so free to engage in hostilities as Sindhia was. Thus Moira's attitude towards the two Maratha rulers, though different, was characteristic enough. The degree of cordiality with which he treated the intriguing and unprincipled Peshwa, till about the last moment of his open hostility, is recorded in the following words: "For some time after, the utmost cordiality seemed to prevail between His Highness (*i.e.,* Baji Rao) and the British Government. Frequent confidential communications passed between the Peshwa and the Resident, and His Highness received a striking proof of the confidence and friendship of the Governor-General in Council, in the communication to His Highness, of our intentions regarding the Pindaris, and the negotiations actually pending with Dowlat Rao Sindhia on the subject, a disclosure which had not been made to any other of the allies of the British Government. On the other hand, no measure or proceeding was either in contemplation or progress which could have tended in the remotest degree to alarm or irritate His Highness' mind."[52]

In contrast to this policy pursued towards Baji Rao, must be reviewed Moira's remarks regarding the suggestions made to him by the Board of Control,[53] and Edmonstone,[54] that, in the operations against the Pindaris, Sindhia's co-operation might be sought.

He declared: "It will not do to sound Sindhia. I will not stain the character of my country so much as to try his dispositions and then shrink from the object in finding them unfavourable...were he to identify himself with the Pindaris he is at war with us, and further discussion is preposterous."[55]

The internal disorder in Sindhia's affairs, which could not have allowed him to offer any very serious resistance to the British, was well known to Moira.[56] But he persisted in cherishing an ardent aspiration to break Sindhia's power completely. How keenly desirous he was to achieve that purpose can be gathered from what he recorded in his Private

Journal on the 23rd Dec. 1816. "It is far better if he be resolved to risk his existence for the support of the Pindaries."[57]

But it was destined otherwise. It was Baji Rao who risked his existence, losing his dominions, and with them fell the hereditary throne of the Peshwa, of which he had been such an unworthy occupant. On the other hand, Sindhia emerged through these troubled years as the only Prince still retaining a semblance of independence. Not only did he not go to war with the Company, but he co-operated[58] with them in the extirpation of the freebooters.[59] Whilst no one would assert that Sindhia was a loyal friend of the British, or devotedly attached to their interests, yet he was sensible enough to see that his security lay, not in opposing the British, but in avoiding a contest with them. The mutual distrust between them arose from Sindhia's dread of the British Power, and the British dislike of his independence. If the two had laid aside their false fears and false pride, and co-ordinated their efforts against the Pindaris, the task would have been comparatively simplified.

But that would not have solved the political problem. As has already been remarked, that constituted only a third, and by no means the most important part, of Moira's political programme. For him, it was an entire scheme, which could not be broken into fragments. "The settlement of Central India is necessary for the safety and stability of our Empire."[60] That was the one task before him, indivisible and urgent, and he meant the resources of his government to be applied to carry it out.

The policy formulated by the Governor-General and so earnestly recommended by him for adoption, failed to receive the support of his Council at Calcutta. Edmonstone, its vice-president, was not convinced of either its soundness or its expediency. He had the support of Seton (until 1816, when he changed his mind)[61] and Dowdeswell.[62] Edmonstone disagreed with Moira in thinking that there was any great or imminent danger on the part of the larger Powers, which were internally too weak, and externally too disunited to open hostilities against the British. The interests and the financial condition of the Company alike demanded a peaceful policy.[63] Edmonstone continued to hold this view of the situation.[64] He was clearly of the opinion that Sindhia was genuine in his desire to suppress the Pindaris and to dissociate himself from their nefarious activities.

He urged, that, even "if we could not obtain the co-operation, we might at least secure the neutrality of Sindhia."[65]

The opposition in Council was not the worst of Moira's embarrassments in putting his plan into execution. The Board of Control and the Court of Directors were most reluctant to sanction any wholesale revision of the existing alliances, with a view to establishing a confederacy of the States of India under British supremacy.[66] The Secret Committee, in repeating their previous injunctions against undertaking extensive operations or forming new alliances, even with the Rajput States, laid down a purely defensive policy for their Indian Government. They were to protect themselves and their allies against specific inroads of the Pindaris, and to punish their aggressions. But "We are unwilling to incur the risk of a general war for the uncertain purpose of extirpating altogether those predatory bands," and further, "extended political or military combinations, therefore, for that purpose we can not at the present moment sanction or approve."[67]

Hampered by his colleagues in Council, and discouraged by his employers at home, as Moira was, he adhered to his own opinions and plans with courage and perseverance. As he acquired greater experience and received outside influence, his opinions developed and were confirmed, although they underwent a partial modification. The keenness of the early days for the formation of a league was wearing away, the righteous indignation at the unjust interference in the affairs of States was losing its warmth when brought into contact with cold, hard facts, and the reaction of feeling produced by Pindari excesses was imperceptibly increasing his determination to crush, along with those freebooters, the power of Sindhia, whom Moira called "the most powerful and the most decided supporter of the Pindaris."[68] This was a natural evolution of his policy, in the light of current events and experiences. It meant only a change in the emphasis from some parts of the plan to others, but in its basic principles it remained unchanged, growing stronger with the progress of time.

Within four months of his arrival in India, Moira wrote in his Private Journal:— "Our object ought to be to render the British Government paramount in effect, if not declaredly so. We should hold the other states vassals in substance, if not in name, not precisely as they stood in the Mogul government, but possessed of perfect internal sovereignty, and only bound to repay the guarantee and protection of their possessions by the British Government with the pledge of the two great feudal duties. *First:*—They should support it with all their forces on any call. *Second:*— They should submit their mutual differences to the head of the Confederacy (our Government) without attacking each other's territories."[69]

This was the goal at which he aimed. Having defined his ideal, he began to apply it. The chapter 3 will be an attempt to review the first steps which he took in that direction.

REFERENCES

1. *Hansard, 31. George III.* pp. 145-7.
2. *Home Misc* Vol. 516-A. pp. 13-15 and 19.
3. Strachey to Moira January 8th No. 8, Bengal Secret Consultations January 28th, 1814.
4. Governor-General's Minute dated April 3rd, No. 4, Bengal Secret Consultations, June, 21st, 1814.
5. No. 4, Bengal Secret and Political Consulations, 21st June 1814.
6. *Ibid.*
7. *Ibid.*

8. The evidence of Sir Richard Jenkins. Parliamentary Papers, 1831-32. (VI) Vol. XIV. pp. 25-26.
9. Edmonstone's Minute, dated 29th April, No. 5, Bengal Secret Consultations 21st June, 1814.
10. *Ibid,* and Seton, another Member of the Council, also opposed the change in the relations with other States. His Minute dated 21st June 1814 No. 10, Bengal Secret Consultations of the same date.
11. His *Private Journal.* 2 Vols. Published 1858.
12. Adam to Metcalfe. November 15th, 1813, private letter. Kaye's *Life of Metcalfe.* Vol. 1, p. 382.
13. Kaye's *Selections from the papers of Lord Metcalfe,* pp. 1-11.
14. Kaye's *Life of Metcalfe,* Vol. 1. pp. 386-388.
15. *Loc. Cit.* 1. pp. 397-398.
16. *Loc, Cit.* p. 449.
17. Minute of December 1st, 1815, No. 5. Bengal Secret Consultations, June 15th, 1816.
18. Kaye's *Metcalfe,* Vol. 1. p. 449.
19. *Ibid.* (Footnote):—

    Compare for instance. Metcalfe's remarks on Jaipur Alliance (Kaye 1. p. 440) with the wording of the Minute on the same subject (paragraph 290), or his remarks on the acquisition of territory, (Kaye, 1. p. 442) with the sentiments contained in (paragraph 126) the Minute.
20. Paragraph 20.
21. Paragraph 25.
22. Paragraph 51.
23. Paragraph 71.
24. Paragraph 84.
25. Paragraph 89.
26. Paragraph 115.
27. Kaye's *Life of Metcalfe.* Vol. I, p. 392.
28. Paragraph 62, of Moira's Minute *op. cit.*
29. Paragraph 275.
30. Paragraph 196.

31. Paragraph 149.
32. Paragraph 272.
33. Kaye's *Life of Metcalfe*. Vol. I. p. 434.
34. Edmonstone in his Minute, dated 29th April 1814, No. 5, in Bengal Secret Consultations 21st June 1814, says:—"We have actually received from them (referring to the Regent and her minister) on more than one occasion, secret overtures to this effect."
35. Malcolm's *Central India. Vol. 1. (1824)* pp. 285-305.
36. Balaram Seth was cruelly murdered. He was Amir Kan's supporter. *Loc, Cit*. pp. 298-299.
37. Grant-Duff. *op. Cit*. III. 325, and also Wilson, Vol. II, p. 191.
38. Extract from a letter from Bengal to the Court of Directors, dated 1st March 1812. Home Misc. Vol. 516A, p. 7.
39. Close to Moira, dated 12th Feb. 114, No. 17, Bengal Secret Consultations, dated 4th March 1814.
40. Close's Despatch, Dec. 4th No. 4, Bengal Secret Consultations, Dec. 17th, 1816.
41. His Minute dated Dec. 1st 1815, paragraph 19, *p. Cit*.
42. *Loc. Cit*. paragraph 26, and also his Minute dated 13th April 1816. *Home Misc. Vol. 604*.
43. Malcolm's *Central India*. (1824) Vol. 1. pp. 283-285.
44. *Ibid* and Sindhia's attempt to establish his influence at Holkar's Court by means of armed forces. Also Prinsep's Transactions. Vol. 1, p. 233.
45. Adam to Metcalfe 14th Oct. 1814. No. 2. Bengal Secret Consultations, 4th Nov, 1814.
46. Hough, *History of Bhopal*. pp. 38, 41, 53, and Malcolm's *Central India* Vol. 1, pp. 373-4, 387, and also Jenkins' *Report on Nagpore Administration* (1827) p. 125.
47. Strachey's Despatch dated 26th Jan. 1815, No. 42, Bengal Secret Consultations, Feb. 14th, 1815.
48. Hastings' Summary of the Operations in India from 1813-1823. Parliamentary Paper, Vol. VIII. 1831-1832. Political Appendix p. 96.
49. He wrote this in a Minute (of the 13th April 1816) in connection with the attempted alliance with Jaipur. (Home Misc. Vol. 604). referring specially to combination between Sindhia and Amir Khan.

50. Aitchison's *Treaties*—(1909) Vol. IV. p. 61.
51. Kaye's *Metcalfe Papers Op. Cit.* p. 4.
52. Secret Letter from Bengal to the Secret Committee, 12th April 1817. Home Misc. Vol. 516A, pp. 67-69.
53. Letter from the Secret Committee dated 26th Sept. 1816, p. 40, *Loc. Cit.*
54. In his Minute of 7th Dec. No. 10 Bengal Secret Consultations 28th Dec. 1816.
55. Governor-General's Minute 6th Dec. 1816. No. 9 *Loc. Cit.*
56. Governor-General himself wrote this about him in his Minute of 15th May 1814. No. 6. Bengal Secret Consultations, 21st June 1814, referring to his proposed league of States under British Supremacy, "Sindhia could be relieved from a grievous tyranny over him by his own army, is sense of which he has several times expressed before servants of the Company. Were he assured of filling the Musnad tranquillit, I have no doubt of his preferring that to the frequent insults which he now undergoes from his troops."
57. Vol. II, p. 154.
58. Lord Hastings *Summary of Operations in India,* printed in Political Appendix—Parliamentary Paper Vol. VIII. 1831-2. p. 101.
59. It can, of course, be argued with considerable force that Sindhia was left no choice in the matter by Moira's military arrangements. But, in a way, that would be only begging the question. If he had felt any inveterate hostility against the British, he could have taken up arms in 1814, 1815, or 1816, before those military movements began, or while the Nepal War was in progress. On the other hand, there was a subsidiary force stationed at the very door of Baji Rao.
60. His Minute of 1st Dec. 1815, *Op. Cit.* paragraph 270.
61. His Minute of 17th April 1816, No. 3 Bengal Secret Consultations, April 20th, 1816.
62. His Minute of 19th April 1816. Home Misc. Series, Vol. 604.
63. His Minute of 22nd April 1814. Home Misc. Series Vol. 604.
64. His Minute of 26th Feb. No. 2 Bengal Secret Consultations 8th March 1817.
65. Edmonstone's Minute of 7th Dec. No. 10 Bengal Secret Consultations, Dec. 28th, 1816.

66. Despatch No. 107 from the Secret Committee dated 29th Sept. 1815 to the Governor-General. *Board's Drafts,* Vol. 5.
67. Despatch No. 118 from the Secret Committee to the—Governor-General dated 5th Sept. 1816. *Loc. Cit.* Vol. 5.
68. His Letter dated 1st March 1820 to the Court of Directors. Home Misc. Series, Vol. 516A, p. 386.
69. Vol. 1, pp. 54-55 on Feb. 6th, 1814. Identical sentiments were expressed in his Minute of 3rd April No. 4. Bengal Secret Consultations, 21st June 1814.

3

Poona and Nagpur

ADVANCE

Maratha power—Peshwaship—a centre of attachment—Baji Rao—Character—conflicting qualities—distracted state of his country in 1803—Uses British alliance to restore his authority and stabilise his government—Elphinstone appointed resident—southern Jagirdars—settlement (1812)—Peshwa forms a contingent—Trimbakji Danglia—Poona-Baroda discussions—Shastri's mission—Shastri's murder-resident demands enquiry—trial and Surrender of Danglia—Peshwa's evasion—secret preparation—indecision—submission-Trimbakji delivered—confined—*Nagpur*—Raghuji Bhonsla's death—Parsoji succeeds—his infirmity—intrigues for Regency between the Dowager Bai and Appa Sahib—Appa Sahib seeks British support—Court intrigues—attempt at reconciliation—failure—Appa Sahib seizes power—secretly concludes subsidiary alliance with the British—treaty—terms—force arrives—British position at Nagpur—*Poona*—Trimbakji escapes—Resident's prompt measures—Peshwa's outward friendliness—Danglia assembles forces—raises a rebellion—Peshwa's secret encouragement—Governor-General's instructions—securities to be demanded from Peshwa after Trimbakji's unconditional surrender—Peshwa's hesitation and cowardice—yields-terms Disclosed—repugnance—submission to demands—new treaty signed—conclusion.

AFFAIRS AT POONA AND NAGPUR

At the time that Moira was striving to establish the supremacy of his Government over the Indian States, it became abundantly clear to him that the greatest rivalry to the British Power was to be expected from the Marathas. The ancient Rajput Kingdoms were in a distressed condition. The Muhammedans, though bold and turbulent, had become too indolent to the dangerous. The power that had successfully organised itself as a menace to the Great Mughal Empire, being the youngest and freshest in the field, was still active, vigorous and restless.[1]

This factor gives to the Treaty of Bassein its great importance. By it Wellesley aimed a blow at the very centre of the Maratha Confederacy. The Peshwa, its ostensible head, was reduced to the position of a dependent on the British Government, and expressly forbidden to deal directly with Foreign States. Thus the other branches of the Maratha Confederacy were boldly separated from the centre, and formally released from the Peshwa's authority.[2] While he was obliged by circumstances to accept those terms out of a sense of self-preservation,[3] it is evident that he could not have liked or welcomed the restrictions they imposed upon his independence.[4] Not only was the British control of the Peshwa's foreign affairs irksome to him, but the Maratha Chiefs themselves were attached to the Peshwa's Masnad, and partly by policy but largely by habit, were "constantly professing their devotion to His Highness and pressing to acknowledge him for their sovereign."[5]

Such was the importance still attached to the position of the Peshwa in the eyes of the people and the Princes of India, in spite of the paper provisions of the Treaty.[6] The state of our relations to the Peshwa has always been much influenced by His Highness's personal character, and it might be interesting to speculate on the form they might assume if the numerous claims and pretensions of this Government were to fall into the hands of an active and warlike Peshwa, who would attend to the improvement of his army, conciliate his Jagirdars, and encourage the former great fendatories of the Empire to look on him as their Chief. It is obvious that in the present state of India, there are fine materials for a powerful confederacy under such a leader; but he must be an extraordinary genius, who could start up with such a character from the midst of a long peace and a Brahmin education."[7] In the above extract we have from the pen of a distinguished Anglo-Indian statesman, who was, during the eventful years 1811-1817, the British Minister at the Poona Court, a picture of the Peshwa's position in the country, and the possibilities that lay before an enterprising and able occupant of that position Baji Rao filled that Gadi at that time, and it is obviously a matter of considerable interest to the student of this period to estimate the character of the man who was placed in that exalted position.

According to the accounts left by contemporary writers and diplomats, who had opportunities of judging Baji Rao and his actions.[8] His character must have been a curious combination of opposing attributes, perplexing these who desired to study his sentiments or foresee is conduct. He possessed many qualities which were wholly inconsistent with "his ruling passion of fear." But for his timidity, he would have been "ambitious, imperious, inflexible and persevering, and his active propensities would probably have overcome is love of ease and pleasure, which are now so strong, from their alliance with his timidity." Eager for power, although lacking in boldness to acquire it, tenacious of authority, though too indolent to exercise it, master of the art of dissimulation, vigilant and vindictive, suspicious and insincere, Baji Rao as not found to be unmixed and pure in anything. He was capricious and changeable, yet showed steadiness in serious designs. Nothing was too low or too crooked, if it satisfied his purpose, or was necessary to ruin the object of his vengeance. His haughty and overbearing nature made him fond of low favourites. He was proud and lofty, but when occasion so required, he could be mean and cringing. His time was divided between fasts, prayers and pilgrimages conducted, as Elphinstone says, with slavish superstition, and scenes of the most disgusting debauchery and coarsest buffoonery.

Against these vices, the Peshwas possessed considerable ability, and was "scrupulously just in pecuniary transactions." Humane, frugal, courteous, and dignified in his manners, he devoted considerable sums of money to public and charitable objects. He was in "a great measure his own minister" and showed considerable ability and statecraft in restoring the government of his country, and in strengthening the central power against the disturbing and rebellious feudatories of his extensive dominions. He smarted under the oppressive alliance with the British, which took away his independence and political prestige. A person such as Baji Rao, could not but have a general distrust of others, and nobody could trust him.[9]

Such was the character of the person who had been driven out of Poona by Jaswant Rao Holkar in October 1802,[10] and whom the British had restored to the Peshwaship on 13th May, 1803, after the Treaty of Subsidiary Alliance had been concluded on 31st December at Bassein.

However unpalatable this dependence on his new allies might have been, Baji Rao utilised it to consolidate. His power and the authority of his Government. At the time of his restoration, he took over the charge of a Kingdom which was only "a dreary waste, overrun by thieves,"[11] over which he had nothing but nominal control. Gujarat and Konkan were the only parts of his territory which were at all settled, and even they were under subedars who disregarded his orders and assumed absolute powers. Even the country along the Bhima—about five miles from Poona—was subject to these ravages.[12] His authority was scarcely known south of the Krishna. "Nobody would rent the lands round Poona, because, being near the seat of government, they were liable to disturbances which His Highness as too weak to restrain." The Forts of Lohagarh and Purandhar were held by rebels. "His Highness was destitute of either power or wealth."[13]

Situated as he was, it was neither his interest nor his desire to throw off the alliance which had supported him against his victorious enemies. He devoted his energies to settling his country and restoring order in his administration. He began by reducing the weaker Jagirdars who were unable to resist him, confiscating the lands of the refractory among them. At the same time, he gradually drew the whole power of the State into his own hands.[14] The Treaty of Bassein included a provision that the Subsidiary Force was to be available "for the overawing and chastisement of the rebels,"[15] and the Peshwa always relied on the assistance of this force in his designs against his recalcitrant nobles.

In 1810, Mountstuart Elphinstone was appointed Resident at the Peshwa's Court, where he arrived in the following year. "When Mr. Elphinstone returned to Poona in 1811, he noticed a marked change in the condition of the country, and the authority of the Prince was gradually restored throughout the territory under his immediate administration."[16]

When Baji Rao had completed the confiscations of the minor nobles and put his authority on a somewhat more secure basis, he looked abroad and contemplated the reduction of the Southern Jagirdars,[17] an object very near his heart indeed. He further repeated his claims on the Gaekwar and the Nizam, and asserted sovereignty over the territories in Hindustan and also over Sindhia, Holkar and Berar. The Peshwa artfully put forward these pretensions but never showed any keenness to bring them up to a speedy settlement.[18]

His relation with the powerful Southern Jagirdars, was, however, a matter which the British government was not prepared to leave either to be settled by the Peshwa according to his own free will, or to remain as an open source of trouble and civil strife. It was a thorny issue. Those Jagirdars were, as a class, useful to the country, which, according to Elphinstone,[19] would have been thrown into confusion by their destruction. Moreover, they had loyally fought[20] with the Duke of Wellington (then Sir Arthur Wellesley), and the British government could not stand by and see them wiped out by their vindictive Savereign. At the same time, it would have been obviously unjust to encourage them to flout the Peshwa's authority, or assume independence from his control.

Minto's Government again went into the whole question and decided to settle it by direct intervention. Elphinstone made minute enquiries into the matter, examining their tenures, and the origins of their various families.[21] Finally he was fully[22] empowered to carry out the measures he proposed. The service which the Jagirdars owed to the Peshwa was enforced by the attendance of their troops. They were made to restore the lands which they had usurped. The British Government guaranteed them their terrtories so long as they fulfilled the terms of the agreement and rendered service to the Peshwa. Both sides were very difficult to manage, and it required all the tact and firmness of the able Resident to bring about the settlement between them. This was not finally achieved without putting armies into motion.[23]

As a result of the security which this arrangement conferred upon his vassals Baji Rao grew jealous of their power. He had often expressed a desire to raise a new force which was to be independent of the feudal militia furnished by the Jagirdars. The Minto Government had been keen on that project, and had instructed the Resident to encourage the Peshwa in that desire. The contingent was accordingly formed, and Captain Ford was selected by the Peshwa himself to command it. This was another achievement of Elphinstone for his Government, who, of course, welcomed the proposal.[24]

The formation of the contingent under British officers, following the settlement of the Southern Jagirdars, increased the Peshwa's dependence on the British, and served to draw closer his alliance with that Government. The Peshwa had often declared and "for a time with sincerity"[25] that the alliance was the most fortunate of events for his security. "1 doubt," wrote Elphinstone, "whether he ever maintained a thought of obtaining an increase of his power at the risk of losing his Alliance with us. That Alliance was, in most respects, exactly suited to His Highness's disposition. It afforded him safety and power of pursuing his favourite plans without any great sacrifice of his case."[26] The presence of the British Force at his capital had not only afforded the Peshwa a safe shelter under which to carry on his schemes of systematic suppression of the nobility, but it also served to give him the strength with which to stabilise his own authority and Government. Baji Rao understood this advantage of the alliance and, as has already been noted, exploited it to the fullest extent.[27]

He continued in this outward friendliness to the British Power for some time, until he raised a low favourite, Trimbakji Danglis, to be his minister. This man had been a spy and courier, and became Baji Rao's associate in his base intrigues and private pleasures. He humoured the Peshwa's avarice by farming the revenues of districts at high figures, indemnifying himself by extortion and oppression of the tenants. He was illiterate, unprincipled and arrogant, and of coarse manners. Trimbakji was strongly prejudiced against Europeans. He rose high in the Peshwa's confidence, and was perhaps the only one to enjoy his affection.[28] Although nominally Sadashev Mankeshwar[29] continued to be the Prime Minister of the Peshwa, Trimbakji held the real influence over the Prince. He was first introduced to the Resident in 1814, and to the latter's keen observation and sound judgment, the first impressions of that vicious person revealed is true nature.[30] Danglia had acquired such a hold over his master that the policy of the Peshwa's Government underwent a great change, particularly in his relations with the British Government.[31] Trimbakji became the centre around which the events of the next three years developed, leading finally to the Peshwa's fall and the disappearance of the dynasty itself.

The discussions which brought about those grievous consequences arose out of the old claims which the Peshwa had over the Gaekwar of Baroda, and these he was pressing with increasing earnestness for a final settlement. The basis of these long standing claims rested on two agreements, one entered into by Damaji Gaekwar with a former Peshwa in 1751 and another made with the Peshwa by Fateh Singh Gaekwar, who contested the succession after Damaji's death in 1768. Under the first agreement Damaji resigned half his possessions in Gujarat to the Peshwa, holding the other half as a tributary of the Poona Court. Under the arrangement of 1768, Fateh Singh agreed to pay the increased annual tribute of seventy-nine thousand nine hundred rupees. In the meantime, under the Treaty of 1802, and in the course of the settlement of Gujarat which was undertaken after this Treaty the British Government had established its ascendancy over the Government of the Gaekwar. The Peshwa's claims to tribute from Kathiawar and Baroda had been wholly neglected. These debts amounted to over a crore of rupees, out of which Baji Rao was prepared to relinquish sixty lakhs. The Baroda Government instead of claiming, that exemption, advanced counter claims against Poona for the revenues of Broach, which without right the Peshwa had alienated to the East India Company, and also for the expenses incurred by the Gaekwar in reducing the rebellious districts of Aba Shelukar for the Peshwa. Then again, the farm of the Peshwa's share of Ahmadabad, which he had been induced to grant to the Gaekwar in June 1804 for a further period of ten years, was also due to expire in 1814.[32]

The Governor-General decided that the settlement of all these disputes on intricate claims and counter claims should be attempted by direct negotiation between the two States, without resorting to the undoubted right of arbitration possessed by his Government under the subsisting Treaties with both these States. Accordingly, Gangadhar Shastri,[33] the able Minister of Baroda, was deputed to Poona, to which place he proceeded under the declared guarantee of the British Government for his safety.[34]

The renewal of the lease of Ahmadabad in which the British Government was equally interested[35] with that of the Gaekwar was positively rejected by the Peshwa, who consequently resumed its control, appointing Trimbakji the Governor of that area.[36]

Other disputes formed the subject of negotiations in which Gangadhar Shastri was engaged on his arrival at Poona. But in them also, the Shastri's efforts produced no better results. The Peshwa maintained his demands with unyielding tenacity. Evasion and intrigues were employed to defeat the purpose of the Shastri's mission. Months rolled away, and still no solution of the outstanding questions was in sight.

At the same time, the Peshwa's energies were directed towards fomenting trouble against the Shastri at Baroda, where he was unpopular and certainly detested by a party headed by Sita Ram, the adopted son and successor in office, for some time, of the former Minister, Raoji Appaji. Sita Ram, who was considered incapable and weak, had been intriguing against the British Government, and had been removed from office.[37] Since his effort to regain power had failed with the British Resident at Baroda, he was now engaged in secret dealing with the Poona Court, to bring about the destruction of his enemy, the Shastri, and to obtain the Peshwa's support in his schemes. He had secured for his side the co-operation of Takhti Bai, a Rani of Baroda. Two agents, Bundoji and Bhagwant Rao, had been carrying message between Poona and Baroda, and at one time, the Gaekwar himself had been made an instrument in the hands of this faction. They also attempted, in union with Trimbakji's agents in Ahmadabad, to arouse a rebellion in Gujarat by inviting the forces of Dhar.[38] All these plans had been laid out to divert, the attention of the British Government and defeat Gangadhar Shastri's object.

Seeing this, the latter decided, with Elphinstone's approval, to return to Baroda. That decision produced an immediate change in the Peshwa's attitude. The Shastri was treated with marked favour, and even cajoled into the belief that he would be offered the ministership at Poona. The Peshwa's sister-in-law was offered in marriage to the Shastri's son, an honour which the Baroda minister accepted with more haste than discretion. It was proposed to adjust the Peshwa's claims on the Gaekwar by the cession of territory' yielding seven lakhs of rupees a year. This proposal was referred to the Gaekwar at Baroda. In the meantime, preparation for celebrating the nuptials were made. When the Shastri did not receive his master's assent to the terms of the settlement he desired the postponement of the marriage. This gave mortal offence to the Peshwa and was a slight which he seemed determined to avenge. Trimbakji became thenceforward more intimate than ever towards the Shastri, and treated him with an uncommon show of affection. The Peshwa proceeded from Nasik, whither he had gone for the purpose of celebrating the proposed wedding, to Pandarpur on pilgrimage. The Shastri, who little realised the trap into which he was walking, accompanied the party, sending away his assistant, Bapu Mairal, and his escort, to Poona. Bundoji, Sita Ram's agent, also proceeded to Pandarpur. A deep plot had been laid by the treacherous Trimbakji to take the Shastri's life. On the night of the 14th July, 1815, after an entertainment given by the Peshwa, Gangadhar Shastri was trickily called back to the temple, at the insistent entreaty of Trimbakji, to join in the worship, and on his way home, the Shastri, who was meagrely attended was murdered by assassins hired for the purpose by Trimbakji Danglia.[39]

The general voice of the country pointed to Trimbakji as the instigator of that crime, made far more heinous in the public eye by the manner and place of the deed and the fact that the victim was a Brahmin. The Peshwa was widely suspected of being involved also.

Elphinstone who was at Ellora, forthwith repaired to Poona[40] and addressed a prompt and spirited note to the Peshwa, demanding diligent measures to discover and punish the culprit of that atrocious crime.[41]

The Resident extended protection to the Gaekwar's Vakil Bapu Mairal, in whose escort the intriguers of Poona incited a mutiny for pay, endangering the life of Bapu himself. Elphinstone advanced him 125,000 Rupees, and gave him full assurance of security.

The Peshwa was filled with alarm, and could not make up his mind. At first he denied Trimbakil's complicity in the murder, for want of adequate evidence, then expressed is helplessness since Trimbakji was powerful, being then in command of his 10,000 horse and 5,000 foot, and in possession of his treasure and jewellery. While he was making evasions and professions of friendliness to the British Government, the Peshwa was secretly raising troops. It appeared to the Resident that the Peshwa was determined to shield his favourite, and might possibly let him escape into the country to raise a rebellion.[42]

Elphinstone was fully prepared for every contingency. He had requistioned the subsidiary force to Poona[43] and had arranged for Trimbakji's pursuit should he decide to fly.[44] The Bombay[45] and Madras[46] armies, and the Nizam's subsidiary force,[47] were placed at his disposal. He was given ample discretion to adopt suitable measures on the spot. If the Peshwa attempted to defy the British demand for Trimbakji's trial, and if persuasions failed, the Resident was authorised to secure Baji Rao's person, and prevent his flight from Poona.[48]

These instructions did not arrive until 1st September.[49] In the meantime, the Resident could not wait. He maintained a pressing demand for Trimbakji's arrest and confinement.[50] On grounds of general policy it was found expedient to confine the accusation to Trimbakji[51] and it was pointed out to Baji Rao that the safest course for him was to surrender his guilty minister to the British Government, who undertook not to inflict capital punishment on him. The Peshwa evaded the Resident's demand with excuses and entreaties. At last, Elphinstone drew up a strong note in the name of the British Government, warning the Peshwa of the serious risk he was running in resisting the just demand of the Governor-General. He told Baji Rao's Government that the subsidiary force would wait four miles outside Poona, to take charge of Trimbakji. Baji Rao's timid mind had already been alarmed. On the night of the 5th September, Trimbakji had been removed to the hill fortress of Wasantgarh, in the expectation that the Resident might consent to that compromise. Elphinstone, of course, was not to be so easily shaken from his resolution. Finally, the Peshwa submitted, and on the 19th September, Captain Hicks, of the Peshwa's Brigade, received charge of Trimbakji and delivered him to British troops on the 25th September. He was confined in the Fortress of Thana, and placed under a European guard. Bhagwant Rao Gaekwar, and Govind Rao Bundoji, Trimbakji's two accomplices, were also surrendered at the same time, and made over to the Gaekwar's Government, by whom they were thrown into the Forts of Bainapur and Gondvaripur[52] in chains.

Thus ended an ugly episode in the relations of the British Government with the Peshwa Baji Rao, which for some time threatened to develop into an open rupture, but which was finally settled without resort to arms, through the most skilful handling of the delicate situation by Elphinstone. The Peshwa's indecision and timidity also contributed to this result. Normal relations between the two States were resumed, and the levying of troops was also abandoned after a few months.[53] Moira wrote to Baji Rao a friendly letter on 20th January, 1816, in which he congratulated the Peshwa on surrendering Trimbakji "The undoubted author of that atrocious crime," and assured him that he could rely on the cordial alliance of the British Government.[54]

After the thick, dark clouds, which had for some time assumed a threatening look at Poona, had dispersed, and the atmosphere there was clear, the British government's political interests attracted its attention elsewhere.

Raghuji Bhonsla, the old Raja of Nagpur, died on the 22nd March, 1816, at the age of 58 years.[55] He left a son, Parsoji, who suffered from mental and physical infirmities. Whilst, by right, he succeeded to his father's throne, it was quite clear to all that the state of the new Raja's health, and his mental imbecility, would necessitate the appointment of a Regent to carry on his administration. Mudhoji Bhonsla, better known by his other name, Appa Sahib, son of Venkaji Munia Bapu, was the young Raja's cousin and, therefore, the heir presumptive to the Masnad of Nagpur, being the next male member in the reigning family.

Intrigues, engendered by personal and political motives, began soon after Raghuji's death and, for a time, the whole Court of Nagpur was enveloped in an atmosphere of uncertainty and factious rivalry, threatening to bring about civil strife. Shridhar Pandit, the aged and respected ex-minister had retired to Benares. Buka Bai, as Raghuji's widow, had a strong claim to the Regency of the State, and to the protection of the Raja's person. Dharmaji Bhonsla, a trusted official of the deceased Raja who was in possession of his treasure amounting to about a crore of Rupees, was in great favour with the Dowager Rani. They seemed to have agreed that, with the Rani as the Regent, Dharmaji would manage the internal government, while Nairoba, who was the Foreign Minister, and Sadik Ali Khan, the head of the army in Raghuji's Government, were to continue in these offices. This would have excluded Appa Sahib from the Regency. It was also rumoured that the Raja was to adopt Raghuji's grandson by his eldest daughter to succeed after Parsoji. With this motive, an unsuccessful attempt was made to exclude Appa Sahib from performing the *Shradh*[56] of Raghuji. Appa Sahib, however, asserted his right, and defeated that object.[57]

The British Resident watched this situation of internal dissension and rancorous intrigue with keen interest. He deliberately refrained from a hurried association with either faction, but reported everything to Moirs. He saw clearly that the state of things was very favourable for the negotiation of a subsidiary treaty, which, after sustained and repeated efforts, it had been found impossible to persuade Raghuji to accept. He very soon received secret messages from Appa Sahib, and was expecting to hear from his opponents, seeking British support.[58] Whilst he was not willing to take a hasty step, at the same time, he did not wish to lose that golden opportunity of establishing a British force in Berar, and British influence at the Nagpur Court. It was certain that the British Government would be appealed to for help (as had already been secretly done), and if a dispute arose, Sindhia, or Holkar, or Amir Khan might be called in. Appa Sahib appeared to him to possess the strongest claim to the Regency, since he was the heir-presumptive. Buka Bai had undoubtedly the right to the Raja's person and Appa Sahib to the Government of the country: but the two rights were indivisible, and therefore he advocated Appa Sahib's cause. Moreover, reported the Resident, the principles of the opposite party were averse to the British connection. Any alliance formed with it would not be acquiesced in by Appa Sahib on his accession. The latter appeared friendly to British interests, and had desired British support. "In supporting Appa Sahib, therefore, we should keep our own party in power." Even if the Bai and Dharmaji succeeded in excluding Appa Sahib, it would be advisable to support him, on the condition of a subsidiary treaty previously concluded with him. Jenkins very ably represented the whole situation to his Government, suggesting that he might "be authorised to take advantage of the earliest offer on the subject."[59]

The matter was promptly taken up. And fully discussed at Calcutta,[60] and immediate instructions were issued to Jenkins for his guidance. He was authorised to avail himself of any overtures from the "legitimate Government of Nagpore." That phrase was explained to imply either the Raja's Government, or in the case of his imbecility, the Government deriving its authority from an individual who had the natural right resulting from the situation, in the State, or in the family of the sovereign, or both. So that, if the Raja's mind were considered unfit, Appa Sahib, as the nearest male relative of competent age and qualification, was to be supported, and the Resident was to receive proposals from him. The draft of the treaty sent down in December 1812, was to serve as a model for the new engagement.[61] Colonel Doveton's force was placed at the disposal of the Resident at Nagpur, to be requistioned when necessary.[62]

In the meantime, affairs at Nagpur remained in suspense. Efforts at reconciliation between the rival parties were proceeding, but no agreement was reached.[63] Appa Sahib continued to solicit earnestly the support of the Resident,[64] who gave general friendly ear to those requests, but did not commit himself to any definite course.

Raja Parsoji, who had been formally installed on the throne with proper ceremonies, became reconciled with Appa Sahib, whom he declared as the Regent of the State.[65]

Negotiations having failed, Appa Sahib took a bold course, and had Dharmaji arrested at his own house on the afternoon of the 11th April. On Dharmaji's imprisonment, his comrade, Nairoba Chitnavis felt alarmed, and fled from Nagpur.[66] Appa Sahib thus made his position secure, and in that security, took severe measures to extort the last farthing of the hoard of wealth which Dharmaji possessed.[67] Nairoba and Sadik Ali, in their alarmed condition, showed their willingness to serve under Appa Sahib, provided he agreed to maintain the foreign policy of Raja Raghuji, and refrained from entering into closer union with the British Power. Appa Sahib kept up a show of friendliness with his opponents, but was at the same time carrying on secret conversations with Jenkins, through the medium of Jaswant Rao.[68]

On the 25th of April,[69] the Governor-General's instructions reached the Resident, but owing to Appa Sahib's impatience negotiations had been opened earlier.[70] On the receipt of these clear orders, the Resident continued the discussions,[71] and after a series of conferences conducted with great secrecy, mostly at the house of Appa Sahib's Diwan,

Nagu Pandit, the draft of the Subsidiary Treaty was drawn up. The principle of the engagement, as laid down by the British Government was readily accepted. The discussion dealt only with the matters of detail, relating to the strength of the Subsidiary Force, the amount of subsidy to be paid, as also the form of security and support which Appa Sahib was to receive from the British Government. The Treaty was concluded on the 27th May, and on the following day it was forwarded by the Resident to Calcutta for ratification.[72]

In concluding this Treaty, the British Resident was naturally able to secure more favourable terms than for other engagements of its type, such as the Treaties of Bassein and Hyderabad. Advantage was taken of the internal jealousies in the State, and consequently, the Treaty of Nagpur had more of the protective element, as explained by Jenkins, and less of equality and reciprocity.[73] In order to appease Appa Sahib's fears it was concluded with him, though in the Raja's name. The Subsidiary Force was to consist of six battalions of Infantry, and a Regiment of Cavalry, with one Company of European Artillerymen. At the special desire of Appa Sahib two battalions were to be stationed at Nagpur, the British Government having the right to requisition one in emergency. The subsidy was settled at Rupees seven lakhs and a half, payable in two half-yearly instalments of equal amounts. The Raja was to abstain from hostilities against other Powers, and to refer his disputes with them to British arbitration. The Nagpur Durbar were not to keep up any communication with foreign States, and the British Government engaged not to interfere in the Raja's internal affairs. The State of Nagpur was to maintain a contingent of 3,000 horse and 2,000 foot, subject to the muster, inspection and general control of the British Resident. The Treaty[74] was ratified by the Governor-General, and returned to Nagpur on the 15th June. It was formally presented to Appa Sahib at a ceremonious Durbar.[75] The pensions which the Resident had promised to Nagu Pandit (Rs. 25,000) and Narain Pandit (Rs. 15,000) were sanctioned by the Governor-General in Council.[76] The Resident was warmly congratulated on his ability and judgment in successfully effecting "the accomplishment of an arrangement so long and earnestly desired by the British Government" and the Governor-General permitted him to retain and wear the diamond ring presented to him by Appa Sahib in grateful recognition of his helpfulness.[77]

The Treaty had been kept secret, and was made known at Nagpur just after the Subsidiary Force, under Colonel Walker, had arrived near the Capital, and the brigade which was to be stationed there had taken station near the Residency.[78] The great indignation which arose in the opposite camp alarmed Appa Sahib. The Bai felt aggrieved at the way in which Appa Sahib, thinking his life was in danger, retired on the 27th June to a garden house outside the city, and resided there until he could overpower his opponents. The Subsidiary Force had been stationed at Pandurna, and the brigade was cantoned about three miles from the city on the 18th June.[79]

The conclusion of the Subsidiary Alliance with Nagpur was an event of very great political importance. Its achievement after Raghuji's death, since it had so long been attempted during his lifetime, was of immense advantage to the British position in the country, both for defence and offence. "In the actual condition of India no event could be more fortunate" according to Malcolm" than the Subsidiary Alliance with Nagpur. It struck a serious blow at the power of the Maratha Confederacy."[80]

The other Powers did not in any way hinder or oppose the removal of Nagpur from the class of independent, to that of Subsidiary States, with the introduction of a British force into it, and the establishment of British control over its strategic position and its military resources. The cycle of political events at the time moved with rare good fortune for the British interests. The Nagpur situation arose after the Poona trouble had been satisfactorily settled at the end of 1815, and it concluded favourably for the British Government just before another storm appeared on the Poona horizon.

After Trimbakji had been safely incarcerated at Thana, the relations of the Peshwa' s Government with the British Power resumed their ordinary cordial course. He began again to look to his allies to support his authority over his disobedient nobles.[81] At the same time, he had not forgotten his friend Trimbakji, the one object of his affections. The Peshwa more than once requested the Resident for his release,[82] and renewed these requests with the servility and allurements[83] of which he alone was capable. At times he promised to pay as heavy a price in money for the liberation of Danglia as might be demanded, and at others, represented it as his disgrace in the public eye that his subject and minister should be imprisoned under a foreign Power.[84] Elphinstone remained quite firm, and never allowed Baji Rao to imagine that the British Government would ever set at liberty the person whom they considered to be the author of an atrocious, cold-blooded assassination.[85]

While the repeatedly expressed desire of the Peshwa for Danglia's release or restoration to the Poona Government had been steadily resisted, news suddenly arrived from Thana that Trimbakji had effected his escape from that fortress on the 12th September, in the disguise of a common labourer.[86]

This incident naturally attracted serious notice. By chance, the Peshwa was at that time absent from Poona—a matter of additional anxiety to the British Resident. The latter promptly dispatched a message to Baji Rao telling him that no blame would attach to the Peshwa if he would seize Trimbakji and re-deliver him into British custody, at the same time warning him against the serious consequences of any attempt or inclination on his part to shield him.[87] The Peshwa showed his readiness to apprehend Trimbakji.[88] But the British Resident was too shrewd and too experienced in Baji Rao's ways, to rely merely either on his own warnings to the Peshwa, or on the latter's professions. He took full military precautions lest Trimbakji should incite an insurrection, and the Peshwa should aid it.[89]

The efforts made to re-arrest Danglia failed. No definite information as to his whereabouts was available for some time.[90]

While the Peshwa was anxious to preserve a show of friendliness and goodwill towards the British, he was reported to be carrying on secret intercourse with the other States, with the view of forming defensive alliances amongst the Maratha Powers.[91] At that very time the Pindaris were committing cruel ravages against peaceful citizens, and Moira indignant at Sindhia's supineness in not checking the evil, had addressed a strong remonstrance to that Prince, asking whether he was at war with the British Government.[92] At the same time, the Governor-General did not wish to lose the support and co-operation of the Peshwa if he could avoid doing so. He wrote to Elphinstone, assuming that the intrigues which were carried on in the Peshwa's name, perhaps did not receive his support. The Resident was desired to acquaint the Peshwa with the policy adopted towards Sindhia. Baji Rao was also to be assured that Trimbakji's punishment was out of no acrimony against him, but was undertaken to save the Peshwa's reputation from being tarnished with the blame for the Shastri's murder.[93]

This method of winning the Peshwa's confidence did not succeed. It was soon heard that Trimbakji was assembling troops in the country, about fifty miles from Poona. During the whole of January and February the recruitment was continuing...The Resident demanded that the Peshwa should quell the insurrection, and that Danglia should be arrested. The Peshwa would not admit any rebellion, but the Resident's information confirmed him in the belief that the Peshwa was secretly helping and encouraging Trimbakji's activities.[94]

All this time, the forces of the insurgents were growing in the neighbourhood of the Mahadeo Hills. Elphinstone sent repeated demands for their suppression, and received answers which professed readiness to act, but evaded compliance.[95] This attitude on the part of the Peshwa aroused the deepest suspicions of the Resident, who felt convinced that he was attempting to stir up war against the English, and restore Trimbakji to power. He immediately explained the situation to the head of his Government, advising him to deal with Baji Rao as an enemy. In that despatch, he discussed the question of the arrangements of the Peshwa's Government.[96]

The Marquis of Hastings (as the Earl of Moira had now been created in recognition of his services in the Nepal War)[97] and his Government, took serious notice of the Peshwa's dubious attitude towards Trimbakji, and his game of duplicity towards the British Government. Elphinstone was at once ordered to deal with him in a severe manner. He had forfeited the confidence of the British Government, and could no longer be trusted without adequate securities. As a preliminary to any other arrangement, Baji Rao was to be required to surrender Trimbakji within a stated time, to be fixed by the British Resident. Should he not submit to that preliminary condition, or should he attempt to leave Poona during the negotiations, or should there be any government of troops in any part of his country, the Peshwa was to be treated as an enemy, his person was to be seized, and war declared on him. But if, on the other hand, the Peshwa agreed unconditionally to deliver up Trimbakji, the Resident was to disclose to him the nature of the securities which would be required as a condition of continuing him on the *Masnad*. They were to consist chiefly in the "maintenance of a preponderating military force in our interests in His Highness's territory, and the appropriation to its payment of a larger portion of His Highness's resources than has hitherto been the case." It was determined to carry out the provisions of the Treaty of Bassein, by requiring the Peshwa to keep up the full body of 5,000 horse and 3,000 foot. "This direct augmentation of a force which, though nominally in the service of the Peshwa, will be, in effect, under our exclusive control" was to be made at a total cost of twenty-nine lakhs of Rupees, to be charged to the Peshwa.

Moreover, Baji Rao was to be requested to renounce for himself and his successors all connection whatsoever with other Maratha States, and to recognise the complete dissolution, both in form and substance, of the Maratha Confederacy, to maintain no vakils or agents at Foreign Courts, and to carry on no communications with them, except through British Ministers. He must renounce all claim over the Gaekwar and all rights and pretensions in Hindustan and over the Chiefs of Malwa and Bundelkhand. He must agree also to the lease, to the Gaekwar, of Ahmadabad in perpetuity. The fortress of Ahmadnagar was to be made over to the British government, and a territorial cession in the Konkan or Kandesh was to be demanded to make up the fund of twenty-nine lakhs for the upkeep of the contingent. These directions were issued to Elphinstone on the 7th April.[98]

The Governments of Madras[99] and Bombay[100] and the Resident at Hyderabad[101] were at the same time requested to support his measures by assembling armies against the Peshwa's possessions without delay whenever the Resident might require that assistance. Since these armies were to be moved towards the Peshwa's dominions, it was thought desirable to co-ordinate and strengthen them by putting them under the single command of Sir Thomas Hislop, who was to be assisted in political duties by Sir John Malcolm, as Agent to the Governor-General in the Commander-in-Chief's Camp.[102] Even if it were necessary to declare war on mature deliberation, the Governor-General thought that the re-establishment of Baji Rao under the prescribed conditions would be the most expedient arrangement.[103]

Owing to an insurrection in Cuttack, the Despatch of the 7th April did not reach Poona until the 10th May. In the meantime, affairs at poona were taking a serious turn. In the country, Baji Rao was believed to be supporting Trimbakji's forces.[104] The Resident was informed by secret agents that the peshwa had given six lakhs of Rupees to Gokhale to raise men.[105] The repair of forts, and the recruitment of horse and men were proceeding. Trimbakji's forces were almost becoming identified with the Peshwa's. Preparations were also being made for the Peshwa's departure from Poona.[106]

Under the circumstance, the Resident did not think it prudent to await the arrival of official instructions,[107] and when he saw that his clear strong warnings to the Peshwa on the 1st and 3rd April[108] did not produce the desired change in Baji Rao's policy, he resolved on a more severe course of action. He interviewed the Peshwa on the 6th, and on the 7th May he sent a note to his ministers demanding a clear undertaking within twenty-four hours, to the effect that Trimbakji would be surrendered within a month from that day, and that the forts of Raigarh, Simbagarh and Purandhar would be made over to the British Garrisons as pledges for the fulfilment of the engagement. The Peshwa passed a night of anxious wavering between flight, resistance and submission. The city was surrounded by Colonel Smith on the morning of the 8th. The forts were occupied by British troops.[109] The Peshwa's indecision, which had lasted long enough, was soon brought to an end. On the 14th May, the Resident presented to him the substance of the conditions which the Governor-General desired to be imposed on Baji Rao, as a condition of his restoration to the former relations of goodwill with the British government.[110] After a few days of further reluctance, Baji Rao yielded to the demand and issued a proclamation offering a reward of two lakhs of Rupees and a village of one thousand Rupees revenue, to any person who would produce Trimbakji, dead or alive.[111]

After this, the full demands of the British Government were made known to Baji Rao on the 28th May. He was shocked at the magnitude of the sacrifices demanded of him, and showed considerable aversion to several of the conditions.[112] Resistance was futile. The Resident was not prepared to listen to any objections urged by the ministers[113] of the Peshwa, and refused to modify his demands. The discussion[114] on the draft of the new treaty did not last long; and the Peshwa signed the definitive Treaty on the 13th June, the same being returned duly ratified by the Government on the 5th July.[115]

It would not be out of place to relate briefly a few salient features of this agreement of far-reaching importance. In the first place, the Peshwa engaged to seize and deliver Trimbakji to the British Government, and to hold his family as hostages.[116] what might be considered politically the most important clause, was the recognition by the Peshwa of the dissolution of the Maratha Confederacy, and an undertaking by him to hold no communication with other Powers, except through the British Resident.[117] His claims on Anand Rao Gaekwar were commuted to an annual payment of four lakhs of Rupees, and no further demands were to be made by the Peshwa on the ruler of Baroda.[118] Baji Rao agreed to cede territory for the upkeep of the contingent to the value of thirty-four lakhs of Rupees a year,[119] which sum included the Peshwa's tribute from the Kathiawar Chiefs.[120] The Fort of Ahmadnagar was to be ceded in perpetuity to the British Government.[121] The Peshwa engaged to admit into his dominion any additional number of British troops which the British Government might think necessary, and to permit them to pass through all parts of his country.[122] Other important parts of the Treaty related to the Peshwa's rights over Bundelkhand[123] Malwa and Hindustan,[124] which he transferred in entirety to the East India Company. The Peshwa's share of the farm of the City and Province of Ahmadabad was leased in perpetuity to the Gaekwar of Baroda, for four-and-a-half lakhs of Rupees annually.[125] And lastly, this occasion was utilised to confirm the Six Articles of Agreement ratified by the Peshwa on the 7th July, 1812, concerning the settlement under British guarantee with the Southern Jagirdars.[126]

These are the main features of the Treaty which Baji Rao was obliged to accept, as a punishment for his past actions, and a security for future behaviour. It greatly diminished his resources, dismembered his dominions, and degraded his position. His power was curtained, his influence reduced and his prestige in the country destroyed. The stern stipulations which he had to sign must have rankled within him as the source and symbol of that degradation and injury which he suffered.[127] Never happy at his dependence on the British, much less friendly with them since Trimbakji's influence, Baji Rao must have become still more bitter towards them after the treaty of Poona. But, for the time being, since it suited both his dissimulating nature and his crippled condition, his discontent was driven underground.

The Treaty was promptly executed[128] and to all appearances the diplomatic relations were restored to their friendly footing; Hastings addressed a letter to Baji Rao consoling him in his new situation and expecting a peaceful attitude from him in future.[129]

The whole transaction which terminated in such utter humiliation for the Peshwa, further raised the reputation of the Resident at his Court with his own Government. Elphinstone, to whose judgment and ability must be largely ascribed the avoidance of open war between the Peshwa and the British[130] emerged with laurels which enhanced his fame for diplomatic skill. His success and conduct at this juncture were reported in terms of high eulogy to the Court of Directors.[131]

The Treaty of Poona, like that of Nagpur, conferred great political and military advantages on the East India Company. The Maratha Confederacy was finally destroyed, although its foundation had been considerably undermined by the Treaty of Bassein and other agreements with the several Princes. But the latter had at heart continued to regard the Peshwa as their head. He was now publicly debased from that position, and that constituted no small political gain to the Company's Government. The territorial cessions obtained from the Peshwa added to that Government's strength and resources. This Treaty afforded the Bombay government an opportunity of consolidating and improving its territories, and of obtaining for itself from the Gaekwar's Government the most important and promising City of Gujarat.[132] The transfer of his claims and rights over the Chiefs of Bundelkhand was even a greater gain to the British Government than a loss to the Peshwa. In the general scheme of extensive operations which Lord Hastings was about to undertake, the acquisition of the rights which the Peshwa had over the Chiefs of Saugor, Jhansi, Jalaun and others, was decidely favourable to the British Plans.[133]

The Treaty with the Peshwa was indeed a substantial step forward towards the goal which Hastings aimed at, and which, in his opinion, constituted the most satisfactory solution of the political problem facing his Government, namely, the establishment of British paramountcy over all the States of India.

Whilst it was an achievement and success which must have gratified Hastings, it was not, of course, in accordance with the policy of the Board of Control. The principles of the Treaty were at clear variance with their settled conviction and declared views. "We feel all the objections" wrote the Secret Committee on hearing of the conclusion of the Treaty "which lie against measures tending to reduce or humiliate those native States which, from the extent of their dominions and from their military habits, were formerly ranked as substantive and protective powers." But it was too late for them to modify the Treaty. They received it as a settled fact. However, they acknowledged, though reluctantly, the necessity for giving new efficiency and solidarity to the connection with the Poona State, and sanctioned the political and military measures involved in the Treaty, declaring it at the same time as "an unwelcome though justifiable exception of the general rule of our policy. The occurrence of such exceptions has been unfortunately much too 'frequent; but however numerous the instances in which we may be driven from an adherence to our rule, nothing in our opinion would warrant a systematic departure from it."[134]

The last chapter was an account of political preparation for the realisation of Hastings' aim; this might be considered as registering a substantial advance towards that aim. The

Treaties of Nagpur in 1816. and Poona in 1817 marked, in their many provisions a distinct and definite progress towards the establishments of the political relationship which was desired by the Marquis of Hastings.

REFERENCES

1. Malcolm's views on this in his letter to Lord Moira d. 17th July, 1817. reproduced in his *"Political History of India"* Vol. II. Appendix No. IV, page clxi, he writes:—"We shall complain most of our Mohammedan Allies; we shall suffer most from the Mahrattas." For Elphinstone's opinion, see Colebrooke's *"Life of Elphinstone,"* Vol. I, p. 292. Metcalfe's views have already been noticed in Chapter 11.
2. Articles 12, 13, 14 and 17 of the Treaty of Bassein, Aitchison, Vol. VI. pp. 55-7 (1909 Ed.) and Grant-Duff *Op. Cit.* (1912) Vol. III, p. 208 and pp. 224-6.
3. Malcolm: *Political History of India*. I. p. 466.
4. Elphinstone's letter to Moira d. 20th Nov. 1815. No. 19. Bengal Secret Consultation 30th Dec. 1815, and also Grant-Duff *Op. Cit.* III, p. 226.
5. Elphinstone to Moira 20th Nov. 1815, *Loc. Cit*.
6. This is evidence by the desire, for example, of Appa Sahib to receive his robes of investiture from the Peshwa in 1816, and again in 1817, of the Nana of Saugor to be allowed to maintain his correspondence with the Peshwa of the Gaekwar (as shown by Elphinstone in his letter of 20th Nov. 1815) to adhere to those forms of allegiance to the Peshwa, although his interests suffered by doing that, and finally Sindhia, inspite of his being independent and comparatively speaking superior in strength, always addressed to the Peshwa messages in which he made a show of compliance to his orders. Sir J. Malcolm speaks of them as "Mahratha Princes and Chiefs, who were before nominally subject to his power, and who still recognised him, in all forms and public acts, as the head of the nation." His *Political History*, Vol. 1, p. 467.
7. Elphinstone to Moira, in his letter of 20th Nov., No. 19, Bengal Secret Consultations, 30th Dec. 1815.
8. Such as Sir John Malcolm, Captain Grant-Duff, Prinsep, and the Hon. M. Elphinstone. The account of the last-named gentleman was based on close personal observation and has been relied upon

in the brief sketch given here. All the accounts agree in their general tenor.

9. Elphinstone's Despatch to Moira of the 20th Nov. 1815, *op. Cit.* also Malcolm's *Political History* Vol. I, 468. Grant-Duff (1912 edition) *Op. Cit.* III, Chap. XVI, and Wilson *Op. Cit. II,* pp. 148-9.
10. Grant-Duff; Vol. III, pp. 206-8, and 225-31.
11. The unsettled condition of the country was described by Arthur Wellesley to Marquis of Wellesley, the Governor-General. in a letter d. 15th Jan. 1804. (*Wellington Despatches:* 1837 Edition, Vol. 11. p. 673.)
12. *Ibid.*
13. Another description of the chaotic condition of the Peshwa's country at the same time:—letter of Sir B. Close to Governor-General Wellesley, 18th Dec. 1803, quoted by Elphinstone in his letter to Moira, 20th Nov. 1815, in Bengal Secret Consultations No. 19, 30th Dec. 1815.
14. Elphinstone's Despatch to Moira of 20th Nov. 1815. *Loc. Cit.*
15. Art. 9 of the treaty. (Aitchison, *Op. Cit* Vol. VI. p. 54, 1909 Ed.)
16. Colebrooke's *Life of Elphinstone,* Vol. 1, p. 246, also Malcolm *Political History*. I. 466.
17. Greater Jagirdars, "particularly the Putwurdhnus. Rastia and the Dessaye of Kittoor." Grant-Duff Vol. III, p. 348.
18. Grant-Duff *Op. Cit.* Vol. III, p. 356 and Prinsep *Op. Cit.* Vol. I, pp. 276-7.
19. Colebrooke's *Life of Elphinstone,* Vol. I. p. 250.
20. Malcolm *Political History,* Vol. I. p. 467. Grant-Duff, *Op. Cit.* III (1912 Ed.) pp. 348-9, Prinsep, *Op. Cit,* Vol. I, p. 275.
21. He submitted his Report in October 1812, Colebrooke's *Life of Elphinstone. Op. Cit.* Vol. I, p. 248.
22. "I had a *carte blanche* for all the disposable force of the Deccan." Elphinstone to Strachey, 12th July, 1813, *Loc. Cit.* Vol. I, p. 252.
23. *Loc. Cit.* Vol. I, pp. 250-55, Grant-Duff *Op. Cit.* Vol. III, p. 349. On this occasion, the Resident made another settlement by which the Rajas of Kolhapur and Sawantwari were made independent of the Peshwa's sovereignty (Prinsep I, p. 275), and those two States were bound down to suppress piracy, and Kolhapur had to cede to the British the port of Malayan. Grant-Duff, *Op. Cit.* Vol. III, pp. 350-1 and Colebrooke's *Life of Elphinstone.* Vol. I, pp. 250-1.

24. Elphinstone's Despatched. 16th Jan. No. 9. Bengal Secret Consultations 19th Feb. 1813. Also Colebrooke's *Life of Elphinstone*, pp. 251 and 253.
25. According to Grant-Duff, Vol. III, p. 335.
26. His Despatch of 20th Nov. 1815, *Op. Cit*.
27. Grant-Duff, *Op. Cit*. (1912) Vol. III, pp. 335-6.
28. Colebrooke, *Op. Cit*. Vol. 1, pp. 292-3. Grant-Duff, III, pp. 356-7, and Wilson, Book II, p. 150.
29. Sadasheo was "a great musician and a composer...and as a statesman possessed of considerable ability." Grant-Duff, III, pp. 334-5, but according to Elphinstone (his Despatch to Moira of the 21st Mar. 1817. No. 9, Bengal Secret Consultations 7th Apr. 1817) he had "not sufficient courage or abilities."
30. Prinsep, *Op. Cit*. Vol. I, pp. 279-280.
31. Prinsep, Vol. I, pp. 319-20,

    Footnote.

    Elphinstone protested against Trimbakji's measures in a note to the Peshwa d. 27th May 1815 (reference to which is also found in the appendix to Minute of 1st Dec. 1815, No. 2, Bengal Secret Consultation 15th June 1816). For Trimbakji's measures indicating his anti-British attitude see also Elphinstone's Despatch to Moira d. 16th Aug. 1815. No. 36, Bengal Secret Consultations, 27th September 1815.
32. Grant-Duff, Vol. III, pp. 365 and 369-70, Prinsep, Vol. I, pp. 270-3 and 278. According to Prinsep the total claims of the Peshwa amounted to over three crores of rupees, and "the Gaekwar had little to set off against these claims." p. 278; Wallace, *The Guicowar and His Relations with the British Government*, pp. 195-6 and 204-5.
33. "A person of great shrewdness and talent, who keeps the whole state of Baroda in the highest order." Elphinstone, (Colebrooke, Vol. I, p. 276). At Baroda he was a supporter of the British influence, and was considered its agent. (Wallace, *The Guicowar*, p. 208). The Shastri was formerly the Bombay Government's Agent at the Durbar of Baroda, and in May 1813 raised to a confidential position by Fateh Singh Gaekwar. (Bombay Government's Despatch to Moira, 26th July, 1815, No. 18, Bengal Secret Consultations, 6th September 1815.)
34. Grant-Duff, Vol. III, p. 371, also No. 2, Bengal Secret Consultations 15th June, 1816, appendix to Governor-General's Minute of 1st Dec. 1815, *Op. Cit*.

35. Grant-Duff, Vol. III, p. 368, and the Despatch of the Secret Committee to the Governor-General in Council of Oct. 26th, 1816, Board's draft No. 120. Vol. 5.
36. Prinsep, Vol. I, p. 279. Grant-Duff, Vol. III, pp. 372-3.
37. Wallace's *Guicowar,* pp. 139-154.
38. Chief Secretary, Bombay Government to Capt. Carnac, Resident at Baroda, 18th Oct. 1815, No. 3, Bengal Secret Consultations, 25th Nov. 1815. In one of the letters which were intercepted these words occur:- "Shastry cannot come back again," It was written by one of Sita Ram's agents to him, on 23rd Aug., 1814.
39. Elphinstone to Moira, Despatch dated the 16th Aug., 1815, No. 36, Bengal Secret Consultations, 27th Sept. 1815; also Grant-Duff, Vol. III, pp 373-5; Prinsep, Vol. I, pp. 282-92; Forrest's *Selection from the Official Writings of M. Elphinstone,* pp. 134-143.
40. Arrived there on 6th Aug. and the Peshwa himself quietly entered the Capital on the 9th in a closed palanquin. (Elphinstone to Moira 16th Aug., No. 36, Bengal Secret Consultations 27th September, 1815).
41. On the 25th July 1815, from Ellora, No. 35, Bengal Secret Consultations, 23rd Aug. 1815. It was followed by another paper sent to the Peshwa on the 15th Aug., in which he protested that the Peshwa had not taken any steps to bring the culprits to trial, and that Trimbakji's guilt had been fully established.
42. Elphinstone to Moira, 18th Aug. 1815, No. 133, 20th Aug., No. 135, also Despatches to Moira, 23rd Aug., No. 139, 28th Aug., No. 142, and 29th Aug., No. 144. Bengal Secret Consultations, 20th Sept. 1815, and another of 6th Sept. No. 70 Bengal Secret Consultations, 7th Oct. 1815.
43. Despatch of 18th Aug., No. 133, Bengal Secret Consultations, 20th Sept. 1815. The first detachment reached Poona on the morning of the 17th August.
44. Private letter from Elphinstone to Doveton, 27th Aug. No. 30, Bengal Secret Consultations, 4th Oct. 1815.
45. Secretary Adam to Bombay Government, 15th Aug., No. 28, Bengal Secret Consultations, 20th Sept. 1815.
46. Another Despatch, No. 29 *Locc. Cit.*
47. Another, No. 30, *Loc Cit.,* and also Russell to Adam, 7th Sept. 1815, No. 16, Bengal Secret Consultations, 4th Oct. 1815.
48. Adam to Elphinstone, 15th Aug., No. 26, Bengal Secret Consultations 20th Sept. 1815.

49. Elphinstone to Moira, 6th Sept. No. 70, Bengal Secret Consultations, 7th Oct. 1815.

50. Elphinstone to Moira, 28th Aug., No. 142, Bengal Secret Consultations, 20th Sept. 1815.

51. Adam to Elphinstone, 10th Sept., No. 22, Bengal Secret Consulations, 27th Sept. 1815.

52. Elphinstone to Moira, 6th Sept. 1815, No. 70, Elphinstone's note to the Peshwa on 4th Sept. No. 71, Elphinstone's despatch to Moira of the 10th Sept., 1815, No. 73, Bengal Secret Consultations, 7th Oct., 1815. Captain Hicks to Elphinstone, 19th Sept., No. 32, and Elphinstone to Moira, 26th Sept.. No. 33, Bengal Secret Consultations, 20th Oct. 1815. Resident at Baroda to Chief Secretary at Bombay, 16th Oct., No. 6, Bengal Secret Consultations, 25th Nov. 1815, and Chief secretary Bombay to Secretary Adam, 17th Oct. 1815. No. 1 Bengal Secret Consultations, 17th Nov., 1815.

53. Elphinstone to Moira, 25th Oct., No. 2, Bengal Secret Consultations, 17th Nov., 1815, despatch 10th Dec. 1815, No. 83, Bengal Secret Consultations, 13th Jan. 1816, and of 20th Feb., 1816, No. 21, Bengal Secret Consultations, 23rd March 1816.

54. Moira to Bajo Rao, No. 11, Bengal Secret Consultations, 20th Jan., 1816.

55. Jenkin's report, *Op. Cit.* submitted to Lord Amherst, (printed 1827), p. 127.

56. Some rites and ceremonies performed for the dead, according to Hindu custom, by the son, and, in his absence, by the nearest relative of the deceased.

57. Jenkins to Moira, despatches of 25th Mar., No. 1, and 29th Mar. No. 2, Bengal Secret Consultations, 15th Apr. 1816.

58. Despatch to Moira of 29th March, *Loc. cit.*

59. To Moira, 29th March 1816. *Loc. Cit.*

60. Minute of the Governor-General, 13th Apr. 1816, No. 3, of Edmonstone, 13th Apr., No. 4, Bengal Secret Consulations, 15th Apr. 1816. Moira strongly urged the advantages of concluding the agreement with Nagpur by supporting the cause of Appa Sahib, on grounds both of justice and of expediency. Edmonstone concurred with him in almost everything.

61. Adam to Jenkins, 13th Apr. No. 5, Bengal Secret Consultations, 15th Apr. 1816. In another Despatch the Resident was also asked to enquire and report what claims Appa Sahib had to the Masnad

in preference to Raghuji's grandson. (Adam to Jenkins, 13th Apr., No. 12, Bengal Secret Consultations, 15th Apr. 1816.)

62. Adam to Doveton, 13th Apr., No. 17, Bengal Secret Consultations, 15th Apr. 1816.

63. Jenkins to Moira, 2nd Apr. No. 17, Bengal Secret Consultations, 20th Apr. 1816.

64. Jenkins to Moira, 5th Apr., No. 18, Bengal Secret Consultations, 20th Apr. 1816, 13th Apr. 1816, No. 3, Bengal Secret Consultations, 4th May, and 22nd Apr., No. 19, Bengal Secret Consultations, 18th May, 1816.

65. Jenkins to Moira, 14th Apr. 1816, No. 3, Bengal Secret Consultations, 4th May 1816.

66. Jenkins to Moira, 13th Apr., No. 3, Bengal Secret Consultations, 4th May 1816.

67. Jenkins to Moira, 22nd Apr., No. 19, Bengal Secret Consultations, 18th May 1816.

68. *Ibid.*

69. Prinsep, Vol. I, p. 362.

70. Jenkins' Despatch of 22nd Apr., Minutes of the Conferences, No. 23, Bengal Secret Consultations, 11th June 1816, also Prinsep, Vol. I, pp. 360-1.

71. Jenkins to Adam. 28th Apr. 1816. No. 9 and No. 10, Bengal Secret Consultations, 11th May 1816.

72. Jenkins to Moira, 28th May 1816, No. 21, enclosing with it the copy of the Resident's letter to Appa Sahib, assuring him of British support, and another to Adam, 28th May, No. 22, also enclosing the full Minutes of the Conferences during negotiations from 22nd Apr. till the conclusion of the treaty, No. 23, Bengal Secret Consultations, 11th June, 1816.

73. Jenkins to Moira, *Loc. Cit.*, also articles 1 and 2 of the Treaty (next footnote).

74. Consisting of 15 Articles, No. 13, Bengal Secret Consultations, 15th June 1816.

75. Jenkins to Moira, 13th July, No. 4, Bengal Secret Consultations, 17th August 1816.

76. Adams to Jenkins, 13th June, No. 14, Bengal Secret Consultations, 15th June 1816.

77. *Ibid.*

78. Jenkins to Moira, 10th June, No. 14, Bengal Secret Consultations 29th June 1816, and Jenkins to Walker, 30th May, No. 9, Bengal Secret Consultations. 22nd June, 1816.

79. Jenkins to Moira, 10th June, No. 14, Bengal Secret Consultations 29th June, and 29th June, No. 6, Bengal Secret Consultations. 23rd July, 1816.

80. His *Political History,* Vol. I, p. 465.

81. Appa Desai was again in revolt, and Elphinstone encouraged Baji Rao in assuming a decided tone in suppressing him. (Elphinstone to Moira, 20th Feb., No. 21, Bengal Secret Consultation, 23rd March 1816.)

82. Elphinstone to Adam, 27th Oct. 1815, No. 8, Bengal Secret Consultations. 27th Nov. 1815. This request was indirectly made.

83. Same to same, 30th Nov. 1815, No. 18, Bengal Secret Consultations, 6th Jan. 1816.

84. Same to same, 24th Feb. 1816. No. 22, Bengal Secret Consultations 23rd Mar., and also 14th June 1816, No 13, Bengal Secret Consultations 13th July, 1816. The Peshwa was even reported to depute a Vakil to Calcutta for obtaining the redress of his grievances, including the liberation of his favourite. (Elphinstone to Adam, 19th Aug. 1816, No. 24, Bengal Secret Consultations, 14th Sept. 1816.)

85. Elphinstone's Despatches 27th Oct. 1815, 30th Nov, 1815, 24th Feb. 1816, and 14th June 1816, referred to in the preceding footnotes.

86. From Judge and Magistrate Thana to Elphinstone, 12th Sept., No. 4, Bengal Secret Consultations, 12th Oct. 1816.

87. Elphinstone to Moira, 14th Sept., No. 3, Bengal Secret Consultations, 12th Oct. 1816.

88. Elphinstone to Adam, 19th. Sept., No. 9, Bengal Secret Consultations, 12th Oct., 1816.

89. Elphinstone to Col. Smith, 15th Sept. 1816, No. 61, Bengal Secret Consultations, 12th Oct. 1816, Elphinstone to Smith, No. 6, Bengal Secret Consultations, 19th Oct 1816. Smith to Colonel Kingscote 17th Sept. No. 7, Bengal Secret Consultations, 19th Oct. 1816.

90. Elphinstone to Smith, 27th Sept. No. 7. Bengal Secret Consultations, 26th Oct. 1816, and Elphinstone to Moira, 3rd Nov. No. 6, Bengal Secret Consultations, 30th Nov. 1816.

91. Elphinstone to Adam, 21st Dec. 1816, No. 3, Bengal Secret Consultations, 18th Jan. 1817. Resident at Poona also enclosed a

copy of an *Akhbar* showing how the Peshwa's Vakils had been sent to Holkar's Court, and to other Maratha Princes. (No. 4, Bengal Secret Consultations, 8th Jan. 1817.).

92. Adam to Resident with Sindhia, 14th Jan, 1817, No. 1, and also No. 2, Bengal Secret Consultations, 18th January 1817.

93. Moira to Elphinstone, 17th January 1817, No. 5, Bengal Secret Consultations, 18th January 187.

94. Elphinstone to Moira, 11th March No. 7, Bengal Secret Consultations, 7th April 1817.

95. Elphinstone sent notes to the Peshwa on 9th and 25th February and 2nd, 3rd, 4th and 7th March No. 8, Bengal Secret Consultations, 7th April 1817.

96. Elphinstone to Hastings. 21st March No. 9, Bengal Secret Consultations, 7th April 1817. This was an important Despatch as it contained the suggestions which formed the principles of the drastic instructions that were issued on the 7th April and on which the Treaty of Poona was eventually based.

97. On 13th February 1817, *Dictionary of National Biography*, (1891), Vol. XXV, p. 119.

98. Adam to Elphinstone, No. 10, Bengal Secret Consultations, 7th Apr. 1817.

99. No. 11, *Loc. Cit.*

100. No. 12. *Loc. Cit.*

101. No. 13. *Loc. Cit.*

102. Governor-General's Minute of 10th May, No. 1, Despatches of the same date to Governor, Fort St. George, No. 2. Sir Thomas Hislop, No. 3,. Sir John Malcolm, No. 5, Bengal Secret Consultations, 10th May, 1817.

103. Adam to Elphinstone, 17th May, No. 3, Bengal Secret Consultations 17th May, 1817.

104. Elphinstone to Hastings, 9th April, No. 29, Bengal Secret Consultations, 10th May, 1817.

105. Elphinstone to Hastings, 7th Apr. No. 25, *Loc. Cit.*

106. Elphinstone to Hastings, 26th Mar. No. 3, Elphinstone to Adam 28th Mar. Nos. 4 and 5, Bengal Secret Consultations 19th Apr. and Elphinstone to Hastings. 19th Apr. Nos. 29 and 30, Bengal Secret Consultations, 17th May, 1817.

107. Elphinstone had fortunately found out through private letters from Adam what the nature of these instructions was going to

be. (Secret letter from Bengal Government to the Secret Committee 9th June, 1817. Forrest. *Official Writings of M. Elphinstons,* p. 175, also Elphinstone's Despatch to Hastings 9th May, No. 17. Bengal Secret Consultations, 31st May, 1817.)

108. Nos. 27 and 28, Bengal Secret Consultations, 10th May. 1817.

109. Elphinstone to Hastings, 9th May, 1817 (Forrest, *Op. Cit.* pp. 209-20. Conference between Baji Rao and Elphinstone, pp. 220-228. Note of 7th May, pp. 229-31).

110. Elphinstone to Hastings, 24th May, 1817, Forrest, *Op. Cit.*, pp. 233-38.

111. Issued on the 21st May, No. 13, Bengal Secret Consultations, 14th June, 1817.

112. Elphinstone to Hastings, 6th June, No. 12, Bengal Secret Consultations, 5th July, 1817.

113. Elphinstone to Hastings, 13th June, No. 2, Bengal Secret Consultations, 7th July, 1817.

114. Notes of Conference, Nos. 13, 14, 15, Bengal Secret Consultations, 5th July, 1817.

115. Elphinstone to Adam, 14th June, No. 24 and No. 25, (Text of the Treaty) Bengal Secret Consultations, 5th July, 1817, also Aitchison, (1909 Ed.) Vol. VI., pp. 64-70.

116. Art. I, *Loc. Cit.*

117. Art. 4, the Peshwa also renounced all claims over Sawantwari and Kolhapur, whose independence of the Peshwa was further confirmed.

118. Art. 5.

119. The Resident suggested this increase over the original figure of twenty-nine lakhs laid down by the Governor-General in Council. (Elphinstone to Adam. 4th June, No. 10, Bengal Secret Consultations, 5th July.)

120. Art. 7.

121. Art. 12.

122. *Ibid.*

123. Art. 13.

124. Art. 14.

125. Art. 15.

126. Art. 16.

127. Elphinstone to Hastings, 15th Oct. No. 36, Bengal Secret Consultations, 21st Nov. 1817.

128. Adam to Elphinstone, 5th July, No. 26, Bengal Secret Consultations, 5th July, 1817, and 25th July No. 2, Bengal Secret Consultations. 15th Aug. 1817.

129. 25th July, 1817. No. 3. Bengal Secret Consultations, 15th August 1817.

130. His motive for not attacking the Peshwa at Poona do him great credit (His Despatch of 9th May, Forrest, *Op. Cit.*, p. 210.)

131. Adam to Elphinstone, 25th July No. 2, Bengal Secret Consultations, 15th Aug. 1817.

132. This transaction will again be noticed later. See the opinion of Captain Carnac, the Resident at Baroda, on the beauty, promise and prosperity of Ahmadabad. (Carnac to the Chief Secretary, Bombay, 26th Aug. 1817, No. 20, Bengal Secret Consultations, 17th Oct. 1817.)

133. Prinsep, Vol. II, p. 10.

134. Secret Committee's letter to Governor-General in Council, 5th Jan. 1818, No. 122, *Board's Drafts*, Vol. V.

4

Moira Applies His Policy

PREPARATION

Pindaris—measures adopted by Minto Government-their settlements southward of the Narbada—Moira's military measures against them—their partial suspension owing to rumoured attack of Amir Khan on Berar—preparations against the Pathans—political measures thought necessary—subsidiary alliance with Nagpur—sustained efforts of the resident—failure—other alternatives—Bhopal threatened by Sindhia and Nagpur—Nawab applies for British protection—Moira forthwith decides to treat with Bhopal—subsidiary alliance offered—similarly Saugor also offered a subsidiary alliance—military preparations to support these alliances—Sindhia's vehement objection—his claims over Bhopal—denied by Moira—further military measures warlike preparations—Sindhia's withdrawal of his forces from Bhopal—Nawab's indifference his duplicity—Moira disgusted—negotiations broken off—Saugor—Nana's hesitation—attempt abandoned—the armies dispressed—Jaipur—Moira advocates alliance with that state—Maharaja's application—entertained—instructions to Metcalfe—Amir Khan's siege of Jaipur—Maharaja's dealings—simultaneous dealings with the British, Sindhia and Amir Khan—negotiations—military measures—armies assembled—Jaipur Government's indifference—terms agreed—extravagant demands—negotiations broken off-summary of the chapter.

Passing mention has already been made that the Minto Government had ordered precautionary measures against the Pindaris. The Commander-in-Chief was instructed to take such steps as would prevent the marauders from making inroads into British territory. At that time, those arrangements were purely military safeguards and bore no political character either in plan or execution. The disposition of the troops had been arranged to meet the contingency of a possible Pindari raid, and was not ordered to provide against the hostility of any States of Hindustan. The latter were not believed to entertain designs against the British Power at that time.[1]

This state of affairs continued from 1812 until the spring of 1814. The Government at Calcutta were kept in constant touch with the position nand activity of the Pindaris, by their Residents with the Princes of Central India, and more particularly by Captain Sydenham. The latter was, at his own suggestion, transferred by the Resident at Hyderabad from Aurangabad to Sandurgaon, a place further north and nearer the Pindari settlements, so that he could obtain fuller and quicker accounts of their doings.[2] The Bengal Government, in their turn, reported regularly to the authorities in England, the intelligence received from their officers relative to the Pindaris.[3] During that period, they had neither attacked the British territories nor molested their subjects in any way.[4]

The Pindari leaders were warring amongst themselves. Although Karim was under restraint at Holkar's Court, his lieutenants, Namdar Khan and Kushal Kunwar commanded strong contingents. Chitu was at that moment the most powerful of them, and was said to possess 10,000 horse, including 5,000 good cavalry, besides infantry and guns.[5] He was attacked by the Karim Shahi Pindaris and obliged to fly. The ruler of Bhopal helped them in driving Chitu from his possessions (except Satwas and Champaner).[6] While Chitu retreated to Ujjain to recover his strength, his pursuers returned to Satwas and besieged that fortress, which contained his family. One of his lieutenants bravely defended it against the attackers.[7]

While these internal dissensions were in progress between the rival parties of Chitu and Karim, other Pindaris under Shaikh Abdulla carried on plundering excursions into Berar and Hyderabad territories; the latter suffered heavily from the destruction of crops, property and villages.[8] It appeared that the Pindaris were steadily extending their settlements to the South. This movement became known in the closing months of the year 1813. Chitu's lands were resumed by Maharaja Sindhia, but Chitu retaliated by laying waste Sindhia's territories to the south of the Narbada.[9] That movement of the Pindaris across the Narbada to the vicinity of Burhanpur and Asirgarh, towards Hundia, became a subject of negotiation between the Governments of Sindhia and the Company. The Resident conferred with the Maharaja's ministers and urged speedy action to frustrate Chitu's plans.[10] The Maharaja was roused to action by the protests of the Resident, although he himself realised, without admitting it to the British Government, that his own army was too scattered and undisciplined to achieve that end.[11] He ordered his generals, (Baptiste and a Maratha commander) to lead an expedition against the Pindaris, and also called upon Raj Rana Zalim Singh, the powerful manage of Kota, to furnish an auxiliary force for the purpose.[12]

As has been remarked a little while ago, the Company's Government had until then pursued a military policy, against the Pindaris, which did not include any political plan. Exceptions to this were the two minor treaties concluded with Rewa and Orchha (also called Tehri), both in Bundelkhand, and the negotiations undertaken to bring the Bhonsla under a subsidiary alliance, which will be noticed hereafter. Until this time, the British government had not contemplated any general action of an extended nature, for the extirpation of the Pindaris. There had even been a time when it had shrunk from arousing expectations in Sindhia's mind of such co-operation with him in that matter as would involve undefined liability on their part.[13]

The Pindaris' movement across to the left bank of the Narbada, and the uncertainty of Sindhia's ability or anxiety to drive them back, led to a change in British policy. Whilst still abstaining from adopting, any political scheme which might lead to hostilitie with other State, they decided to employ the subsidiary force of the Nizam at Jalna to attack the Pindaris and prevent their settling on the southern side of the river. With that object, orders were issued on the 8th February, 1814, to the Resident at Hyderabad.[14] A few days after this decision to take the offensive against the Pindaris, Moira's Government reconsidered that order in view of the persistent rumours that Amir Khan was contemplating an attack on the territories of Raghuji Bhonsla.[15] On February 26th fresh instructions were issued to the Resident suspending the former orders in view of these rumours about Amir Khan's designs on Nagpur. The Nizam's subsidiary force was to be kept in readiness to cover Berar from the Pathan incursion. Although the projected attack on the Pindari positions was suspended, (not abandoned), yet the Resident was instructed to block the passes of the Deccan against the Pindaris.[16] News of Amir Khans hostile designs on Berar continued to pour in all through the first half of 1814.[17] The British Government was naturally desirous of defeating his evil designs, not only as an act of far-sighted sagacity, but also in order to protect the dominions of their ally, the Nizam. These adjoined Nagpur territory, which they were bound to defend against all foreign aggression. Brisk military preparations were undertaken, the Peshwa's subsidiary force being ordered to be kept in readiness at Serur. Simultaneously, the available force in Bundelkhand was to assemble at an advanced position on the frontier of that province.[18] The Government of Bombay was also asked to despatch the force under Lieutenant-Colonel Dowse to Jalna, and to be prepared for any further military and political acting that might be taken. The troops from Bombay were required to reach Jalna by the 1st September.[19]

From this military activity the Pindaris and the Indian States must have gained the impression that something decisive was in contemplation. Lord Moira on his part, felt that his government had to protect its vast dominion against so many dangers that its military strength was insufficient for the purpose.[20] On the 1st Feb. 1814, he wrote that the frontiers or the British provinces were exposed to constant danger from the Pindaris, more particularly the unprotected part bordering on Raghuji's territory.[21] These strategic defects in the military position led him (Lord Moirs) to the conclusion that he could not wisely restrict himself to measures of a military nature only. Political action appeared to him to be necessary also. He himself had formulated the principles on which that action should be based,[22] but since his policy and programme were unacceptable both in the Council and in England, he cold not bring his plan into systematic operation at once.

But there was one political step which he found himself at liberty to take. He approved it, as it had the merit of strengthening the strategic position of the Company's territories. It consisted of persuading Raghuji Bhonsla of Nagpur to enter into a subsidiary alliance with the Company.

In 1809-10, the Raja's territories had been attacked by the forces of Amir Khan, the Pathan Chief, and Wazir Muhammad of Bhopal. Without any request on the part of the Bhonsla, the Minto Government sent a force under Colonel Barry Close, to save his State. The Raja was consequently able to repulse his enemies.[23] As a result of their unsolicited assistance the British Government expected the Raja to accept a permanent British contingent in his country, and bind himself by ties of subsidiary relations. A draft treaty was sent down to the Resident at the end of 1812[24] and for a time it appeared[25] to Jenkins that the attempt would succeed. If that plan had come about, the British line of unprotected frontier would have been greatly reduced. A British subsidiary force would have been stationed in Nagpur territory, and consequently some of the richest of the British districts would have been better guarded against the Pindari menace. The Raja's territory, too, would have been saved the almost annual visitations of their plundering hordes. "The objects of the proposed arrangement are to secure the military command of the territories and resources of Nagpur for purpose of general defence," wrote the Bengal Government approvingly to their representative at Nagpur.[26] The efforts to realise this purpose began in the time of Minto, and continued unremittingly for nearly two years. The Moira government pressed them with great keenness. All kinds of political pressure, and a full measure of diplomatic skill, were employed to achieve that end, on which the Bengal Government had set its heart, and which was obviously of great importance to their interests.[27] Amir Khan's projects against the Raja afforded a suitable occasion for the renewal of those efforts, while the timid Raja was under the fear of that invasion, and the knowledge of the wretched condition of his own army.[28] But he remained indifferent, and evaded the demands made of him, even when threatened by the Pathan Chief, Jenkins, an exceedingly able and sagacious officer, continued in his optimism for some time. Those of the ministers who were favourable[29] to the proposed alliance with the Company's government, also cherished similar hopes. The Raja, however, remained unmoved, and turned a deaf ear to all the suggestions and advice which were pressed on his attention by the Resident and by his ministers. Nothing would persuade him to accept the suggesteu course. By the middle of June, Jenkins informed Moira that the Raja seemed determined to resist his overtures. Neither, political pressure nor diplomatic entreaties, nor even a sense of immediate danger, could persuade him to change his mind. He was prepared for the worst, and would "rather resign his dominions, and go to Calcutta" than submit to the hateful alliance. "Jealousy of his independence is the leading principle that prompts that repugnance." The Resident informed the Governor-General in the same long letter how the "ministers Sreedhur Pundit and Juswant Rao, the Rajah considers, as wholly devoted to our interests," and the latter whom he had taken back in his service at Lord Minto's insistence, "has not only lost the Raja's confidence, but is the object of His Highness's aversion." Jenkins believed that the adverse influence which swayed the Raja's mind came from the opposite party, which favoured his allying with the Peshwa.[30] Although Jenkins assured the Governor-General that he would do his utmost to continue in his efforts, he had by that time lost all hopes of any success; and a few weeks later, on the 26th September, he apprised Moira of Raghuji's final refusal to enter into a subsidiary alliance.[31] This news reached Moira when he was proceeding up the river for his tour of the upper provinces.

As chances of the Nagpur alliance became less hopeful, the Governor-General looked round for another plan to realise the same political object and acquire the same military position in Central Indian affairs, which would have been acquired by that eagerly-sought alliance.

The great influence which Metcalfe exerted on Moira's mind in shaping his policy, has already been noticed. It is very interesting to see how, in the selection of a plan which could be an adequate alternative to the Nagpur treaty, and equally beneficial in its effect, the first suggestion came from man other disciple of the Wellesley school. It was Mr. (Late Sir Richard) Jenkins, the able Resident, and eventually the Administrator, of Nagpur who was the author of the idea.

Long before the British Government had thought of undertaking any great political measures to strengthen their position in Central India, before Moira had shaped is own policy, and certainly before his Government was prepared to approve that forward step.[32] Jenkins informed the Bengal government that he had hinted to the Raja of Nagpur that in the event of his remaining obstinate, the British might adopt other measures in the determination of which the interests of the Raja would not be consulted. The resident had in view the Plan[33] of forming a connection between the British and the Chiefs of Bhopal and Saugor.[34]

These two principalities lie in the heart of Central India, on the northern side of the Narbada, in a region adjoining the Pindari homes, and included in the scene of their activity. By an alliance with these Malwa States, the British Government could realise the same advantages against the Pindaris, as it expected from the Nagpur alliance, with the additional gain of isolating the Raja of Nagpur, and cutting him off from Sindhia's territories.

The principles of Moira's political programme, formulated at an early period of his term of office, included the scheme but which Bhopal was to be taken under British protection. Since the Bhonsla remained so obstinately indifferent to British overtures of alliance, it was proposed "to annex to the dominions of the Nawab of Bhopal those territories of the Rajah of Nagpore which lie to the north of the Narbada. That boon and the security to be derived from our protection would make the Nawab very ready to place his state on the footing of dependence on our government, with the obligation of resisting any force hostile to us which should attempt to pass through his country."[35]

Consequently, on receipt of the long letter from Jenkins of the 14th June, already referred to, reporting the repugnance of the Nagpur Government towards the British alliance Moira confidentially directed that the Nawab of Bhopal should be secretly sounded. Care was to be taken not to precipitate hostilities with the Pindaris, or excite Sindhia's suspicion, whilst Jenkins was to attempt to discover what inducements would be required to render Bhopal a useful ally.[36]

This was the first practical step which Moira took in the direction of the ideal that he set before himself. The negotiation with Nagpur had been opened by his predecessor, and had that alliance matured, it would have received the approval of the Board of Control in England also,[37] although they were unwilling to sanction the dismemberment of the Raja's dominions to secure that object.[38] This alternative plan of attaching Bhopal and Saugor and interposing British influence in the very centre of the disturbed region had no sanction from England. Jenkins was told clearly that, although, for the time being, objections existed against the proposed arrangement with Bhopal, it was the wish of the British government, as soon as a favourable opportunity occurred, to improve its means of operating against marauders with vigour and success on a comprehensive scale.[39]

By the combination of certain events the plan of extending protection to Bhopal and Saugor, which was thus seriously under contemplation at the headquarters of the Governor-General, came up for a speedier decision than he had intended. The chief of them has already been noticed. The Bhonsla Raja, after two years of evasion and vacillation, finally refused to accept the British subsidiary treaty. This news reached Moira in October. Another event, the reported alliance between the Nagpur Raja and Sindhia, also precipitated that decision. In view of the confused condition of Central India, and the jealousy which the independent Princes and the Pindaris undoubtedly felt for the British Power, Moira greatly feared this alliance.

He had been informed by Jenkins that Raghuji would look to Sindhia for help against Amir Khan,[40] and had assurance of support from the Peshwa.[41] Moreover, he knew that Sindhia was meditating another attack on Bhopal, and if that had succeeded, the Governor-General's plans, as a preclude to a more comprehensive political programme, which he had in mind, would have been frustrated.

So he made up his mind to take a bold step without any further hesitation. Just at the time when unfavourable news came from Nagpur, the Nawab of Bhopal transmitted to the British Resident at Delhi[42] overtures for an alliance. He wished to secure protection against Sindhia's forces. Without any loss of time, Moira instructed Metcalfe at Delhi, to avail himself of the Bhopal Vakil's presence and conclude an agreement with that State.[44] He furnished the Resident with an outline of the proposed engagement containing the conditions on which the final treaty would be based. The terms included the dependence of Bhopal on the British Government in all external relations and disputes, freedom for the British troops to enter into the Nawab's territory at all times, and the eventual reception of a permanent British force and cession of a fort as a military depot within his State. The British Government was to undertake to protect it against its external enemies.[45]

Similar instructions were issued in the similar though less important case of Saugor, to Wauchope, the superintendent of Political Affairs in Bundelkhand. Govind Rao, Nana of Saugor, occupied nearly the same position, both politically and strategically, as Bhopal, and so received a like treatment.[46]

Without loss of time, the Residents with Sindhia and Bhonsla were informed of the decision.[47] Strachey, at Sindhia's Court was directed to act immediately on the receipt of intimation from Metcalfe and Wauchope, of the adjustment of the preliminaries with the agents of Bhopal and Saugor. He was to signify to Daulat Rao's government that Bhopal had been taken under British protection, and that he was to desist from his enterprise against that State. A similar demand was to be made by Jenkins to the Raja of Nagpur. At the same time, both these Princes were to be assured that the British Government did not contemplate any aggression against them, and that those measures were directed chiefly against the Pindaris.

It was a bold stroke of policy indeed, and Lord Moira fully realised the seriousness of the course he had taken, particularly, in its consequences on Sindhia's mind. It would effectively curb his influence and give a blow, as intended, to is power in Deccan politics.

Moira, therefore, ordered the military forces of the British Government to advance towards Bhopal in order to support the alliance which was under negotiation with that State. A direct communication was made to Colonel Doveton, Officer Commanding Nizam's subsidiary force, to march to Ellichpur to defend Bhopal against Sindhia and the Raja of Berar, although this object was not made public. The ostensible cause of the movement was to be the protection of the country against the Pindaris.[48] Similarly, Lord Moira addressed urgent letters to the governors of the two presidencies of Bombay[49] and Fort St. George,[50] to prepare for the emergency.

Moulvi Nizam Udin, who had gone to Delhi on his private business and who was authorised by Wazir Muhammad Khan, the ostensible Nawab of Bhopal, to transmit his overtures to the Resident there, stated that he was not authorised to conclude an agreement in the name of the Nawab. The Resident could not therefore, confer with him on the subject of the desired alliance.[51] On account of the nearness of the seat of the Superintendent of Political Affairs in Bundelkhand, the negotiations with Bhopal were also entrusted to that officer (Wauchope), who was to open direct communications with the Nawab.[52] Wauchope lost no time in disclosing the terms to Wazir Muhammad Khan, and asked him to depute his agent to discuss them.[53] He received a hopeful answer from the Chief of Bhopal, in which it was represented that he was awaiting the return of Moulvi Nizam Udin from Delhi. All the conditions of the proposed agreement save two, were acceptable to him. The question of the situation of the British troops and their depot for supplies, and that relating to the expenses of the troops, were the two points which needed deliberation and discussion. He therefore informed the British officer that he would depute a trusted agent to proceed to Banda and confer with him[54] soon after the Moulvi's arrival.

Wauchope informed Strachey of Wazir Muhammad Khan's general acceptance of the terms, for such he took to be the meaning of the latter's communication. The Resident at Sindhia's Court waited on the Maharaja and broke the news that the British Government had taken Bhopal under their protection, and therefore demanded that his general, Baptiste, should forthwith be ordered to refrain from an attack on that principality.[55] On the 29th November[56] the conference took place in which the ministers, Gopal Rao Bhao, Anaji Bhaskar and Gokul Parekh took part, the Maharaja himself showing keen interest. The discussion, which grew warm on Sindhia's side, was led by Gopal Rao.[57]

The ministers questioned the right of the British Government to interfere with Bhopal, which had been a dependency of Sindhia's. That action for the British Government was described by Sindhia's Durbar as a violation of the treaty between the two States, which clearly laid down that the English should have nothing to do with the tributaries of the Maharaja in Malwa. It was asked, what was the meaning of the friendship that was declared to subsist between the two Governments when the British were trying to detach Bhopal, Sindhia's dependency, from his Government. Gopal Rao added that the petty state of Bhopal alone was of no use. The British were using it as a step to further aggrandizement. The British Resident denied the right of the Durbar to prevent his Government from entering into an engagement with Bhopal. It was, and had been, an independent State, which did not come under the Treaty of 1805. Therefore, the British were at full liberty to conclude a separate alliance with it. The conference ended without any understanding or agreement on the contended issue. The Maharaja did not concede to the Resident's request, further repeated through his Munshi three days later,[58] that the Maharaja's forces under Baptiste should be ordered to withdraw from Bhopal. Sindhia declared to Munshi Aisudin:— "Very well, if this is the case, each party will act according to its own views of expediency."[59]

From the prevailing condition of public law, and the rules governing inter-state relations in India at that time, the legal issue raised in that controversy over Bhopal could not be easily settled.

Between the principality in Malwa, and Maharaja Sindhia, there had always existed an "implied connection," according to Malcolm. He says: "Madhajee Sindhia had been throughout his life, looked upon as the friendly protector of the Afghan principality; and though no actual supermacy was either asserted or admitted, still there was, from the policy of both parties, an implied connection. This led to a considerable importance being attached to the Khelaut or honorary dresses, which Dowlet Row Sindhia sent to the Nabob and to Vizier Mahomed Khan,"[60] Sindhia was known to demand and levy tribute from the Chief of Bhopal.[61] The Duke of Wellington (then Sir Arthur Wellesley) thought that "there is no doubt that he (Sindhia) had a claim upon the Nabob of Bhopal, and it is more than probable that he had one upon Saugor."[62] This long-standing claim of Sindhia over Bhopal, maintained from the time of Mahadji, combined with the undefined provision of the treaty,[63] strengthened the force of the arguments on Sindhia's side. That treaty specifically allowed Sindhia to count the ancient and autonomous ruling houses of Mewar and Marwar among his tributaries, to the exclusion of British interference in their affairs. Therefore, according to the prevailing notions of Maratha sovereignty, he cold, with justice, lay his pretensions over the more recent and less important State of Bhopal also.

But the Governor-General was not prepared to give Sindhia the benefit of the doubt, by interpreting the clause of the treaty in his favour. Bhopal was not mentioned in the treaty, nor had the British ever clearly admitted Sindhia's claim of suzerainty over that Afghan principality. It was notorious that it had heroically resisted Sindhia's encroachments.[69] And Bhopal had never admitted Sindhia's supermacy. In these circumstances, Moira felt justified in believing that the British Government was not in any way precluded from entering into an agreement with Bhopal. This view of the issue was maintained by the Governor-General throughout the difficult discussions that ensued. Sindhia followed up his oral protest to the British representative at his Court, by a written complaint. He despatched to letters to Moira with his agent, Raja Kamal Nain, through the Resident at Delhi.[65] But Moira remained firm and denied

Sindhia's claim to sovereignty over Bhopal.[66]

The issue involved was not simply a question of the interpretation of treaties for the settlement of the rights of the contending parties. It was very largely a political problem, involving the relations of powerful and mutually suspicious rivals. The ground relinquished by one was not merely a simple loss to that side, but was feared to be the positive gain of the other.

How clearly Moira foresaw the fury with which his policy would be received by Sindhia, can be judged from what he wrote in that connection:— "I desired that this communication be made in the most conciliatory tone, and the Resident would not report to me the violent language with which it would probably be met by Scindia, so as there might not be any affront to discuss...Scindia, as was unofficially imparted to me, received the intimation with all the vehemence of language which I had expected."[67]

Moira was therefore not wholly unprepared for the threats which issued from Sindhia. In October he had ordered the armies from Madras, Bombay, Poona, Hyderabad, and Gujarat, to support his plans in Bhopal.[68] When the account of the interviews of Strachey and his Munshi with Sindhia arrived, the former plans were enlarged, and vigorous measures were ordered to bring into play the full strength of the British Government in the Deccan.

Since October, events in another quarter had been increasing the British difficulties. The serious reverses in the first campaign of the Nepal War demanded the concentration of the resources of the Bengal Army in the hills, against the Gurkhas.[69]

Undeterred by these obstacles, however, Moira adhered to his plans. He wrote to Strachey to assure Sindhia in a courteous and conciliatory manner that no aggression on his rights was contemplated by the negotiations with Bhopal, and that his claims would be given full consideration by the British Government. The Governor-General wanted to afford him every opportunity of calmly reflecting on the consequences of his obstaincy on an untenable point. The Resident was instructed to ask for a promise not to attack Bhopal, but at the same time, not to insist on the immediate fulfilment of this promise.[70] Moira wanted a little time to collect his forces and improve his position in the possible contest for which he was providing. In the same despatch, he wrote to the Resident, that the interval which would occur would be a gain on the British side.[71] With the same object, he issued instructions to Wauchope, who was directed to require Wazir Muhammad candidly and explicitly to avow his relations with Sindhia. No means were to be adopted to expedite the deputation of the Vakil from the Nawab, and, lastly, he was told not to execute a preliminary Agreement, but to conclude a definite treaty. Instructions were also laid down on the two points raised by the Nawab in his letter to Wauchope (already referred to). He was to be asked to cede the Fort of Raisen, and the amount of subsidy to be paid by Bhopal was fixed at four lakhs and a half. But on both these points, the Nawab's counter-proposals were to be admitted, if put forth.[72] Appended to the despatch was a draft treaty containing the conditions of the alliance, with secret article sat the end, by which the Company engaged to endeavour to recover the lands wrested from the Nawab by Sindhia and the Pindaris.[73]

In the meantime, extensive and very efficient military preparations were being carried on. The largest possible force which could be drawn from all parts and presidencies of India, was ordered to assemble on the northern border of the British Deccan. The resources of Madras[74] and Bombay,[75] the subsidiary forces of the Peshwa,[76] and the Nizam[77] were marshalled out in full force to meet, what Moira considered, "the Crisis.[78] The Bengal Army was fully occupied in the *Tarai* and the hills against Nepal in the North. The Deccan and the Gujarat Armies were, therefore, to be relied upon to deal with the Marathas. Moira viewed the situation with great seriousness, and doubted whether the British resources were sufficient against the enemies whom he was preparing to encounter. He complained that even on a "peace" establishment, the British Army in India was inadequate, and that at that particular moment it urgently needed augmenting.[79] He took upon himself the responsibility of adding three Regular Regiments of Indian Infantry to the Bengal Army.[80] He further strengthened his available resources by instantly relieving the regular army from civil duties, by calling out the Grenadier Companies of the regiments of the line, and forming them into separate battalions, and lastly, by ordering the recruitment of considerable levies of Irregular horse and foot.[81] In order that nothing might be left to chance, in addition to the grand preparation and the efficient military equipment already described, Moira applied to the Governors of Ceylon,[82] the Cape of Good Hope, and Mauritius,[83] for the help of their spare forces to support him in meeting the danger in India.

The plan of operations which he sketched to for the British army was revealed in his letter to the Governor of Madras. Besides the defence of British and allied territory, the object was to reinforce the divisions of Colonies, Doveton and Smith, and enable them to attack Sindhia's territories with vigour and effect. The Deccan forces were to advance to a position from which they could operate against his southern possessions, and watch the Raja of Nagpur, with the view of menacing his territory and, if necessary, opening hostilitie against him.[84]

These plans and preparations on a grand scale, were produced by the attitude adopted by Sindhia in the Bhopal affair. The Governor-General laid more importance on Sindhia's indignation and credited the Maratha Powers, particularly Sindhia and Bhonsla, with a great sense of unity, than was perhaps warranted by their antecedents. It was only natural for him to imagine that the rulers who, in common, had suffered from the British the loss of their territory, and were "wounded by the same degradation of their dignity" should cherish a "common object".[85] The correspondence that took place at the time of the Bhopal discussion between Raghuji and Daulat Rao Sindhia confirmed him in his conviction.[86] Any reasonable person in his place would have a *priori* been led to the same conclusion. Little could he understand that disunion and mutual jealousy were strongly ingrained in the very nature of the Indian Princes, even on occasions when from common interest, they might be expected to join forces in common action. Bringing a fresh outlook with him, born of his experiences in Europe and America, it is no wonder that Moira took that view. And it is equally natural that his colleagues in the Council, who had known India longer and more intimately, should have disagreed with him in that opinion. They admitted that if the Indian States "combined, they must perhaps be accounted irresistible," but they pointed out to him in their reply to his minute of the 9th February, 1815,[87] that their combination was difficult and highly improbable. The collision of other strongly conflicting interests and natural enmities would always prevent them from combining against the British. Before opening hostilities against the British, each State would fear the alliance of its rivals with the British against itself.[88]

When the Residents at the Courts of the Indian Princes acquainted them with the plans of taking Bhopal under British protection, the Peshwa expressed his utmost satisfaction,[89] the Nizam was quite indifferent, and took no interest either way,[90] the minister, Chandoo Lall, however, entered into the affair with the greatest zeal and cordiality.[91]

Even the Raja of Nagpur, with his show of claims over Bhopal,[92] did not indicate greater dissatisfaction than was expected from his disappointed hopes and his sacrifices to Sindhia.[93] He even agreed in a good humoured manner, to send clear orders to his general, Sadik Ali Khan, to withdraw his troops from Bhopal.[94]

The military preparations of the Company's Government must have alarmed the Indian Powers,[95] and it an be imagined that if their traditional jealousy and perpetual distrust of each other had allowed, Sindhia, Holkar and Bhonsla would have agreed to unite in a defensive coalition against the British. When the financial and other distresses[96] of Holkar's Government led to the mission of its minister, Tantia Alekh, to Sindhia's Court,[97] his minister suggested that as an expedient policy an appearance, at least, of the union of the three States might be announced.[98] But it seems that they could not make even a show of unity.[99] The threatening attitude adopted by Sindhia in resenting British intervention with Bhopal and the other Malwa Chiefs, amounted to little more than mere wordy indignation. Although he had refused to refrain from attacking Bhopal, when requested by the Resident, Sindia took the first opportunity of quietly withdrawing his forces from that region.[100] A suitable occasion soon arose for this retirement. The two generals, Jaswant Rao Bhao and Jean Baptiste, fell out, owing to Baptiste's refusal to advance money for Jaswant Rao's disorderly troops.[101] The result was, that Baptiste attacked the latter and in an action that took place on the 18th November, 1814, Jaswant Rao was beaten, and forced to fly, losing many guns and leaving three hundred and fifty killed on the field, Chitu and Karim's party fought for Jaswant Rao in that battle.[102]

For some time Baptiste pursued Jaswant Rao towards Bhopal,[103] lingering for a while in that vicinity. During this time he received loyal communications from Wazir Muhammad,[104] and later withdrew towards Ujjain.[105]

Although he abandoned his plans against Bhopal, Sindhia, this is obvious, must have noticed the movement of the Company's forces with considerable apprenhension. The alliance with Bhopal, proposed by the British Government, followed by military preparations, proved a signal of alarm for Daulat R o Sindhia. His jealousy of the British was redoubled by these grand preparations,[106] and although he did not make any effort to oppose the British by an open rupture, the two Governments thenceforward drew steadily apart. The British thought that war with Sindhia was "a contest not long to be avoided."[107] Sindhia on his side, was affected in his attitude towards the Pindaris. Whatever might have been his former intentions against them, his reluctance against co-operating with the British in their suppression, must have increased after the incidents of the winter of 1814-1815. His general, Jean Baptiste, actually made efforts to bring the Pindaris under the control and discipline of the Maharaja's Government. Written engagements were concluded with their leaders to abstain from plunder; they were given lands, and were also required to maintain a body of horse attached to the Maharaja's army.[109] These engagement s conferred five, three and seven *mahals* on Chitu, Namdar Khan, and Muhammad Wasil Khan respectively. They were ratified by Daulat Rao in June.[109] These measures of doubtful utility, were the only military preparations undertaken by Sindhia during the critical period of those discussions.[111]

During the months, November 1814 to March 1815, that two Governments were carrying on irritating negotiations about the control of Central India, and thousands armed men were consequently assembling in the Deccan and Gujarat. Yet the ostensible cause which had provoked these events was silently disappearing from under their feet. Wasir Muhammad, the ruler of Bhopal, was binding his time, and playing off one rival against the other. By offering to accept British protection, he saved his small estate from an attack by the united forces of Sindhia and Raghuji. After Baptiste's withdrawal and Sadik Ali's diversion from Bhopal, he found that the immediate danger had been removed. He next wished to see if he could further save his own independence also by avoiding an alliance with the Company's Government. As the armies of the Maratha States were withdrawing, and those of the British Government were advancing, he kept in constant correspondence with the commanders of both the withdrawing and advancing armies. Even after Baptiste had definitely withdrawn from Bhopal, he negotiated with him. Lord Moira was informed of a ceremonious meeting between Wazir Muhammad and Baptiste at which Wazir persisted the latter with a horse and a Khilat.[112] News also arrived that he had accepted Baptiste's terms, and sent a Vakil to Sadik Ali Khan, the commander of the Berar forces.[113] While these secret communications were in progress, the Chief of Bhopal was keeping up an appearance of the utmost friendliness and loyalty towards the British. He addressed letters to the Residents at Delhi,[114] and at Sindhia's Court,[115] and also to Major-General Marshall,[116] and Colonels Smith[117] and Doveton.[118] All these letters were replete with expressions of gratitude and attachment. He professed in every one of them his great eagerness to become an ally and a dependent of the Company.

To Wauchope, Superintendent for Political Affairs at Banda, he wrote that he would send a Vakil to settle the terms of the treaty, after the remaining thirteen days of the month of mourning (*Ramzan*) were over.[119] But none was sent until the 18th March, or more than five weeks after the expiry of that month, and over four months after the receipt of Wauchope's first letter to him.[120]

In the meantime, Moira received reports of Wazir Muhammad's secret relations with Baptiste. This disgusted the Governor-General, who decided to put an end to those negotiations in which the British Government had been so insincerely treated.

On the 29th March, orders were issued to Wauchope to discontinue the discussion with Bhopal, whose ruler had acted in an indefensible manner. The Nawab's secret dealings with Baptiste after the removal of the immediate danger of the latter's attack, together with his repeated evasion and delay in sending a Vakil to Banda, naturally produced this result. The Vakil was to be told that the Governor-General was convinced that the Nawab had endeavoured to gain the favour of both sides by a double negotiation. The conduct of Wazir Muhammad Khan was summed up in these three words, "duplicity, insincerity and evasion." The Vakil was therefore to be dismissed after the assurance that no resentment or unfriendliness would be shown to his State. Wauchope was also told to receive any representation or explanation that the Vakil had to offer.[121] As was expected, the Nawab renewed his requests with explanations of his delay in sending a Vakil. However, Moira saw no ground for modifying his former resolution, and the negotiations were broken off for the time being.[122]

The attempt to take Bhopal under British influence still appeared to Moira to be a sound and desirable policy. However, the Nawab's insincere attitude left him no option but to close the affair. The British had contested Sindhia's claim over the Nawab on the ground that he could not advance any evidence to prove that Bhopal was his tributary. "But this absence (of) testimony," wrote Moira, "was remedied by the Nabob of Bhopaul. In a paper delivered by him to Baptiste he acknowledged by implication Sindhia's rights over him, by stating that he had always faithfully discharged the military service which he owed to the Maharajah, thereby invalidating our argument of his owing no such duty."[123] It cannot be wondered at that after such a response from the Nawab, Moira decided to let matters stand on their former footing.

Whilst the Bhopal correspondence was proceeding, the Superintendent at Banda was conducting allied negotiations with the State of Saugor, of which Govind Rao was the nominal ruler. The real power was wielded by Binayak Rao, the manager. He had allied himself with Rukmini Bai, the widow of the late Nana Abba Sahib, who had held the chief authority since her husband's death.[124] At first the Nana, with whom the subject was opened, showed great eagerness to avail himself of British protection,[125] but this was followed by dilatoriness and evasion.[126] There were three chief points on which agreement could not be reached with the Nana Firstly, he was unwilling to surrender lands in Mahoba province,[127] adjoining British territory, to which Lord Moira attached a great importance.[128] Secondly, he would not abstain from correspondence with all the other States (including the Peshwa). And lastly, the Nana desired that the British army should be available when required to uphold his authority within his State.[130] It was felt that the Nana would not agree to the treaty, unless the manager were reduced or expelled.[131] Wauchope sounded the manager separately,[132] but his terms also were extravagant, and therefore unacceptable to the British Government.[133] In these circumstances, Moira decided to give up his plan regarding Saugor also, particularly since there was no great advantage to be gained in pursuing it apart from the Bhopal alliance. Therefore, Wauchope was instructed not to proceed further.[134]

The decision was conveyed to the Residents with Sindhia,[135] Bhonsla,[136] and the Peshwa,[137] who were directed to inform those Princes that owing to Wazi Muhammad's fickle conduct the Governor-General had decided to withdraw from the arrangement. Nevertheless, the British claimed a perfect right to enter into negotiations with Bhopal and reserved full liberty to avail themselves of it, if it should be expedient in the future. Sindhia, in particular, was to be assured of the British desire to remain on friendly relations with him, but he was to be told quite clearly that the eighth article of the Treaty of 1805 could not be applied to Bhopal, which was not recognised as his tributary.

The crisis having thus subsided, Moira ordered the "grand army" of the Madras Government which had assembled at Bellary under Sir Thomas Hislop,[138] and the Gujarat force under Colonel Holmes,[139] to retire to their ordinary stations from the advanced positions which they had taken up. All the extra staff appointed as a consequence of the assemblage of these forces, was to be reduced. The Mysore Silladars were also to be returned and the Karnul Regiment to be disbanded. Only the forces under Colonels Doveton and Smith were required to maintain their forward positions in the following monsoon.[140] By the end of the spring, the threatening war-clouds which had hung so heavily over Central India in the winter months of 1814-15, began to disperse. Apparently, mutual confidence was restored, and normal relations resumed their course.

In the meantime, the information relative to the Bhopal-saugor negotiations reached the authorities in England,[141] who did not concur with their Governor-General. They ascribed the preparations of Sindhia and the Raja of Berar, not so much to an intention of attacking Bhopal, as to the alarm caused by the movements of the British troops, and the rebellion amongst the follower of Sindhia himself. They declared plainly that if the engagements with Bhopal and Saugor had not been concluded, and "if the state of negotiations admit of it, we desire that no further steps may be taken for the purpose of concluding the engagement." Even if Sindhia and the Raja of Nagpur should be reconciled to these projects, they said, they did not flavour them, and considered them as having a tendency to produce embarrassments, which it was their earnest wish to avoid.[142] On the receipt of these clear views of the Board of Control, Moira had no alternative but to carry out their declared wishes. He felt bound[143] to acquaint the Resident with Sindhia, of the new policy. Instructions were accordingly issued, and the Resident, Captain Close, was told that while he was not to make any gratuitous announcement (which would amount to an invitation to Sindhia to conquer Bhopal),[144] he was to understand clearly that the policy of the British Government would be, not to interfere in any way between Sindhia or any other Power and Bhopal. He was to regulate his proceedings in conformity with that resolution.[145]

Another step, which Moira advocated in accordance with his political principles described in chapter 2, was the alliance with the Rajput State of Jaipur.[146] To his mind, it had practically the same advantages, and it commended itself to Moira's flavour in almost the same manner, as the other attempted alliances with Nagpur and Bhopal. In its many features, it particularly resembled the case of Bhopal, already discussed. And since it bears that family likeness to the Bhopal affairs, its logical place is in this chapter, in spite of its belonging chronologically to a late time.[147] It was expected that by taking Jaipur under British protection, the Company would derive in Western India the same strategic advantages that the Bhopal Treaty would have afforded them in Central India. The British troops could advance westward up to Ajmer and southward to the vicinity of Bundi without having to seek the leave of any foreign Power.[148] The territory and resources of Jaipur would thus be rendered available for supplies, and the co-operation of the Bombay and Bengal armies would be faciliated.[149] Valuable advantages would be reaped in the facility of attacking the territories of Sindhia and Holkar,[150] and protecting those of the other Rajput States.[151]

Moreover, the Company's Government was not restrained by any treaty from extending their alliance to Jaipur.[152]

The Treaty concluded with Jaipur in 1803 by Wellselsy had been denounced in 1806 under Sir George Barlow's orders, in spite of the warm protests of Lord Lake, then Commander-in-Chief of India.[153] The justice of that step, especially in view of the fact that the Jaipur Government, on Lake's testimony, had rendered very willing help to Major-General Jones' force,[154] had been considered "extremely questionable."[155] On these grounds, the Secret Committee, after considering the matter, directed their Government in India to enter into a subsidiary engagement with Jaipur.[156] That order arrived in Bengal in June 1814. The Government was then engaged in a general discussion of political relations, and of the best mode of meeting the menace of the Pindaris. That reason, combined with the entanglements arising out of the Nepal War, led to the postponement of the execution of this alliance to a later date, as part of a more comprehensive scheme dealing with the situation as a whole.[157] This postponement was approved by the authorities in England.[158]

At the end of 1815, when the War with Nepal was drawing to a close, and Moira's views had taken a more decided and final form, he urged the adoption of the plan of the Jaipur alliance. As it happened, the Maharaja of Jaipur, at that very time, renewed his request for the formation of that alliance.[159] His earnest requests were occasioned by the return of Amir Khan to Jaipur on a round of his usual extortions. The ex-minister,[160] who had lost power in the State, intrigued with the Pathan leader, inviting his aid to regain his position. Amir Khan took advantage of the internal dissensions of Jaipur, to advance against the capital, and lay siege to it. The Jaipur army resisted the attack with great pertinacity.[161]

Moira strongly wished to seize the opportunity of Jaipur's difficulties to open negotiations with that Government. The occasion was most opportune, since both parties were willing. "The political interest which turns on the fate of Jaipur is very important."[162] It was not only important, but very urgent. "The matter requires immediate decision. If we are to act at all for the rescue of Jaipur, we must act instantly, for it is on the brink of perdition. There is no time for asking orders from home."[163] In these words, Moira showed his anxiety to conclude the agreement with Jaipur before the strength of that State was added to that of Amir Khan, "which was better composed, higher disciplined, and more fashioned to service than is professed by any other Chieftain in India." Moira did not fear a union between Amir Khan and Sindhia; he regarded the British strength as ample against their combination. But he thought it highly unlikely that Sindhia would oppose the British plans about Jaipur.[164] The question was fully discussed at the Council Board. Moira's colleagues did not all fall in with his views on that important question. The Vice-President, Edmonstone, recorded his dissent on the ground that the alliance was not a necessary step for the suppression of the Pindaris.[165] Since the Governor-General desired it to pave the way for a general scheme for the revision of political relations, he (Edmonstone) felt bound to oppose its immediate adoption. In his view, that matter came by implication under the spirit of the orders of the Secret Committee, which clearly laid down that their affairs were "to be maintained in the same relative state under which our possessions have, now for ten years, continued in a state of tranquillity."[166] Edmonstone thought that the Jaipur question could not be raised without disturbing the system which it was desired to maintain.[167] With this view another member, Dowdeswell, agreed in thinking that Moira's plans were opposed to the policy of the Court of Directors. Seton, although he had opposed the Jaipur alliance in 1814, changed his mind in 1816.[168] He saw that the conditions had altered, and since no danger was to be fared from the side of Nagpur,[169] since acute internal dissensions were threatening Jaipur at the moment (in 1816), and since the Pindari evil had been greatly aggravated, he emphatically supported Moira.[170]

After a sharp discussion, Moira's view was carried by a majority vote, and it was forthwith decided to entertain the overtures of the Maharaja of Jaipur. Metcalfe, the British Resident at Delhi, who had also received solicitations from that Court, was entrusted with this important duty. He was fully acquainted with the principles on which the agreement with the Jaipur Government was to be concluded. A subsidiary force was to be established in the State, the expenses of which (in whole or part) were to be met by that State. The external relations of Jaipur were to be controlled by the British Government, excluding all foreign influence or authority. The military power and resources of the Sate were to be at the disposal of the British Power, to be utilised for all purposes connected with the Alliance, and the welfare of the two States. The Jaipur Raj was to maintain a contingent of horse, to be disciplined by British officers, and open to occasional inspection and muster by British authorities. Exclusive of the stipulated contingent, the Maharaja's Government was to engage to bring forward his whole military force and employ all the resources of his country in case of a joint war. Provision was to be made that all questions arising between Jaipur and other States, embracing Sindhia's and Holkar's claims to tribute, were to be referred to the arbitration and award of the British Government. And lastly, a fort, conveniently situated, was to be demanded from the Jaipur durbar to be used as a depot for the supplies of the British force.

On its part, the British Government was to agree to defend Jaipur against all enemies, foreign and domestic, to guarantee its integrity and the independence of its Government, and to afford the aid of British troops in restoring the Maharaja's just authority in case of rebellion. He was to be assured that the British Government would exercise no interference in his intrenal administration, nor in any way interpose between him and his subjects, except at his express desire.

The strength of the subsidiary force, would, it was suggested, consist of six battalions of Infantry, two regiments of Cavalry, and a field train with suitable strength of artillerymen. The right to increase the Force was to be retained, but the Raja of Jaipur would not have to bear the extra expense.

These were the principles which were enunciated for the guidance of the resident at Delhi, who enjoyed the full confidence of the Supreme government, and was therefore given ample discretion to settle the details of the treaty including the amount of subsidy to be charged.[171]

The negotiations with Jaipur to which Moira attached so much importance, were to be adequately supported by military preparations. A strong force at each of the two stations, Rewari and Muttra, on the frontiers of Jaipur, was to be posted, fully equipped and ready to enter into Jaipur. The troops at these two places were to number no less than 18,000 effective fighting men, placed under the command of Sir David Ochterlony and Major-General Marshall respectively. A reserve corps was to be formed at Cawnpore, to act as a check on Sindhia, and if necessary, to take the offensive against his possessions in that region. Sir John

Horsford was appointed an extra Major-General on the Field Staff, and placed in charge of the force at Cawnpore.[172] The subsidiary force of Poona, Hyderabad, Baroda and Nagpur, were to be kept in readiness for action and to be moved forward. A strong force was to be assembled in Bundelkhand thus connecting up the whole line of defence right across the country. Besides this, the frontiers were to be strongly guarded, both on the Punjab side (at Karnaul and Firuzpur) by the contingents of the Chiefs of Dadi and Firuzpur, and on the gujarat side by the Bombay army. The strength of the fighting forces which were to assemble at all these places, Muttra, Rewari, Cawnpore, Bundelkhand, Jalna, Ellichpur, Hushangaba, and in Gujarat, came to roughly 40,000 Infantry, 12,000 Cavalry and appropriate artillerymen, exclusive of the contingents of the States of Alwar, Bharatpur, Dadi an Firuzpur, the rulers of which were also to be invited to co--operate with the British Army.[173]

While these grand arrangements were ordered, and great expectations were entertained of extending British influence in Western India, it became apparent, soon after the negotiations had been opened, that the Jaipur Government was not so keen to seek British protection, as it had been when the first offer was made.[174] The history of the previous year was repeating itself, and Bhopal experience was reproduced in many ways. As has been already noticed, the two were remarkably alike. Not only were Moira's motives similar with regard to Bhopal and Jaipur, but the conduct of these States and their dealings with the British Government also resembled each other. Bhopal's duplicity played Sindhia against the British, Jaipur used the same tactics with Amir Khan. The Maharaja's Government sought help from Sindhia[175] against the immediate danger of the Pathan Chief, at the same time using the show of British alliance for the same purpose. Moreover, concurrently with the conversations at Delhi between the British Resident and Maharaja Jagat Singh's agents, overtures were made to Amir Khan, dissuading him from molesting the country.[176] The British attempt to bring Jaipur within the sphere of its political influence had the same result as the attempted alliances with Bhopal and Saugor. The engagement did not come about in 1816.

The one point in which the Jaipur case differed from that of Bhopal was that Sindhia, although his political and material interests were affected in the same manner, cold not object to British interference in Jaipur. It was feared that he would claim his right to collect tribute from the latter State. But he could not invoke any provisions of the standing engagements between his State and the British, which could restrict the latter's freedom to treat with Jaipur. The Treaty with that State was dissolved in 1806, while the engagement with Sindhia had been concluded in 1805. The British government could not, therefore, be restricted from renewing the relation which subsisted between it and Jaipur at the time, and after the conclusion of the Treaty with Sindhia.[177] Sindhia's jealousy of the British and his alarm must of course have been increased by the attempt to establish their authority over Jaipur, but no open attempt at obstructing the British Plans in that quarter was apprehended.[178] Not only was it impossible to urge any plea of violated agreement, but the general condition of Sindhia's Government, and of his political relations, also made it highly unlikely that he would attempt a conflict with the British.[179]

When entreated by the Maharaja of Jaipur, Sindhia sent a small force[180] to act under Bapu Sindhia, with the object of rescuing Jaipur from the extortion and oppression of Amir Khan.[181]

While the Pathans were besieging Jaipur, the Maharaja's Vakils were engaged, with a great show of earnestness, in conducting negotiations with Metcalfe. After prolonged discussion which lasted several weeks, the parties arrived at an agreement on the terms, and proceeded to draw up a treaty. The amount of the subsidy formed a subject of keen dispute and controversy. Metcalfe demanded twenty-five lakhs as the annual charge. The Maharaja's Vakils said that their State could not afford more than two and a half lakhs of rupees. The Resident offered to accept fifteen lakhs as the permanent annual amount, and to admit reduction of its for the first few years. It was then agreed that there should be no demand for the first year, five lakhs each for the second and third years, ten lakhs for each of the next five years, and fifteen lakhs thereafter.[182] On renewed representations, the amount for the fourth and fifth years was further reduced by two lakhs. When no apparent obstacle remained to hinder the immediate conclusion of the treaty, the representatives of Jaipur demanded the provinces of Rampura and Tonk, which had formerly belonged to Jaipur, and were then in Amir Khan's possession.[183] The Resident naturally rejected this demand, and consequently, the negotiations were broken off. A party at the Jaipur Court was opposed to British connection, and its influence, in Metcalfe's opinion, brought about that attitude on the part of the Jaipur Government.[184]

That party was further strengthened in its confidence by the success with which the Jaipur forces were able to harass Amir Khan. Even after maintaining a persistent offensive against the capital of the State, he did not succeed in reducing it, and was compelled to raise the siege and retire from Jaipur.[185] With that event came the much needed and desired relief for Jaipur Sate. But it was found that the Maharaja's Government continued to negotiate with the Pathan Chief and Bapu Sindhia, even after the former's withdrawal.

Realising that Jaipur Durbar was no longer in earnest about its alliance with the British Government, Metcalfe did not wish to protract the negotiations. He discontinued the conferences with the Jaipur Vakils, and requested Major-General Marshall to reduce the military establishment.[186]

The Maharaja of Jaipur again expressed a desire to form an alliance,[187] and negotiations were renewed in November with the arrival of the agents from Jaipur. Some difficulty arose on the question of referring all disputes to British arbitration and award. The Jaipur Vakils suspected that the British Government might thereby acquire the claim of adjudicating on the right of the Maharaja, Jagat Singh, to his throne, more especially since there was a rival claimant living. When Metcalfe had cleared up this misunderstanding, negotiations finally broke down on the question of the ratification of the treaty.[188]

Thus ended another great measure by which Lord Moira attempted to improve the political relations of the Company's Government with a view to bringing about its ascendancy in the councils of the Indian States, and enabling it to suppress all predatory' bodies.

With that single end before him, he endeavoured to effect subsidiary alliances with the Raja of Berar, with the Nawab of Bhopal, with the Nana of Saugor, and with the Maharaja of Jaipur. All those successive attempts failed one after the other, and the projected engagements could not be concluded. The indifference manifested by those States to a closer union with the British Power was attributable to "the general reluctance felt by the petty independent Princes to make any indissoluble alliance on terms calculated to interfere with the unrestrained latitude of political action they had hitherto enjoyed."[189] This was as true of Nagpur and Jaipur as it was of Bhopal and Saugor. They realised fully that an alliance with the Company involved a character of helpless dependence on its Government, and consequently it was not palatable to them.

It has been seen how the first steps taken by Moira in pursuance of his own outlook failed, and also, why they failed. Yet these attempts were not entirely without result. While it is true that the desired treaties were not effected, and that the British political influence could not be authoritatively established in the regions of the Narbada and the Chambal, one must not, however, overlook the fact that the diplomatic efforts which were made, produced indirect results of considerable significance. Bhopal was saved from possible destruction at the hands of Sindhia and Raghuji, and these Powers were arrested from carrying their aggressions further into Central India. But more than even that was the important moral effect produced by those events. It became quite evident that the British Government was no longer willing to remain behind the "Ring Fence" which it had set up in the time of Barlow and Cornwallis in 1805 and 1806. It had abandoned that position, and was vigilant and ambitious, ready to advance to those positions, where dissensions called for settlement and disorders needed suppression.

Of course this change of attitude was disquieting to all the independent Sovereigns, particularly to Sindhia. Their interests and those of the British Government at that time of this undoubted predominance but unacknowledged supermacy, were not wholly consistent. This incongruity and clash of interests became more clearly emphasised by these events.

The controlling authority in England, the Board of Control, was still closely wedded to its old policy of maintaining the existing relations. They reminded the Governor-General that they were against "undertaking extensive operations with the view of remodelling our political relations and extending our influence or control...We feel it, therefore, necessary to repeat our injunction against the formation of new Alliances without our previous sanction." They did not favour any extended system of alliances with the Rajput States, and even with Nagpur they preferred "an ordinary defensive Alliance" to the permanent establishment of a Subsidiary Force in the Raja's dominions.[190] Though the Board were not converted to Moira's views, the accounts of the vigorous measures pursued in India must have prepared them for the inevitable change which was destined to come, and which Moira was eager to bring about. On these grounds, the events narrated in this chapter are more correctly a record of political preparation than one of political failure.

Within his own Council, Moira's difficulty was partially reduced by the change of views in Seton's mind, thus enabling the Governor-General to carry his projects against the powerful and deliberate opposition of his able Vice-President, Edmonstone.

After more than ten years of break and reaction following Wellesley's period, Moira could not be expected to start building where his great predecessor had left off. The first two years and a half were naturally occupied with these attempts, which certainly succeeded in preparing the ground for his measures in warning the Indian Princes, in trying to convert his employers in England and his colleagues at Calcutta, and in infusing a new spirit into the political outlook of the Bengal Government.

REFERENCES

1. Pindari Papers. Home Misc Series Vol. 516A p. 13.
2. Russell to Moira—29th April 1814. No. 3. Bengal Secret Consultations, 20th May 1814.
3. Pindari Papers. *Op. Cit*. 516A. pp. 1-23.
4. *Loc. Cit*. p. 20. Letter to Secret Committee 7th Dec. 1813.
5. Sydenham to Russel. 24th April. No. 4, Bengal Secret Consultations of 20th May 1814.
6. Secret Letters No. 6—Sydenham to Russell. 1st May 1814, Jenkins to Russel—No. II. 1st May 1814. in Bengal Secret Consultations of 20th May 1814.
7. Akbar (News) received by Sydenham dated 29th April 1814, No. 2, in Bengal Secret Consultations—20th May 1814.
8. Sydenham to Russell—26th March, No. 6. Bengal Secret Consultations of 15th April 1814.
9. Resident at Sindhia's Court to Moira dated 15th Nov. 1813, No. 12. Bengal Secret Consultations of 7th Jan. 1814.
10. Resident to Moira—of 8th Jan. No. 8, Bengal Secret and Political Consultations of 28th Jan. 1814.
11. See for instance:—(a) The Resident's Letter dated 15th Nov. 1813. No. 12. The Secret Consltations of 7th Jan. 1814. (b) Another Letter from the same gentleman of 20th Jan. 1814. No. 7. Bengal Secret Consultations of 11th Feb, 1814. (c) Another letter from him of 19th May—No. 6. Secret Consultations of 3rd June 1814.
12. Resident to Moira—17th April, No. 2. Bengal Secret Consultations of 29th April 1814.

13. Letter to the Resident at Sindhia's Court, 28th Jan. 1814. No. 9. Bengal Secret Consultations of 28th Jan. 1814.

14. Pindari paper. *Op. Cit.* pp. 21-22.

15. Letter from the Resident with Sindhia 3rd Jan. (containing reports of Dec. 24th, 26th and 27th 1813) No. 8, Bengal Secret Consultations of 21st Jan. 1814. Also *Memoirs of Amir Khan*, p. 426.

16. Letter to the Resident of 26 Feb. Bengal Secret and Political Consultations of 4th March 1814. Also see Pindari Papers (Home Misc. No. 516a) p. 23.

17. (a) Letter from Sydenham to Russell of 28th Feb, 1814. No. 6. Bengal Secret Consultations of 25th March.

    (b) Despatch of Jenkins to Bengal Government of 3rd March 1814. No. 9. *Loc. Cit.*

    (c) From Wauchope, Superintendent Political Affairs in Bundelkhand, of 16th April 1814. No. 3. Bengal Secret Consultations of 29th April 1814.

    (d) Russell to Moira, of 29th April 1814. No. 3. Bengal Secret Consultations.

18. Letter to the Resident at Hyderabad, of 26th Feb. 1814 No. 8. Bengal Secret Consultations, of 4th March 1814.

19. Despatch to the Governor in Council, of 20th May 1814 No. 9. Bengal Secret Consultations, of 20th May 1814.

20. His Private Journal. Vol. I, pp. 40-48.

21. *Loc. Cit.* p. 42.

22. His Minutes of the 3rd April and 15th May 1814. *Op. Cit.* (In the last Chapter.)

23. Report on Nagpur by Jenkins, *Op. Cit.* p. 125.

24. See Jenkins' Letter to Bengal government, of 1st Feb. 1813, No. 24. Bengal Secret and Political Consultations of 19th Feb. 1813.

25. *Ibid.*

26. Letter to the Resident at Nagpur of 19th Feb. 1813. No. 25. Bengal Secret Consultations of the same date.

27. Jenkins to Moira of Jan. 20th. No. 15. Bengal Secret Consultations 11th Feb. 1814.

28. Despatch from the same to the Government of 3rd March 1814. No. 9, in Bengal Secret Consultations of 25th March 1814, and

another Letter from the same to Moira 23rd March 1814. No. 7, in Bengal Secret Consultations of 13th April 1814.

29. *Ibid* and also his long Despatch to Moira of 14th June 1814. No. 14, in Bengal Secret Consultations of 5th July 1814.

30. *Ibid.*

31. Jenkins' Despatch of 26th Sept. No 37. Bengal Political Consultations of Oct. 18th, 1814.

32. Their Letter to Jenkins of 11th Feb. 1814 clearly discouraged him from giving out that hint of dealing with Bhopal which the British Government could not fulfil. No. 16, in Bengal Secret Consultations of 11th Feb. 1814.

33. Jenkins to Moira of 20th Jan. No. 15. Bengal Secret Consultations of 11th Feb. 1814.

34. There is a noticeable family resemblance in the views on the subject of Jenkins in his Despatch, paragraph 26 (of 3rd March 1814. No. 9. in Bengal Secret Consultations of 25th March 1814) and those employed by Moira in his Minute of 3rd April 1814, quoted in the text.

35. His Minute of 3rd April 1814. No. 4. Bengal Secret Consultations of 21st June 1814.

36. Adam to Jenkins of 8th July. No. 7. Bengal Secret Consultations 19th July 1814.

37. Vol. 16. *Bengal Secret Letters*. p. 289- "had received the entire approbation of your honourable committee and the honourable court of Directors" paragraph 2. Secret Letter from Governor-General to the Secret Committee, 11th Aug. 1815.

38. Despatch No. 107. 29th Sept. 1815 of the Secret Committee to the Governor-General.

39. Letter to Jenkins 8th July, already referred to.

40. Resident's Letter of 23rd March 1814. No. 7, in Bengal Secret Consultations of 18th April 1814.

41. His Letter of 14th June. No. 14. in Bengal Secret and Political Consultations of 5th July 1814, addressed to Moira.

42. Letter from the Resident at Delhi of 20th Oct. 1814. No. 24, in Bengal Secret Consultations of 19th Nov. 1814.

43. In 1809 Wazir Muhammad had applied for the same protection. But the British Government desired to avoid the embarrassment which an alliance would involve and therefore rejected the overtures. (See Malcolm's *Central India* Vol. 1. pp. 393-5.)

44. Adam to Metcalfe marked "most secret" dated Cawnpore 17th Oct. 1814. No. 2, in Bengal Secret Consultations of 4th Nov. 1814.
45. *Ibid. and also Prinsep. Transactions* etc. Vol. 1. p. 238.
46. Adam to Wauchope of 17th Oct. 1814. No. 9, in Bengal Secret Consultations of 4th Nov. 1814. (Conditions in paragraph 4.)
47. These "most secret" communications were issued on the 17th Oct. 1814, from the Governor-General's Camp at Cawnpore. Secret Consultations of 4th Nov. 1814 to Nagpur resident. Nos. 3 and 4, the former in Moira's own handwriting, and to the Resident with Sindhia, No. 5.
48. Adam to Colonel Doveton of 17th Oct. No. 8, in Bengal Secret Consultations of 4th Nov. 1814.
49. Moira to Governor of Bombay, No. 10. *Loc. Cit.*
50. Moira to Governor of Fort St. George. No. 11. *Loc. Cit.*
51. Metcalfe to Adam of 20th Oct. No. 24, in Bengal Secret Consultations of 19th Nov. 1814.
52. From Adam to Wauchope, of 26th Oct. 1814. No. 11. Bengal Secret Consultations of 19th Nov. 1814.
53. Wauchope to Adam. Bengal Secret Consultations. No. 27, of 29th Nov. 1814.
54. Translation of the Nawab's letter to Wauchope—received 24th Nov. 1814. No. 14. Bengal Secret Consultations of 20th Nov. 1814.
55. The communication was premature. The agreement had not been concluded. Moira himself regretted later (his Letter of 11th Aug. 1815 to the Secret Committee, paragraph 22, in *Bengal Secret Letters* Vol. 16) that the discussion was brought about earlier than he expected and before he was prepared to meet it.
56. Both Prinsep (Vol. I, p. 244) and Hough (in his *Brief History Bhopal* p. 97) give the 30th Nov. as the date of the Conference. But is appears that it took place not on that date but on the 29th Nov. as Strachey used the words "last night" for it in his Despatch which was written on the 30th Nov.
57. Strachey to Lord Moira of 30th Nov. 1814. No. 33, in Bengal Secret Consultations of 20th Dec. 1814.
58. Strachey to Lord Moira of 2nd Dec. 1814. No. 34, in Bengal Secret Consultations of 20th Dec. 1814.
59. The Residency Munshi had that interview on the 1st Dec. reported by Strachey in the letter of 2nd Dec. *Loc. Cit.*

60. Malcolm. *Central India,* Vol. 1. p. 387. But from this it is not to be supposed that Malcolm would have accepted Sindhia's claim. Elsewhere he writes:— "The Nabobs of Bhopal had never been tributary to the family of Sindhia, though they had been occasionally obliged to pay large sums to its chiefs for aid and protection against the attacks of other states," His *Political History.* Vol. 1. p. 449.
61. *Ibid,* p. 389, Prinsep 1, 243, and also Letter from the Resident with Sindhia of 15th Nov. 1813, No. 12. Bengal Secret Consultations of 7th Jan. 1814.
62. *Wellington Despatches,* (1837 Edition) Vol. III. p. 665, his Letter to Colonel B. Close of 4th March 1805.
63. Appeal was made to Article 8 of the Treaty of Nov. 1805 between Daulat Rao Sindhia and the East India Company, which runs thus:— "The Honourable Company engage to enter into no treaty with the Rajahs of Odeypur, and Jodhpur, and Kotah, or other chiefs, tributaries of Dowlat Rao Sindhia, situated in Malwa, Mewar or Marwar, and is in no shape whatever to interfere with the settlement which Sindhia may make with them," Aitchison. *Op. Cit.* Vol. IV, p. 61. (1909).
64. See the graphic description of the last siege of Bhopal by Malcolm in his *Central India.* Vol. I, pp. 396-410, (1824).
65. Substance of which was reported by Metcalfe in his Despatch of 31st Jan. 1815. No. 85, in Bengal Secret Consultations of Feb. 25th 1815.
66. Adam to Strachey, of 29th March 1815. No. 60. Bengal Secret Consultations of 2nd May 1815.
67. Summary of Operations, etc., Parliamentary Papers—Vol. VIII. 1831-32. Political Appendix, p. 96.
68. On the 17th October, *Op. Cit.*
69. Prinsep, Vol. I, pp. 86-90.
70. Letter to the Resident of 6th Dec. 1814. No. 9, in Bengal Secret Consultations of 29th Dec. 1814.
71. As Hastings wrote about it some years later "The gain of time was everything to me, when I was disciplining recruits in all quarters for the augmentation of our force." His Summary of Operations, etc., Parliamentary Papers. Vol. VIII. 1831-32. Political Appendix p. 96.
72. Adam to Wauchope of 6th Dec. No. 11. Bengal Secret Consultations of 29th Dec. 1814.

73. No. 12. *Loc. Cit.*

74. Moira's Letter to the Governor, Fort St. George, marked "most urgent" of 6th Dec. 1814. No. 4. Bengal Secret Consultations of 29th Dec. 1814.

75. *Loc. Cit.* No. 5, Moira to Governor of Bombay.

76. *Loc. Cit.* No. 7, Adam to the Resident at Poona.

77. *Loc. Cit.* No. 8, Adam to the Resident at Hyderabad.

78. His Minute to the Council of 9th Feb. 1815. No. 1. Bengal Secret Consultations of 21st March 1815.

79. His Despatch to the Court of Directors (also meant for the Secret Committee) of 26th Oct. 1814. *Bengal Secret Letters* Vol. 15. pp. 405-13.

80. Moira's Despatch to the Secret Committee of 9th Dec. 1814. *Bengal Secret Letters* Vol. 15. p. 435.

81. Prinsep. Vol. I. pp. 248-9.

82. His Letter to Governor Fort St. George of 6th Dec. No. 4. Bengal Secret Consultations of 29th Dec. 1814.

83. Moira to Lord Somerset, the Governor of the Cape of Good Hope. No. 37, and to governor of Mauritius. No. 38, both of 17th May, Bengal Secret Consultations of June 6th 1815. These communications indicate that Military aid had been requisitioned from these quarters.

84. Despatch of Dec. 6th. No. 4. Bengal Secret Consultations of Dec. 29th 1814.

85. As he wrote in a Letter to the Secret Committee of 26th Oct. 1814,- *Bengal Secret Letters,* Vol. 15. p. 407.

86. (a) Jenkins to Moira of 11th Dec. 1814. No. 11, in Bengal Secret Consultations of 3rd Jan. 1815.

    (b) Resident with Sindhia's Despatch to Moira of 15th Jan. 1815, No. 29, of 7th Feb. 1815.

87. No. 1, Bengal Secret Consultations of 21st March 1815.

88. Council's Minute tc the Governor-General of 21st March No. 17. Bengal Secret Consultations of 21st March 1815.

89. Elphinstone to Moira of 18th Jan. No. 116. Bengal Secret Consultations of 5th. Feb. 1815; and see also. Moira's Letter to the Secret Committee of 11th Aug. 1815, paragraph 53.

90. Russell to Moira of 22nd Jan. 1815. No. 93. Bengal Secret

Consultations of 25th Feb. 1815.

91. Moira to the Secret Committee of 11th Aug. 1815, paragraph 55. The Resident at Hyderabad in his Letter to Moira, had reported also that his Communication to Chandu Lal, had been full and confidential regarding the British plans about Bhopal. (Also last Footnote.)

92. Raja's Paper showing his claims, received by the Resident on Jan. 15th, No. 38. Bengal Secret Consultations of 14th Feb. 1815. (See also Jenkins' Letter to Moira of 14th Dec. 1814. No. 14. Bengal Secret Consultations of 3rd Jan. 1815.)

93. Adam to Jenkins of 2nd Jan. 1815. No. 6. Bengal Secret Consultations of 7th Feb. 1815, and also Moira to Secret Committee 11th Aug. 1815, paragraph 50.

94. Jenkins Secret Letter to Moira of 21st Dec. 1814. No. 88. Bengal Secret Consultations of 10th Jan. 1815., and more particularly, his Letter to Adam of 24th Dec. 1814. No. 98. Bengal Secret Consultations of 6th June 1815, where Jenkins says:— "Nothing seems further from the thought of the Rajah at the present moment than any attempt to oppose our plans by force of arms."

95. For example—Jenkins' Letter to Moira of 16th April 1815. No. 127. Bengal Secret Consultations of 16th May 1815—chiefly paragraph 3.

96. Metcalfe to Adam, No. 31. Bengal Secret Consultations of 14th Feb. 1815.

97. Resident with Sindhia to Moira of 1st March. No. 131. Bengal Secret Consultations of 21st March 1815.

98. *Ibid*.

99. Lord Moira, himself, reported in his Minute (11th Aug. 1815) to the Secret Committee that in the Bhonsla-Sindhia correspondence, each discouraged the other—(paragraph 46) and that the Sindhia-Holkar communications took no definite shape either. (Paragraph 47.)

Prinsep gives greater importance to this combination than it perhaps deserves. In his excellent narrative he declares, (Vol. 1. p. 245):—

"There was still reason to doubt that both these Courts (referring to Sindhia and Bhonsla) were heartily bent upon the combination, which accounts from every quarter, during the months of November, December and January, reported to be organising against British Power. Mahrattas. Putans, and Pindaries, seemed for the moment to have forgotten all their mutual jealousies, under the notion that the moment was near at hand, which would give the opportunity of a successful rise against our galling superiority."

That this language is an over-statement of the situation can be gathered from the reports received during those months of November, December and January about the same Powers.

100. It is known, for instance, that the Pathan leader was applying for a Jagir under the British. (Adam to Metcalfe of 7th April 1815. No. 15. Bengal Secret Consultations of 2nd May 1815.) And so were the two foremost Pindari Chiefs. Chitu and Namdar, to serve under the British. (Resident with Sindhia to Adam of 15th Feb. 1815. No. 58. Bengal Secret Consultations of 7th March 1815.)

The Pindaris were still sharply divided amongst themselves, and the quarrel between Jaswant Rao and Baptiste, Sindhia's generals, drew Chitu to the former's side, and Dost Muhammad to that of the latter. Jaswant Rao and Chitu attacked one of Baptiste's posts at Tal, burned the town, and put the garrison to the sword. (Wauchope to Adam of 29th Dec. 1814. No. 97. Bengal Secret Consultations of 10th Jan. 1815.).

101. Then again the Holkar-Sindhia relation were not better. Ram Din, a Holkar officer, was molesting Sindhia's territory. (Resident with Sindhia to Moira of 15th Jan. 1815. No. 29. Bengal Secret Consultatons of 7th Feb. 1815.) Far from joining in an anti-British confederacy, the Regent of Holkar's government (Tulsi Bai), was making overtures to the British Government for a closer alliance, in order to free herself from the thraldom of Amir Khan. (Sydenham's Letter to the Resident at Hyderabad of 9th April. No. 123. Bengal Secret Consultations of 16th May 1815.)

102. From the Raja of Nagpur, according to the very reliable judgment of Jenkins:— "there was no fear of any armed opposition... His Highness has given every proof that would have been expected, of his determination to avoid any measure calculated to give us offence... He feels he is at our mercy... He has no confidence in Sindhia's character and little in his own power." (His Letter to Secretary Adam of 24th Dec. 1814. No. 98. Bengal Secret Consultatoins of 6th June 1815.)

Moreover, Raghuji was bitter in his complaints against Sindhia's policy towards him. (Resident with Sindhia to Moria of 1st March 1815. No. 131. Bengal Secret Consultations of 21st March 1815.)

From all these facts, there appears to be a greater measure of truth in the Council, who thought a combination amongst the powers highly unlikely, certainly not of an offensive nature.

(Besides the Council Minute already referred to, see also Edmonstone's Minutes of 31st July, 1815 and 2nd Oct. 1815.) No. 2. Bengal Secret Consultations 7th Oct. 1815.

(1) Prinsep. Vol.1 p. 251, also Sindhia's Letter to Moira of 6th Jan. 1815. No. 1. Bengal Secret Consultations of 24th Jan. 1815.

(2) Resident with Sindhia to Moira of 21st Nov. 1814. No. 113. Bengal Secret Consultatiosn of 6th Dec. 1814.

(3) Resident with Sindhia to Moira of 3rd Dec. 1814. No. 36. Bengal Secret Consultatiosn of 20th Dec. 1814., also from the same to Adam dated 26th Nov. 1814. Bengal Secret Consultatiosn of 13th Dec. 1814.

103. Resident with Sindhia to Moira of 3rd Dec. (in the last Footnote).

104. Wauchope to Adam of 25th Dec. 1814. No. 95. Bengal Secret Consultations of 10th Jan. 1815.

105. Resident with Sindhia to Moria of 15th Jan. 1815. No. 29. Bengal Secret Consultations of 7th Feb. 1815.

106. Prinsep-Vol. 1. p. 232.

107. As Moira wrote to the Secret Committee on 26tth Oct. 1814, in *Bengal Secret Letters,* Vol. 15.

108. Resident with Sindhia to Moira of 20th May 1815. No. 89. Bengal Secret Consultations of 6th June 1815.

109. Resident with Sindhia to Moira of 13th June 1815. No. 75. Bengal Secret Consultations of 4th June 1815.

110. "No military preparations are going forward in this camp." reported the Resident at his Court to Moira on 16th Dec. 1814. No. 25. Bengal Secret Consultations of 29th Dec. 1814.

111. Except an order to Anand Rao, the Chief of cavalry in Baptiste's camp to increse his force. But the Resident who reported about it in his Letter to Lord Moira (last footnote) thought that it might have been with a view to collect Jaswant Rao's scattered fugitives and thus weaken the force of that rebellious commander.

112. Wauchope to Adam of 25th Dec. 1814. No. 95. Bengal Secret Consultations of 10th Jan. 1815, also reported by the Resident with Sindhia to Moira dated 6th Jan. 1815. No. 41. Bengal Secret Consultatiosn of 24th Jan. 1815. And his deputing an agent, Syed Inayet Massih, to Baptiste, was reported by Superintendent Political Affairs in Bundelkhand to Adam, 4th March 1815. No. 133. Bengal Secret Consultatiosn of 21st March 1815.

113. Jenkins to Moira of 17th Jan. 1815. No. 37. Bengal Secret Consultations of 14th Feb. 1815.
114. Metcalfe to Adam of 26th March 1815. No. 52. Bengal Secret Consultations of 18th April 1815. Another Letter from his agent, Moulvi Nizam Udin, also contianed the same sentiments as his master's.
115. Received on 25th Dec. 1814 by the Resident. No. 116. Bengal Secret Consultatiosn of 10th Jan. 1815.
116. Letter from Wauchope to Adam of 4th March 1815. No. 133. Bengal Secret Consultations of 21st March 1815.
117. Elphinstone to Adam of 16th March 1815. No. 50. Bengal Secret Consultations of 11th April 1815.
118. Doveto to Jenkins of 13th March 1815. No. 100. Bengal Secret Consultations of 6th June 1815.
119. Wauchope to Adam of 18th Feb. 1815. No. 60. Bengal Secret Consultations of 7th March 1815.
120. All these dates were carefully examined by the Governor-General. (Adam to Wauchope, 18th April 1815. No. 19. Bengal Secret Consultations of 9th May 1815.)
121. Adam to Wauchope of 29th March 1815. No. 27. Bengal Secret Consultations of 2nd May 1815.
122. Adam to Wauchope of 18th April. No. 19. Bengal Secret Consultations of 9th May 1815.
123. Governor-General to Secret Committee dated 11th Aug. 1815. *Bengal Secret Letters*, Vol. 16, paragraph 65.
124. Wauchope to Adam of 26th Dec. 1814. No. 91. Bengal Secret Consultations of 17th Jan. 1815.
125. Wauchope to Adam of 22nd Oct. 1814. No. 30. Bengal Secret Consultations of 19th Nov. 1814.
126. From same to same of 30th Nov. 1814. No. 27. Bengal Secret Consultations of 29th Dec. 1814, also see from the same to same of 15th Dec. 1814. N. 16. Bengal Secret consultatiosn of 3rd Jan. 1815.
127. Same to same of 5th Dec. 1814. No. 30. Bengal Secret Consultations of 29th Dec. 1814, and also 15th Dec. 1814. Nos. 16 and 17. Bengal Secret Consultations of 3rd Jan. 1815.
128. Adam to Wauchope of 30th March 1815. No. 58. Bengal Secret Consultations of 2nd May 1815.

129. Wauchope to Adam of 15th Dec. 1814. (*Op. Cit.)*, and also same to same of 11th Jan. 1815. No. 43. Bengal Secret Consultatiosn of 24th Jan. 1815.

130. *Ibid.* This object was described in these words:— *"Intizam Amurat Mutalik Khangi,,"* implying domestic management of Saugor.

131. Wauchope to Adam of 26th Dec. 1811. No. 91. Bengal Secret Consultations of 17th Jan. 1815.

132. *Ibid.*

133. Answers put down by Binayak Rao to the questions sent by Wauchope. No. 44. Bengal Secret Consultatiosn of 24th Jan. 1815.

134. Adam to Wauchope of 30th March 1815. No. 58. Bengal Secret Consultations of 2nd May 1815.

135. Adam to the Resident of 29th March 1815. No. 60. Bengal Secret Consultations of 2nd May 1815.

136. Of same date No. 63. *Loc. Cit.*

137. Dated 30th March 1815. No. 70. *Loc. Cit.*

138. Moira to the Governor, Fort St. George. 30th March 1815. No. 67. Bengal Secret Consultations of 2nd May, and also Moira to Hislop. No. 69. *Loc. Cit.*

139. Moira to the Governor. Bombay. No. 68. *Loc. Cit.*

140. Moira to the Governor. Fort St. George, 30th March No. 67. Bengal Secret Consultations of 2nd May 1815.

141. Moira's Despatch to the Court of Directors (also meant for the Secret Committee) of 26 Oct. 1814. Bengal Secret Letters. No. 15. p. 405 onwards.

142. Secret Committee to the Governor-General (*Board's drafts* Vol. 5. Despatch No. 107 of 29th Sept. 1815.)

143. Governor-General's Minute of April 5th, 1816. No. 13. Bengal Secret Consultations of 6th April 1816.

144. Moira's Minute, *Ibid.*

145. Adam to Close of 5th April 1816, No. 14. Bengal Secret Consultations of 6th April 1816.

146. Moira's Minute of 1st Dec. 1815, paragraph 152 and again paragraphs 276 and 37. *Op. Cit.* (Chaps. 1 and 2.)

147. Bhopal Negotiations already discussed were broken off in April 1815. Jaipur Negotiations were begun in April 1816.

148. Lord Moiora's long Minute of 1st Dec. 1815, para. 302.

149. *Loc. Cit.* Paragraph 152.
150. *Loc. Cit.* Paragraph 302.
151. *Loc. Cit.* Paragraph 304.
152. *Loc. Cit.* Paragraph 288.
153. Malcolm's *Political History*, Vol. 1. p. 369.
154. *Ibid.*
155. Letter of Court of Directors. of 2nd Sept, 1807.
156. Secret Committee's Despatch of 23rd Dec. 1813. (*Board's Drafts.*)
157. Prinsep. *Op. Cit.* Vol. 1. p. 370.
158. *Board's Drafts,* Secret Committee to Governor-General-in-Council. No. 104. of 19th May 1815.
159. His Letters to Moira received on 15th Dec. 1815. Nos. 58, 59 and 60. Bengal Secret Consultations of 19th March 1816. He deupted Rai Ram Singh to convey his wishes to the Governor-General. Another letter was received on 15th March 1816. No. 61. Bengal Secret Consultations of 19th March 1816.
160. Rai Chaturbhuj approached Amir Khan to remove Manji Das from the ministry (pp. 447-448, *Memoirs of Amir Khan.*)
161. *Loc. Cit.* pp. 449-453.
162. Moira's Minute of 13th April 1816, paragraph 24, No. 1. Bengal Secret Consultations of 20th April 1816.
163. *Loc. Cit.* Paragraph 23.
164. *Ibid.*
165. Who were, he urged, to be distinguished from the Pathans under Amir Khan.
166. Of 29th Sept. 1815. (No. 107. *Board's Drafts.* Vol. 5.)
167. Edmonstone' Minute of 16th April 1816. No. 2. Bengal Secret Consultations of 20th April 1816.
168. His Minute of 17th April 1816. No. 3. Bengal Secret Consultations of 20th April 1816.
169. Subsidiary alliance with that State which was unsuccessfully attempted in 1814 was then being favourably negotiated with the Regent, (the Raja having expired) and was concluded in May 1816.
170. Seton's Minute of 17th April 1816. No. 3, Bengal Secret Consultations of 20th April 1816.

171. The instruction issued to Metcalfe embodied the principles, on which the Treaty was to be concluded. Secretary Adam's "most secret" Despatch to him, 20th April, No. 6. Bengal Secret Consultations of 20th April 1816.

172. Governor-General's Minute of 5th June 1816. No. 5. Bengal Secret Consultations of 11th June 1816, contains these proposals, which were adopted by the Council and executed accordingly.

173. These military arrangements were explained to Metcalfe in the Despatch to him of 20th April, already referred to; also in Moira's Minute of 5th June. (last footnoe) and in the Despatches addressed on 20th April 1816 to Sir D. Ochterlony, No. 7, to the Adjutant-General, No. 8, to Resident with Sindhia, No. 9, Resident at Poona, No. 11, Resident at Hyderabad, No. 12, Governor of Fort St. George, No. 13, Governor of Bombay, No. 14, in Bengal Secret Consultations of 20th April 1815. The figures as reported by the Governor-General to the Court of Directors, for the different arms of the British force to be mobilised on this occasion were:—6 Troops of Horse Artillery, 3 Regiments of European Dragons, 13 Regiments of N. Cavalry, 4 Companies of Independent Cavalry, 7 Battalions of European Infantry, 41 Battalions of Native Infantry. Despatch of 28th Sept. 1816) also Prinsep *Op. Cit.* Vol. 1, pp. 374-5.

174. Metcalfe to Resident with Sindhia of 26th May 1816, No. 8. Bengal Secret Consultations of 15th June 1816.

175. Resident with Sindhia to Moira of 22nd May 1816. No. 28. Bengal Secret Consultations, June 11th 1816.

176. Metcalfe to Adam. 19th Aug. No. 7. Bengal Secret Consultations of 7th Sept. 1816.

177. Adam to Resident with Sindhia of 20th April 1816, No. 9, Bengal Secret Consultations of 20th April 1816.

178. Resident with Sindhia to Moira, 22nd May 1816. No. 28. Bengal Secret Consultations of 11th June 1816.

179. This was Moira's opinion, and also that of the Resident at Sindhia's Court. Governor-General's Minute of 5th June 1816, Adam's Despatch to Metcalfe of 20th April 1816, Adam to Resident with Sindhia, 20th April, and the latter's Despatch to Moira, (last footnote).

180. Bapu Sindhia had with him 3,000 men, to which were to be added the contingents of the other Commander, son of Hindaul Khan, 2,000 men. Jaswant Rao ws ordered to join Bapu with his force of 3,000 men. Sindhia sent from his camp a body of 1,500, bringing the total to 9,500. (Resident with Sindhia to Moira 22nd May, No. 28. Bengal Secret Consultations of 11th June 1816.)

181. It was feared, however, that Bapu Sindhia and Amir Khan had an understanding between themselves, since they maintained Vakils at each others camps, and that therefore Bapu might not act effectively against Amir. (Resident with Sindhia to Moira, of 9th May 1816. No. 32. Bengal Secret Consultations 25th May 1816, and 2nd May 1816. No. 28. Bengal Secret Consultations of 11th June 1816.)

182. Private Correspondence, Metcalfe to Adam, 3rd July. No. 3. Bengal Secret Consultations 3rd Aug. 1816.

183. *Loc. Cit.* Metcalfe to Adam. 7th July 1816.

184. Metcalfe to Adam. 7th Aug. No. 5. Bengal Secret Consultations of 7th Sept. 1816.

185. *Ibid.* His decision to withdraw might have been due also to the fear of his 200 cannon. Amir himself, found an excuse, as he gave it, in the request that the Rani (Maharaja Jagat Singh's wife, and the daughter of Maharaja Man Singh of Jodhpur, Amir Khan's friend and patron) addressed him not to destroy her State. Similar instruction was also issued to him by Tulsi Bai. (*Memoirs of Amir Khan*-pp. 449-53.)

186. The negotiations were begun in May (Resident's Despatch 26th May, No. 7. Bengal Secret Consultations, 15th June 1816.) Amir Khan withdrew his forces in July (3rd July 1816. No. 3. Bengal Secret Consultations 3rd Aug. 1816) and negotiations were broken off in August (19th Aug. No. 7. Bengal Secret Consultations of 7th Sept.) These negotiations were also reported to the Court of Directors in Governor-General's Letter of 28th Sept. 1816.

187. His Letters to the Governor-General and Edmonstone. Nos. 17 and 18. Bengal Secret Consultations 12th Oct. 1816.

188. Metcalfe to Adam, of 27th Nov. No. 2. Bengal Secret Consultations 17th Dec. 1816.

189. Prinsep, *Op. Cit.* vol. 1. p. 378.

190. Despatch of the Secret Committee to Governor-General of 5th Sept. 1816, No. 118. *Board's Drafts.*

5

War and After

Jealousy of British power—Sindhia-Ranjit Singh-Nepal-Maratha confederacy, attempts in 1815/16—Peshwa. The moving spirit—Sindhia-Holkar-Bhonsla-Pindaris, their inroads in the Deccan and south India—Sindhia unable to control them—his attitude—British decision for their suppression—grand preparations—military schemes carefully laid out—Sindhia faced with a treaty which he accepts—relations revised—Amir Khan detached, signs an agreement—progress of the operations against the Pindaris—the Peshwa becomes restive—preparations—hostilities—battle of Kirki—defeat—flight—battle of Astha—Satara Raja rescued and restored to his state—Peshwa's country appropriated by the British-Nagpur Raja follows Peshwa's example—war—his defeat—restoration under restricted authority—second attempt—arrested—sent to Allahabad—escapes—becomes a fugitive—an infant, Raghuji's grandson, seated on the throne—Holkar's government—Tulsi Bai's leanings towards British alliance—British attitude—negotiations—failure—Bai murdered-military chiefs for war-battle of Mahidpur—Holkar becomes dependent ally—new treaty—Pindaris destroyed and their chiefs surrender—Baji Rao meets Malcolm—terms offered—accepted—sent to Bithur on a pension—the fall of Asirgarh-treaty with Bhopal-Saugor-administration assumed by the British-

British political success and acquisition of extensive territory—Hastings' aim realised.

It has already been noticed that the rising power of the Company excited general distrust among the leading States of India. They realised that the predominance which the British Government was requiring meant the loss of their independence and political importance. The events of the first three years of Hastings' period of office increased that feeling of jealousy. The movements of the British forces in October 1814, in the beginning of 1815, and again in the summer of 1816 (already alluded to) must have worked up their fears to a high degree. The negotiations by which it was attempted to take Bhopal and Jairpur under subsidiary alliance, fed the same feeling. And not the least of these contributory factors were the discussions at Poona in the autumn of 1815, leading to the confinement of Trimbakji under British custody, and again those in 1817, resulting in the conclusion of the humiliating Treaty in June of that year. All these incidents could not fail to arouse still further the feelings of discontent in the various Princes of the country.

Persons, and even parties, were to be found at the Courts of these Princes who earnestly pressed on their masters' attention, plans and proposals for concerting measures for the overthrow of the British Power. The influence which those persons exercised on the rulers differed in different States according to the character of the Prince.[1]

Daulat Rao Sindhia and Maharaja Ranjit Singh, the Sikh ruler of the Punjab, often exchanged letters and presents, and it was at times believed that the correspondence subsisting between them was not a mere act of courtesy, but was prompted by political motives, for the formation of an alliance.[2] Although such an engagement did not come about,[3] the desire for its attainment was in index to the minds of the ruling Princes of the time.

Similarly, reports were received relating to the exchange of letters between the Maharaja of Nepal and Sindhia. The former sent a Vakil also, but the envoy received no very warm reception from the Maratha Prince,[4] and in spite of the earnest complaints from Nepal, Sindhia remained cold and unresponsive.[5]

But it would appear that the secret negotiations which went on among the Maratha Princes themselves were more sustained and earnest than those carried on with the remoter States of Lahore and Kathmandu. What the British Government watched with an anxious and vigilant eye was the possible attempt at the revival of the Maratha Confederacy.

The prime mover in the affair was, of course, the Peshwa, whose attitude towards the British grew steadily worse under Trimbakji's influence. It was later discovered that as early as 1814, Baji Rao had sounded Sindhia and Holkar, to combine with him against the British, but nothing came of the attempt.[6] About the same time, in the autumn of 1815, when the British Government were pressing for the arrest and surrender of Trimbakji as the person responsible for the murder of, Gangadhar Shastri, the Peshwa was engaged in a studious but secret propaganda to interest the Bhonsla, Sindhia and Holkar in his affairs and to persuade them to make common cause with him against the British.[7] Whilst the position of the Peshwa still commanded a real respect from the independent members of the one-time Maratha Empire,[8] yet they did not trust the man who now filled that position. Baji Rao's messages were received with seeming readiness and loyalty which was only skin-deep. Raghuji Bhonsla, and Daulat Rao Sindhia both returned very polite answers, expressing their willingness to follow the Peshwa if he should give them the lead, and requisition their aid in his own writing[9] a condition, which they knew perfectly well, the Peshwa's position would never permit him to perform. Balaji Kunjar, an aged man of repute who had formerly been a minister of the Peshwa, went round on a visit to the Maratha Princes; in the autumn of 1815 he proceeded from Sindhia's Court to that of the Raja of Berar. Although he professed a complete indifference to politics, and gave out that he was going to a place of pilgrimage, to spend the rest of his life in retirement, it was believed that his mission had the object of awakening those rulers to a sense of unity, and rallying them all under the standard of the Peshwa.[10] But Raghuji was not converted by Balaji's persuasion, and soon wished that his expensive guest would leave his capital.[11] Thus the secret efforts towards unity made in 1815. chiefly on the initiative of Baji Rao, had produced no result, and through the firmness of Elphinstone, the Peshwa had been obliged to surrender his low favourite.

The important events of 1816 found Sindhia disinclined to avail himself of the opportunities which arose. Raja Raghuji Bhonsla and Wazir Muhammad, the respective rulers of Berar and Bhopal, died in March of that year. Those States were both strategically and politically very important, and Daulat Rao Sindhia was aware that the British would surely take advantage of the distractions that were bound to arise in those quarters. However, as though the British attitude in 1814 on the Bhopal negotiation had so completely frightened him, he took no interest in the intrigues that followed Raghuji's death at Nagpur, nor did he show any inclination to take part in the affairs of Bhopal.[12] He even expressed satisfaction when he received the intelligence that the disorders at Nagpur had terminated in Dharmaji's arrest, and the establishment of British influence at that Court.[13] Another occasion which concerned Sindhia far more intimately arose in the shape of the difficulties of Jaipur, which was again being harassed by Amir Khan. The Jaipur Durbar appealed to Maharaja Sindhia earnestly for help against the Pathans.[14] But in spite of the inveterate enmity which he cherished against Amir Khan, and the alarms produced by the diplomatic and military measures of the British with regard to Jaipur, Sindhia made little attempt to profit by the comparatively advantageous situation. His only efforts consisted of the Tardy support of a body of 1500 men, sent out from his own camp, and loose orders issued to his two reluctant and disobedient generals, Bapu Sindhia and Jaswant

Rao Bhao, to proceed to the rescue of Jaipur.[15] Although he was strongly desirous of driving Amir Khan from Jaipur, and also of preventing it from falling under British control, he showed no energy or decision in attempting to achieve those ends.[16] Later, he became markedly indifferent to the requests of that Prince.[17]

The condition of Holkar's Government was growing steadily worse. Sindhia failed in his desire to obtain control and influence over its affairs. Amir Khan was the real obstacle. The Pathan was Sindhia's great rival in the Rajput country, and not only were Jaipur and Jodhpur under his control, but it was feared that Mewar would also be lost to Sindhia in the same way. In any case, any union between Sindhia and Holkar remained an impracticable proposition, in spite of Sindhia's wishes[18] and Holkar's distress.[19] The Regent Tulsi Bai was eager to free herself from the control of the military under Ghafur Khan.[20] Matters grew steadily worse owing to the further dissensions between Mina Bai and Tulsi Bai, the former being keenly suspicious of the Regent Bai's attitude towards her. These internal jealousies left Amir Khan free to pursue his own designs abroad, and he showed no inclination to take any advantage of the disputes.[21] The condition of Holkar's Sate, at the time, made it "neither useful in alliance nor formidable in hostility."[22]

The changes which took place in another Maratha State have been reviewed in the chapter 3. After Raghuji's death, Nagpur became a subsidiary State, and Hastings naturally relied upon it as having passed out of the list of probable enemies. But this feeling of security was not of long duration. Appa Sahib was attached to his allies only from selfish interest, in order to draw support from British strength against his enemies at Nagpur. He supported that alliance with earnestness, so long as he required their help. But very soon he grew cold, and once his object was attained, his attitude began to undergo a perceptible change. During his Regency, his position was not wholly secure. His hopes as the presumptive heir to the throne were still awaiting fulfilment. However, he did not have to wait long. On the 1st February. 1817, Raja Parsoji Bhonsla was found murdered in his bed-room,[23] and as the rightful claimant to the vacant throne, Appa Sahib succeeded him.[24] This event represented the final fulfilment of his personal ambitions, and then followed the change in his attitude. The old ministers, Nagu Pandit and Narain Pandit fell into disfavour because they were considered to be the supporters of the British alliance. Negotiations with the Vakils of the Peshwa and also of Sindhia and Holkar were secretly carried on by the Raja without the knowledge of the British Resident. The latter had to protest against the change in the ministry and the secret conversations with foreign envoys against the terms of the Treaty.[25] At that very time, the Peshwa was screening Trimbakji, and secretly designing to unite the other Maratha States with himself against the British. The new Raja showed great eagerness in the affair and held anxious conferences with the Poona Vakils at the time. The Resident was given the usual assurances of faithful attachment, but Jenkins did not fail to use all the necessary precautions. It was at is instance that Lieutenant-Colonel Adams posted suitable detachments, properly equipped under European officers, at Nagpur, Betul and Hushangabad.[26]

This sketchy review of the situation at the different Courts shows how circumstances had conspired to produce a growing estrangement between the Maratha Princes and the Company's Government. This coolness was a common feature of all the four principal States. That the attempt to revive the Maratha Confederacy in 1817 did not bring forth equal efforts and sacrifies from them all, is to be ascribed to the differing mentality and condition of the four Princes. The Peshwa was smarting under British dependence, particularly after the last treaty. He was the most active of all, and harboured the most hostile motives. The new Raja of Nagpur appeared to be ready to follow his lead. But both were placed under strict checks imposed by the treaties, and by the presence of British forces in their-States. The condition of Holkar had been reduced to "extreme debility and insignificance.[27] There was no outstanding personality at that Court capable of striking a bold line of policy or of marshalling its resources with any vigour or definite purpose. Daulat Rao Sindhia was undoubtedly "looked up to as the great support of the native States against the aggrandisement of the British Power, and he no doubt feels his own importance by giving encouragement to that idea.[28] But he lacked enterprise and earnestness. Indecision and lethargy were his growing characteristics. Moreover, he was convinced of the utter futility of taking any bold step against the British. Captain Close, the British Resident that his Court, was of this opinion, and reported that "Sindhia, however desirous he has always shown himself to bring about a re-union of the Mahrattas, seems never to have thought of forming a general confederacy out of all the neighbouring States." It appeared to him that the Marathas had formerly been guided by a national feeling, but that after their division into separate States, they could not act together.[29] Sindhia had, moreover, come to realise the relative strength of his State, and that of the Company's Government. "Anxiety and alarm were fast succeeding to the jealous rivalry and contentious spirit which the violent among his courtiers still vainly flattered him was the policy warranted and demanded by his relative position among the Powers of India.[30] It was in this frame of mind that after the summer of 1817, the various Maratha Sovereigns carried on secret attempts to bring about a combination of their strength and resources. The Peshwa's agents were engaged in urging Holkar[31] and Amir Khan, Sindhia and Bhonsla[32] to make common cause against the foreign Power.

All the secret correspondence which went on among the Indian rulers, was fully known to the British Government, as were also, naturally, their plans and intentions. The Residents and Political Officers maintained a close and highly efficient staff of secret news writers and local agents at the different camps and capitals of the Princes. They kept their Government fully and regularly informed of what was passing. Even the conversations held in strict privacy behind closed doors came to be reported, more or less in detail, to the Residents.[33] Nothing escaped the vigilant eye of the British Government. In all the schemes which they adopted for the establishment of their power and the tranquillity of the country, they made full allowance for the possibility of having to deal with potentially hostile States, seething with discontent, and smarting under their political control. Therefore, whilst this element was never absent from the grand military preparations which Hastings decided to make in 1816-17, the ostensible justification of these measures was furnished by another factor, which he could no longer ignore.

As before remarked, the Pindari Chiefs had entered into definite engagement with Sindhia in the summer of 1815, agreeing to abstain from plunder and to settle on the lands allotted to them.[34] But they lost no time in violating these conditions, and they very soon renewed their former occupation of plunder and rapine with increased cruelty and audacity.[35] As soon as the season of 1815-16 opened, they carried their inroads into the Deccan. Although the Nizam's dominions,[36] suffered most, their depredations inflicted cruelties and violations on the subjects of Bhopal.[37] Nagpur[38] and the Peshwa,[39] not excluding those of Sindhia himself.[40] The Deccan expedition returned with rich booty.[41] They were encouraged by their successes, and in the beginning of 1816 they fitted out a second expedition which set out for the Deccan in February.[42] This incrusion reached even further than the last inroad, and caused greater injuries to the life and property of the people of the Company's Madras Presidency. Going beyond Hyderabad, passing through Musalipatam, they appeared at Guntur. They attacked that civil station and "committed various depredations attended with acts of the most outrageous violence."[43] This inroad of the Pindaris was the worst that had been experienced by the people in the South. It was attended by the grossest forms of cruelty, torture and violence to women. A number of villages were burned; poor people fled into the jungles to escape the horrors of Pindari oppression. A general panic ensue. The moral injury resulting in the loss of confidence was even greater than the material injury they suffered.[44]

It became abundantly clear that Sindhia was incapable of exercising any control over the Pindaris. Since he kept up "the farce of considering them subject to his authority, and they, in return, affect to acknowledge themselves his obedient and humble servants,"[45] the British Government very naturally remonstrated with him about the Pindari outrages. Sindhia was conscious of the blame which would attach to him, and the odium that he would incur from the States which the Pindaris devasted.[46] He was anxious to restrain their activities and curb their mischievous power. The British Resident renewed his protests several times, complaining against Sindhia's indifference towards the suppression of those freebooters.[47] This state of affairs continued throughout 1816 and part of 1817.[48] For the greater part of the year 1816 Sindhia's best force was fully occupied in an attempt to reduce the rebellious Raja of Raghugarh.[49] Moreover, he could not make up his mind as to what could be done to put an effective check on the Pindari leaders. Besides "the pecuniary difficulties, the mutinies and the numerous embarrassments to which this Government (of Sindhia) continue to be subject,"[50] his evasive and uncertain attitude towards the Pindaris must be ascribed to "his habitual and increasing love of ease and indolence."[51] Captain Close ably summed up his situation in these words; "His Highness certainly has in this case to contend with numerous conflicting interests and feelings. If he were seriously to restrain the plundering incursions of the Pindaris; the effect must be to turn them loose on his own possessions, should he be sensible of his inability to act against them, he must yet be alarmed at the probable consequences of such a confession. Should he sincerely and honestly concur in measures for their destruction, he would lose the aid of a powerful body on whose existence he may perhaps count for the preservation of a fancied independence."[52]

With the perpetual fear and distrust of British Power at the back of his mind, Sindhia had also the consciousness of his inability to deal a decisive blow at the powerful Pindaris. It was a difficult situation for him. And yet he knew, and admitted, that since he claimed them as his subjects, the British had a just right to call upon him to restrain them. He seems to have had a vague desire, which is pride forbade him to avow openly, that the British would offer to co-operate with him in suppressing the Pindaris. Hints were even thrown out by his ministers with that object, but the British Resident had no authority to give any undertaking of the kind.[53]

When the British Government, naturally impatient at Sindhia's hollow promises, learnt that as soon as the season of 1816-17 had opened the Pindaris again commenced their in roads,[54] they decided to take a stern course of action. The Resident with Sindhia was required to wait on the Maharaja to demand from him an explanation of the Pindari outrages, and to ask him to declare whether he was at war with the British Government.[55] That attitude had a serious effect on Sindhia, if only for a time. He ordered a force of 5,000 horse and six battalions of infantry to move out under Bala Rao Inglia.[56] Bapu Sindhia and Jaswant Rao Bhao were also instructed to join that contingent, which eventually went under Jacob, since Inglai did not wish to stir out of his Jagir.[57] These measures, following the threatening letters which Daulat Rao Sindhia had issued to Chitu and Namdar Khan,[58] showed that he meant to carry out his intentions against the Pindaris.[59] But it seems that those preparations were directed more out of an anxiety to avoid a rupture with the British[60] than with any real zeal to uproot the Pindari evil. His Government possessed neither the energy nor the proper means to effect that purpose.[61] This was exemplified by the indifferent progress which the expeditionary forces made in the fulfilment of their mission, and the violent differences which occurred amongst the commanding officers themselves.[62]

In the meantime, the subject was undergoing a thorough discussion in the councils of the British Government, both at Calcutta and in London. The Government of Bengal came to the unanimous conclusion that vigorous measures for the suppression of the Pindari marauders were indispeusable.[63] This important decision was arrived at on the 21st December, 1816, but, owing to the lateness of the season its systematic execution was postponed until the opening of the next season, about the month of September.[64]

Just after the Board of Control in England had issued their strict instructions of 5th September, 1816, in favour of a pacific policy, they received the account of the Pindari excesses committed on the subjects of the Company's Government in the spring of 1816. "Warmest indignation," was excited their minds, and forthwith fresh instructions were issued to the Governor-General-in-Council authorising the adoption of a bold policy for the suppression of the marauders. Whilst a distinction was still maintained between warlike policy for a remote political advantage and a military exertion in defence of their subjects, the Government in India was given full discretion to employ adequate defensive measures and to demand co-operation from the Indian Princes.[65]

These concurrent decisions, taken almost simultaneously, but independently, by the authorities in England, and by their Government at Calcutta, gave Hastings the opportunity of undertaking the plans which he had been vainly urging on his colleagues and employers for three years. Very naturally, therefore, he made the fullest preparations to put those plans into execution.

Military measures against the Pindaris were continued in the winter of 1816 and the spring of 1817.[66] But the full scheme for exterminating them root and branch, was timed to begin in September, 1817, when the grandest preparations were undertaken.[67] The resources of the British Government were brought into full play, and a mighty army was marshalled to round up the Pindari hordes, hunt them out of every corner of the land, and destroy them completely. It consisted of a force of about 115,000 strong, both regular (91,000) and irregular (24,000)[68] and its distribution and movements as regards time and rendezvous were carefully arranged. The plan embraced the whole of Central India and Rajputana.[69] The Governor-General was to take the field in person, in command of the centre division. The Commander-in-chief of the Madras Army, Sir Thomas Hislop, had been asked to assume the charge of the Deccan Army, with Sir John Malcolm in his camp as the Political Agent of the Governor-General.[70]

The thorough and extensive plan of operations against the Pindaris, including the careful provisions for a possible war with the Maratha States, together with the events that followed, fall within the province of a military historian. In this limited study concerning the political relations of the States one has to be content with the bare mention of the military actions that took place.

In the summer months of 1817, Maharaja Sindhia was still wavering between an open and determined attack on the Pindari Chiefs and a weak policy of bringing them under his control through negotiation.[71] During this time, Hastings was maturing his schemes for drastic action, and in the month of September Sindhia's Government was confronted with the unalterable determination of the British to have their way.[72]

The assent of the Board of Control for the suppression of the Pindaris had by this time been received in India. But the Governor-General thought that something more was needed to meet the situation. He declared again his "settled conviction that no system of measures which did not comprehend the reform of the greater States of Central India and the revision of our relations with them all would effect the extirpation of the predatory system (in which sense alone the extirpation of the Pindaris is an object of any consequence)." He therefore took upon himself the "unparticipated responsibility" for the comprehensive measures which he adopted.[73]

Lord Hastings left Calcutta in July, and arrived at Cawnpore in September. From Cawnpore, he sent down definite conditions to be put Daulat Rao Sindhia for acceptance. If he rejected them, he was to be treated as an enemy. He was required to furnish his troops to act with the British force against the Pindaris, distributing his infantry, cavalry and artillery as desired by the British Government. No Pindaris were to be sheltered or employed by him. He was not be raise any further troops without the concurrence of the British Government. The Maharaja himself was to engage to remain at Gwalior or at any other place which might be designated for him, during the operations. And finally, since Sindhia had failed after long expectations to suppress the Pindaris whose re-union must be prevented, and since the British Government had resolved to take that step, the subsisting Treaty between Sindhia and the British Government was to be considered virtually dissolved. Therefore, Hastings felt that the British were free to enter into treaties with the substantive States on the left bank of the Chambal. Securities for the observance of these conditions were considered desirable, and consequently Sindhia was asked to surrender some of his best forts during the operations. If the Maharaja declined to accede to the terms, the Resident was to take leave, quit Sindhia's Camp, and withdraw to the Governor-General's headquarters. In any case, operations were to be commenced, either against the Pindaris or against Sindhia.[74] This action was followed by a draft treaty, embodying the terms demanded from Sindhia, and defining the changed relationship.[75] The British Government's firm attitude naturally alarmed the Maharaja,[76] but no further wavering or procrastination on his part was admissible. Hastings demanded clearly "I must learnt once whether he be a friend on whom I am to place reliance, or whether I must resort to the procedure which his standing in the light of an enemy would impose on me."[77] The discussion on the Treaty opened on the 6th October.[78] The Maharaja's Government showed surprising indifference on the question of allowing the British the freedom to enter into an alliance with the Rajput States,[79] on which point some resistance was expected.[80] Obstinate reluctance was shown in giving up the fortress of Asirgarh.[81] The time to be allowed to Sindhia to decide was to be so regulated by the resident as "to bring him to a determination by the 26th October, when the centre and right division will have effected the passage of the Jumna."[82] The Maharaja assented to the terms, and on the 5th November he signed the Treaty, which was ratified by the Governor-General on the very next day.[83]

This engagement was prefaced with the expression of the mutual desire to destroy the predatory system, and to prevent its renewal.[84] Its main provisions dealt with the measures to be adopted towards these ends. The lands in the possession of the Pindaris were to be restored to their rightful owners. The Maharaja agreed to provide 5,000 efficient horse to act against the Pindaris. He was not to augment his army, which during the war would occupy certain positions allotted to it by the British Government. British garrisons were to be admitted into his two forts of Asirgarh and Hundia, which were to be restored to him after the close of the war. The Government of Sindhia released the Company from the restriction imposed upon them by Article Eight of the Treaty of 1805, by which the British were precluded from entering into an alliance with the States of Hindustan. At the same time, the British Government disclaimed any interference with those States which were clearly and indisputably the tributaries of the Maharaja Sindhia.

This Treaty settled in a peaceful manner an issue which had always been doubtful, namely, Sindhia's attitude in the war against the Pindaris. He was practically disarmed by the British, the Treaty itself conferring many advantages on the British in their immediate object against the Pindaris. The British were released from the galling restriction of the former treaty—a point to which they rightly attached great importance. The Treaty was a great achievement and the Government felt justly elated over it.[85] It brought out clearly the relative strength and position of the contracting parties in their reality. The weaker of the two had to submit to conditions imposed on it by the stronger. But theoretically and constitutionally, Sindhia continued to remain an independent ruler, whose relation with the Company Government was merely that of "amity and friendship."

Hastings had never ceased to smart under the restrictive provision (Article 8) of the Treaty of 1803.[86] and now that it was removed, he meant to reap to the full the advantages of the change. The policy he applied towards the Rajput States as a result of that liberation merits separate treatment. In the meantime, it is interesting to follow the events in Central India which developed into a Maratha War.

Amir Khan, another powerful Chief, second in strength perhaps only to Sindhia, was a force to be reckoned with.[87] It was desired "to waken a little the hopes of Amir Khan with a view to detach him from the rest of the predatory bands."[88] The negotiation, which had been discouraged earlier, was re-opened through the Resident at Delhi. At first Amir asked for rather extravagant terms in exchange for his security and maintenance.[89] But the shrewd Pathan understood his interests, and agreed to Metcalfe's proposals.[90] He signed a Treaty on the 9th November.[91] The British Government guaranteed him the independent possession of his lands and territory. Amir Khan undertook to disband his army, to dispose of his artillery to the British, and to refrain from all aggression on other States. His force was to serve on the requisition of the British Government.[92] His son was to proceed to Delhi as a hostage for the due fulfilment of the terms of the Treaty.[93] Thus a fairly powerful Chief, who might have been a possible enemy of the British, was successfully converted into a peaceful ally. Once a plundering Pathan, who preyed upon the Princes and their subjects he was now settled as the head and found of a State, and became His Highness the Nawab of Tonk. The arrangement, though viewed with doubts and dissatisfaction by some sagacious persons,[94] was justified by its results.

Having secured the neutrality of Sindhia and Amir Khan by means of negotiation and diplomatic effort, Hastings' military operations commenced under fortunate suspices indeed. On the 16th October he crossed the Jumna to take command in person. The different divisions of the Deccan army were already on their way converging on Malwa. Three British officers were sent to take up their positions in the three divisions of Sindhia's army, under Generals Baptiste, Bapu Sindhia and Jaswant Rao Bhao.[95] General military action against the Pindaris had been commenced before the close of the rainy season, and their leaders soon began to realise that they had to meet a formidable attack. They experienced great difficulty in finding an asylum for their families, for no Prince would admit them into his territory.[96]

It is now time to refer to the events which made the Pindari campaign develop into a war against the Maratha Rulers (except Sindhia and the Gaekwar). The first among them to strike that line of action was, as one would naturally imagine, the Peshwa.

His last humiliation still rankled and, although by his deep dissimulation he was able to persuade Malcolm[97] that he had no warlike designs, he had been hatching such a plan. On the pretext of raising men to co-operate with the British against the Pindaris, as recommended by Sir John Malcolm, Baji Rao began vigorous preparations. He even took other steps with the same object, such as requiring the Jagirdars to recruit men for his army, and conciliating the Raja of Satara and his own brother.[98] On the occasion of the Dashera, on the 19th October, a great military display took place, which the Resident witnessed. The latter at once wrote to Bombay for a European Regiment, and requested General Smith to send back reinforcements. The Peshwa, with his habitual indecision, could not decide on definite action, and was still deliberating with his council on the attack.[99] The Resident had a most anxious time on the night of the 28th October; but Baji Rao, with his usual hesitation, lost his opportunity. The British battalion arrived on the 30th,[100] but the Peshwa had gone too far to retrace his steps. The action took place on the 5th November at Kirki.[101] The British Residency was burnt, but the British forces met and repulsed the Peshwa's heavy numbers. The day went against the Peshwa, who lost heavily in the number of killed and wounded, as compared with the Company's troops.[102] Moro Dikshit, the Peshwa's prominent officer, lost his life in the battle, defending his master's standard.[103] Brigadier-General Smith returned to Poona on the 13th November, attacking the town on the 16th, and on the following day the Peshwa and his army abandoned his camp.[104] Thenceforward, Baji Rao became a wandering fugitive, his pursuit being taken up by Brigadier-Generals Smiths and Pritzler with energetic action.[105]

On receipt of the news of the outbreak of hostilities at Poona, Hastings sent down prompt instructions for the Resident's guidance. Baji Rao was not to be restored to the Government of Poona on any terms. It was decided to annex the Peshwa's country, and to exclude Baji Rao and his House from sovereign authority for all time. He was to be expelled from the Deccan or his person seized. Jagirdars were to be continued in their possession, excepting Baji Rao's adherents, such as Gokhale, whose lands were to be confiscated. The Raja of Satara was to be set up as a separate Jagirdar, or established in a small and compact sovereignty to conciliate Maratha sentiment. Elphinstone was allowed full discretion in applying these principles. The Governor-General appointed him as the Sole Commissioner of the conquered territories, fully empowering him to administer the country and settle its civil government.[106]

The Peshwa was chased from place to place,[107] his forts[108] were attacked one after another and reduced. His troops came into action with the Company's forces more than once. A battle took place at Koregaon on the 1st January, 1818,[109] and another at Ashta on the 20th February following. Baji Rao was defeated at the latter spot and had to flee, leaving his brave general Gokhale dead on the field. The British gain in the action included the rescue of the young Raja of Satara and his family.[110] Considering the decision arrived at relative to the future of the Peshwa's Government, the recovery of the person of Shivaji's descendant was a notable political advantage, of which Elphinstone at once made full use. He treated the young Prince with becoming courtesy. He was taken to Satara, where Elphinstone waited on him on the 4th March.[111] He had already issued a proclamation in the name of the British Government, declaring the annexation of Baji Rao's dominions to the British possessions. He also announced the intention of placing the Raja of Satara "at the head of an independent sovereignty of such an extent as may maintain the Rajah and his family in comfort and dignity."[112]

Hastings' determination to abolish the Peshwaship for even rested in the belief that this institution was bound to claim the allegiance of the other Maratha Sovereigns, whose implicit obedience would always be rendered to the Peshwa, no matter what pledges they might give to the British Government, or what individual filled that office. Hastings came deliberately to the conclusion "there must then be no Peshwa."[113]

Thus whilst Baji Rao and the Peshwaship were disposed of simultaneously, events in Nagpur had taken a similar turn. It has been previously noticed that at heart the Raja agreed with Baji Rao and sympathised with him in the discussions preceding the Treaty of June, 1817. The Resident (Jenkins) was taking full precautions against him. After the Peshwa had opened hostilities against the British, the Raja received the Khilat (robes of investiture) sent from Poona, with great devotion and ceremony, inspite of the Resident's warnings.[114] This was, of course, a forecast of future events. After making preparations, and learning that Baji Rao had already led the way, the Raja opened war on the British. In the fierce fighting that caused at the Battle of Sitabaldi, on the 26th and the 27th November, in which both sides, lost heavily, the Raja's side was defeated.[115]

As soon as Hastings learnt of the happenings at Nagpur, he instructed the Resident to remove Appa Sahib from the throne, and to place Raghuji's grandson on it.[116] These instruction did not reach Jenkins until he and Brigadier-General Doveton, who arrived there on the 12th December, had decided to offer terms to the Raja.[117] They were presented to him on the 14th, and he was forced to submit to them on the morning of the 16th December, on which day the Raja repaired to the Residency at 9 A. M. The British proceeded to occupy the city of Nagpur.[118] The Raja's Arab soldiers resisted the British attack, and repulsed the British on the 24th, but were eventually forced to retire and leave the town on the 30th December, when Doveton occupied Nagpur.[119] When Jenkins received the Governor-General's instructions of the 19th, December he already stood committed to Appa Sahib's restoration.[120] But as he explained in his despatch of the 16th January, in his action he had anticipated the salient features of the instructions, with the one exception of Appa Sahib's removal. The plans adopted included the securing of the complete command of the country. Whoever might become the ruler, no substantial authority was to remain in his hands. Jenkins advocated "the principle of governing the State ourselves through responsible ministers, making such a provision for the Prince and his family and dependents as may make him respectable." The settlement was to follow the Mysore arrangement, with this difference, that "I should introduce more direct and constant interference in every branch than was there found expedient."[121] So that, in essence, and apart from the person of the ruler to be recognised, the Resident's action was not in any way less drastic than that which the Governor-General had directed him to take. A fresh treaty was prepared for the Raja, which was signed and executed on the 6th January. It laid down that he retained his *Masnad* until the pleasure of the Governor-General was known, on the conditions that he ceded certain territories (parts of the country on either side of the river Narbada, Berar. Gawilgarh, Sirguja, Mandala, Sohagpur):[122] the government of the country was to be conducted by ministers in the confidence of the British Government, according to the Resident's advice. All those forts which the British Government might demand were to be delivered immediately.[123] These terms were accepted by the Raja, and approved by the Governor-General,[124] and the

Raja returned to his palace on the 9th January. The Resident took measures to arrange for the government of cede and reserved territories.[125]

The conditions of the Raja's restoration must, of course, have made him more unfriendly to the British Power. Very soon, his sympathies with the cause of Baji Rao reasserted themselves, and revealed his real feelings. He planned to join the ex-Peshwa near Chanda. But the Resident was vigilant as usual, and seized Appa Sahib before he could achieve his object.[126] Since the Resident reported that proofs[127] had been obtained that Appa Sahib was connected with the murder of Raja Parsoji Bhonsla in the preceding year, and in view of Appa Sahib's correspondence with Baji Rao, it was decided to send him, with his two ministers. Nagu Pandit and Ram Chandra, to Allahabad, under a proper guard.[128] Jenkins was directed to raise the grandson of Raghuji, who was the rival claimant to the throne when the British supported Appa Sahib in 1816, and to invite the Dowager Rani, Buka Bai, to assume the regency. The infant ruler ascended the *Masnad* on the 26th June, 1818, and the Bai became his guardian. Hastings was in favour of selecting a minister or two to carry on the administration. But before his sentiments could be made known to the Resident, the latter had chosen European Superintendents for several divisions to function under his control.[129]

On the morning of the 18th May, Appa Sahib himself escaped from the escort of Captain Brown, who was conducting him to the Fort of Allahabad, and fled indisguise.[130] He joined the Cond Chiefs, and organised their forces in opposition to the British, but they were easily dispersed, and he was obliged to fly for his own life as a desperate fugitive, reaching Asirgarh to seek shelter there with Jaswant Rao Lar.[131]

Baji Rao and Appa Sahib, both very impatient and disgusted at the strict and increasing control of the British imposed by the presence of British forces in their dominions, attempted to shake off their dependence. Both lost their

Kingdoms and were reduced to a miserable condition. Appa Sahib, on the fall of Asirgarh, made his escape to Hindustan. He next retired to Jodhpur, where he died in 1840.[132] Before taking a final glimpse at the declining fortunes of Baji Rao, it is only fit that a short account should be given of the transformation through which Holkar's State passed in this time of crisis. For this, we must revert to the autumn of 1817.

Holkar's position was, similar to that of Sindhia, independent (by treaties) of British control. Although not so powerful as his rival, the State of Malhar Rao Holkar still commanded great resources, which his weak Government was incapable of organising or controlling. Hastings applied to this State the same principles with which he had reduced the proud position of Sindhia. He directed Metcalfe to tell Holkar's administration, that the British Government considered it an indispensable branch of its duty to settle the disorders of that government, which was in a state of decay and dissolution, since the Regent Bai had lost all authority over its affairs. She was unable to restrain the soldiery or to oppose the Pindaris. "If Holkar's Government," said the despatch, "possess neither the power nor the inclination to bear its part in a duty incumbent on every substantive State in India, it must incur the consequences of its inability to discharge that duty, and must either submit to be considered as an accomplice of the freebooters, or must place its resources at the disposal of a Power which will direct them to their proper object." The despatch went on to affirm that "No power in India is capable of assuming that direction of affairs of the Holkar family, excepting the British Government, which, in the failure of those States whose more immediate duty it was, has been compelled to take the lead in the important work of destroying the Pindari powers." On these grounds it was urged that "in fact the dissolution of Holkar's Government and its absolute incapacity to maintain the relations of peace and amity have nullified the engagements concluded with Jaswant Rao Holkar in January, 1806, and have absolved the British Government from any necessity for respecting the provisions of that Treaty, which is not imposed by general equity without reference to specific convention." Hastings made it quite plain that if Holkar did not submit to his conditions, he was determined to treat the State as an enemy to be destroyed with the predatory bodies. The Regent Bai and the boy Maharaja were required to place themselves under British protection, and to reside at some place in Khandesh or on the Narbada until their country was settled by the British Power. The latter were to be released from the restriction of the Treaty of 1806, thus becoming free to conclude separate treaties with the Rajput Princes; and, finally, the State must aid the British in their operations against the Pindaris, and recognise whatever arrangements they might come to with Amir Khan. These instructions were issued on the 1st October, from the Governor-General's Camp at Cawnpore,[133] and Metcalfe attempted, though in vain, to carry them out.[134]

Since the increasing desire of Tulsi Bai to obtain freedom from the oppression of the Pathan party was well-known, the negotiations were expected to yield results satisfactory to the British interests. At this time, the Assistant Resident at Sindhia's Court, Captain James, Tod, was sent to Kota to concert measures with Raj Rana Zalim Singh and the Maharao of Bundi for their aid in the Pindari War, and he was desired, by reason of his vicinity to Holkar's capital, to open negotiation with that Government, and to avail himself of the dissensions of the Court.[135]

While such were the expectations with which Metcalfe had charged Tod's mission towards Malwa, circumstances precipitated the crisis, and turned the course of events at Holkar's Court. The Deccan army, under Hislop, was advancing. In the early days of December, its Third Division under Malcolm was chasing energetically but unsuccessfully the Pindari leader Chitu.[136] The division of the Deccan army approached Holkar's Dominions, and matters had to be settled with that Government, either by its submission or by open rupture. Therefore, Malcolm opened negotiations.[137]

As has been already seen, on the 6th November, the Peshwa, and on the 26th of the same month, Appa Sahib, the Bhonsla Raja of Nagpur, had opened hostilities against the British. The War against the foreigner had begun. Holkar's army was requistioned by the head of the Maratha Confederacy. This factor rapidly changed the situation. The military party was in favour of supporting the Peshwa, and fighting the British as the common enemy. This was the dominant voice in the councils of Holkar's government. The *Sardars* resolved on, war. Preparations were commenced. Vakils sent to the British camp for conducting negotiations were recalled. The Regent, Tulsi Bai, who had formerly evinced a desire to enter into alliance with the British, was seized and the young Maharaja was put under strict guard.[138] The Pathan Chiefs, Ghafur Khan, Raushan Beg and Raushan Khan, decided in council to punish Tulsi Bai with the penalty of death. Accordingly, she was taken down to the bed of the River Sapri early in the morning of the 19th December, and was publicly be headed.[139] No further doubt remained as to the attitude of Holkar's Government.

Hislop and Malcolm had fully anticipated that attitude before the murder took place. They combined their forces at Ujjain on the 12th December, and marched towards Mahidpur, where Holkar's army was assembled. When the negotiations failed to bring about an agreement, the British army advanced, and an attack was made on the carefully drawn up forces of Maharaja Malhar Rao at Mahidpur on the 21st December. The charge was led by Malcolm himself, and a deadly battle ensued, lasting from mid-day till 3 o'clock. Malcolm was loyally served by his European and Indian soldiers, and both displayed great bravery and resolution under the hottest fire from the guns on Holkar's side.[140] The Company's army lost heavily, but Holkar's was destroyed.[141]

This decisive action put Maharaja Malhar Rao in the hands of the British. The Princes was hardly eleven years old, but he and his State had to suffer in full measure the consequences of the action of the military Chiefs. Malcolm opened negotiations with Tantia Jog, Holkar's able minister, whom he received in his camp on the 3rd January. The term he offered were the confirmation of Amir Khan's independence and his engagement with the British, the cession of Holkar's claims on the Rajput States, the fight to Raj Rana of the four districts which he had rented from Holkar, and lastly, the cession in perpetuity of the whole of Holkar's possessions to the south of the Satpura Range, including Khandesh Tantia Jog earnestly protested against the harshness of these terms. He pleaded piteously that Holkar's loss in territory to the British, to Amir Khan and to Zalim Singh was far too great, and that the terms involved an undue humilitation for his master, and that he would be deprived of some of the most cherished and ancient possessions of the Holkar House.[147] All these entreaties proved to be in vain. The vanquished party was to be deprived of all possible means of ever rising in arms against the British power.[143] Tantia Jog could only appeal for a kinder consideration at British hands. The minister realised as fully as Malcolm, that in the position to which his master had been reduced, nothing more could be done. But in dealings between States, feelings of kindness seldom affect public interests. Malcolm remained firm and did not relax his demands. On the 6th January, the Treaty was signed, and Holkar was obliged to accept the British terms in their entirety.[144]

This Treaty of Mandasor revised the relations between the British and Holkar. The former position of equality between the two became one of subsidiary and subordinate alliance. Beside the renunciation of all claims over the territory of Amir Khan, the Parganas in the possession of Zalim Singh of Kota, and the tributes from the Rajput States, Holkar was bound down to receive a British force in his territory to keep internal order. He had to reduce his own sperfluous troops, to maintain a contingent of 3,000 horse to serve with the British force, to submit all foreign disputes to British arbitration and to abstain from any communications with other Powers. Lastly, it was provided that the British Government would not permit the Peshwa[145] to exercise any sovereignty over Holkar.[146]

This was another achievement of Hastings for his Government. Holkar was debased from the position of a free Power to that of a protected State in subordinate alliance with the Company. The settlement with Holkar squared even more completely with Hastings' aims and ambitions than that arrived at with Sindhia. British ascendancy was established, and the military power of the State was broken. The height of Hastings' triumph was reached by this Treaty. The aim of his early days was realised. Within a few months from October 1817 to January 1818, that high political purpose had been accomplished, chiefly through military successes. Although military operations continued for some time longer against the Peshwa, the Pindaris and the Raja of Nagpur, it became quite evident that what remained was only the necessary but less important part of what had already been achieved. Hastings was able to report to the Court of Directors on the 8th February that all essential operations (except those in the State of Poona) had terminated and that the Company's arrangements had assumed their destined shape.[147]

The military operations which were continued to round-up the Pindaris, and to pursue the Peshwa, need not occupy much more space. Jaswant Rao Bhao, Sindhia's rebellious general, was attacked by Major-General Brown. He fled into the deepest fastnesses of Mewar to Kumbhalmer, but was pursued by the forces under Major-Generals Donkin,[148] and Malcolm, and surrendered to the latter on the 14th February.[149] A day later, Karim Khan, the Chief of the Pindaris, surrendered at Jawad after wandering as a fugitive in the hills and jungles and remaining hidden in disguise for some time. He gave himself upto Malcolm on a promise of pardon and future subsistence.[150] Karim and other Pindari Chiefs accepted the arrangements, which Malcolm offered them for the allotment of lands in the Gorakhpur District in the Upper Provinces, and were sent off to settle there.[151] Chitu, another Pindari leader, was found killed by a tiger in the jungle, whither he had gone to seek safety from the incessant pursuit of Malcolm's men. His sword, his horse and his bones were found. His son Muhammad Panah surrendered to Malcolm.[152]

During the task of pursuing and destroying the freebooters in Malwa, Malcolm received unstinted support from Holkar's Government under its prudent minister, Tantia Jog.[153] He learnt that Baji Rao was moving towards him, and this news roused the soldier-diplomat's natural keenness, and his spirit of energy and ambition. He made preparation to meet the contingency.[154]

The first indirect offers from Baji Rao reached Malcolm on the 14th May,[155] direct overtures being received on the 17th of that month, when an emissary from the fugitive Prince arrived in the British General's camp.[156] In the meantime, military arrangements were pushed forward. Baji Rao had no hope even if he thought of resistance. With Doveton in his rear at Burhanpur, and the forces of Malcolm and Colonel Russell close by, he was completely surrounded.[157]

Thus Baji Rao and Malcolm, who had previously made each other's acquaintance in the field of diplomacy, met again, but in very different circumstances, Malcolm, favoured by destiny at every turn of his eventful career, the Maratha depressed and defeated, alarmed and sorrowful. At the long and painful interview which took place, Baji Rao was told clearly that the British had made up their minds, and that nothing on his part could alter their decision. He must give up all hopes of regaining even a shadow of his sovereignty.[158] If he delayed submission, he would merely bring ruin upon himself. The terms proposed for his acceptance, were, his resignation for himself and his heirs of all claim to the Poona Government in exchange for a liberal pension from the British Government, which Malcolm engaged would not be less than eight lakhs a year. He was to retire to some place in Hindustan. Further, his adherents would be treated liberally.

These terms were to be accepted within twenty-four hours.[159] The inevitable happened, and Baji Rao moved to Malcolm's Camp on the 3rd June, pitching his tent within half a mile of the General's.[160] Thus ended the career of the last of the Peshwas. He was moved to Bithur, where he lived for many years on the handsome pension to which Malcom had committed his unwilling Government.[161]

With the disposal of Baji Rao and the final disappearance of the Peshwa from the public scene, Hastings' political measures achieved their end. The military activity, which began to slow down by the formal dissolution of "the Deccan Army" at the end of March 1818,[162] did not complete its operations until the fall of the famous Fort of Asirgarh. Its commander, Jaswant Rao Lar, held out, in apparent defiance of his master, Maharaja Sindhia, and in opposition to the British demand for surrender. Malcolm suspected that Appa Sahib had taken refuge in the fortress and Chitu was certainly hovering about in the neighbourhood. When Jaswant Rao Lar showed a hostile attitude towards the British, the latter obtained Sindhia's consent to take possession of the place. On Lar's resistance, Sir John Doveton invested the fort which fell on the 19th April 1819, after a three weeks' close siege. In the subsequent search for Baji Rao's jewellery, which the British officers conducted, they accidentally came across a letter in Sindhia's own handwriting directing his commander, Lar, to obey Baji Rao's orders and to resist the British. This detection might have had a very damaging effect on Sindhia's relations with the British Government. The document discovered was conveyed to Sindhia by Hastings' orders, and as a penalty, the British decided to retain Asirgarh in their own possession. Beyond this, no further discussion took place between the two States.[163]

Whilst the military part of the Maratha War ended with the fall of Asirgarh and its loss by Sindhia, as the political side might be considered to close with the submission of the Peshwa to Malcolm, the arrangements made with the two minor States of Bhopal and Saugor, although not forming any part of the Maratha War, might be noticed at this stage. Their inclusion in this chapter is justified partly by the favourite position they occupied in Hastings' political discussions of that period, and partly by the important connection which they had, in his opinion, with the general political problem he set out to tackle.

The young Nawab of Bhopal who succeeded Wazir Muhammad in March 1816, repeatedly begged the British to take him under their protection.[164] But since the instructions of the Board of Control against that arrangement had been clearly laid down, the offer was politely declined,[165] although Hastings (then Earl of Moira) strongly favoured the alliance.[166]

But he abandoned this attitude when he set out from Calcutta for Cawnpore to lead the general operations against the Pindaris and the Marathas. He clearly avowed that he would holdly advance the political interests of the Company, and would fully avail himself of the situation in order to settle the country in a permanent state of tranquillity. So that, when military operations commenced, Hastings authorised Hislop and Malcolm to conclude a treaty with Bhopal.[167] Malcolm opened negotiations by encouraging the Nawab to accept the terms offered him by Jenkins,[168] who had addressed a letter to the Nawab through Lieutenant-Colonel Adams, asking him to accept conditions of defensive and subordinate alliance. Bhopal was to come forward to aid the British against the Pindaris in every way, surrendering its external independence.[169] The Nawab accepted these conditions, and faithfully helped the British against the Pindaris.[170] This agreement was later emboided in a formal Treaty which was submitted to the Governor-General on the 27th February 1818, and ratified by him on the 8th March.[171] Thus Bhopal passed from a precarious condition to one of pledged protection under British Power, and has remained in that position ever since. On account of its central situation, its alliance was then a coveted object. The conclusion of this Treaty was a part of the settlement of Central India as originally planned by Hastings.

The sister State of Saugor, owing to internal causes, offered a slightly stiffer problem for British diplomacy to deal with. The Nana, the nominal ruler, was kept away from actual administration by the manager, Binayak Rao, who really ruled to the exclusion and consequent discontent of Nana Govind Rao. Apart from this dissension, the British Government found another method of handling the Saugor case. The Peshwa had always claimed nominal sovereignty over the Chiefs of Saugor, Jalaun and Jhansi, and these he had transferred to the British government by the Treaty of Poona (Article XIII). Hastings stepped forward to take full advantage of that transfer. He directed his agent in Bundelkhand to require the Manager to render to the British, who stood in the Peshwa's place, the allegiance which they owed to him. British protection was offered to him and to the State. In return, a fortress and a tribute of 50,000 Rupees a year were demanded. Binayak Rao was to be told how much he would profit by entering into the agreement. If Binayak Rao did not fall in with that proposal "he will be dispossessed of that territory should it suit the views of the British Government to support the pretensions of Govind Rao, which it must be considered at full liberty to do." The Manager was asked to make a prompt decision on the point.[172] But when these negotiations failed to make an impression on the Manager, a treaty was concluded with the Nana himself, by which he recognised British supremacy, and placed himself under their protection. He agreed to submit all disputes with other States to the British Government who, in return, engaged not to contract any agreement with the Dowager Bai or Binayak Rao, detrimental to the Nana's claims. The Nana ceded to the Company the territory of Mahoba pargana and certain other villages.[173]

Binayak Rao remained in different and would not recognise the Treaty. When diplomacy failed to win him over, force was resorted to and Major-General Marshall was directed to march his army against the Manager. The Political Superintendent was also ordered to join the Major-General.[174] The Manager could, of course, offer no further resistance. The

Bai and Binayak Rao were removed and pensioned, and the administration was taken over by the British. The Nana retained the title, and the net revenues of the State were made over to him, after payment of the cost of administration, the pensions of the Bai and Binayak Rao, and deduction of the tribute due to the British Government.[175] Thus Saugor, though its settlement was a little more difficult than Bhopal, received far more drastic treatment. It ceased to exist, not only as a political problem, but also as a political entity.

Before closing this chapter on the Maratha War and the changes which it brought about, mention might be made of another agreement which took place between the Company's Government and that of Sindhia, in June of 1818.[176] It did not possess any political importance, but involved the exchange of certain territories. It is worth mentioning because of the cession to the Company by Maharaja Sindhia of the important town and district of Ajmer, which is to-day a flourishing little spot of political value under British occupation, surrounded on all sides by the ancient States of Rajasthan. Ajmer was made over by Bapu Sindhia to Wilder on the 28th July, the latter being appointed its first Commissioner. Sindhia was also asked to make over to Bhopal the fort of Islamnagar, to which the Nawab and his family had a particular attachment.[177]

Thus the war between the Maratha States and the English ended with the realisation in full measure of the Governor-General's early aim and ambition. Not only had the Pindaris been completely destroyed but the power of the major States of Hindustan had been broken, their political independence shattered, and the paramountcy of his own Government fully established. Sindhia, though nominally an independent ally, was greatly reduced in strength, and stood "insulated and precluded from any extraneous assistance...girdled round by States which we have raised to the power of resisting him, even without our aid."[178] Holkar was a smaller Power after the war, dependent on the British. Berar, which was also greatly reduced in size, was under British control owing to the Raja's infancy. The Peshwa, the chief source of embarrassment to the British and the rallying centre of Maratha nationalism, was finally uprooted.

The war resulted in the acquisition by the British of vast territories, although Hastings had not set out with that end in view, and disclaimed it as his principal motive for extending the political power of the Company. The dominion of the Peshwa, with the exception of a small area separated for the Raja of Satara, were annexed to British territories, and Elphinstone was organising its civil government, while Brigadier-General Thomas Munro was employed in settling the country south of the Krishna.[179] Large and rich territories were acquired from the Raja of Nagpur. Molony was appointed Commissioner of that part acting under the supervision of Jenkins.[180] The provinces of Khandesh and parts of Malwa acquired from Holkar were assigned to Malcòlm, who restored order and peaceful life to that part of the country in the years 1818-1820.[181] Major Marjoribanks was governing Saugor.[182] Great and extensive as were the material gains of the Company in territory, still greater were the political advantages which resulted and which had been primarily the object nearest Hastings' heart. The new treaties gave the Company a clear ascendancy over the States of India. Their sovereignty in external affairs was taken away, and even in internal matters it was greatly circumscribed, more so in actual practice than in the words of the treaties themselves. The British Political Agents at the different Courts were not so much the ambassadors of a friendly Power, as the influential guides of the Indian rulers. A Resident was stationed at Holkar's Court. Major Agnew held that position temporarily, succeeded by Wellesley as the permanent incumbent of the post. They acted under Malcolm's supervision. The influence exercised by the Resident over the internal government became increasingly felt as something real.[183] Captains Briggs[184] and Dyson[185] were employed to settle respectively Khandesh and the States of Banswara and Dungarpur. Captain Henley was deputed to Bhopal as the British Resident at that Court.[186] The States of Rajputana were placed under the charge of Sir David Ochterlony, as the Resident-General of that province. Jenkins at Nagpur was practically the ruler himself, and was administering the country through European superintendents, the Raja being a minor.

Such were the arrangement following the extensive operations undertaken by Hastings in the season of 1817-18. The consequences flowing from them completely satisfied his sanguine expectations.[187] In the previous chapters, an attempt was made to sketch his plan and programme with their early preparation, followed by the first steps of advance towards that aim. This chapter has briefly described its fulfilment, and may be considered as marking the time of his achievement.

REFERENCES

1. Hindu Rao Ghatke, at Sindhia's Court, Sita Ram Rao, at Baroda, Nairoba Chitnavis, later Ram Chandra Wagh and Paras Rao Bhao at Nagpur. Trimbakji, also Sandasheo Mankeshwar and Gokhale at Poona, the Pathan party at Holkar's Court, Manji Das at Jaipur, are examples. Similar influences existed at Mysore, Lucknow and Hyderabad also.
2. Resident at Delhi to Adam, 23rd Oct. 1815, No. 3, Bengal Secret Consultations, 15th Nov. 1815, and Resident with Sindhia to Adam, 26th May 1816 No. 29, Bengal Secret Consultations, 11th June, 1816.
3. Resident with Sindhia to Adam, 3rd Mar. 1816, No. 23, Bengal Secret Consultations, 23rd March 1816.
4. Resident with Sindhia to Moira, 23rd April No. 11, Bengal Secret Consultations, 11th May, 1816.
5. Raja Bikram Shah Shamsher Jang's letter to Sindhia, 4th February 1816, and Sindhia's reply, 13th Apr. 1816, No. 30, Bengal Secret Consultations, 11th June, 1816.
6. The evidence of this is to be found (for what it is worth) in the replies furnished by the Pindari leader Karim Khan, after his surrender, to Capt. Stoneham who was asked by Hastings to examine Karim on that point. (Hastings to the Secret Committee, 31st May, 1820, *Bengal Secret Letters*. Vol. 19, and Capt. Stoneham to Hastings, 6th May, 1820, *Enclosures to Secret Letters from Bengal*, vol. 21.)

7. Jenkins to Elphinstone, 22nd Sept., No. 35, Bengal Secret Consultations, 20th Oct, 1815, 8th Oct., No. 21, Bengal Secret Consultations, 27th Oct. 1815. Elphinstone to Adam, 14th Oct. 1815, No. 10, enclosing copy of letter from Hindu Rao Ghatke to Dajiba Deshmukh, 11th Sept., No, 11, Bengal Secret Consultations, 10th November 1815.
8. In a Treaty concluded secretly between Sindhia and Holkar in 1815-16, the first article described the common allegiance due from them to the Peshwa. (No. 22, Bengal Secret Consultations, 14th Aug. 1818.)
9. Elphinstone to Adam, 14th Oct, 1815, No. 10, Bengal Secret Consultations, 10th Nov, 1815, and Resident with Sindhia to Moira, 10th Sept., No. 31, Bengal Secret Consultations, 4th October 1815.
10. Jenkins to Adam, 31st October, No. 1, Bengal Secret Consultations, 17th November 1815.
11. Jenkins to Adam, 4th December 1815, No. 16, Bengal Secret Consultations, 6th January 1816.
12. Resident with Sindhia to Moira, 3rd April, No. 21, Bengal Secret Consultations, 20th April 1816, and 23rd April, No. 11, Bengal Secret Consultations, 11th May, 1816.
13. Resident with Sindhia to Adam, 31st May, No. 10, Bengal Secret Consultations, 15th June 1816.
14. Resident with Sindhia to Resident at Delhi, 19th May, No. 27, Bengal Secret Consultations, 11th June, 1816. Resident with Sindhia to Resident at Delhi, 4th June, No. 25, Bengal Secret Consultations, 22nd June, 1816.
15. Resident with Sindhia to Moira, 22nd May, No. 28, Bengal Secret Consultations 11th June 1816. Bapu Sindhia was known to be friendly with Amir Khan.
16. Resident with Sindhia to Adam, 2nd June 1816, No. 11, Bengal Secret Consultations, 15th June 1816. Jaipur Vakil complained to Sindhia about Bapu Sindhia's delay and evasion. Resident with Sindhia to Resident at Delhi, 4th June, No. 25, Bengal Secret Consultations, 22nd June, 1816. Resident with Sindhia to Adam, 22nd June, No. 12, Bengal Secret Consultations, 13th July, 1816.
17. Resident with Sindhia to Resident at Delhi, 6th Aug., No. 6, Bengal Secret Consultations, 24th Aug. 1816. Resident with Sindhia reported to Moira "The Jeypore question is now very little thought of," (Aug. 13th, No. 9, Bengal Seccret Consultations, 7th Sept., 1816.)

18. In fact, a Treaty was concluded between Sindhia and Holkar in 1815-16 for a defensive union. The Resident came to know about it three years later. (Stewart to Adam, 23rd July, No. 21, Bengal Secret Consultations, 14th Aug. 1818. The text of the Treaty No. 22, *Loc. Cit.*

19. Acting Resident with Sindhia to Adam, 8th Dec. 1815, No. 21, Bengal Secret Consultations, 6th January 1816.

20. Same to same, 18th Dec. 1815, No. 22, Bengal Secret Consultations, 6th January 1816.

21. Resident with Sindhia to Moira, 3rd April, No. 21, Bengal Secret Consultations, 20th April 1816.

22. As Moira expressed it in his letter to the Secret Committee of 11th Aug. 1815 (*Bengal Secret Letter,* Vol. 16, p. 289 onwards).

23. Jenkins found evidence late to show that Appa Sahib was responsible for Parsoi's secret assassination. (His Despatch dated 14th April 1818, No. 25, Bengal Secret Consultations, 10th July 1818, and his private letter to Adam. 12th March, No., 6, Bengal Secret Consultations, 24th July, 1818.)

24. Formally installed himself on 21st April 1817. (Jenkins' *Report Op. Cit.*, p. 132).

25. Jenkins to Adam, 3rd May, No. 28, Bengal Secret Consultations, 31st May 1817, Jenkins to Hastings, 9th May, No. 11, Bengal Secret Consultations, 24th May 1817.

26. Jenkins to Hastings, 30th May, No. 2, Bengal Secret Consultations, 21st June 1817.

27. Adam to Metcalfe, 24th May, No. 3, Bengal Secret Consultations, 24th May, 1817.

28. Close to Adam. 26th May, No. 29. Bengal Secret Consultations, 11th June, 1816.

29. *Ibid.*

30. Prinsep. *Op. Cit.* Vol. 1, p. 388.

31. Elphinstone to Adam, 18th July, No. 35, Bengal Secret Consultations, 13th Aug. 1817, and 27th July, No. 22, and also No. 23. (the intelligence received from the camps of Holkar. Amir Khan, Zalim Singh of Kota, of Sindhia's Hirkarras at Poona. etc.) Bengal Secret Consultations, 22nd Aug. 1817.

32. Jenkins to Hastings, 30th May, No. 2, Bengal Secret Consultations, 21st June 1817.

33. For example, the paper of intelligence forwarded by Close to Adam, No. 4, Bengal Secret Consultations, 24th Aug. 1816, and another, No. 18, Bengal Secret Consultations, 21st June, 1817. Baji Rao complained to Malcolm at Maholi against Elphinstone, that the latter so completely watched him that he knew "the very dishes that were served at his meals." Colebrooks's *Life of Elphinstone,* Vol. 1, p. 303. Similarly, the Resident at Lucknow received "hourly" reports from his "news writers and Hirkarras" (Baillie to Moira, 13th July, 1814, *Oude Papers, Home Misc.* Vol. 518, p. 615, and Cole at Mysore "employed secret spies" for procuring information (despatch to Madras government, Feb. 10th, No. 3, Bengal Secret Consultations, 18th Mar. 1814).

34. Close to Moira, 20th May, 1815, No. 89, Bengal Secret Consultations, 4th July, 1815, and Wauchope to Adam, 19th Aug. No. 146, Bengal Secret Consultations, 20th Sept. 1815.

35. Jenkins to Adam, 20th Oct. No. 14 and No. 15, (Intelligence Paper) Bengal Secret Consultations, 10th Nov. 1815. Russell to Adam. 2nd Nov., No. 33, Bengal Secret Consultations, 25th Nov. 1815. Col. Doveton to Russell. 28th Oct., No. 34, and 30th Oct., No. 41. Close to Adam, 6th Nov, 1815, No. 43, Bengal Secret Consultations, 23th Nov. 1815.

36. Russell to Adam. 21st Nov. 1815, No. 10, Bengal Secret Consultations, 6th Jan. 1816.

37. Resident with Sindhia to Adam, 4th Dec., No. 6. Bengal Secret consultations, 23rd Dec. 1815.

38. Jenkins to Adam, 17th Nov., No. 4, and 21st Nov., No. 5, Bengal Secret Consultations, 8th Dec. 1815.

39. Elphinstone to Moira, 10th Dec. 1815, No. 83. Bengal Secret Consultations, 13th Jan, 1816.

40. Resident with Sindhia to Adam, 4th Dec., No. 6, Bengal Secret Consultations, 23rd Dec. 1815.

41. Acting Resident with Sindhia to Adam. 1st Feb., No. 55, (Big merchants of Ujjain were sent for in Chitu's camp to buy the valuable jewellery brought from the Deccan), No. 56, Bengal Secret Consultations, 2nd Mar. 1816.

42. Acting Resident with Sindhia to Adam, 3rd Mar. 1816, No. 16, Bengal Secret Consultations, 23rd Mar. 1816, and Wauchope to Adam, 7th Mar, No. 57. Bengal Secret Consultations, 16th Mar, 1816, also Jenkins to Adam, 13th Feb. No. 9, and 15th Feb. No. 10 and No. 11, Bengal Secret Consultations, 9th Apr. 1816.

43. Magistrate Guntur to Secretary Judicial Department, Fort St. George Government, 11th Mar. No. 2, Bengal Secret Consultatins, 6th Apr. 1816, and of 12th Mar., pp. 35- (*Papers Relating to Pindari and Maratha Wars*, printed, *Home Misc. Series*, Vol. 516a).

44. A Commission was appointed to enquire into the injury inflicted on the people of Madras province by the Pindari in road of Mar. 1816. Their Report pp. 50-63 Vol. 516a, *Op. Cit*.

45. Acting Resident with Sindhia to Adam, 8th Dec. 1815, No. 21, Bengal Secret Consultations, 6th Jan. 1816.

46. *Ibid,* and a Despatch of 25th Apr. No. 12, Bengal Secret Consultations, 11th May 1816.

47. Close to Moira, 13th Aug., No. 9. Bengal Secret Consultations, 7th Sept. 1816.

48. Adam to Resident with Sindhia, 14th Jan. Nos. 1 & 2, Bengal Secret Consultations, 18th Jan. 1817; and of 15th Feb., No. 5, Bengal Secret Consultations, 15th Feb. 1817; Close to Hastings, 9th July, No. 34, Bengal Secret Consultations, 25th July, 1817 and 26th Aug. No. 18, Bengal Secret Consultations, 12th Sept. 1817.

49. Close to Moira, 23rd Apr. No. 11. 11th May 1816. Although Raghugarh fell on 3rd Sept. (Despatch of 4th Sept. No. 3, Bengal Secret Consultations. 21st Sept. 1816). Raja Jai Singh kept on harassing the possessions of Sindhia after that time. (Despatch to Moira, 7th Jan. No. 1, Bengal Secret Consultations, 28th Jan. 1817.)

50. Close to Moira, 9th May, No. 32, Bengal Secret Consultations, 25th May 1816.

51. Tod to Adam, 9th June, No. 3. Bengal Secret Consultations, 28th June 1817.

52. To Moira, 3rd Apr. No. 21. Bengal Secret Consultations, 20th Apr. 1816.

53. Resident Close expected that a proposal for a system of co-operation "would be made by Sindhia." (His letter 25th Apr., No. 12, Bengal Secret Consultations, 11th May 1816.) The Maharaja's minister did discuss the question on those lines later, but the Resident gave him no decisive answer, (13th Aug., No. 9, Bengal Secret Consultations, 7th Sept. 1816); also his Despatch of 26th Nov., No. 7, Bengal Secret Consultations, 28th Dec. 1816. Elphinstone wrote to Lord Keith on 26th Nov. 1816 "The Resident with Sindhia is of opinion that if the demand were seriously made, Sindhia would at once agree to all the measures requisite to enable us to crush the Pindaris." Colebrooke's *Life of Elphinstone,* Vol. 1, p. 341.

54. Resident at Nagpur to Resident with Sindhia, 6th Sept., No. 49, Supt. Political Affairs. Bundelkhand, to Adam, 17th Sept., No. 52. Bengal Secret Consultations, 28th Sept. 1816; Adam to Jenkins 23rd Nov., No. 8, Bengal Secret Consultations, 23rd Nov, 1816; Collector Ganjam to Board of Revenue, 6th Jan, 1817, and Secret Letter from government Fort St. George, 27th Jan. 1817, pp. 47-8, *Home Misc,* Vol. 516a.

55. Note of Instructions, No. 2 Bengal Secret Consultations. 18th Jan. 1817.

56. Close to Adam. 7th Feb., No. 1. Bengal Secret Consultations, 1st Mar. 1817.

57. Tod to Adam, 29th May, No. 17. Bengal Secret Consultations, 21st June 1817.

58. No. 6, Bengal Secret Consultations, 28th Dec. 1816.

59. Resident with Sindhia was of this view. His Despatch No. 5. Bengal Secret Consultations, 28th Dec. 1816.

60. A paper forwarded by Tod to Adam (23rd May 1817) No. 18, Bengal Secret Consultations, 21st June, 1817. and Close to Adam. 7th Aug. No. 4. Bengal Secret Consultations, 30th Aug. 1817.

61. Resident with Sindhia to Moira. 7th Jan. No. 1. Bengal Secret Consultations, 28th Jan. 1817.

62. Tod to Adam, 9th June, No. 3, Bengal Secret Consultations, 28th June, 1817.

63. Secret Letter from Bengal, 21st Dec. 1816, *Home Misc.* Vol. 516 a, p. 43, also the Minutes of the Governor-General, 6th Dec., No. 13 of 16th Dec., No. 17. Edmonstone's Minutes, 7th Dec., No. 10, 13th Dec., No. 9, of 12th Dec., No. 14.and 21st Dec. No. 18; Seton's 8th Dec, No. 11, 14th Dec. No. 15, and Dowdeswell's 10th Dec. No. 12 and 14th Dec. No. 16, Bengal Secret Consultations, 21st Dec. 1816. In the general decision to destroy the Pindaris the whole Board agreed, although Edmonstone held to the view that Sindhia was genuinely desirous of joining in their suppression, and did not think there were any schemes involving the accession of strength of Sindhia or Holkar to the Pindaris.

64. Governor-General's Minute *Op. Cit.* No. 17. Bengal Secret Consultations, 21st Dec. 1816.

65. *Home Misc.* Vol. 516a. pp. 40-42. Despatch was dated 26th Sept. 1816.

66. Particularly Colonel Walker's operations inpursuing them. Adam to Jenkins, 23rd Nov., No. 8. Bengal Secret Consultations, 23rd

Nov. 1816. Resident with Sindhia to Secretary Adam, 26th Nov., No. 7, Bengal Secret Consultations, 28th Dec. 1816. Secret letter from Fort St. George 27th Jan. 1817. *Home Misc.* Vol. 516 a, pp. 47-48.

67. Hastings did not wish to let Sindhia know of these plans in advance. (His Minute No. 17. Bengal Secret Consultations, 21st Dec. 1816). The Resident with Sindhia was later even instructed to tell Sindhia that "The British Government is aware of the embarrassments which have prevented him from taking immediate steps against the Pindaris, and that his failure would not be misconstrued by the Governor-General-in-Council." (Adam to Resident with Sindhia, dated 21st June, No. 15, Bengal Secret Consultations, 21st June, 1817.)

68. Grant-Duff, *Op. Cit.*, (1912) Vol. III, p. 399.

69. The military plans are described by Prinsep. *Transactions,* Vol. II, pp. 11-17.

70. Governor-General's Minute, 10th May, No. 1, Bengal Secret Consultations, 10th May, 1817.

71. Tod to Adam, 29th May, No. 18, Bengal Secret Consultations. 21st June 1817. Resident to Hastings, 9th July, No. 24, Bengal Secret Consultations, 25th July, 1817, 30th July, No. 34, Bengal Secret Consultations, 22nd Aug., 7th Aug., No. 4, Bengal Secret Consultations, 30th Aug. and 15th Sept., No. 11, Bengal Secret Consultations, 10th Oct. 1817.

72. Resident told Sindhia's minister "Our plans are laid and nothing could now change them." (Resident to Hastings, 27th Sept. No. 35.) and three days later Sindhia had given permission for the passage of Hislop's forces through his territory (to Adam, 30th Sept., No. 37, Bengal Secret Consultations, 17th Oct. 1817.)

73. His Minute for the Council, addressed to Edmonstone, 28th Oct., No. 1. Bengal Secret Consultations, 28th Oct. 1817.

74. Adam to Resident with Sindhia, 28th Sept., No. 4, and draft of a note to be presented to Sindhia, No. 5. Bengal Secret Consultations, 28th Oct. 1817.

75. Adam to Resident with Sindhia, 28th Sept., No. 4, and draft of a note to be presented to Sindhia, No. 5. Bengal Secret Consultations, 28th Oct. 1817.

76. Close to Adam 6th oct. No. 21 Bengal Secret Consultations 7th Nov 1817.

77. Hastings to Close, 26th Oct., No. 9. Bengal Secret Consultations. 14th November 1817.

78. Resident's Despatch, 14th October, No. 56. Bengal Secret Consultations. 11th November 1817.

79. *Ibid.*

80. Resident's Despatch of 3rd October, No. 42. Bengal Secret Consultations, 28th October 1817.

81. Resident's Despatches of 15th Oct., No. 67 and 16th Oct., No. 69, and 20th Oct. No. 72. Bengal Secret Consultations, 14th November 1817.

82. Instructions to the Resident, 28th September *Op. Cit.*

83. Adam to Close, 6th Nov., No. 18, Bengal Secret Consultations, 21st Nov. 1817.

84. The preamble of the Treaty, No. 16. Bengal Secret Consultations. 21st November 1817.

85. His Private Journal, Vol. II., pp. 231-33.

86. *Loc. Cit.* Vol. 1, p. 301. also his Minute of 1st December 1815. paras 79. 84, 89 and 115. *Op. Cit.*

87. Governor-General's Minute of 1st December 1813. paras 25 and 26 of 13th April 1816, *Home Misc.* Vol. 604. 5th June 1816. No. 5. Bengal Secret Consultations, 11th June, 1816.

88. Hastings to Metcalfe, 5th May, 1817. Kaye's *Life of Metcalfe.* Vol. I. pp. 457-8.

89. Metcalfe to Adam. 10th August, No. 39. Bengal Secret Consultations. 5th September 1817, and Adam to Metcalfe 1st October. No. 13. Bengal Secret Consultations, 28th October 1817.

90. He found himself placed between the forces of General Donkin and Sir D. Ochterlony (*Amir Khan's Memoirs,* pp. 463-5.)

91. Metcalfe to Adam, 9th November, No. 16. Bengal Secret Consultations 28th November 1817.

92. The Treaty of Six Articles, forwarded by Metcalfe, on 10th November, No. 22, Bengal Secret Consultations, 5th December 1817.

93. Metcalfe to Adam, 11th November No. 32. Bengal Secret Consultations, 5th December 1817.

94. Such as Captain Sautherland and Sir David Ochterlony. (Kaye's *Life of Metcalfe,* footnote in Vol. 1, p. 464.)

95. Adam to Ochterlony, 21st November, No. 7, and to Malcolm, No. 8, Bengal Secret Consultations, 12th December 1817.
96. Resident with Sindhia to Hastings, 26th August, No. 18, Bengal Secret Consultations, 12th September 1817.
97. Malcolm went round on a political mission to visit the different Courts of Mysore, Hyderabad, Nagpur and Poona, before taking up his duties in Sir Thomas Hislop's camp. He met the Peshwa at Maholi, on 9th August 1817. Kaye's *Life of Malcolm,* Vol. 11, pp. 169-70; also Colebrooke's *Life of Elphinstone,* Vol. 1, p. 286.
98. Colebrook's *Life of Elphistone,* Vol. 1, p. 371.
99. *Loc. Cit.,* p. 372.
100. Colebrooke's *Life of Elphinstone,* Vol. 1, pp. 372-5 and 379.
101. Elphinstone to Hastings, 6th Nov. 1817, *Home Misc.* Vol. 516 a, pp. 119-121.
102. Forrest's *Official Writings of M. Elphinstone,* pp. 180-7.
103. *Ibid,* 187, and Prinsep, *Op. Cit.,* Vol. II, p. 61.
104. Prinsep, Vol. II, pp. 64-5.
105. *Home Misc.* Vol. 516a, pp. 137-41.
106. Adam to Elphinstone, 15th Dec. 1817, *Home Misc.* Vol. 516a, pp. 266-8
107. *Loc. Cit.* pp. 197-201.
108 Strong fort of Simlegarh fell on 2nd March 1818, *Home Misc.,* Vol. 516a. p. 245.
109. *Loc. Cit.* pp. 180-1
110. *Loc. Cit.* pp. 219-19.
111. *Loc. Cit.* p. 238.
112. Issued on 11th February, *Loc. Cit.* pp. 245-7.
113. His letter to the Court of Directors, 20th June, 1818, *Loc. Cit.* pp. 362-3.
114. Jenkins to Hislop. 24th Nov, 1817, No. 136, Bengal Secret Consultations, 26th December 1817.
115. Lieut-Col. Scott to the Adjutant-General of the Deccan Army, 30th Nov. 1817, *Home Misc.,* Vol. 516a, pp. 133-5.
116. Adam to Jenkins, 19th Dec. 1817, No. 2, Bengal Secret Consultations, 9th January 1818.
117. Jenkins to Adams, 15th Dec. 1817, No. 4, Bengal Secret Consultations, 9th January 1818.

118. The Battle of Nagpur, after which the Raja's ammunition and 75 guns were captured by the British. General Doveton to the Adjutant-General, 19th December, *Home Misc.* Vol. 516a. pp. 148-30.

119. The whole series of incidents summed up in Hastings' letter to the Secret Committee, 21st August 1820, *Loc. Cit.* pp. 426-30.

120. Jenkins gave his motives in keeping Appa Sahib on the throne. His Despatch of 6th January 1818, No. 39. Bengal Secret Consultations. 20th Feb. 1818.

121. Jenkins' Despatch to Adam. 16th Jan., No. 30. Bengal Secret Consultations, 27th February 1818.

122. These were very fertile parts, yielding a net revenue of Rs. 22,47,200; Prinsep Vol. II, p. 101.

123. These were the main provisions of the Treaty. (Full text in Aitchison's *Treaties, Op. Cit.*, (1909), Vol. 1, pp. 424-5.)

124. Adam to Jenkins, 22nd January, No. 16, Bengal Secret Consultations, 6th March 1818.

125. Resident to Adam, 15th February, No. 27. Bengal Secret Consultations, 10th April 1818.

126. Jenkins' *Report, Op. Cit.*, p. 135.

127. Jenkins to Adam (private letter). 12th March 1818. No. 6, Bengal Secret Consultations, 24th July, 1818.

127. Jenkins to Adam (private letter). 12th March 1818. No. 6. Bengal Secret Consultations, 24th July, 1818.

128. Jenkins' Despatch, 6th May, No. 38, Bengal Secret Consultations, 28th May. 1818.

129. Governor-General to the Secret Committee, 21st August 1820, *Home Misc.*, Vol. 516a. pp. 435-46. His instructions to the Resident, 28th June, Nos. 3 and 4. Resident's Despatch, 26th June, No. 14. Bengal Secret Consultations, 24th July 1818.

130 Jenkins' Despatch. 17th May, No. 59. Bengal Secret Consultations, 5th June, and also p. 338. Vol. 516a.

131. Jenkins' *Report. Op. Cit.* p. 135.

132. Aitchison, *Op. Cit.* Vol. I, p. 88.

133. Adam to Resident at Delhi, 1st Oct. 1817, No. 13, Bengal Secret Consultations, 28th Oct. 1817.

134. Metcalfe to Adam, 17th Oct., No. 48, Bengal Secret Consultations, 14th November 1817

135. Metcalf to Adam, Nov. 15th, No. 37, Bengal Secret Consultations, 5th Dec. 1817; 21st Nov., No. 108, and Metcalfe to Tod, 21st Nov., No. 109, Bengal Secret Consultations 10th Dec. 1817.

136. Malcolm to Hislop, 13th Dec. 1817, "I never was within fifty miles of the freebooters, and their flight was too rapid to afford me the least chance of reaching them." Kaye's *Life of Malcolm,* Vol. II. p. 197. (Footnote.)

137. The letters exchanged between Malcolm and Holkar, *Home Misc.* Vol., 516a. p. 186.

138. Malcolm to Adam, 24th Dec. 1817, *Loc. Cit.* pp. 184-6.

139. William's letter, 29th Dec., *Loc. Cit.* p. 162.

140. Malcolm to the Adjutant-General of the Deccan Army. Kaye's *Life of Malcolm,* Vol. II, pp. 212-15.

141. Hislop to Hastings *Home Misc.,* Vol. 516a, pp. 166-9. The description of the battle by an English eyewitness. Kaye's *Life of Malcolm.* Vol. 11.

142. Malcolm to Adam, 6th Jan, 1818 *Home Misc.,* Vol. 516a, pp. 188-90.

143. Kaye's *Life of Malcolm,* Vol. II, p. 226.

144. With one minor exception, 9 unimportant villages of Walgaun (the birthplace of Holkar) were to be restored to Holkar if the Governor-General were satisfied with his conduct, *Home Misc.,* Vol. 516a, p. 190.

145. This clause was welcomed by the minister, and was inserted at request. Malcolm to Adam, 7th January, *Loc. Cit.,* p. 192.

146. Text of the Treaty of 16 Articles, p. LXXXVI, and Malcolm's Despatch of 7th January *Loc. Cit.,* pp. 190-2.

147. *Loc. Cit.,* p. 203.

148. *Loc. Cit.,* pp. 236-7.

149. Kaye's *Life of Malcolm,* Vol. II, p. 230 and also *Home Misc.* Vol. 516a p. 237.

150. *Loc. Cit.,* pp. 237, and 253-4.

151. *Loc. Cit.,* p. 260. Captain Stoneham was appointed to that duty to act as superintendent of Pindari Chiefs. Despatch to him, 10th June, No. 34, Bengal Secret Consultations, 26th June 1818.

152. Watson to Wellesley (Resident at Indore), Feb. 27th, No. 61, Bengal Political Consultations, April 3rd, 1819.

153. And also from Raj Rana Zalim Singh (Malcolm to Hastings 10th May, *Home Misc.* Vol. 516a, pp. 296-9.)

154. Malcolm to Low, 17th May 1818. Kaye's *Life of Malcolm,* Vol. 11, p. 237.

155. *Home Misc.,* Vol. 516a. p. 300.

156. *Loc, Cit.,* p. 337.

157. As Baji Rao himself told Malcolm, Kaye's *Life of Malcolm* Vol. II, p. 246

158. *Loc. Cit.,* pp. 353, 354-6.

159. *Loc. Cit.,* p. 352.

160. *Loc. Cit.,* Malcolm to Adam. pp. 356-9 and to Hastings p. 356.

161. The amount of eight lakhs a year was considered too extravagant by Lord Hastings. It later formed the subject of a bitter controversy in which Malcolm defended himself. (Extract from his Despatches and private letters in Kaye's *Life of Malcolm,* Vol. II, pp. 254-263). cf. Hastings to Secret Committee, 17th Oct. 1822, *Home Misc.,* Vol. 516a, pp. 455-8.

162. Commander-in-Chief's general order of 31st March 1818, *Loc. Cit.,* pp. 262.

163. Hastings to the Secret Committee, 17th October 1822, *Loc. Cit.,* pp. 462-66, Account of the Siege *Life of Malcolm.* Vol. II, pp. 286-98.

164. Wauchope to Adam, 1st May, No. 21 and Nawab's letter to Supt. No. 22, Bengal Secret Consultations, 18th May 1816, and another in July 1816, No. 11, Bengal Secret Consultations, 9th Nov, 1816, No. 11, Bengal Secret Consultations, 11th Jan. 1817, in Feb., No. 7, Bengal Secret Consultations, 22nd Mar. 1817, two visits by the Nawab's Agent to the Resident at Nagpur: Jenkins to Adam. 25th Jan. 1817, No. 1, Bengal Secret Consultations, 22nd Feb. 1817.

165. Adam to Wauchope, 9th Nov. 1816, No. 1, Bengal Secret Consultations, 9th Nov. 1816.

166. His Minute of 1st Oct., No. 12, contained his sentiments, with which Seton agreed, Minute of 6th Oct. The whole Council agreed to refer the matter again to the Secret Committee, No. 13 and No. 15, Bengal Secret Consultations, 9th Nov. 1816.

167. Hastings to Hislop, 28th Oct., No. 29; Adam to Malcolm, 28th Oct., No. 30, Bengal Secret Consultations, 21st Nov. 1817.

168. Malcolm to Adam, 24th Oct., No. 44, Bengal Secret Consultations, 14th Nov. 1817.

169. Jenkins to Adam, 15th Oct., No. 26, Bengal Secret Consultations, 21st Nov. 1817.

170. Hastings to the Court of Directors, 8th Feb. 1818, *Home Misc.*, Vol. 516a, p. 206.

171. *Loc. Cit.*, pp. 333-5, and Aitchison (1909), Vol. IV, pp. 296-8.

172. Adam to Wauchope, 29th July 1817, No. 12, Bengal Secret Consultations, 30th Aug. 1817. These instructions were carried out; Despatch from Adam to Wauchope, 9th Sept., No. 17, Bengal Secret Consultations, 26th Sept. 1817.

173. Wauchope to Adam, 30th Oct., No. 153, Bengal Secret Consultations, 19th Dec. 1817, forwarding the Treaty itself.

174. Adam to Wauchope, 15th Feb. 1818,, No. 41, Bengal Secret Consultations, 13th Mar. 1818.

175.

Tribute to British Government		Rs. 1,00,000
Military Service		1,59,840
Expenses of Administration		69,800
Provision for the Bai and Manager		2,50,000
		Rs. 5,79,640
Surplus payable to the Nana		Rs. 1,18,360
	Total	Rs. 6,98,000

Hastings to the Secret Committee, 1st Mar. 1820, *Home Misc.*, Vol. 516a, pp. 412-414.

176. Treaty dated 25th June 1818, Aitchison, Vol. IV, p. 69 and 73.

177. Adam to Resident with Sindhia, 8th Feb., No. 18, Bengal Secret Consultations, 6th Mar, 1818, also Hastings to the Secret Committee, 1st Mar. 1820, *Home Misc.*, Vol. 516a, p. 403.

178. Hastings speech in July 1818 to the European citizens of Calcutta, (reproduced in an Appendix) to White's *Considerations on the State of India*, p. 434.

179. Hastings to the Secret Committee, 17th Oct. 1822. *Home Misc.*, Vol. 516a. p. 451.

180. *Loc. Cit.*, 21st Aug. 1820, p. 438.

181. Malcolm to Hastings, 10th May 1818, pp. 296-9, *Loc. Cit.* other letters, Kaye's *Life of Malcolm*, Vol. II, pp. 307-11, Instructions issued to him 24th Apr., No. 6, Bengal Secret Consultations, 15th May 1818.

182. Hastings to the Secret Committee, 1st Mar. 1820, *Home Misc.*, Vol. 516a, p. 414.

183. Hastings' letter, 1st Mar, 1820, *Home Misc.*, Vol. 516a, vol. 516a, pp. 399-400.
184. Despatch of 4th Mar., No. 352, Bengal Secret Consultations, 24th July, 1818.
185. Despatch of 2nd July, No. 59, Bengal Secret Consultations, 7th Nov. 1818.
186. Hastings' Despatch 1st Mar. 1820 *Home Misc* Vol. 516a p. 404.
187. His speech of July 1818 at Culcutta, White, *Op. Cit.* pp. 421-437.

6

The Nepal War

Racial relations: treatment of Eurasians: condition of native India: the Nepal War.

The Earl of Moira, whom, anticipating a little, we call by his better known name, Marquess of Hastings, was nearly fifty-nine when he became Governor-General. Hitherto distinguished chiefly for being 'on term' of the closest and most expensive intimacy with the Prince Regent'.[1] he departed from all the probabilities by rendering over nine year's service of a quality which has been under rated. He was shrewd, patient, independent, holding his opinions modestly and under continual revision; from his diary, as from his actions, emerges the image of a man experienced and humane. He proved once more that an astringent despair, if accompanied by rigid views of duty, can achieve almost as much as hope itself:

> 'I feel a bond that will never allow me to relax in effort as long as my health will suffice. I at times endeavour to arouse myself with the hope that I may succeed in establishing such institutions, and still more such dispositions, as will promote the happiness of the vast population of this country; but when the thought has glowed for a moment it is dissipated by the austere verdict of reasons against the efficiency of exertion from an atom like me. They Almighty wills it; it is done

> without the mediation of an instrument. The notion of being useful is only one of those self-delusions with which one works oneself through the essentially inept vision of life.[2]

He attacked his own ignorance by at once undertaking an extensive tour up-country, during which he comments repeatedly, in the strongest, most contemptuous terms, on the racial estrangement which was to run its deepening course until the tardy improvement in our own post-War world. But he was unable to do more than by example confirm in courtesy those who had no temptation to fail in it, thereby staving off the worst insolence on one side and the worst humiliation on the other, for a few years longer. He could not re-establish friendly intercourse. He and his wife, Lady Loudoun, managed to do a little for the self-respect of Eurasians. Learning that the ablest freelance in India, the celebrated Captain Skinner—who after quitting Sindhia's service in 1803, had served the Company, and much distinguished himself by his enterprise, his intrepidity, and his judgment',[3] qualities much to seek in the conduct of military affairs at this time—was again in the market for any native State, disgrunted at being liable to 'find himself under the orders of possibly a very inexperienced youth', Hastings 'requested' him to 'assume the honorary title of Lieutenant Colonel', and

> 'apprised him of my intention to propose to Government that a rank in the Irregulars should entitle the officer holding it to rank as youngest field-officer of the line, and to command accordingly all captains and subalterns.'[4]

The veteran was extraordinarily moved by this act of consideration.

> 'To understand this warmth of feeling, one ought to know the excessive depression in which the half-castes are held by the Company's servants. Till Lady Loudoun gave a private hint that colour never would be noticed,

half caste ladies, though of the best education and conduct, and married to men in prominent stations, were not admitted to the government House.'

Yet whatever might be done for a Skinner the lot of Eurasians, who did the immense mass of the actually indispensable work of administration in the uncovenated services, remained what it has been to our own day—the most inexcusable stain in even the records of Anglo-Indian snobbery. A Governor-General's sister exclaims, twenty years later.[5]

> The "unconvented service" is just one of our choicest Indianisms, accompanied with our very worst Indian feelings. We say the words just as you talk of the "poor chimney sweepers" or "those wretched scavengers"—the unconvented being, in fact, clerks in the public offices. Very well-educated, quiet men, and many of them very highlly paid; but as many of them are halfcastes, we, with our pure Norman or Saxon blood, cannot really think contemptuously in fact of them."

During his tour Lord Hastings was shocked by repeatedly discovering men rooting in jail for ancient offences which seemed to him long over-expiated. This resulted in an important reform in procedure. Believing that the Company's personnel could now be trusted to wield magisterial as well as administrative functions, he joined the offices of magistrate and collector. Thus British India for minor offences was given something of the 'non-regulation' methods which obtained in such regions as Delhi, the most effective in newly annexed districts, the most popular with those who administered and in the main liked by those who were administered unto—swift and summary, dispensing with much formality and highly paid roguery.

Had it been possible, he would have done away with the whole legal hocus-pocus. He wrote (November, 1817):

> 'Nothing can more strongly make the prematurity of our attempt to force upon the Indian population our judicial

system than the abhorrence which every man of family among the natives entertains against being summoned, even as a witness, into one of our courts. On this account, it is almost impossible to obtain the testimony of any of them in criminal cases, where they have been present at the perpetration of the act. They will, in the preliminary examination, admit their having been present, but will stoutly swear that they did not happen to notice what was going forward, and can say nothing on the subject. With the lower classes the system is equality unpopular. The security which they enjoy in person and property is duly estimated by them; but that they refer entirely to the principle of Government. The inconvenience, the expense, and the delay which they experience in our civil proceedings, make them unreservedly lament that they are pot subjected to military decision.[6]

But the contrast between the abundance of wisdom wrested from experience and the slight prevalence of that wisdom in human affairs, despite the many enlightened men in influential places, is one of the most powerful reasons for pessimism. It remains mildly mysterious how the legal system, so condemned by the wisest and noblest of the conquerors, became securely fastened down on India. To-day, when the unemployed Indian lawyer is so abused that the uninstructed reader might judge—*does* judge, in fact—that he willfully ate of poisonous fruit and is suffering in his person the proper penalty of foolishness, it is worth remembering how reluctantly India accepted Western justice. We are told that during Lake's Laswari campaign, whole populations fled in terror, not from 'the brutal and licentious soldiery,' but from the 'High Court' which was believed to be accompanying them.!

In language strangely prophetic,[7] Lord Hastings, who saw 'around me the elements of a war more general than any which we have hitherto encountered in India', immediately diagnosed the almost universal hatred of the Company. It was useless to pretend that native States were sovereign Powers so long as the British kept in them subsidiary forces. These subsidiary forces made tyranny safe, and constantly had to put through dirty jobs for contemptible rulers; those rulers hated their overlord, and oppressed their subjects. With every year Hasting's certainty of the 'disgust and estrangement' set up by these relations deepend. Whatever the princes had been when Wellesley began his vigorous dealings with them, they were now —except Ranjit Singh and the Gurkha Maharaja, who were both outside the Company's sphere—vassals in fact, and vassals in a condition of smouldering disaffection. Most of Lord Hasting's time was occupied with the wars he foresaw, and with efforts to set onto some plane of logic and honesty the Company's relations with such States as survived. He sought opportunity to bring them all where they would accept control, of their armies, and submit their mutual quarrels to British arbitration. Before he succeeded, there was to be desperate kicking against the pricks.

Looking over India, he surveyed a dreary scene; and in his despondent conclusions the best British opinion concurred. Sir John Malcolm found in Haidarabad.[8] (1817)

> 'a broken and oppressed race. I am, indeed, disposed to believe that no country was ever more miserably governed. What, indeed, can be expected when the prince is a melancholy madman, and the minister a low Hindoo, who owes his power to the support of our Government, and pays the price of subservience to our Resident for continuance in office? Where power is without pride there can be no motive for good government. I am told it is impossible to maintain our connexion, on a better footing. I can only reply, it is impossible there can be a worse...'

Metcalfe was urging the Governor-General to abolish the mischievous fiction of 'the King' in Delhi, the Mogul establishment, whose pomp was inflated as their importance was small, were abominable neighbours to his authority. Lord Hastings acknowledged that

> 'nothing has kept up the floating notion of a duty owed to the imperial family, but our gratuitous and persevering exhibition of their pretensions—an exhibition attended with much servile obersance in the etiquettes imposed upon us by the ceremonial of the court.[9]

But he had his hands too full to handle a problem so intricately bound up with questions of legal and historical right. Never can Governor-General have felt more distracted, as he listened to the representations of his ablest servants, each convinced that his particular trouble was the one most desperately needing settlement. Munro was pleading for drastic reorganisation of India's internal polity, and in a long letter[10] lamented the subsidiary system's

> 'inevitable tendency to bring every Native state into which it is introduced, sooner or later, under the exclusive dominion of the British Government...Even if the prince himself were disposed to adhere rigidly to the alliance, there will always be some amongst his principal officers who will urge him to break it. As long as there remains in the country any high-minded independence, which seeks to throw off the control of strangers, such counsellors will be found. It have a better opinion of the natives of India than to think that this spirit will ever be completely extinguished; and I can therefore have no doubt that the subsidiary system must everywhere run its full course, and destroy every government which it undertakes to protect.'
>
> 'This very Peishwah will probably again commit a breach of the alliance. The Nizam will do the same: and the same consequences, a farther reduction of their power for our own safety, must again follow.'

> 'This very Peishwah will probably again commit a breach of the alliance. The Nizam will do the same: and the same consequence, a farther reduction of their power for our own safety, must again follow.'

'The usual remedy of a bad government in India is a quiet revolution in the palace or violent one by rebellion, or foreign conquests. But the presence of a British force cuts off every chance of remedy, by supporting the prince on the throne against every foreign and domestic enemy. It renders him indolent, by teaching him to trust to strangers for his security; and cruel and avaricious, by showing him that he has nothing to fear from the hatred of his subjects. Whereever the subsidiary system is introduced, unless the reigning prince be a man of great abilities, the country will soon bear the marks of it in decaying villages and population.'

Readjustment of relations had to be postponed, however, for in 1814 border raids and boundary disputes passed into a war with Nepal. This for a time was 'regarded as a mere affair with a troublesome Raj of the frontier.[11] When its magnitude emerged, the Governor-General himself organised four distinct attacks 'on a frontier of about six hundred miles...But, unfortunately, four out of five generals employed displayed extraordinary incompetence in different fashions.'[12] The first to so distinguish himself was General Gillespie, of Vellore and Java fame, who on October 30 was killed trying to storm the Kalunga stockades. At a second attack on them (November), the troops hung back and sacrificed their leaders. The two attempts cost 740 casualties, 'considerably more than the entire number' of the defenders of 'this petty fortress'.[13] It was invested and cut off from water, and its confined space subjected to intensive bombardment, measures resulting in its evacuating three days after the repulse of November 27. The Gurkha commander and the seventy unwounded men of his 'defiant garrison'[14] slipped unnoticed through the besieging lines, leaving Kalunga 'in a shocking state, full of the mangled remains of men and women killed by...our batteries'.[15]

It is pleasant to remember that this terrible compaign was marked not only by great suffering but by mutual kindness. The gurkhas were such an enemy as the Company had never encountered:

> 'None ever displayed so much bravery in action or so much system, skill, and conduct, so much prudent caution, and so much well-timed confidence. None other ever possessed a country so easily defended, and so difficult to the invader.'[16]

They gave, as well as extorted, respect. Baurial of the dead was 'a courtesy they never refused...and not the only one we experienced at their hands'.[17]

The invaders fought blind, while all the eyes were with their foes, who moved easily round them in the dense forests and towering hills. Gillespie's rout was followed by others. On December 25 a European storming party was chased from Jaituk, and the sepoys following them even outstripped them, fleeing so expeditiously that they were back in their camp, the whole force having lost 500 men, by ten o'clock in the morning.[18] General Wood was defeated at Jitgarh. Yet another army lost two detachments amounting to over a thousand men, the Gurkhas rushing their camp and burning the tents and pursuing the fugitives in every direction. The loss of officers was unprecedented; they were so often left unsupported. Only the fourth army, General Ochterlony's by, sheer caution, building roads and bringing up heavy guns, had escaped serious humiliation, and its leader.

> 'was steadily pursuing his plan by slow and secure manoeuvres, but had yet gained no brilliant advantage over his equally cautious antagonist.'[19]

The impression made in India was deep and wide. Metcalfe, than whom no one was now more influential with the Governor-General, wailed (January 15, 1815):

> 'We have met with an enemy who show decidedly greater bravery and greater steadiness than our troops possess; and it is impossible to say what may be the end of such a reverse of the order of things. In some instances our troops, European and Native, have been repulsed by inferior numbers with sticks and stones. In others our troops have been charged by the enemy sword in hand,

> and driven for miles like a flock of sheep. In a late instance of complete rout, we lost more muskets by a great number than there were killed, wounded and missing. In short, I who have always thought our power in India precarious, cannot help thinking that our downfall has already commenced. Our power rested solely on our military superiority. With respect to one enemy, that is gone. In this war, dreadful to say, we have had numbers on our side, and skill and bravery on the side of our enemy. We have had the inhabitants of the country disposed to favour us, and yet overawed, nothwithstanding our presence and partial success, by the character of our enemy.

One division (Gillespie's, and then Martindel's) had lost a third of the numbers with which it had set out from Meerut. The failures were instantaneously reflected in the attitude of the Maratha chiefs and Ranjit Singh's armed watchfulness at Lahore. It was now that seeds of the next Maratha War were sown.

The British, for whom 'an uninterrupted course of easy victory' had bred 'precipitancy and want of caution,'[20] set themselves to learn from their brilliant teachers. The Gurkhas, on their part, erred by being satisfied with a successful defensive war. Pushing home no advantages they 'were abundantly satisfied with repulsing an attack or cutting off an outpost'. When the British themselves erected stockades, the war became one of 'continuance, that is...length of the purse', and of strong points.

Ochterlony, who changed all this, received no help from his brother commanders. Gillespie's successor, in particular, had managed to infect his whole army with his own imbecility, thereby reinforcing the enemy's decisive individual superiority. A distressing incident took place at Chamalgarh, where two hundred Gurkhas, being surrounded by two thousand irregulars, resolved to die fighting. This heroic expedient proved unnecessary; the mere sight of the stout countenance which they showed caused their besiegers to flee precipitately, 'this unlooked-for result of their interpidity' giving the victors

> 'so much confidence, that they never afterwards failed to attack a post of irregulars, whenever palced within their reach; and even when stock added, they generally succeeded.'[21]

But Ochterlony plodded on, despite minor defeats, and did well enough to overrun Kumaon; and in May, 1815 the Gurkhas made overtures for peace. Negotiations failed on the Company's demand to have a Resident at Khatmandu; and an intercepted letter from the Gurkha leader to his prince showed why he was willing to risk everything rather than this. He insisted and this attitude is one of the reasons why the independence of Nepal survived, when that of other kingdoms, also formidable in battle, went down—that if a treaty were made, it must be honourably kept. 'Lands transferred under a written agreement cannot again be resumed', though 'if they have been taken by force, force may be employed to recover them'. It was better to make no peace, he argued, but to let the war sleep for two years, while the British, in temporary possession of the malarious Terai, were steadily weakened by climatic ravages. The prayers of Brahmins, if these were bought by promises of *jagirs* in the event of victory, would be weakening them still further. Then the war could be strongly reawakened.

The writer of this letter was thinking along lines now common to all native India.

> 'After the immense preparations of the enemy, the will not be satisfied with all thee concessions, or if he should accept of our terms, he would serve us as he did Tipu, from whom he first accepted an indemnity of six crores of rupees in money and territory, and afterwards wrested his whole country. If we were to cede to him so much country, he would seek some fresh occasion of quarrel, and at a future opportunity would wrest from us other provinces.

...When our power is once reduced, we shall have another mission, under pretence of concluding a treaty of alliance and friendship, and founding commercial establishments. If we decline receiving their mission, they will insist; and if we are unable to oppose force, and desire the to come unaccompanied with troops, they will not comply. They will begin by introducing a company; a battalion will soon after follow, and at length an army will be assembled for the subjection of Nipal. You think that if for the present the lowlands, the Doon, and the country of the Satlej were ceded to them, they would cease to entertain designs on the other provinces of Nipal. Do not trust them!...if you had in the first instance decided upon a pacific line of conduct...the present contest might have been avoided. But you could not suppress your desire to retain these places' (Butwal and Sheoral), 'and by murdering their revenue officer excited their indignation, and kindled a war for trifles...In this place I am surrounded, and daily fighting with the enemy...I must gain two or three victories before I can accomplish my object of attaching Ranjit Singh to our cause. On his accession...the chiefs of the Deccan may be expected to join the coalition, as also the Nawab of Lucknow...If we are victorious, we can easily adjust our differences; and if we are defeated, death is preferable to peace on humiliating terms....'

Fighting was resumed early in 1816, and Ochterlony won important victories. The Gurkhas hurriedly made peace, at the price of loss of territory and acceptance of a Resident. A more valuable result yet was the lasting character of the agreement. The contending parties had learnt mutual respect, and understood the limits to which each could be pushed with safety.

REFERENCES

1. *Oxford History of India*, 620.
2. *The Private Journal of the Marquess of Hastings, January* 1, 1816.

3. *Op. cit. i.* 293.
4. *Op. cit. 8. 294-5.*
5. The Hon. Emily. Eden, *Up the Country,* 140 (June 9, 1838). 15
6. *Private Journal,* ii. 229.
7. 'In our treaties with them we recognise them as independent sovereigns. Then we send a Resident to their courts. Instead of acting in the character of ambassador, he assumes the functions of a dictator; interferes in all their private concerns; countenances refractory subjects against them; and makes the most ostentatious exhibition of this exercise of authority. To secure to himself the support of our Government, he urges some interest which, under the colour thrown upon it by him, is strenuously taken up by our Council: and the Government identifies itself with the Resident not only on the single point, but on the whole tenor of his conduct. In nothing do we violate the feelings of the native prince so much as in the decisions which we claim the privilege of pronouncing with regard to the succession to the musnud. We constantly oppose our construction of Mahomedan law to the right which the Moslem princes claim from usage to choose among their sons the individual to be declared the heir-apparent. It is supposed that by upholding the right of primogeniture we establish an interest with the eldest son which will be beneficial to us when he comes to the throne. I believe nothing can be more delusive. He will profess infinite gratitude as long as our supper is useful to him; but, once seated, has subsequent attachment will always be regulated by the convenience of the day. He, too, will in his turn have to feel our interference in the succession as well as in minor instances.' (*Private Journal,* i. 47 ff.)
8. An incident in the summer of 1814 had shown how completely Haidarabad, as well as Oudh, had become dependent. The Nizam's two youngest sons were in the habit of ranging the capital with a gangster band. The Resident tried to round them up: they barricaded themselves in a palace: he blew its gates open 'with some six pounders he had with him' (Prinsep, i. 264). Then the princes were banished, and some of their boon companions executed.
9. *Private Journal,* i. 320 (January, 1815).
10. *Life of Sir thomas Munro,* 247 (August 12, 1817).
11. Henry T. Prinsep, *History of the Political and Military Transactions in India during the Administration of the Marquess of Hastings,* 1813-23, i. 133.

12. *Oxford History of India*, 621-2.
13. Prinsep, i. 92.
14. *Life of Lord Metcalfe*, i. 393.
15. Prinsep, i. 94.
16. Metcalfe, January 15, 1815
17. Prinsep, i. 107.
18. *Op. cit.* i. 99.
19. *Op. cit.*. i. 130
20. *Op. cit*. i. 135.
21. *Op, cit i*. 160.

7

Rajput States

Their importance—Treaties with them embody Hastings' policy—his determination to reduce them under British influence—instructions to Metcalfe—the latter's activity—Karauli treaty signed in November 1817—terms—among the independent Rajput states—Kota the first to ally with the British—Zalim Singh—treaty—supplementary article—remarks—Tod concludes treaty with Bundi-Jodhpur engagement signed at Delhi—Marwar Governments fears—point raised—treaty with Mewar signed—terms the same as others—Mewar envoy's memorandum—Kisangarh and Bikaner—Jaipur negotiations protracted—treaty signed—tribute question—Banswara-Pratapgarh-Dungarpur—finally Jaisalmer—the nature of the treaties—their intention compared to their application—Mewar—Ruined state of the country—usurpation of feudatories and foreign powers—Tod's settlement of the government—improvement—returning peace and prosperity—Marwar-Maharaja resumes power—resists British interference—oppresses his feudatories—Jaipur—Mohan Ram's rule—Maharaja's death—Rani Mother regent—disorders and intrigues—British view—An agent—deputed—interference decided on Kota—Maharao's death—the new Maharao and the Raj Rana's son—differences—disorder—British support of the Raj Rana—

Maharao's flight-return—battle of Mangrol-Maharao retreats—submits—restoration—review—interference—general treatment of the Rajput states—tribute question—conclusion.

While it is beyond question that in the history of the relations of the British Government with the Indian States, Lord Hastings' term of office should be considered of great importance, the name of that Governor-General is still more particularly associated with the settlement of the Rajput States, which he finally drew within the sphere of British influence. A treaty had been concluded with Jaipur in Wellesley's time,[1] but, as has already been observed, with the change in the policy of the Company's Government, it was cancelled by Cornwallis and Barlow. The Agreement formed with Jodhpur by Lord Lake in 1803 never came into force at all[2] since it was not ratified by the Maharaja. So that with the minor exceptions of Alwar[3] and the two Jat principalities of Bharatpur[4] and Dholpur,[5] the whole block of Rajput country on the western bank of the Jumna and extending its frontiers to the Punjab, Sindh, Gujarat and Malwa remained for political purposes a stretch of uncontrolled territory. This position continued until 1817, when Hastings embarked on his grand operations to tranquilise Central Indian and establish paramountcy in the country.

There are many good grounds for giving separate treatment to his dealings with the Rajput Princes. In the first place they formed then, as in many respects they do now, a group by themselves very similar to each other and yet very different from the other States in historical traditions, social conditions and political institutions. Moreover at that time their special interests were certainly not identified with those of the Maratha Princes whom Hastings set out to reduce. In fact the Rajput States found in British alliance a much needed relief and deliverance from the miserable conditions to which they had been reduced by Maratha oppression for half a century, owing to the destruction of their resources in wealth, population and political prestige. Since they furnished a source of strength and a field of prey for the Maratha Rulers and Amir Khan, the real rivals of British Power, the Rajput States were embraced by Hastings as the nature friends of his Government. He saw in their alliance not only a check to the extension of the power of Sindhia, Holkar and Amir Khan, an object of considerable value in his estimation, but the acquisition of immense strategic advantages for the Company's military and political position in Central India. "The establishment or our influence over those States would interpose strong barriers between the Sikhs and those Powers which might be expected to aid them.[6]

He also expected to utilise the resources of the Rajput country for defensive and offensive purposes, against internal and external enemies of the Company.[7] It was not merely in the British attitude towards them that the Rajput States offered a problem for special treatment. Even after the conclusion of the treaties, their execution presented peculiar difficulties in those States on account of local conditions, which will be observed as this account progresses further.

Another interesting feature about the treaties binding the Rajput states in political relation with the Company is worth mentioning. They contain essentially those principles which Hastings, at the very commencement of his term of office, laid down as the ideal political arrangement. In this case he found almost untrodden ground on which to enter and chalk out his own plans for the foundation of the future edifice of political relationship. And so the treaties with these States were fashioned after Hastings' policy.

When he left Calcutta for the Upper Provinces of Hindustan personally to direct operations in the field he had set out with a determination to bring the Rajput States within the pale of British protection. It was principally on this point that he decided, on his own personal responsibility, to overstep the limits laid down for him by the Board of Control.[8] He was not prepared to postpone action any longer. This again was the principal and most important motive in his mind for presenting to Sindhia a new treaty to modify the old one, concluded by Barlow in 1805, the restrictive clause of which Hastings had always resented. While Maharaja Sindhia was still considering the articles of the proposed agreement in October 1817, instructions had at the same time been issued to Metcalfe, the Resident at Delhi, to open negotiations with the Rajput Rulers. It was indeed unnecessary to wait for the final result of the conversations at Gwalior. The Governor-General had made up his mind.[9] If peaceful negotiations failed he was determined to achieve his purpose even by a war with Sindhia, should that extreme step be deemed necessary to obtain for the British Government the required freedom to treat with the Western Powers of Hindustan. While the definite measures for defining the relations with them could be suspended until Sindhia's attitude had been ascertained, no delay was to be allowed in arriving at a general understanding with them. The twofold object of that policy was "to establish a barrier against the revival of the predatory system or the extension of the power of Sindhia and Holkar beyond the limits assigned to it by the measures now in progress".

It could be achieved by one of two alternative plans, "either by combining them (the three principal Rajput States at least) in a common league under the paramount authority of the British Government or by concluding separate engagements with each State on the conditions best adapted to its peculiar circumstances and situation." But owing to the distractions prevailing in them, and their mutual pride and jealousy, a system of confederation was difficult, and the latter mode was, therefore, considered preferable. It was desired to contract relations of alliance with Udaipur (Mewar), Jaipur (or Dhundar), Jodhpur (Marwar), the smaller States of Kota and Bundi (Harauti) and Karauli, and also with the three principalities of Banswara, Dungarpur and Pratapgarh (the off-shoots of the Udaipur House) situated on the Gujarat border and with the distant States of Bikaner and Jaisalmer. The instructions issued in 1816 to the Resident at Delhi for conducting negotiations with Jaipur were to form the basis of the terms he was asked to offer to the various Rajput States. However, Metacalfe was not to insist on the cession of a fort by the contracting State. The question of tribute was also to be re-examined in view of the possibility that Sindhia and Holkar might accept British terms without resort to warfare. In that case, the British Government would guarantee them the tributes from the different States, which had been regularly paid to the two Maratha Princes. But, "the question of Sindhia's and Holkar's tribute is to be treated as one between the British Government and the two latter Powers exclusively. So that all direct intercourse between the Rajput States and Maharattas shall cease." Hastings was keen that the negotiations should not be delayed or hampered by these minor details. If the engagements could not be concluded with all, they were to be formed with as many as possible. "Every step we take is so much gained, and offers a fairer probability of combining the rest in the same arrangement." Metcalfe was asked to invite the co-operations of the Chiefs in suppressing the Pindari freebooters, and in preventing their revival. The general object of securing their co-operation to the extent of their means was deemed much more important than the conclusion of definite agreements, since it was believed that such co-operation would lead to their dependence on the British Government. These instructions formed the contents of an important despatch, issued from the camp of the Governor-General on the 8th October.[10] Metacalfe soon became busy. The States were duly informed of the wishes of the Governor-General, and negotiations were set on foot with the agents of many of them at Delhi, in accordance with the directions sent out from the headquarters at Cawnpore.[11]

On the 9th November, the same day on which Amir Khan's agreement was signed, Metcalfe reported that the Maharaja of Karauli had accepted a Treaty through his Agent at Delhi.[12] Karauli had been a tributary of the Peshwa, and by virtue of the Treaty of Poona,[13] the British Government had acquired all rights over his tributaries in Hindustan and Malwa. The Maharaja acknowledged the supremacy of the East India Company, and in return was taken under its protection. No tribute was imposed upon the State, but it was stipulated that the Maharaja would furnish troops at the requisition of the British Government, according to his means. The Treaty bound the principality of Karauli in subordinate alliance to the Company's Government, without whose consent, no negotiations with other Powers were to be carried on.[14] The Treaty was approved and ratified by the Governor-General on the 15th November.[15]

Excluding the case of Karauli, which was an acknowledged dependency of the Peshwa's, the first of all the independent Rajput States to respond to Metcalfe's communication was the small but well-to-do State of Kota, then under the clever management of Raj Rana Zalim Singh who, by his tact and sagacity, had acquired a great name. He had completely eclipsed the hereditary ruler of the State. Whilst the latter was acknowledged as the nominal sovereign, the Raj Rana himself wielded the real power. By his clever manipulation of the various contending interests and warring powers, not only had he saved the little State of Kota from Maratha and Pathan devastations, but he himself had become a factor of considerable importance in almost all the inter-state matters of Malwa. He remained friendly with all the Powers, paying tributes to Amir Khan and Sindhia, and farming districts belonging to Sindhia and Holkar, keeping on good terms with everyone—especially the most powerful.[16] He arbitrated in their disputes[17] and, above all, guarded the interest of his own State with remarkable foresight, maintaining a highly efficient force. The country was extremely well-governed. Such a shrewd statesman as Zalim Singh would not be slow to discern the path of safety and self-interest, since he had watched the rising power of the Company. Not only did he offer a contingent of fifteen hundred tingly equipped men, and co-operate in every way with British in the Pindari campaign, but he readily came forward to form an alliance with them.[18]

The Raj Rana, therefore, led the way in this matter, and the Treaty which Metcalfe concluded with his Agent at Delhi on the 26th December, 1817, became the model for similar agreements with the other States of Rajasthan. By it, the Maharao of Kota entered into a relation of "perpetual friendship, alliance and unity of interest" with the East India Company. He accepted its protection, agreeing to have no dealings with other States, to refer all disputes to British arbitration, to act always in "subordinate co-operation with the British Government, and acknowledge its supremacy." He also agreed to pay that Government the tribute payable to the Maratha Chiefs, and lastly, to furnish the troops of Kota according to the means of his State, at the requisition of the British Government. In return for the surrender of his political independence, the Maharao of Kota and his successors were recognised as "absolute rulers of their country," into which the civil and criminal jurisdiction of the British government would not be introduced. This Treaty[19] was ratified by the Governor-General on the 6th January.[20] A tribute schedule was drawn up, and it was agreed to pay the amounts due to Sindhia, Holkar and the Pawars for Kota proper, the seven Kotris and Shahabad, into the British treasury at Delhi.[21] In the following year, the British Government relinquished the Shahabad tribute, and ceded to Kota the districts of Dig, Pachpahar, Ahora and Gangrar.[22]

Two years later another question arising from this Treaty became a source of serious embarrassment. It related to the rights and authority of the titular as against the real ruler of Kota. Raj Rana Zalim Singh was the actual ruler, managing the affairs of the State in the name of its hereditary Prince Maharao Umed Singh, with whom, at the request of the Raj Rana himself, the Treaty had been concluded. Zalim Singh's agents at Delhi required an assurance from Metcalfe in the name of the British Government, that his position as the Premier of Kota would pass on to his heirs and successors, and he was anxious to have that guarantee embodied in the Treaty itself. Considering the loyal services rendered to the British Government by Kota under Zalim Singh's administration, the Resident at Delhi was willing to meet his wishes.[23] Hastings supported his Agent in the matter, and the Treaty was modified by means of a supplementary article to "more effectually secure to Raj Rana Zalim Singh and his heirs, the authority and the privileges in the State of Kota which he now exercises."[24] It is not to be wondered at that this apparently innocent assurance to the Raj Rana, for whose friendly exertions the gratitude and consequent loyal support of the British Government was a just recompense, later became the cause of trouble and civil strife in Kota. The British Government entered into a solemn agreement, the provisions of which were capable of incompatible interpretations.[25] They guaranteed to Zalim Singh and his heirs the authority of the chief manager of the State, (thereby creating a hereditary Premier) and at the same time (by Article 10 of the Treaty), engaged always to recognise the Maharao (the rightful sovereign of Kota) and his heirs as "absolute" rulers of the country. What ruler could be really absolute whose premier was chosen for him by a outside authority, and in perpetuity? The germ of instability was inadvertently laid in the agreement itself, and in course of time it developed to mischievous dimensions. In the meantime, most amicable relations had been established between the two Governments. The services of the Kota Durbar were warmly appreciated by Hastings in personal letters[26] to the Maharao and to the Raj Rana, and Tod delivered to the State the possession of the territories north of the Narbada, which had been taken from Holkar by the Treaty of Mandasor and were given to Kota[27] in appreciation of its sacrifices in the British cause.[28]

Metcalfe had concluded the Treaty with Kota at Delhi, with Thakur Sheodan Singh, the Agent of Zalim Singh, who arrived there before Tod could begin his political duties in Harauti. But the conclusion of a similar engagement with the sister State of Bundi was left to be completed by Tod. That small State had always maintained a friendly attitude towards the British, and had suffered terribly from the exactions of the neighbouring Powers. Considering those facts, it was Hastings' wish to require no tribute at all from the Maharao of Bundi.[29] When issuing those instructions, the Governor-General was under the impression that the tribute which it owed to Sindhia amounted only to the trifling sum of Rs. 10,000. But Metcalfe very shrewdly kept the question open, and desired Tod to include in the Treaty the stipulation that Bundi would pay to the British Government the amount which it regularly paid to Maharaja Sindhia.[30] As it turned out, the latter claimed that his share of tribute from Bundi was Rs. 1,05,000 per annum. Although this figure was reckoned to be far in excess of the amount normally received, yet it appeared that Sindhia's claim was too substantial to be relinquished. Beyond the instructions regarding the settlement of tribute, there was no difficulty to surmount. The conditions were to be "but few and simple, providing for protection and guarantee on the one hand, and political dependence and subordinate co-operation on the other.[31]

Tod left Kota on the 6th February, arriving at Bundi on the 8th. Discussions on the terms of the treaty began on the 10th. But, as he reported, the ruined condition of the country and the benefits of British connection, made any discussion unnecessary. The Maharao was all along cordial, grateful and appreciative. The Treaty was soon concluded, the tribute chargeable being Rs. 80,000. The Maharao gave in a memorandum of the places belonging to his State, which were then in the wrongful possession of other Powers. His particular grievance was against his astute neighbour, Zalim Sing, who had contrived to keep for himself the fort of Indragarh, a place specially dear to the Bundi Raj.[32] The Treaty was approved and ratified by Hastings on the 1st March.[33] Before Tod had completed his political mission in Harauti, and set out for Mewar, whither he was deputed to proceed, Metcalfe had cast his net over two of the leading States of Rajputana, and converted them into subordinate allies of the Company.[34]

He had opened negotiations with the Agent of the Maharaja of Jodhpur (Marwar) at Delhi in October. That State was very cautious in yielding to the terms demanded by the British Resident;[35] but their fears and prejudices were overcome by giving the necessary assurances. The Government of Marwar were afraid that the British would extend their interference from external affairs to internal administration, and wished to be quite sure that the Company's Government would not enter into separate engagements with the feudatories of the State. The Maharaja wished to resume the Jagir given under coercion to Amir Khan, and to recover, by armed force if need be, their fort of Amarkot, lost to the Chiefs of Sindh through the treason of their own officer. He was also desirous of retaining the province of Godwar, which had been given to Jodhpur by the Mewar Government several generations ago, in the time of Maharaja Bijai Singh. The custom of giving shelter and protection to those who sought it was a time-honoured tradition with the Rajput States, and the government of Jodhpur were anxious to preserve it. They also desired that the services of their contingent should not take their men beyond the Narbada. These were the Chief points raised by the plenipotentiaries of Jodhpur, on which Metcalfe gave suitable and satisfying assurances. He removed their fears by referring to Article Nine of the Treaty by which the British Government were precluded from entertaining the applications of the Maharaja's Thakurs, or nobles, and further reassured them that his Government had no wish to introduce its laws or jurisdiction into Marwar. The Treaty was concluded on the 6th January at Delhi, with the usual provisions of defensive alliance, perpetual friendship, protection and subordinate co-operation. Article Eight laid down that the Jodhpur State would furnish a contingent of 1500 horse for the service of the British Government, and that whenever necessary, the whole of the disposable forces of the State would join the British Army.[36] The conclusion of this Treaty further increased the political prestige of the Company. An important State, with extensive dominions in Western Rajputana, was reduced to dependence.

Only a week later, Metcalfe concluded an agreement with the ambassador of Udaipur, Thakur Ajit Singh. On account of the fame of its past history, Mewar holds the premier rank amongst the several States of Rajputana. It illustrious rulers had always fought chivalrously to protect their honour. For generations, Mewar had given to the country a succession of wise rulers, brave generals, heroic leaders, and even some fine poets.[37] But in the eighteenth century the fortunes of the country steadily declined. And just before Hastings' period of office, Mewar was perhaps the worst sufferer from Maratha and Pathan exaction. The depopulation and decay, the ruin and desolation, which the repeated inroads of Bapu Sindhia and Amir Khan caused in Mewar had reduced the position of its ruler and the condition of its people to a low and miserable level indeed.[38] Therefore, when the British turned their attention to the Rajput States in 1817, they found the proud name of the ancient house of the Maharana humiliated, the fertile country, with its rich natural resources lying desolate, and many parts of it usurped by refractory nobles or Maratha generals.[39] From his high title of the "King of the Hindus," Metealfe had anticipated some objections on the part of the Rana of Udaipur to accept the terms of "supremacy" and "subordinate co-operation" with the British Government. As he reported to the Governor-General:—On account of these high pretensions, I expected some opposition to the third article, and was prepared to modify it as might have been requisite or expedient."[40] Instead, the Rana's envoy raised another objection of a similar nature, but since he did not insist on it, the objection was eventually dropped.[41] So that the Treaty, as it was finally signed on the 18th January, embodied provisions almost identical with those contained in the engagement with Kota and Jodhpur.[42] The Mewar envoy presented to Metealfe a memorandum of the claims for the restitution of territories in the wrongful possession of other Powers—Sindhia, Amir Khan, Holkar, Jodhpur, and Kota, and for the restoration of the Rana's sovereignty over the Chiefs of Banswara, Dungarpur and Pratapgarh, the former feudatories of Mewar.[43]

Although the company's Government, under Hastings, was at this time at the height of its power and political prosperity, there can be doubt that the indirect moral result of such a treaty as that concluded with Udaipur greatly enhanced its prestige in the country. The Ranas of Udaipur had never before so definitely, formally and effectually surrendered their independence to any other Power, not even to the Mughal Empire, as they did to the Company in 1818.

In the month of March, Metcalfe induced two more States to form an alliance with the British Government on practically the same conditions as the others. The Rathor States of Kishangarh,[44] a tiny principality in the neighbourhood of Ajmer, and Bikaner,[45] became allies of the Company, and agreed to recognise its supremacy. In neither of the two cases, was it deemed necessary to charge any tribute. By Article Seven of the Treaty with Bikaner, the British Government engaged to help the ruler in restoring his authority over his nobles and other subjects who had thrown it off. The State undertook to meet the cost of the military assistance which it might require for that purpose. With the conclusion of the Treaty with Bikaner, the sphere of British control was pushed further towards the frontiers of the Punjab and Sindh.

Of all the important States which formed these alliances with the British Government, the State of Jaipur was the last to capitulate. Negotiations with that Government had given no small amount of embarrassment and disappointment of Metcalfe in 1816. And the State was maintaining its former tradition in 1817 and 1818 also, by the way in which its embassy conducted itself at Delhi.[46] Metcalfe expected that the advance of Ochterlony's force towards Jaipur territory would "bring the procrastinating counsels of the Rajah to a decision in favour of the immediate conclusion of the alliance."[47] It was perfectly obvious that with the submission of one State after another, both big and small, Jaipur could not held out for any length of time. But with a view of accelerating the settlement which was, of course, inevitable, Metcalfe tried two effective plans for the wavering government of Jaipur. Not only did he not raise any objections to, but he even connived at, Amir Khan's occupation of some parts of Jaipur territory. And secondly, he encouraged the feudatory Chiefs and nobles of Jaipur to enter into separate agreements with the British Power. With this object, the Raja of Khetri, one of the leading nobles of Jaipur, sent his son, Kunwar Bakhtawar Singh, to Delhi, and a conditional engagement was concluded with him. Others would have been similarly treated if the Jaipur Durbar had not felt alarmed at this clever move of the British Resident, whose aim was twofold, either to frighten the Court of Jaipur into concluding a treaty, or to undermine its authority by forming separate alliances with the nobles of that State.[48] Metcalfe's diplomacy succeeded, and jaipur negotiations became more earnest. The tribute question further prolonged the discussion.[49] But eventually an agreement was reached, and the Treaty was signed on the 2nd April. The main conditions of the engagement were the same in essentials as those agreed to by the Maharana of Mewar. The amount of tribute was adjusted on a sliding scale by which the State was excused from its altogether for the first year, and agreed to pay four, five, six, seven and eight lakhs of rupees respectively for the second, third, fourth, fifth and sixth years. After that, the amount was to be eight lakhs as year until the revenues exceeded forty lakhs per annum, when the State was to pay five-sixteenths of the additional revenue above eight lakhs.[50]

This Treaty was ratified by the Governor-General on the 15th April, 1818. With the submission of Jaipur, the whole of Rajputana lay prostrate, and British paramountcy came to be acknowledged over that historic country. Formal engagements still remained to be concluded with the smaller States of Banswara, Dungarpur, Deolia, Pratapgarh and the Bhati State of Jaisalmer. The three former, of Sisodia stock, had, in the dark days of its decay, shaken off their allegiance to Mewar, and desired independent recognition. The British Government naturally favoured the latter plan.[51] In the unsettled times when the Mewar Government was so completely disintegrated, they were overpowered by Holkar and by the Pawar States of Malwa, who levied tributes from them whenever possible. As has been mentioned at the end of the last chapter, Sir John Malcolm with a few able assistants was engaged in tranquillising Malwa. The settlement of Banswara, Dungarpur and Pratapgarh, was left to him. He deputed Lieutenant Dayson to enquire into the conditions prevailing in those States,[52] and that officer addressed himself to the task with singular zeal and care. His enquiries revealed how these petty States were reduced to desolation and poverty owing to the depredations of the times.[53]

On the 16th September, Metcalfe concluded a Treaty with the Agent of Banswara, which Hastings ratified on the 10th October, 1818.[54] But the Maharawal denied that he had sent any agent to Delhi with authority to conclude an agreement with the British.[55] And so, on the 25th December, 1818, another engagement was concluded between the Maharawal and the British Government at Banswara, by Captain Caulfield, another of Malcolm's assistants, being ratified at Calcutta on the 18th February following. The second treaty resembled the first in all essential matters, with the addition, at Malcolm's instance, in the second of a security for the regular payment of the stipulated tribute. Authority was given to the British Government to collect the town duties of Banswara, should punctual payment be not made. This Treaty, unlike the engagements with other States, gave to the British the power of interposing their advice in settling the affairs of the State, a provision which was deliberately inserted.[56] And finally, the Treaty provided for the payment to the British Government of arrears of tribute due to the Pawar Chief of Dhar (or any other State).[57]

The connection of Pratapgarh with the East India Company began in 1804, but the engagement concluded in that year was dissolved under the policy of Cornwallis.[58] Between that time and the period of Malcolm's regime in Malwa, this principality suffered heavily from Holkar's Government. The people of Pratapgarh felt bitter against that Government from the memory of the affections and oppressions to which they had subjected them. The Jagirdars usurped the lands of the State, and committed acts of plunder in times of general disorder. Having endured all these wrongs and losses, the Maharaja of Pratapgarh sought relief in the alliance and protection of the British Power.[59] In concluding an engagement with this State, Malcolm had to consider and settle Holkar's claims to tribute from it.[60] Another hitch in the signature of the Treaty was the security for the payment of tribute, on which point again Malcolm showed great firmness.[61] The Treaty was concluded by Caulfield at Nimach on the 5th October, with the usual stipulations for protection, tribute and subordinate isolation. Although it was declared that the British would not interfere in the internal government of the State, the Ruler agreed "to be guided by the advice of the British Government." The security for the regular payment of the tribute was duly provided for, as in the case of Banswara, by the authority given to the British Government to receive the town duties in case of failure.[62]

A Treaty was concluded with the third State of this group on the 11th December, 1818, on exactly the same terms as those concluded with Banswara, mentioned above.[63] The Treaty with Pratapgarh formed the model for both of them, with this one difference, the Dungarpur and Banswara owed tributes to Dhar,[64] and Pratapgarh to Maharaja Holkar.

Before the close of 1818, the great year of the Rajput treaties, Metcalfe had concluded another treaty at Delhi in the 12th December. This last engagement was with the State of Jaisalmer. The terms of this Treaty were simple and general, and it was in itself expressive of the position of security and superiority which the British had attained. The relations were defined in a few short sentences comprising only four articles. The complete establishment of the British Power in the country made it unnecessary to define the relations with jaisalmer with any great precision. No tribute was imposed. This State was remote from the scene of the Maratha and Pathan depredations and consequently did not owe them any tribute.[65]

Thus the group of States which now comprise Rajputana had all been taken under the Company's protection before the end of 1818, with the solitary exception of the small Chiefship fo Siroohi, with which no treaty was concluded until a few years later,[66] owing to the undecided claims of the Maharaja of Jodhpur to its tribute and allegiance.[67]

An examination of the treaties concluded at this time reveals, as was remarked at the beginning of this chapter, that they essentially embody the principles advocated by Hastings on his arrival in India. His object was to form a Confederacy of all the internal States of India, with the British Government as the senior controlling member. The two main duties of the vassal States were to be *firstly* the settlement of their disputes through the arbitration of the paramount Power, instead of by war, and *secondly,* the furnishing of their forces at the call of that Power at any time.[68] Both these principles were included in all the engagements which have been noticed in this chapter. The policy of interposing British arbitration in inter-state disputes, for the suppression of mutual warfare and the extension of the political control of the Company was an old one, and Hastings also adopted it. But the second part of his scheme was his own. None of his predecessors had so uniformly demanded that the entire resources of the allied States should be available at the requisition of the British Government. It was a bold step in advance on existing political conditions, which meant the accession of new and substantial strength to the Company's prestige in its dealings with the Indian States. And the latter fully realised the significance of the change. Not only was the feudal stipulation to furnish the State forces whenever required included in every treaty, but the Governor-General preferred that the obligations of the contracting States of afford the services of their troops, should be kept general, rather than specified to a precise number.[69] On this important ground, these treaties represented the attainment of his cherished goal and the complete success of his efforts to plant the British domain permanently in India.

His idea of the British Confederacy in India was a group of internally independent State "possessed of perfect internal sovereignty,"[70] having no external relations whatsoever with other States, excepting through and with the paramount Power, namely, the British Government. He had deplored in strong language past interference with the internal affairs of the States, leading to great discontent, disharmony and even bitterness amongst the princes.[71] It has been seen how the new relations that Hastings formed embodied the two basic principles he had early laid down. It remains to be seen whether in the execution of these treaties he was equally successful in carrying out his principles of confederal relationship and avoiding the errors he had condemned in the policy of his predecessors. With this object, it is worth while to review briefly the developments that took place after the treaties had been signed and ratified. Therefore, it would be interesting to examine the course of the relations of the British Government with the leading States of Rajputana, namely, Udaipur, Jodhpur, and Jaipur.

It has been seen how the historic State of Mewar had been the worst sufferer from the Pathans and the Marathas. After concluding the Treaty with Bundi, Tod was required to proceed to Mewar, to settle the affairs of that unfortunate land.[72]

It was apparent that the conclusion of the Treaty with the Maharana, affording him and his Government the protection of the superior power of the Company, would be insufficient to meet the situation. The Maratha and Pathan inroads had so completely unsettled the authority of the Rana, that a deep wound had been caused in the body politic of Mewar, which had grown into a disease, and it was not, therefore, enough, merely to remove the original cause of the evil. It was felt desirable to apply a more positive and prompt treatment to restore the State and save it from further decay.

When Tod entered into Mewar in February, 1818, he found that some of the richest and most valued forts and districts belonging to the Maharana were in foreign possession. Kota held the distant Pargana of Jahazpur, the famour Fort of Kumbhalmer was garrisoned by Jaswant Rao Bhao's men, Bapu Sindhia had become the master of Rajnagar, Raipur, Kuakhera, and Sangramagrh. Several other very fertile parts, such as Nimach, Jawad, Jiran, Gangapur, Godwar and Nimbahera had been lost to Mewar through the weakness of its rulers and the aggression of its neighbours.[73] Hastings realised that it was "an object of importance with reference both to the restoration of the prosperity of that State and to the direct interests of the British Government to recover as large a portion of them as possible."[74] This was not the only relief that Mewar cried for. Under the new Treaty the restitution of her territories, foreibly seized or usurped by unscrupulous adventurers, would fairly come within the province of British interference, as the paramount arbitrary Power. But mewar was then suffering from more ills than one. Taking advantage of the disorders of the time, the powerful Chiefs and feudatories of the Maharana had also usurped large parts of the State (Khalsa) Lands, and had disregarded the claims of service and tribute due from them to their suzerain, the head of the State. This aristoneracy of the nobles of Mewar, most of whom are descended from the reigning house itself, is, in its traditions, dignity and privileges unquie in the whole of India. The unsurpations of the State territory and the adjustment of the Rana's claims on their service was a much more perplexing problem than it at first appeared.[75] Moreover, it was clearly a matter of internal concern. Before the Government of Mewar could be placed in a stable working condition, it was desirable to settle these two outstanding matters, namely, the restitution of the usurped territories and the restoration of the Rana's authority over his recalcitrant Chiefs.

Only a partial solution of the first was practicable[76] Those territories which had long remained in the possession of other States—Sindhia, Holkar and Marwar—could not be retaken. But the more recent usurpations were restored to the Maharana. General Donkin's force advanced into Mewar and easily recovered Raipur from Bapu Sindhia's agents.[77] Tod arrived just in time to recover Kumbhalmer without any fighting, by paying off the arrears of Bhao's garrison which made over the fort without further resistance.[78]

From Kumbhalmer Tod proceeded to Udaipur, arriving there on the 8th March. There he saw with his own eyes the excessive poverty of the Rana, the utter destitution of the country around and the deplorable weakness of the governmental authority, which was at once the cause and the consequence of the ruined condition of the State. In such a situation as Tod found himself " it will be difficult" he wrote" to avoid immediate interference, but it would have the worst effect to allow them to know I wished to abstain from it."[79] Hastings himself perceived that "in the actual state of the Court of udaipur, some more active interference on your part than would be justifiable in a more wholesome condition may not only be excusable, but actually indispensable for the success of the measures in view." Tod was told, however, to exercise that intervention "with utmost moderation, caution, and discretion and in the form of private advice, not of authority."[80]

He addressed himself to that task very soon after his arrival, a task at once urgent, yet bristing with enormous difficulties. The Maharana himself was a person of shreed understanding, fully conversant with the history of his House, and the privileges attaching to his position. Although not devoid of talents, and certainly possessed of the best intentions, Maharana Bhim Singh was weak, fickle and generally incapable of managing men or affairs. His ministers were selfish and corrupt. The nobles flouted his authority and quarrelled amongst themselves. The two factions of the Chundawats and the Sakatawats had been irreconcilable for many generations. At this time, Rawat Gokul Das of Deogarh was the leader of the former (although the senior Chief of the clan is the Rawat of Salumbar), while Maharaj Zorawar Singh of Bhindar was the head of the Saktawats. Not only the Chiefs of the first rank (called the "sixteen" from the original number in the premier class), but also the lesser nobles, such as the Rao of Bhadesar, had displayed a rebellious attitude towards the Maharana during the time of his declining fortunes.[81] The Maharana accused them of wrongfully extending their possessions in Khalsa land, of levying customs duties which were due only to the central Government of the Rana, and of delinquency in service at his Court by personal attendance, and in furnishing foot and mounted forces at the capital according to usage.

Tod held conferences with the Maharana and the different nobles. On the 27th April, 1818, an assembly of the Chiefs was convened, at which the terms of the proposed arrangement, as previously settled between the Maharana and Tod were explained to them. Another session of the assembly originally arranged for the 1st May, was, at the wish of the nobles, convened on the 4th of that months. A prolonged discussion ensured. Objections, excuses, postponement and opposition were urged one after the other. The Rana displayed remarkable firmness and judgment during that fifteen hours' sitting, after which, at last, the agreement was signed by all the Chiefs present—the Rawat of Begun setting the example, followed by his kinsmen of Amet and Deogarh. The Maharaj of Bhindar was the last to append his signature. The terms of settlement comprised the surrender of all Khalsa land seized by the nobles and jagirdars since the Sambat, 1822 (1766 A.D.). The nobles were to abstain in future from levying *Dhani Bilswa*—a rateable impost on agricultural produce. *Rahbari Bhum* (a new toll charged from travellers in chaotic times for immunity from plunder) was disallowed. The terms and times of the service of the nobles by personal attendance, and the presence of their quota of irregular forces at the Capital were defined for future observance. The authority of the Rana's executive for enforcing these terms and for commanding the unfailing obedience of the nobles, was recognised. This was the substance of the *Kaulnama* (i.e. agreement), which was adopted under Tod's signed guarantee.[82]

Difficult as was the settlement of these internal feuds, and, therefore, great as was his achievement in obtaining the signatures of all these proud Chiefs, the enforcement of the conditions was still more difficult indeed. For several months, Tod had to employ all his tact and firmness in persuading the nobles, (particularly the Maharaj of Bhindar) to restore the usurped lands, and to discontinue the collection of customs dues, (for instance, by the Rawat of Deogarh at the passes leading into Marwar). By patient endeavour and an uncommon spirit of loyalty, Tod achieved a large measure of success in re-establishing the Rana's government over his State. Very soon the results of those sincere efforts began to appear in the rising populations, returning trade, and reviving financial prosperity of the country.[83]

Although complete restoration to normal conditions and the reconstruction of a strong Central Government from the wretched state to which the jealousies of the selfish nobles[84] and the corruption of the ministers had reduced Mewar, could only be gradual, it is certainly true that the recovery had set in and further, that its steady start was due chiefly to Tod's exertions and advice.[85] His influence was exercised in a almost every branch of public administration; the system of land revenue naturally received his particular attention, for on it depended the regeneration of the State.[86] It is even still more remarkable that his advice was welcomed by the Rana, who reposed a high measure of confidence in Tod personally, and expected useful support from the powerful Government which he represented. This state of affairs continued throughout Hastings' period of office.[87]

The Rathor State of Marwar, before entering into alliance with the Company in 1818, had suffered nearly as badly from Amir Khan's oppression as the sister State of Mewar.[88] For some years earlier Maharaja Man Singh had been forced to withdraw from public affairs under a supposition of insanity, and the engagement had been concluded in his name with his son, Chhattar Singh, who was made Regent. The young Prince died within a few weeks of the conclusion of the

Treaty, and the Government was carried on by his minister, Thakur Salim Singh and Akahai Chand. But after the death of the heir-apparent, the Maharaja gradually removed his mask, and grasped the power of the State. As soon as his position became secure, he wreaked full vengeance on his former enemies, the ministers and nobles who had reduced him to a mere figure-head and driven him into seclusion. Twelve persons of rank, some of them nobles, were mercilessly put to death, and many more were thrown into parison.[89] He then began to rule with a strong hand. Intending to chastise his disobedient Chiefs, he applied to the British Government for the loan of two battalions to act strictly under his orders.[90] He particularly hoped to deal a blow at the Thakur of Nimaj who had openly revolted against the Jodhpur sovereign.[91]

In view of this increasing difference between the Maharaja and his feudatories, and the general instability of the administration at Jodhpur,[92] the British Government had to decide on their line of action. Both Maharaja[93] and the ministers[94] whom he had treated cruelly were opposed to British intervention in their State administration. The attitude which Hastings desired his local representative to adopt in the matter was "on the one hand the maintenance of the lawful authority of the Rajah, and the acknowledged rights and privileges of the Thakurs of the State of Jodhpure, the exclusion of foreign and the suppression of domestic plunderers, and the establishment of order and tranquillity throughout the Province of Marwar, and on the other, the accession of the military strength and local political influence of the Government of Jodhpore to the views and measures of the British Government for the general tranquillity of India, and specially of Rajpootana, and the security of the tributary and feudal rights confirmed or acquired by the Treaty." It was further laid down that "the performance of our pledge to the State of Jodhpore requires that when we are called on to take part in support of its interests, we should exercise the power of effectual interference, to the full extent demanded by the nature of the case." But by the policy and the duty as imposed by the spirit of the Treaty, that interference was to be limited to general political arrangements, and its extension to internal affairs was to be avoided. "Desirable as this forbearance may be, however, the circumstances of the country may be such as to compel us as in the case of Jaipur and Oodeypore to take a more direct and ostensible part. If this be so, the Governor-General-in-Council would not, out of a scrupulous refinement which would defeat the expediency of the case, refuse to meet the exigency, but he would at once assume the necessary tone."[95]

When the trouble between Maharaja Man Singh and his Chiefs became more acute, and the former sought British military assistance, he was required to disclose fully his motives, and the purpose for which he required a British force, before it could be sent to his aid, so that "the Governor-General-in-Council may judge of the justness of the measures which we are called upon to support.[96] But as has been before remarked, the Maharaja was very averse to admitting British counsel in his own affairs.[97] He was a deep, dissimulating character, and did not in the least relax in his determination to crush his nobles. He achieved his purpose by using the name of his British allies, and the impression of their power, without actually calling in their arms. The dreaded threat of employing British troops against them was sufficient to throw the nobles into despair. Their lands were sequestered, their forts besieged, some of them seized and imprisoned, others killed in defending their homes and property. The Maharaja completely estranged his Chiefs, who left Marwar, and from their temporary asylum in the neighbouring States, made a spirited appeal for British mediation.[98] They waited for over a year in patience, but in vain.[99] Man Singh succeeded in his plans ruining his feudatories through the potential aid of the British, without actually making use of it.

The policy which was defined for Jodhpur could not be applied there. But a greater scope for its use was found in the affairs of Jaipur, which continued to give great trouble.

After the conclusion of the treaty with that State, Ochterlony then the Resident in Rajputana, proceeded to Jaipur in May 1818. That State had a most dissolute Prince as its ruler.[100] Maharaja Jagat Singh impressed Ochterlony with an eagerness to purify his administration by reorganising the ministry.[101] He selected Nazir Mohan Ram as his chief minister (Mukhtiar) and begged the British Resident to support his nominee.[102] Mohan Ram served the State with understanding and industry. General improvement began to appear in various branches of the administration, including the revenue system.[103] Matters had hardly settled down, when suddenly Maharaja Jagat Singh died on the 21st December, 1818, thereby ending a reign incompletely redeemed by his late attempts at reform from the disgrace of earlier debauchery and dissipation.[104] This event was followed by intrigues, disorders and party jealousies, which for many years threw the Government into great confusion. It was also a period during which the British attitude in the matter of interference in its affairs underwent a clear and deliberate development.

The adoption, to the *Gadi,* of a minor from the Narwar house, a remote branch of the family, carried out by the Nazir, threatened to produce a serious dispute in the State.[105] But the country was saved from that misfortune by the birth of the junior Rani on the 25th April, 1819 of a posthumous son of the Maharaja. That event threw the Nazir's action regarding the adoption into oblivion, and brought to the fore the more important one of the formation of the Government. Ochterlony had again arrived at Jaipur to take a personal part in the discussions at that Court.[106] He favoured a policy of interference, and tried indirectly to maintain his favourite, Mohan Ram, in power.[107] But he failed in that object, and could not prevent the power from passing into the hands of Rawat Beri Sal, who became the head of the administration with the Dowager Maharani as Regent.[108] The Governor-General had no objection to this, and wished to avoid direct interference as long as possible. It was, however, recognised that "the ministers of a petty Court so supported by a paramount Power almost inevitably become tyrants over their prince, and usurpers of his sovereignty." Therefore, the Resident was required to watch the regency with strict attention and to give his advice when necessary.[109]

This view, adopted in 1819, was reaffirmed in the following year. Although this time (in 1820) a slight change in the attitude was visible in the declaration that "it is our right and duty to prevent the diminution or defalcation of the revenues, more especially during a minority," Hastings was still inclined to put off interference.[110]

Rawat Beri Sal, however, was not secure in his position. Palace intrigues and jealousies widened the difference between the two Dowager Ranis. The junior Maharani, as the mother of the infant Maharaja, asserted her right to supreme authority in the State. At the end of 1820, serious disorders took place at Jaipur. Thirty-five persons lost their lives, including Fauji Ram, a favourite official of the Rani Rathorni. Rawat Beri Sal's position became extremely precarious. It transpired that the Rawat was in the good books of the Maharani, and distrusted by the Rani Mother who began to exercise power through her son favourite, Jota Ram, still allowing Beri Sal to retain the rank of the Mukhtiar. Ochterlony, in reporting these occurrences, represented the advisability of appointing a European officer at Jaipur.[111]

The proposal was forthwith sanctioned, and Captain Stewart, Resident at Gwalior, was chosen for the duty.[112] The stationing of a permanent British political functionary met with unanimous opposition from all parties at the Court.[113] This triangular tussle went on for some time, but Stewart did not wish to remain there merely as a passive spectator or an honoured guest. He soon showed his impatience at not being consulted.[114] The administration was suffering from corruption and inefficiency. The revenues were falling. Jota Ram, the Rani Mother's favourite, was associated with the Rawat in all his public functions.[115] The British knew that although the Rawat was neither able nor honest, their best course under the circumstances lay in supporting the Mukhtiar. At a private interview, Steward explicitly promised him that support.[116] Ochterlony was again urging on his Government the need and desirability of effectual control over Jaipur affairs.[117]

The Resident's proposal was adopted. Thus came the final phase of British policy when Hastings formed "his deliberate opinion that the condition of affairs at Jaipur ... has at length imposed on the British Government the absolute necessity of exercising that direct and decided interference," which was conceived to be in the best interests of the State. The policy was justified and grounded on the provision of "protection" embodied in the Treaty. He was therefore "determined to authorize the requisite degree of interference in the internal administration of that Government." And that interference was to embrace not merely the revenue branch, but others too, particularly the spending of the revenues. The British Government, it was declared, as "the guardians of the interests of the minor Rajah" were bound to secure his State against embezzlement.[118] This decided course was also made known to the Jaipur Government.[119] It was in keeping with this changed attitude that Stewart's action in pledging his Government's support to Beri Sal should be fully approved.[120] The British Agent at Jaipur carried out the above orders with spirited vigilance.[121] Rawat Beri Sal assumed a decided tone in his affairs, being assured for the support of the British Government. In consultation with Stewart, he even considered the advisability of expelling the evil counsellors of the Rani, and removing the minor Prince from her care. He also desired the presence of a British detachment at Jaipur.[122] British support of the Rawat was continued, but no drastic measures were considered desirable during the Raja's minority.[123]

These unstable conditions at the Jaipur Court continued for many years until the Rani's death in 1833.[124] The misgovernment and disorders at the end of 1822 compelled Ochterlony to revisit the State in January, 1823, to attempt for the third time a solution of its complications. By that time Lord Hastings had left India.

The sketch of British relations with the three leading States of Rajputana gives to the student an idea of their development. Although further enquiry into the affairs of more minor principalities would involve unnecessary repetition, this review of Rajput relations with the British Government would be incomplete without a brief reference to what occurred at Kota as a result of the anomalous provisions of the Treaty with that State. That event merits a short notice on account of the important issues which it involved.

The titular sovereign of Kota, Maharao Umed Singh, died on the 21st November, 1819. His eldest son, Kishore Singh, aged forty, succeeded to his father's *Gadi*. The new Maharao was "a man of some talents, and considerable energy of character." Although mild in temper and demeanour, he had sufficient pride of position to feel the indignity of being reduced to a mere cypher in his own State.[125] And that is precisely what was required of him by the supplementary article to the Treaty of December, 1817, concluded by the British Government in the February following, in favour of Zalim Singh, and his eldest son, Madho Singh and their heirs.

Kishore Singh was willing to allow to the old Raj Rana (at that time in his eightieth year) the full and unfettered powers that he had been exercising in the State. But the new Maharao was not prepared to surrender to Madho Singh his rights and privileges of ruling his own country. Zalim, on the other hand, was only too anxious that his powers and position should descend to his eldest son in their entirety. He was clever enough to obtain British support, in the shape of the supplementary article, for the furtherance of this ambition. Occasion for the inevitable dispute soon presented itself, when the old Regent had an attack of paralysis, and, according to the practice which Zalim had been careful to maintain for several years, Madho Singh discharged his father's functions during his illness. The Maharao appeared determined to assert his authority, and the affair threatened to develop into a serious breach. Tod arrived at Kota on the 22nd February, 1820, and examined the state of the parties on the spot. He found that the Maharao of Bundi supported Kishore Singh. Moreover, his younger brother, Maharaj Prithi Singh, and the younger son of the Raj Rana himself, Goverdhan Das, were loyally attached to the Maharao. As later events showed, and as could very well be expected, the nobles and people of Kota naturally sympathised with his position. Madho Singh had his own party, and in spite of his inferior character and reputation, he had the advantage of Zalim Singh's name and influence, and the support of the British Government.[126]

The latter declared unambiguously in favour of Zalim Singh. They recognised him as the *de facto* ruler of Kota. "The titular Rajah was no more thought of as the ruler of Kota" averred the British Government in justification of their attitude " than the Rajah of Satara was as the leader of the Marathas or the Great Moghul as the Emperor of Hindustan." Hastings' Government clearly laid it down that their obligation, from which they could not depart, was due only to the Regent and that Zalim Singh had alone the power to release them from it. "No pretensions of the titular Rajah can be entertained by us in opposition to this positive engagement."[127]

In the meantime, matters grew daily worse at Kota. Maharao Kishore Singh, aided by the impetuous counsels of Prithi Singh and Goverdhan Das, made up his mind to recover his position. In the spirit of the Tenth Article of the Treaty he demanded that he should be the sovereign of Kota, and maintained that the subsequent guarantee to Madho Singh "reduced the Gadi of Kota to a simple heap of cotton."[128] The estrangement between the Maharao and Madho Singh increased. The situation seemed serious when arms were collected on both sides and the general tranquillity was threatened. Instead of attacking the Maharao, the Political Agent and the Regent decided to blockade the fort and the palace in order to bring about his surrender. Kishore Singh, rather than submit to the humiliating terms, marched out of the palace, followed by a party of his adherents. In this seemingly hopeless situation, Tod acted with great tact and succeed in bringing the Maharao back to Kota. He also impressed on him the futility of his resistance, and insisted on the surrender of his friend, Goverdhan Das, who was exiled from the State. Affairs reverted to their normal course. Public reconciliation was brought about between the Maharao and the Raj Rana, and also Madho Singh. At Tod's request in August 1820, the Maharao bestowed the customary Khilat on Madho Singh.[129]

This reconciliation was only short-lived. Maharao Kishore Singh and Madho Singh had disliked and distrusted each other from boyhood. Moreover, Kishore Singh could never remain content with nominal sovereignty. Trouble again broke out in December, with the appearance of Goverdhan Das in Malwa. At Kota, the Maharao won over a large portion of the regular battalion of the Regent under Saif Ali, a trusted old officer. They mutinied. The old Regent attacked the Maharao's party with artillery. The Maharao with his brother, Prithi Singh, escaped from Kota into Bundi, and the Raj Rana quelled the disorders within a week. Order was restored in the town, but the Maharao became a fugitive. The British Government at once took serious notice of the affair. A cavalry detachment from their cantonment at Nimach was ordered to pursue Goverdhan Das and arrest him, dead or alive, whilst the commanding officer was also required to be ready to offer any aid asked for by Zalim Singh.[130]

After a short stay at Bundi, the Maharao proceeded to Brindaban (a place of pilgrimage) and thence to Delhi, passing Bharatpur on his way. He represented to the British Government, through their resident at Delhi, that the rebellious conduct of the Raj Rana had deprived him of his just rights.[131] His appeal produced no effect at Calcutta. His action was treated as a violation of the authority of the Regent and his flight from Kota was considered as an abdication of his *Gadi*.[132] However, Kishore Singh's spirit was implacable and uncompromising towards Madho Singh.[133] Not only was the sympathy of the people and Chiefs of Kota on his side, but public opinion among the Rajput Princes was strongly in favour of his cause.[134] In his indignation Kishore Singh turned back towards Kota, in the vain hope of achieving by force that which he had failed to obtain through negotiation. As he approached, his followers increased in numbers, many of his nobles rallying to his standard with characteristic Rajput loyalty. The Raj Rana and the British Agent concerted measures to check his progress.[135] Negotiations having failed, the two opposing parties met in a pitched battle at Mangrol on the 1st October where, although the Maharao's men fought with great bravery, he lost the contest, and had to retire, osing his brother, Prithi Singh, who died of wounds receivved in fighting.[136] The Maharao learnt the bitter lession that he had no chance of success against his rival so long as the superior might of the Company was being Zalim Singh. Although Hastings realised, though very late, the anomalous situation created by the Treaty, and the impolicy of deposing a Prince whose cause was so popular in the *Rajwara,* yet he was not ready to relax the terms on which along Kishore Singh could be restored. British support of Zalim and his son Madho Singh was consistent and unalterable,[137] and it was finally decided to raise his younger brother, Bishen Singh, to the *Gadi* of Kota, if the Maharao should refuse to submit unconditionally to the terms offered him.[138]

Realising the hopelessness of any further efforts, and having to chose between utter ruin and merely nominal rank as ruler, the Maharao abandoned further resistance.[139] After securing the consent of the Raj Rana to the conditions laid down for the Maharao by the authorities at Calcutta, Tod obtained Kishore's submission to them. The conditions were presented to him on the 18th November, and the agreement signed and exchanged on the 25th at Nathdwara (in Mewar). He returned to Kota on the 29th December, and was formally reinstalled on the *Gadi* of his ancestors.[140] Maharao Kishore

Singh agreed to submit the supremacy of Zalim Singh, Madho Singh, and their heirs in the Government of Kota, and further undertook to recruit no troops beyond personal guards.[141] Tod also drew up some articles which Madho Singh signed, agreeing to respect the dignity of the Maharao and render him all customary honours and homage. The Maharao's allowance was fixed at Rs. 1,04,000 annually, which amount was to be paid regularly.[142]

The protracted dispute which led to bitterness and bloodshed was at last settled. The Maharao resigned himself to his fate. No one could look upon this as a satisfactory solution. It could not be expected that Kishore Singh would forget his indignity, nor that he should feel anything but the deepest distrust of Madho Singh.[143] Hastings himself would have liked to separate the two by making a separate provision for the Raj Rana and his heirs. But he declined to quit the line he had once chalked out for his course. Since, however, the root of the trouble remained, the remedy, which he contemplated, had to be applied later (in 1838) when a separate principality was created for Zalim's descendants, and the real cause of the strife, the fateful supplementary article of 1818 was removed.[144]

The Kota incident, although it made the Company unpopular with the Rajput State, established its paramountcy over them by all by fear of their irresistible power. All those States,[145] big and small, realised either by example or by experience the change in their situation. The Princes no longer possessed the unrestricted authority to which they aspired. Not only was their independence and with it their international status finally and formally taken away, but in internal affairs also, although technically autonomous their Governments were not in reality free to do as they liked. Their relations with the feudatory nobles, the way in which they managed their finances, the regulation of succession to the thrones, and sometimes even the choice of their ministers, were all subjects on which the British Government did not always adopt an attitude of neutrality. Hastings' early determination to abstain from interference in the internal affairs of the allied States could not be maintained. It was inevitable in the nature of such wholly unequal alliances that he would be unable to adhere to his original ideal. The temptation was too strong, and the conditions were too trying, for any Government. It has been seen how slowly, haltingly, yet inevitably he authorised the policy of interference in the States of Rajputana and now it was unsuccessfully tried in Jodhpur, partially applied in Jaipur, and effectively carried out in Kota and Udaipur. The consequence was that the Princes and their Governments became still more dependent on the British Power, and less self-reliant than would have been the case had Hastings remained firm in his original intentions.

It must be observed that the Rajput States did not range themselves in opposition to the British government. In fact, they were, as characterised by Hastings, the "natural allies" of the British.[146] But their independence was reduced to the same extent, and subjected to the same conditions as those Governments were which had been hostile to the company. Indeed Hastings' treaties with the Rajput States indicate their subordination in a more explicit manner than those concluded with other Powers in an earlier period (or with Sindhia in Hastings' own time). This invidious distinction is indeed noticeable. Tod's devotion to the chivalrous traditions of the Rajputs is well-known. He lamented deeply the miserable conditions to which they had been reduced, and earnestly wished "for the restoration of their former independence."[147] But he was not the only person to feel the wrong inflicted on the Rajputs. The matter received the attention of the Court of Directors and orders were drafted in 1829 for the improvement of the relations with the States of Rajputana.[148] It was though advisable to revise the treaties in order to remove some of the humiliating clauses precluding those Princes from communicating with their peers, binding them to submit their disputes to British arbitrating and engaging them to furnish their contingents when required. The articles relating to the payments of tributes were to be modified, and the Political Agents were to be withdrawn from their capitals. This change was to be more-or-less formal, out of deference to their former rank and dignity, and from a regard for their sentiments. The proposed change was not to have any material effect on the British right to interpose their influence in the concerns of the States and to call for their co-operation in time of need. It was expected as a result that the Rajputs would feel considerably more attached to the alliance. But these proposals never took shape and the instructions which had been drawn up were never issued.[149]

A few words might be added on the particular question of the tributes levied from the Rajput States, on which account Hastings has been criticised.[150] Their underlying principle meant the continuation of the oppressive practice of the Pathans and Marathas. "The quota to the British Government was fixed precisely on the same scale. A change had occurred, but principally in name. The humiliating consciousness of subjection still remained.[151]

But the imposition of tribute on the Rajput States had a certain justification which must not be overlooked before coming to any definite conclusion on his interesting question. The British Government, who undertook to protect them against external enemies, claimed that the contracting States should share, according to their means, the cost of defence. Their tributes represented this contribution. Moreover, the Company's Government, in order to mark their supremacy over their subordinate allies, fixed the payment of tribute as the indication of that relationship. Another argument urged in favour of the tributes is that, by the operation of the treaties, the States greatly increased their revenues "of which it would have been an act of wanton profusion to make a distribution purely gratuitous."[152]

These apparently convincing points put forward in favour of the levy of tributes do not fully explain the policy which authorised them. Several States were exempted[153] from that payment altogether, although protection was extended to them in the same measure as to the tribute paying Princes. Then, again, it was not necessary to receive permanent annual payments to charge the States with their share of the cost of defence against external enemies.[154] Agreements could have been made that on such occasions the actual expenditure incurred in military operations would be chargeable to them, (the method actually adopted, for example, in the cases of Bikaner and Alwar).[155] If tribute were to be the outstanding feature of the feudatories' fealty to the supreme Government, and the proper share of the common expenditure on military defence, the levy ought to have been proportionately uniform and certainly universal. But that was not the case. A different policy was pursued in the case of the larger States. From them "No subsidy, no concession humiliating to their national dignity was demanded. Why not preserve the same exalted conduct to the smaller States?"[156] The arguments urged in defence of the tribute, therefore, only partially explain the underlying motives of the policy.

Whilst the historian judges the deeds of the statesmen in cool moments, and applies to them the tests of strict logic or high morality, the latter has to "act in the living present." Hastings set out on his grand military enterprise determined to crush the Pindaris and extend British supremacy over all the States—Maratha and Rajput. This he wished to achieve, by peaceful means if possible, but by war if necessary. His Government was solemnly bound by an agreement with the Marathas (Sindhia and Holkar), not even to negotiate with the Rajput States of Mewar and Marwar. In these difficult and anxious circumstance, the only bait which he could offer to obtain Sindhia's assent to the otherwise drastic terms was that his revenues from the Rajput States (originally imposed by coercion) would be secured to him, even after he gave the British freedom to treat with them. This is what Hastings did. This is the chief (not the only) cause and motive for levying tributes. It was an act of expediency which yielded a great political advantage.

It is true that the Rajput States were subjected to tribute which was humiliating, and that, as has been seen, British intervention was authorised and even exercised in their domestic matters, thus reducing their independence, an object highly prized throughout Rajput annals. Yet it is only fair to remember that through British alliance they received a timely rescue from a cruel, crushing and degrading system. British influence over those States restored the elements of peace, prosperity and settled Government. It is undeniable that the permanent effects of helpless dependence are demoralising and deeply injurious to any community; but when it is borne in mind that these ancient Governments were, in Hastings' time, gasping for the last breath of their existence, the price paid will not appear as heavy as would otherwise be the case.

REFERENCES

1. In 1803 and ratified by the Governor-General on January, 15th 1804. Aitchison, *Op, Cit.* Vol. III, pp. 102-103.
2. The Treaty, *Loc. Cit.* pp. 157-158.
3. Treaty of 1803 and another engagement of 1811. *Loc. Cit.* pp. 322-323 and 324-325.
4. *Loc. Cit.* pp. 275-277.
5. *Loc. Cit.* pp. 292-296.
6. His minute of December 1st 1815, *Op. Cit.* para. 84.
7. *Loc. Cit.* paras. 89, 152, 302, 303.
8. His letter to the Vice President of the Council from Cawnpore, October 10th, No. 1, Bengal Secret Consultations, 28th October 1817.
9. Hastings to Metcalfe October, 5th, 1817, Kaye's *Life of Metcalfe*, Vol. I, pp. 459-60.
10. Adam to Metcalfe, 8th October, No. 26, Bengal Secret Consultations, 28th October, 1817.
11. Metcalfe to Adam. 18th October, No. 30, Bengal Secret Consultations, 14th November, 1817.
12. Metcalfe to Adam, 9th November, No. 17, Bengal Secret Consultations, 28th November 1817, and 10th November, No. 23, Bengal Secret Consultations, 5th December 1817.

13. Article 14 of the Treaty of June 1817, *Op. Cit.*
14. The text of the Treaty, Aitchison (1909), Vol. III, p. 281-5.
15. Adam to Metcalfe, 15th November, No. 30, Bengal Secret Consultations 5th December 1817.
16. Close to Hastings (then Moira) 23rd April, No. 11, Bengal Secret Consultations, 11th May, 1816. Metcalfe to Adam, 13th August, No. 39, Bengal Secret Consultations, 5th September, 1817.
17. For example, between Sindhia and the Raja of Raghugarh (Resident with Sindhia to Moira, 13th August, No. 9, Bengal Secret Consultations, 7th Sept. 1816) and between Tulsi Bai and Amir Khan (Malcolm's *Central India* (1824) Vol. I, p. 306).
18. Close's Despatch of 23rd April 1816, *Op. Cit.* Tod's Despatches to Adam. 26th November 1817, No. 10 Bengal Secret Consultations, 2nd January 1818, and 10th December 1817, No. 53, and 5th December 1817, to Malcolm, No. 50, Bengal Secret Consultations. 9th January 1818. Metcalfe to Adam, 18th Oct., No. 50, Bengal Secret Consultations. 14th November 1817. As regards Zalim's administrative success. Tod wrote:—"I need say nothing of Zalim Singh. He might instruct me. I could little benefit him by advice." Tod to Ochterlony, 11th August, No. 104, Bengal Secret Consultations, 7th November 1818. But it must be said that the Raj Rana's rule was high-handed and oppressive to the people, p. 1568, Tod's *Annals and Antieuities of Rajasthan* (1920), Vol. III.
19. Text of the Treaty, No. 61, and Metcalfe's Despatch, Dec. 30th 1817, No. 60, Bengal Secret Consultations, 30th Jan. 1818.
20. Adam to Tod, 6th Jan., No. 17, Bengal Secret Consultations, 6th Feb. 1818.
21. Despatches on the disputed claims on Kota tribute, Adam to metcalfe, 19th Jan., No. 19, Bengal Secret Consultations, 6th Feb. 1818, and Metcalfe to Adam, 20th Jan., Nos. 109 and 110, Bengal Secret Consultations, 6th Feb. 1818, also the Schedule of the Treaty.
22. Aitchison, (1909), Vol. III, p. 372-3.
23. Metcalfe to Adam, 8th Jan., No. 69, Bengal Secret Consultations, 30th Jan. 1818.
24. Adam to Metcalfe, 19th Jan., No. 19, Bengal Secret Consultations, 6th Feb. 1818. The supplementary article was concluded at Delhi, on 20th Feb., and ratified by the Governor-General on 7th Mar. 1818. Aitchison, (1909), Vol. III, p. 372.

25. Edmonstone later referred to this unfortunate provision as capable of producing, unless abrogated, "interference on our part of the most vexatious, injurious and embarrassing nature" (written evidence for the House of Commons Select Committee), *Parliamentary Paper*, 735-VI 1831-1832 Vol. XIV, p. 113.

26. Governor-General to the Maharao and to the Raj Rana, 3rd Feb., No. 13, Bengal Secret Consultations, 27th Feb. 1818.

27. *Ibid,* and Tod to Adam, 26th Dec. 1817, No. 16, Bengal Secret Consultations, 13th Feb. 1818.

28. Article 3, p. LXXXVI, *Home Misc., (Pindari and Maratha War Papers).* Vol. 516a.

29. Adam to Metcalfe, 8th Oct., No. 26, Bengal Secret Consultations, 28th Oct. 1817.

30. Metcalfe to Tod, 21st Nov. 1817, No. 103, Adam to Metcalie, 28th Nov. No. 105. Bengal Secret Consultations, 19th Dec. 1817.

31. Adam to Tod, 20th Jan. No. 21, Bengal Secret Consultations, 13th Feb. 1818, Tod made full enquiries into the subject of Sindhia's share of tribute, and his information was that for (a) Crila (b) The Mahals of Kurwar and Barundini (c) The Chouth of Khalsa lands, Sindhia received for 5 years net amounts varying between 39 and 49 thousand Rs. a year, to which would be added Sindhia's share of (d) Patan, amounting to Rs. 40,000 p. a. (Tod to Adam, 24th Jan., No. 19, Bengal Secret Consultations, 13th Mar. 1818). The British Government had induced Holkar's Govt. to give up its claim on Bundi by Treaty of Mandasor, Art. A *Op. Cit.*

32. Tod to Adam, 15th Feb., No. 19, Bengal Secret Consultations, 15th May, 1818.

33. Adam to Tod, 1st Mar., No. 9, Bengal Secret Consultations, 27th Mar. and 20th Mar., No. 20, Bengal Secret Consultations, 15th May, 1818.

34. Tod made Political Agent in Mewar. Adam to Tod 3rd Feb., No. 7, Bengal Secret Consultations, 6th Mar. 1818.

35. Metcalfe to Adam, 18th Oct., No. 50, Bengal Secret Consultations, 14th Nov. 1817.

36. Metcalfe to Adam, 8th Jan. No. 66, Text of the Treaty, No. 67, Bengal Secret Consultations, 30th Jan. 1818. Same to Same, 20th Jan.., No. 102, Bengal Secret Consultations, 6th Feb. 1818. The tribute was fixed at Rs. 1,08,000 (after all deductions) in Jodhpur Rupees, to be paid half in specie, and half in goods. (22nd May. No. 22, Bengal Secret Consultations, 12th June 1818).

37. Bapa Rawal, Samarsi Ranas Hamir, Lakha, Sanga, Kumbha, Pratap, Raj Singh, are illustrious names not only in the history of Mewar, but also in the annals of Hindustan. Tod's *Rajasthan* (1920), Vol. I, Chapters, 2, 5, 6, 8, 9, 11, 12, 13, etc..
38. Tod's *Annals and Antiquities of Rajasthan* (1920, Ed. by Crooked), pp. 545-548, Vol. I. References of Bapu Sindhia's depredations in Mewar, in 1814, in the Despatch of the Resident with Sindhia to Moira, No. 15, Bengal Secret Consultations, 15th July, 1814.
39. Adam to Metcalfe, 8th Oct., No. 26, Bengal Secret Consultations, 28th Oct. 1817.
40. Metealfe to Adam, 18th Jan., No. 107, Bengal Secret Consultations, 6th Feb., 1818.
41. It seems strange that the Udaipur envoy should have failed to secure better terms for his State, which Metcalfe was prepared to concede. It is possible that Thakur Ajit Singh was not disinterested enough in the execution of his duty. This explanation is confirmed by later correspondence between Tod and the Political Secretary. (Tod to Adam, 1st Feb., No. 31, Bengal Secret Consultations, Feb. 20th, 1818; Tod to Metcalfe, Nov. 39th. 1820, No. 9, and Swinton to Tod No. 10, Bengal Secret Consultations, Jan. 6th, 1821. In this last Despatch Tod was asked explicitly to warn the Thakur that since he "appeared to be the chief cause of this lamentable state of affairs in Mewar" and since he was "opposing the establishment of tranquillity and good order" it might "ultimately become necessary for this government to require his exemplary punishment on that account."
42. The Treaty was ratified by the Governor-General on 22nd Adam to Metcalfe. No. 14, Bengal Secret Consultations, 13th Feb. 1818. There was no specific number of horsemen mentioned for service, as in the Jodhpur Treaty. The tribute was fixed at one-fourth of the revenue for five years and afterward at three-eighths of the revenue.
43. Memorandum of claims containing 21 items, No. 29, Bengal Secret Consultations, 20th Feb. 1818.
44. Metcalfe to Adam, 28th Mar., No. 77 and Treaty itself, No. 78, Bengal Secret Consultations, 17th Apr. 1818. Ratified on 7th Apr., No. 6, Bengal Secret Consultations, 24th Apr. 1818.
45. Adam to Metcalfe, 4th Apr., No. 16, Bengal Secret Consultations, 1st May 1818.
46. Metcalfe to Adam, 29th Jan., Bengal Secret Consultations, 20th Feb. 1818, and 18th Oct., No. 50, Bengal Secret Consultations, 14th Nov. 1817.

47. Metcalfe's instructions to Ochterlony, 21st Nov., 1817, No. 112, Bengal Secret Consultations, 19th Dec. 1817, which were approved by the Governor-General. Adam to metcalfe, 3rd Dec., No. 5, Bengal Secret Consultations, 26th Dec. 1817.
48. Metcalfe to Ochterlony, 21st Nov. *Op. Cit.*, and Metcalfe to Adam 29th Jan., No. 26, Bengal Secret Consultations, 20th Feb. 1818.
49. Metcalfel to Adam, 27th Feb., No. 21, Bengal Secret Consultations, 21st Mar. 1818, and 24th Mar., No. 74, Bengal Secret Consultations, 17th Apr. 1818. Metcalfe demanded 15 lakhs and the Jaipur Delegation offered Rupees 2,40,000 to begin with.
50. Text of the Treaty, No. 26, Bengal Secret Consultations, 24th Apr. 1818. (Art. 6 of the Treaty about tribute.)
51. Instructions to Metcalfe, 8th Oct. 1817, Metcalfe's reply of 18th Oct., already referred to, and Adam to Tod. 3rd Feb., No. 7, Bengal Secret Consultations, 6th Mar. 1818.
52. Malcolm to Adam, 2nd July. No. 59, Bengal Secret Consultations, 7th Nov. 1818.
53. His full Reports on Banswara and Dungarpur, No. 96, Bengal Secret Consultations, 31st Oct. 1818, and Memorandum on Pratapgarh, 20th June, 1818, No. 60, Bengal Secret Consultations, 7th Nov. 1818.
54. Metcalfe to Adam, 22nd Sept., No. 4, and the Treaty itself, No. 5, Bengal Secret Consultations, 10th Oct. 1818.
55. Dyson to Malcolm, 17th Sept., No. 97, Bengal Secret Consultations, 31st Oct., 1818.
56. Metcalfe wrote thus referring to this provision in his own treaty with Banswara. "The Fifth Article was introduced in order to secure us the right of interposing our advice and authority for the settlement of the disturbances which at present prevail in the State of Banswara." His Despatch of 22nd Sept., No. 4, Bengal Secret Consultations, 10th October 1818.
57. The Treaty, Aitchison (1909) Vol. III, pp. 67-69.
58. *Loc. Cit.*, pp. 81-82.
59. Dyson's note, 20th June, No. 60, Bengal Secret Consultations, 7th November 1818.
60. Malcolm to Adam, 26th September, No. 61, to Agnew 26th September, No. 62, Bengal Secret Consultations, 7th November, 1818.
61. Caulfield to Malcolm, 6th October, No. 63, and Malcolm to Adam, 13th October, No. 64, and Malcolm to Caulfield, 10th October, No. 66, Bengal Secret Consultations, 7th November, 1818.

62. The Treaty was ratified by the Governor-General on 7th November 1818, Aitehison (1909) Vol. III, pp. 83-85.
63. *Loc. Cit.*, pp. 55-57. Both these treaties were ratified on the same day 13th February 1819.
64. Dyson to Malcolm, 17th September, No. 97, Bengal Secret Consultations, 31st October 1818.
65. Malcolm to Adam
66. In 1823, *Loc. Cit.*, pp. 210-212.
67. Metcalfe to Adam, 20th January, No. 102, Bengal Secret Consultations, 6th February 1818, and Wilder to Ochterlony. 11th February, No. 19, Bengal Secret Consultations, 14th April, 1821. Tod repudiated the claims of Jodhpur over Sirohi as untenable, His *Travels in Western India*, (1839), pp. 61-64.
68. This was Hastings' aim as recorded by him in his *Private Journal* in Feb. 1814 (pp. 54-5), and publicly in his Minute of 3rd April 1814 (reference to these has already been made in Chapter II).
69. Adam to Metcalfe, 19th January, No. 19, Bengal Secret Consultations, 6th February 1818. (Instructions relating to Kota.)
70. *Private Journal*, Vol. I, p. 54.
71. His Minute of 3rd April, No. 4, Bengal Secret Consultations, 21st June, 1814.
72. Adam to Tod. 3rd February, No. 7, Bengal Secret Consultations, 6th March 1818.
73. Memorandum furnished by the Udaipur envoy to Metcalfe at Delhi No. 29, Bengal Secret Consultations, 20th February, 1818.
74. Adam to Tod, 3rd February, No. 7, Bengal Secret Consultations, 6th March 1818.
75. Tod to Adam, 22nd April, No. 67, Bengal Secret Consultations, 5th June, 1818.
76. *Ibid.*
77. Donkin to Adam, 11th February, No. 108, and to Tod, 12th February, No. 11, Bengal Secret Consultations, 13th March 1818.
78. Donkin's Despatch, 26th February, No. 43, Bengal Secret Consultations, 21st March 1818, and Tod to Adam, 27th February, No. 22, Bengal Secret Consultations, 15th May, 1818. Other parts, such as Hurda, Chhoti Sadri, Kanera, and Rajnagar, were also duly restored. Jahazpur came much later. (Tod's Despatch of 22nd April, No. 67, Bengal Secret Consultations, 5th June, 1818.)
79. Tod to Adam, 11th March, No. 23, Bengal Secret Consultations, 15th May, 1818.

80. Adam to Tod, 20th March, No. 23, Bengal Secret Consultations, 15th May, 1818.
81. Tod's *Rajasthan* (1920, Vol. 1, pp. 369-70.
82. Tod to Adam, 22nd April, No. 67, and to Ochterlony, 7th May, No. 69, Bengal Secret Consultations, 5th June, 1818.
83. Tod to Ochterlony, 11th August, No. 104, Bengal Secret Consultations, 7th November, 1818.
84. Tod wrote:—"I have paid deepest attention to the past history of this State, and can safely pronounce that all (its) past misfortunes may be dated from the period that the counsel of the Omrahs was admitted into the Government." To Metcalfe, 26th April, No. 30, Bengal Secret Consultations, 12th June, 1819.
85. "I had long foreseen they would he compelled to apply to me, and was prepared." Tod to Metcalfe, a long Despatch". *Ibid*.
86. Tod's statements of the income for Mewar, Nos. 31 and 32, and his Memorandum to the Rana, No. 33, Bengal Political Consultations, 12th June, 1819. The British Government approved of the plan of giving the farmers their guarantee to lease the crown lands. Metcalfe to Tod, 12th June, 1819, No. 34, Bengal Secret Consultations of date.
87. Tod to Metcalfe, 25th February, No. 41, Bengal Secret Consultations, 15th April 1820, 29th November 1820, No. 9, Bengal Secret Consultations, 6th January 1821, to Secretary Swinton, 16th July, 1821, No. 19, Bengal Secret Consultations, 6th October 1821, and Tod's final report on Mewar, before his departure for Europe in June 1822, addressed to Ochterlony, 26th May, No. 6, Bengal Secret Consultations, 2nd August 1822.
88. His aid was first sought by the State in the dispute which Jaipur over the hand of the fair Princess Krishna Kumari of Udaipur. Once having gone in, the Pathan Parasite stayed on and treated the whole State as the spoils of his adventure. (Tod's *Rajasthan*, *Op. Cit.*, Vol. II, pp. 1086-1092.
89. Wilder to Ochterlony, 22nd February, No. 14, Bengal Political Consultations, 31st March 1821.
90. Maharaja's letter to Ochterlony, No. 6, Bengal political Consultations, 23rd September 1820.
91. A letter from Jodhpur received by Ochterlony, No. 7, Bengal Political Consultations, 23rd September, 1820, and Wilder to Ocherlony, 22nd February, No. 14, Bengal Secret Consultations, 31st March, 1821.
92. Ochterlony to Secretary to Governor-General, 25th August, No. 13, Bengal Secret Consultations, 19th September 1818.

93. Tod's *Rajasthan, Op., Cit.*, Vol. II, pp. 1093-4.

94. Ochterlony to Adam. 11th August, No. 12, Bengal Secret Consultations, 5th September 1818.

95. Adam to Ochterlony, 5th September, No. 17, Bengal Secret Consultations, 5th September 1818.

96. Metcalfe to Ochterlony, 23rd September, No. 8, Bengal Political Consultations, 23rd September, 1820.

97. He rejected the offer of British troops to settle his State, made by Wilder, who was deputed to his Court in 1818, and later again showed the same attitude when Tod advised him to rely on British support. (Tod's *Rajasthan, Op. Cit.*, Vol. II, pp. 1093 and 1095-6.

98. The translation of their letter to the Political Agent, Western Rajputana States, reproduced in Tod's *Rajasthan*, Vol. 1, pp. 228-30.

99. *Loc. Cit.*, Vol. II, pp. 1097-1101.

100. *Loc. Cit.*, pp. 1364-5.

101. Ochterlony to Adam, 21st May, No. 22, Bengal Secret Consultations, 19th June, 1818.

102. Ochterlony to Adam, 22nd August, No. 9, Bengal Secret Consultations, 12th September, 1818. Rawat Beri Sal, who had concluded the Treaty at Delhi as the Jaipur envoy, was not only excluded from the ministry, but was coerced by the Maharaja to surrender the large parts of State (Khalsa) lands, which he had usurped. He had expected that the British would support him in his resistance, but Ochterlony did not favour his disloyalty to his master.

103. Ochterlony thought very highly of the integrity and achievements of Mohan Ram. In his opinion, the Nazir was the ablest Prime Minister that Jaipur had known. (Despatches to Metcalfe, 29th April, No. 28, Bengal Political Consultations, 22nd May, 1819, and to Hastings, 31st May, No. 18, Bengal Political Consultations, 23rd June, 1821.) But 'the system of chicanery and force by which he attempted to carry his object, savoured more of self-interest than of loyalty." Tod's *Rajasthan*, (1920 Ed.), Vol. III, p. 1373.

104. Tod's *Rajasthan, Op. Cit.*, Vol. III, pp. 1364-1369.

105. Mohan Ram to Ochterlony, received 4th February, No. 43, Jaipur Vakil at Delhi to Metcalfe, No. 44, Bengal political Consultations, 20th February, 1819. Protests were received from the Maharaja of Kishengarh, Nos. 87, 89 and 111, from the Thakur of Jhalai, No. 88, Bengal Political Consultations, 3rd April, 1819. Tod also

criticised the adoption adversely, as violating the succession law of the Rajputs. Tod's *Rajasthan* Vol. III, pp. 1370-71, (1920).

106. Ochterlony to Metcalfe, 10th April, No. 40, Bengal Political Consultations, 1st may, 25th April, No. 29, Bengal Political Consultations, 14th May, 1819. No. 27, Bengal Political Consultations, 22nd May 1819.

107. His conference with Beri Sal, who resisted the British desire to interfere. (Octherlony to Metcalfe, 7th may, No. 19, Bengal political Consultations, 3rd June, 1819.) He addressed letters to Bhatianiji (the junior Maharani) to dissuade her from joining the senior Maharani, also advising her to support Mohan Ram. No. 20, Bengal Political Consultations, 3rd June, 1819.

108 A written agreement from Beri Sal and other Thakurs and officials, to serve the State faithfully. The former also engaged to leave the person, property and dignity of Mohan Ram undisturbed. Ochterlony to Metcalfe, 25th may, No. 19, and No. 21, Bengal Political Consultations, 11th September 1819.

109. Metcalfe to Ochterlony, 3rd June, No. 24, Bengal Political Consultations, 3rd June 1819.

110. Metcalfe to Ochterlony, 28th October, No. 20, Bengal Political Consultations, 28th October 1820.

111. Ochterlony to Swinton, 17th December 1820, No. 4, Bengal Political Consultations, 13th January 1821, 10th January, No. 7, No. 8, (Intelligence) 20th January, No. 9, 10, (intelligence). Bengal Political Consultations, 10th February 1821.

112. Swinton to Stewart, No. 11, Bengal Political Consultations, 10th February, 1821.

113. Stewart arrived at Jaipur on 17th April. His Despatch to Ochterlony, 26th April, No. 7, Bengal Political Consultations, 26th May, 1821, and to Swinton, 18th May, No. 15, Bengal Political Consultations, 23rd June 1821.

114. Stewart to Swinton, 7th June, No. 7, Bengal Political Consultations, 30th June, 1821.

115. Stewart to Swinton, 18th May, No. 15, 11th June, No. 20, Bengal Political Consultations, 23rd June, 1821, and 18th July, No. 14, Bengal Political Consultations, 11th August 1821.

116. Stewart to Swinton, 25th August, No. 7, Bengal Political Consultations, 22nd September 1821.

117. Ochterlony to Hastings, 31st may, No. 18, Bengal Political Consultations, 23rd June, 1821.

118. Swinton to Ochterlony, 30th June 1821, No. 8, Bengal Political Consultations, 30th June, 1821.
119. Governor-General's letters to the infant Maharaja and Rawat Beri Sal. No. 7, Bengal Political Consultations, 30th June, 1821.
120. Swinton to Stewart, 22nd Sept., No. 10, Bengal Political Consultations, 22nd Sept. 1821.
121. He demanded the land revenue settlement for three years, required the State to produce for his inspection these statements (a) *Jamabandi,* Land Revenue Account, (b) *Tankha* land, that is territory held by officials in lien of pay, and (c) *Jagir* land, held as fiefs. He even deputed two of his own officials to watch the proceedings at the Diwan Khana. But he later withdrew them on the protest of the Rani and on her promising to furnish all the required information (Stewart to Swinton, 25th Aug., No. 7, Bengal Political Consultations, 22nd Sept. 1821).
122. Stewart to Swinton, 17th Dec. 1821, No. 18, Bengal Political Consultations, 11th Jan. 1822.
123. Swinton to Ochterlony, 11th Jan., No. 19, Bengal Political Consultations, 11th Jan. 1822.
124. Aitchison, *Op. Cit.,* (1909), Vol. III, p. 91.
125. Tod to Metcalfe, 2nd Dec., 1819, No. 15, Bengal Political Consultations, 1st Jan. 1820.
126. Tod to Metcalfe, 12th Mar., No. 15, of 28th Mar., No. 16, Memorandum about the persons and parties of Kota, No. 17, Bengal Political Consultations, 22nd Apr., 1820.
127. Metcalfe to Tod, Apr. 22nd, No. 20 Bengal Political Consultations, 22nd Apr. 1820.
128. Tod's *Rajasthan,* Vol. III, p. 1589 (1920).
129. Tod to Metcalfe, 14th Apr., No. 24, Bengal Political Consultations, 6th May, 1820. 22nd May, No. 16, Bengal Political Consultations, 15th July, 1820, 17th June, No. 10, Maharao's letter to Tod, No. 11. Bengal Political Consultations, 22nd July 1820, Tod to Metcalfe, 10th Sept., No. 29, Bengal Political consulations. 14th Oct. 1820, & Tod's *Rajasthan* (1920), Vol. III, pp. 1590-4.
130. Tod to Swinton, 31st Dec., 1820, No. 8, to the Raj Rana, 31st Dec. 1820, No. 10, to Lieut.-Col. Ludlow, 31st Dec., No. 11, to Swinton, 3rd Jan. 1821, No. 12, to Lieut.-Col. Ludlow, 3rd Jan., No. 18, Bengal Political Consultations, 3rd Feb. 1821.

131. Maharao to Ochterlony, No. 16, Bengal Political Consultations, 24th Feb. 1821, of 7th May, No. 9, Bengal Political Consultations, 9th June, 1821, and another, No. 16, Bengal Political Consultations, 16th June, 1821.
132. Swinton to Tod, 10th Mar. 1821, No. 34, Bengal Political Consultations of date.
133. Tod to Swinton, 24th Apr., No. 12, and Maharao to Tod, No. 13, Bengal Political Consultations, 12th May, 1821.
134. Tod to Swinton, 2nd Apr., No. 23, Bengal Political Consultations, 5th May 1821, Ochterlony to Swinton, 31st Jan., No. 15, Bengal Political Consultations, 24th Feb. 1821, Tod to Metcalfe, 17th June, No. 10, Bengal Political Consultations, 22nd July, 1820, also Tod's *Rajasthan*, Vol. III, p. 1597.
135. Tod to Swinton, 15th Sept., No. 21, Bengal Political Consultations, 6th Oct. 1821, Tod ordered the battalions from the British cantonments at Nimach and Nasirabad.
136. Tod gives a graphic description of this battle (his *Rajasthan, Op. Cit.*, Vol. III, pp. 1602-6), in which the chivalry of the *Haras* was exhibited. The Raj Rana was always uncertain about the loyalty of his men, so unpopular was his cause (*Rajasthan*, Vol. III, pp. 1599-1600.) also Tod to Swinton, 2nd Oct., No.4, Bengal Political Consultations, 20th Oct., 1821.
137. Swinton to Tod, 9th June, No. 14, Bengal Political Consultations, 9th June 1821.
138. Swinton to Tod, 20th Oct., 1821, No. 5, Bengal Political Consultations of the same date.
139. Tod to Swinton, 26th, Oct., No. 14, Bengal Political Consultations, 14th Nov. and 31st Oct., No. 36, Bengal Political Consultations, 24th Nov., 1821.
140. Tod to Swinton, 29th Nov., 1821, No. 13 Political Consultations, 3rd Jan., 1822, and 5th Feb., No. 6, Bengal Political Consultations, 16th Apr., 1822.
141. Aitchison (1909), Vol. III, p. 373.
142. *Loc. Cit.*, pp. 374-6.
143. Caulfield to Ochterlony, Sept. (no date given) 1822, No. 11 Bengal Political Consultations, 11th Oct., 1822. Zalim Singh's distrust of the Maharao was equally persistent. (Ochterlony to Swinton, 3rd Oct., No. 1, and Caulfied to Ochterlony, 1st Nov., No. 2, with correspondence that passed between Zalim and the Maharao. Bengal Political Consultations, 7th Dec., 1822.)

144. Treaty of 1838, by which Jhalawar was set up by dismembering Kota, Aitchison, Vol. III, pp. 393-5 (1909).

145. The Treaty with the State of Alwar, since it had been formed in a earlier period, conceded, by its formal wording rather than in its actual working, a comparatively better status to the Alwar Government. (Alwar Treaty of 1803, Aitchison (1909), Vol. III, pp. 322-3). But Alwar possessed no greater independence than other States, as is evidently from another engagement that the Maharao Raja had to sign in 1811, not to enter into any negotiation or agreement with other States, without the consent of the British Government; Aitchison (1909), Vol. III, pp. 324-5. No tribute was levied from Alwar. Similarly the treaties concluded in 1805 and 1806 subsisted between the Company and the Jat States of Bharatpur and Dholpur. (Aitchison, (1909.) Vol. II, pp. 275-7, and 299-301). Alwar, Dholpur and Bharatpur sent contingents to aid the British in the Pindari operations, (Metcalfe to Adam. Nov. 1st. No. 14. Bengal Political Consultations, 28th Nov. 1817.

146. His Minute of Dec. 1st, 1815, *Op. Cit.*, Para. 84.

147. His dedication of *"The Annals and Antiquities of Rajasthan"* to Kings George IV and to William IV.

148. Edmonstone's written evidence for the Parliamentary Select Committee. *Paper* (735-VI) 1831-32, Vol. XIV, p. 101.

149. Edmonstone's Note, Oct. 27th, 1829, *Loc. Cit.* pp. 112-3.

150. Their amount was considered excessive by Sutherland and Tod. Sutherland *Op. Cit.*, p. 180. Tod's written evidence for the Select Committee. *Parliamentary Paper* (735-VI) 1831-32, Vol. XIV, pp. 123-4.

151. *Considerations on the State of British India*, by A. White, p. 230.

152. Prinsep uses these arguments in favour of the tributes levied by Hastings, *Op. Cit.*, Vol. II, pp. 349-351.

153. Such as Holkar, Bikaner, Kishengarh, Jaisalmer.

154. White would not admit this contention as sound. "Where was the enemy?" He asks, the Pindaris and Pathans had been swept away. "There remained no predatory force to disturb Central India." *Op. Cit.*, p. 231.

155. Alwar (Art. 5 of the Treaty of 1803) and Bikaner (Art. 6 of the Treaty of 1818); Aitchison (1909). Vol. III, pp. 322 and 343-4 respectively.

156. White; *Op. Cit.* p. 231.

8

Subsidiary States

No fundamental change in their position in Hastings' time—*Oudh*—treaty of 1801—the resident's interpretation and action—Nawab's resentment—Minto government urge reforms in administration—Moira's arrival—change in British policy—same treaty differently interpreted by different parties—Nawab Sadat Ali's death—his successor meets the Governor-General—complains against the resident—withdraws the statement—Baillie instructed not to interfere minutely in Nawab's affairs—company takes loans from the Nawab—Nawab assumes the kingly title—*Mysore*—Wellesley's arrangement of 1799—Maharaja assumes powers in 1811—resident's distrust of Raja's capacity—Hastings' policy—*Travancore and Cochin—the Gaekwar*—1802 treaty—British loans—assignments in territory—internal Government regulated by the resident, Colonel Walker—Kathiawar settlement—intrigues in 1815—Sita Ram's surrender demanded—treaty of 1817—death of Fateh Singh and Anand Rao—Siyaji Rao Gaekwar succeeds to the Gadi—Elphinstone goes to Baroda—relations defined—interference definitely withdrawn—Kathiawar tribute question settled *the Nizam of Hyderabad*—relations—Sikander Jah—his ministers—their appointment—Chandu Lal—his character—Nizam's sons—their misconduct—force sent against them—their confinement at Golkunda—Nizam's contingent—reform and reorganisation—Hyderabad Government—disorder, oppression and decay—Russell's attempts at reform—Metcalfe becomes the resident—William Palmer & Co.—dealings with the state—sixty lakh loan—court of directors disapprove—Metcalef's distrust of Chandu Lal, and dislike of Palmer & Co.'s dealings—his reforms—Chandu Lal's jealousy—estrangement between Metcalef and Hastings—question of interference—Metcalfe proposes to clear the Nizam's debts to Palmer & Co.—plans enforced—treaty of 1822—*Conclusion.*

Mention has been made in an earlier chapter of a number of important States which had been reduced by Wellesley's subsidiary treaties to an alliance with the East India Company, thus surrendering their independent rights of making war and peace with other States, and agreeing to accept and pay for a British force stationed in their territories. The Peshwa had belonged to this class of States. Hastings added Nagpur to the list in 1816 and Holkar in 1818. These three cases have already been reviwed.[1] Other subsidiary States of India did not undergo any fundamental change in their relations with the British Government during Hastings' period of office. This is true in the sense that their constitutional position as fixed by Wellesley remained unaltered in all essential matters, as distinguished, for example, from the case of Holkar and that of the Rajput States. But the changed position of the Company after its victorious emergence from the war of 1817-18 necessarily reacted on its relations with these States. Therefore, the working of these relations also forms an interesting part of this narrative of Hastings' dealings with the States of India.

Oudh

The relations of the Bengal Government with the Ruler of Oudh formed a subject of pressing importance till the very last days of Minto's stay in India, and consequently early became one of the first objects of Hastings' attention. Those relations had been settled by the Treaty of 1801, which forced Nawab Sadat Ali to cede to the Company nearly half his dominions, yielding an annual revenue of a crore and thirty-five lakhs of Rupees. That Treaty,[2] and another document[3] defining the final arrangements as arrived at after a conference between Wellesley and Sadat Ali in February 1802, were expected to smooth away all difficulties in future, and to usher in a period of harmony. Whatever might have been the intentions of the authors of those instruments of amity, it is not surprising that, worded as they were their working produced results very opposite indeed from those desired of them. The Sixth Article of the Treaty, while guaranteeing the remaining territories to the authority of the Nawab and his heirs, also laid down that "he will establish in the reserved dominions such a system of administration (to be carried into effect with his own officers) as shall be conducive to the prosperity of his subjects and be calculated to secure the lives and property of the inhabitants; and his Excellency will always advise with and act in conformity to the counsel of the officers of the said Honourable Company." By the same Treaty the Company agreed to defend the Nawab Wazir[4] against all foreign and domestic enemies, at the same time engaging that after the cession of the territory no further demands would be made on his treasury for the services of British troops, whether employed to repel a foreign enemy or suppress rebellions in Oudh itself.[5] The able Nawab, Sadat Ali, took a personal interest in his affairs. He dealt vigorously with the big landlords and in many cases resumed their grants, when they resisted his demands. He was extremely parsimonious, though not mean. His aims were the acquisition of wealth for the treasury and the consolidation of the central power of his Government.[6]

The Resident at his Court, Major Baillie, constantly demanded that the Government of the country should be carried on under his advice. He claimed, indeed by a literal interpretation of the Treaty that the Nawab Wazir's obligation to consult the wishes of the British Government extended "to all affairs connected with the *ordinary* government of your dominions and with the *usual* exercise of your authority."[7] Even the domestic concerns of patronage and the granting of pensions and Jagirs to the officials and courtiers of the Nawab became subjects of a most bitter and prolonged controversy between the two Govenments.[8] Nor was the manner in which these representation were made always tactful, or considerate to the Nawab's dignity or authority in his own State.[9] The discussion centred chiefly round the question of the reform of the revenue administration in the reserved territories. The revenues were collected by Amils, to whom the lands were formed out on a loose system of contracts. This frequently leld to extortion and oppression, with the result that the Zamindars put up armed resistance against the State. To quell the revolt of the landlords the Nawab Wazir had to call in the aid of British troops, as was permitted by the Treaty.[10] This meant that the British arms were employed apparently in the interest of law and order, but also at times to support oppression, possibly injustice. The British Resident claimed that just as British troops were required to help the Nawab Wazir's administration, so the latter must agree to rule the country in accordance with British counsel. He further required that the system of revenue collection should be altered, and a better one introduced in its place. The Governor-General, Lord Minto, gave full support to that proposal. After a protracted discussion on the subject, he made definite suggestions to Sadat Ali for his immediate acceptance. The principles of reform urged by Minto consisted of "an essential change in the system of assessment, management and collection" of the Nawab's revenues.[11]

Either because he was convinced of the impracticability of the suggested reforms, or because he saw in them the further loss of his authority and importance, the Nawab did not feel any great enthusiasm for them. But they were pressed upon him with such insistence and unabated vigour by the Resident and the Governor-General[12] that Sadat Ali had neither the courage nor the means to withstand the decisive tone adopted by the British Government. When open resistance appeared vain, he adopted the method of evasion, and, whilst apparently submitting to the will of the Resident, he postponed action in spite of repeated remonstrances.[13]

Minto had left the matter in this unsettled state when Hastings (then Earl of Moira) took over charge. The new Governor-General, was definitely opposed to the exercise of interference in the affairs of the Indian Princes, and also to the lowering of their status and dignity. He had already heard that the Nawab of Oudh was held in a "painful and degrading thraldom"[14] and he took a different view of the situation from his predecessor. An occasion soon presented itself for the demonstration of the change in policy. A courtier of the Nawab Wazir, Tehsin Ali Khan, died on the 27th August, 1818,[15] appointing the British Government executor of his property amounting to nearly a lakh and a half of Rupees.[16] Considering Tehsin Ali's services to the British Government, Minto had authorised the Resident to accept the execution of his will.[17] The Nawab Wazir claimed that, as his master and sovereign, he had the reversioning right to Tehsin Ali's personal property.[18] Hastings decided to withdraw from the position taken up by Minto, and made over the property to the Nawab.[19] He considered that public faith and equity required that the Nawab should be left free to exercise his independent rights over his subjects and servants. The Resident was instructed to avoid any future agitation in minor matters, which might cause irritation, and to reserve the influence of the British Government for more important affairs.[20] The authorities in England approved of this attitude.[21]

The question of reforming the revenue system was still in suspense. The conciliatory policy was extended to that sphere also.[22] The Nawab had undertaken some partial measures in the direction suggested by the British Government, but their limited scope and extent did not satisfy the Resident.[23] It was felt that the Nawab had an inward repugnance to carrying out the reforms. It was of little use to force him to adopt them, for since they had to be worked by his won officers, it was in his power to defeat the spirit of these changes.[24] Moreover, the principles of compulsion could not be adopted without violating the spirit of the alliance. Therefore, "the conclusion appears to the Governor-General-in-Council to be inevitable, namely, that the specific plan of reform proposed to the Vizier by Lord Minto must be relinquished, or insisted on as the alternative of a resolution on our part, which would amount to a dissolution of the existing relations between the two States. The principles of justice and good faith, as well as of political expediency, appear to the Governor-General-in-Council to forbid the adoption of the latter course, and thus to impose on the British Government the necessity of desisting from the further prosecution of the object."[25] This extract contains Hastings' view, which again met with the entire approval of his employers at home.[26]

It is interesting to pause here for a moment to consider how the same instrument (Wellesley's Treaty of 1891) was differently interpreted by the different parties concerned.

Baillie, the British envoy at Lucknow, concentrating his attention on the letter[27] of the engagement, was clearly convinced that the British were unquestionably entitled to require the Nawab to act in accordance with their wishes in all his concerns.[28] In this construction of the Treaty, Minto fully agreed with his Agent.[29] On the other hand, the Nawab Wazir imagined that, after depriving him of a large part of his territory, the Treaty was intended to leave him reasonably free to rule the reserved dominions without the Resident's minute intervention in his domestic affairs. In fact, he thought that the dismemberment of his State was the price with which he had purchased that autonomy,[30] and that in future he would consult the British envoy only on extraordinary matters.[31] While the two parties viewed the position from different angles, it was not easy to attain any satisfactory solution of the outstanding problem. And although, under the inspiration of fear or intimidation, he might agree to abide by the advice imposed on him, his own conviction was that the he was being unfairly treated. By a strict interpretation of Article Six of the Treaty, Minto and Baillie were justified in exercising the minute control which they attempted over the Oudh government. But that construction of the terms of the Treaty would have logically led to the conclusion that the Company's Government was to be the sole judge of the occasion and the extent of British interference in the Nawab's ordinary administration. It is unlikely that such a complete subordination of the Nawab in matters relating to his reserved territories was intended.[32]

By restricting the right reserved to the British, to interfere with advice and remonstrance, to those affairs which might injuriously affect British interests, Hastings attempted to reconcile the Nawab's view to the words of the Treaty.[33] He considered "that in all other respects the administration of the Nawab is to be free; but, indeed, it is evident from the whole tenor of the treaty, that an uninterrupted exercise of his own authority within the reserved dominions was assured to him in order to qualify the very strong step which we took in appropriating to ourselves (as an exchange for the subsidy) so large a portion of his territories. The Nawab is consequently to be treated in all public observance as an independent prince. Essentially he must be subservient to the British Government."

Before Hastings could formulate these definite views on the Oudh question, a number of incidents and events had occurred to give him an intimate acquaintance with the real situation at Lucknow, not the least of which was his visit to that city in the autumn of 1814. (25th October to 11th November)[34]

While the negotiations for the introduction of reforms were still pending, Nawab Sadat Ali suddenly died on the 11th July 1814,[35] leaving an accumulation of several millions sterling in his treasury.[36] His eldest son was quickly declared Nawab, the claims of Sadat Ali's second and favourite son Shamsudaula, being ignored. The deceased Nawab had trusted and trained Shamsudaula in the governmental duties.[34] The new Nawab, Ghazi-ud-din Haider-Rafaut-Daula, perceived the value of the British Resident's help in the removal of his rival, and was, therefore, obviously anxious to keep Baillie pleased,[38] at any rate until he felt secure against his ambitious brother. The latter Prince was eventually removed to Benares, on an annual pension of two lakhs of rupees[39] The new Nawab, though learned in philosophy philology and literature, did not possess his father's ability as a ruler.[40] For the time being he readily accepted the Resident's advice, and accordingly, measures were undertaken to reform the revenue and judicial administration.[41] But the new arrangement was hardly better in its working, and certainly not more popular. As in the past, British troops were still required to uphold the authority of local officers.[42] And lastly, the Nawab Wazir himself did not like the change.[43] Very soon the relations between the new Nawab and the old Resident reverted to the state of pension that had existed in the time of Sadat Ali.

The young Nawab the Governor-General met at Cawnpore on the 13th October, 1814, whence they both proceeded to Lucknow. Hastings again received accounts of Baillie's overbearing conduct towards the Wazir, and the latter's wish for the Resident's removal.[44] These complaints, which were expressed by the Nawab Wazir in a paper to the Governor-General, and also orally expressed to him and his Aide-de-Camp, Captain Gilbert, were later withdrawn, first through his servant Agha Mir, and later personally to the secretaries of the Governor-General. The unconvincing explanation offered was that the Nawab had been incited to that action against the Resident by the evil counsels of his European officers, McLeod, Law, Clarke and de L'Etang.[45] The latter, of course, denied the imputation, and McLeod offered to prove to Hastings' satisfaction that the Nawab's charges were basely untrue, and further that it was owing to Agha Mir's intimidation, presumably on the Resident's support, that the Nawab had withdrawn his complaints.[46] The whole incident revealed an ugly and deplorable situation, made even disgusting by the timid and base behaviour of the Nawab Wazir. His clear denial made any further enquiry a very delicate business.[47] The Nawab did not, however, escape punishment for his cowardly act, for as a result of the intrigue he had to accept Agha Mir, a low servant, as his minister.[49] He would have preferred Hyder Mehdi, the clever and tried administrator whom Baillie disliked.[50] Agha Mir (who assumed the title of Muhamud-daula) and Raja Daya Krishna became, respectively, the Peshkar and Diwan of Oudh, and began to rule the country with the Resident's support.[51] As might have been expected, the Nawab considered them as unwelcome checks on his own authority, and very soon his distrust of them became openly manifest.[52] He had only himself to thank for what followed. Hastings did all he could to uphold his dignity and restore his authority in his realm.

Clear instructions were laid down for the British Resident, that "in all intercourse, the Resident should consider himself as the ambassador of the British Government to an acknowledged sovereign. A respectful urbanity and a strict fulfilment of established ceremonials should thence be preserved by the Resident towards his Excellency."[53] On other points, too, all the wishes expressed by the timid Wazir were met by the Governor-General in an open-hearted manner. It was recognised that 'the treaty unquestionably in every fair construction purported to leave the Nawab Vizier an independent sovereign within the reserved dominions. The clause by which the interference of the British Government with advice or remonstrance, through the Resident, is acknowledged as a right, can never in any decent acceptance be understood to mean a meddling with the Vizier's family and domestic concerns."[54] By enforcing the principles of his early policy,[55] Hastings had restored amicable relations with the Ruler of Oudh who must have experienced a sense of relief for which he had been pining for many years. This benevolent effect did not remain unappreciated.[56]

Nor was the gratitude wholly one-sided. Another transaction between Hastings and Oudh which took place at the same time as the incidents already described, and which must have influenced the policy adopted, deserves mention Just when the Nepal War was progressing, and the Company's Government was in financial difficulties, when the market was indeed very unfavourable for procuring loans, and when Hastings badly needed money to fight the Gurkhas in the Hills his eyes turned to the Hoarda left by Sadat Ali. A crore of rupees was offered by the Nawab as a fight but accepted as a loan at six per cent.[57] It was a very timely, useful and substantial help to the Company, and was acknowledged as such the financial need of the Company, and the protracted operations against Nepal necessitated a second application to the Nawab Wazir who advanced another crore a few months later on the same conditions.[58] On the conclusion of the Nepal was as the spoils of victory the British received the district of Khairagarh and some part of the *Tarai.* These tracts were comparatively unproductive and certainly a great trouble to the Company to hold.[59] Hastings made them over to the Wazir in full satisfaction of the second loan which was cancelled by a formal Treaty.[60] This arrangement was naturally very gratifying to Hastings who knew that it could not have been brought about excepting through the Wazir's wish to adopt his recommendation.[61]

Whilst the public relation between the two Governments were thus improved the personal relations between the Nawab and the Resident grew worse Baillie ascribed that estrangement to the encouragement of private intrigue by the Governor-General himself.[62] Hastings was obliged to reply and point out Baillie's domineering disposition which both Nawab Sadat Ali and Ghaziudin Haidar had rightly resented.[63] Baillie's presence at Lucknow was regarded as incompatible with the harmonious relations which should subsist between the head of the Government and his Agent in Oudh and so his removal was ordered.[64] Baillie fell a sacrifice to that anomalous system which had been set up by the Treaty of 1801 although it is true that his zeal more mistaken than discreet and his manners contributed to that consequence.

Although this policy of non-intervention inaugurated by Hastings considerably smoothed the relations between the Government of the Company and of Oudh it could not wholly cure the evil system which had its root in the treaty of 1801, namely, the calling in of British troops to suppress the Zamindars who took up arms against the Wazir's administration. This continued as before. "In the beginning of 1822 about seventy of their forts in the vicinity of Sultanpur, were occupied and dismantled by a British detachment."[65] (Wilson.)

During Lord Hastings' time and with his deliberate encouragement the Nawab Wazir assumed the title of the King of Oudh.[66] Hastings' fear of the revival of the Mughal House, and its possible danger to the British, led him to hint to the Nawab that it rested entirely with him whether he was to continue the old servile forms of respect to the Delhi family.[67] He was informed that the British had dropped that unbecoming mark of submission. That diplomatic observation was expected to produce its effect. The Resident was further advised to work upon the Nawab's reflection. If consulted by him about his desire to assume the kingly title, "he should seize it and bring it immediately to a distinct understanding intimating his persuasion that the British Government would readily recognise such a title of assumed by the sovereign of Oude, provided it made no change in the relations and formularies between the two States or altered the manner in which British subjects. . . had hitherto been received."[68] The higher title was accordingly readily assumed. As had been expected, this was received with undisguised indignation at the Court of Delhi, which its turn produced a keen resentment at Lucknow the net result of it was "an irreparable breach between the two Mahomedan States" which afforded Hastings "extraordinary satisfaction."[69]

He has been criticised for taking this step, but much of the strength of this condemnation is washed away by the fact that his critics attack him from two almost opposite positions. In the first place, it has been said that "This was perhaps the most sterile stroke of the sterile science of diplomacy that was ever conceived or executed. The title never took much root out of Lucknow."[70] On the other hand, Wilson, writing long after Hastings' term of office, declared that names are sometimes as real as things and the King of Oude is not for any purpose the same Potentate as the Nawab Vizier," and doubted "whether identity of religion and community of interest will not outweigh all other considerations, and whether the King of Oude will not be as willing as the Nawab Vizier to place his resources at the foot of the imperial throne."[71] The above criticisms represent two extremes. This act of Hastings' diplomacy could, however, be considered consistent with his general policy towards the States of India, namely, that of dignified, though subordinate isolation. But his avowed motives for taking that step must lead the student to the conclusion that it was certainly an unnecessary, though not wholly a sterile, course of action, the product rather of fantastic fears than of bold statesmanship.

Mysore

In this class of subsidiary States, Mysore bore a certain resemblance with the Kingdom of Oudh since in both cases the British had, by treaty, reserved to themselves the right to offer advice and to be consulted in matters of internal administration.[72] In the last Mysore War, the British and the Nizam, the victorious allies, indemnified themselves with a large portion of the territories of Mysore. The remaining portion was restored to a minor belonging to the family of the old Hindu Rajas whom Haidar Ali had dispossessed.[73] The Maharaja, thus restored by Wellesley, was only three years old. The Treaty defining his relations with the British Government, bound him tightly to the performance of his subsidiary obligations. In the case of his failure to fulfil them, it empowered the Company to take over the management of the State into their own hands, in that case allowing a lakh of pagodas and a fifth of the net revenue of his State for the Maharaja's subsistence.[74] The Government of Mysore, was placed in the hands of an able Brahmin minister Purniya who worked under the supervision and general counsel of the British Resident. Purniya was a clever administrator, and by his tact and prudence conducted the affairs with great regularity and dissection. There was little interference on the part of the Resident during the later years of Purniya's ministry.[75] The knowledge of the right interposing had proved sufficient of itself to prevent any frequent or urge necessity for its exercise.[76] Purniya's rule was absolute, and in his anxiety to fill the treasury, he frequently injured the true interests of the State and the resources of its people. The latter suffered from extortion.[77]

While the Government was carried on by this powerful minister the education of the minor Prince was sadly neglected. He "was led to the enlightened tuition of his mother, grandmother, and other lad of the Harem."[78] As he grew in years, he became jealous of Purniya sole authority and aspired to assume the reins of Government which was little fitted to hold.[79] In 1811, he took the direction of affairs in his own hands. Purniya, unwillig to share his authority with anybody else, resigned, and died shortly afterwards. The Maharaja was sixteen years of age when he thus began to rule. He found a full treasure (Purniya left two crores of rupees in the State coffers) and a settled Government.[80] Though possessed of an amiable disposition, an excellent temper, and a liberal heart, the Maharaja Krishna Raja Odiyar very superstitious, credulous, unreliable and in many ways an indifferent rule. He was very jealous of British interference and extremely tenacious power, wishing to do everything himself. His ambitions in this directly were always fed by the counsels of the personal favourites, was surrounded him.

In the relations between the Mysore State and the Company Government, during the time of Lord Hastings, nothing of sufficient importance took place, to alter fundamentally the position as define by the Treaty of 1799. But, as in the case of Oudh, Mysore is illustration both of the way in which the working of treaty provision led to friction, irritation and constant difficulty, and of Hastings views. The Mysore story has such a close parallel to that of Oudh as to appear almost identical with it. At Mysore, we find the Resident, Cole, who, like Baillie, displays a keen sense of duty and an extraordinary zeal in purifying the Maharaja's Government. He offers his advice, and insists on its acceptance, in almost the same tone and manner as Baillie at Lucknow. The Raja receives the Resident's counsel in the same way as the Wazir, with outward deference but inward indignation. Cole employs the same modes of secret spies for procuring information as Ballie at Lucknow. In desiring the Raja to introduce all the new Amildars to him before they were sent out to their districts, Cole took the same action as Baillie took in Oudh in revenue matters. These methods produced the same annoyance to the rulers at both places. We find the Raja sending his secret agent, Shri Niwas Rao to Madras, with the same object as Sadat Ali had in McLeod's visit to Calcutta, to obtain emancipation from the Resident's control. Cole put up his own nominee, Bakir Sahib, for the ministers post, just as Baillie supported Agha Mir, and both these persons, who were at first in the good books of their respective sovereigns, later lost their confidence, presumably because they looked to the Resident for support in their power.[81] In short, in their exuberant zeal for a better administration the British representatives at the two Courts, assumed a decided tone in demanding from the Princes concerned a ready compliance with the measures of reform suggested by themselves.[82] The resemblance continues still further in the policy adopted by Hastings in the two cases.

Whilst giving credit to Cole, as in the case of Baillie, for his integrity and honourable zeal, Hastings directed the Government of Madras to unstuck the Resident to abstain from that minute and irritating interference in the details of the Raja's Government. "While the external defence of the Kingdom of Mysore was entrusted to the British Government, and the internal tranquillity of the country maintained by the presence of the British force, the charge of the civil administration, both in its general outline, and subordinate details, devolved on the Rajah, a general superintendence and control being vested in the British Government, and certain provisions made for the preservation of our paramount influence in the State and for the surety and security of resources from which the subsidy is derived." A distinction was to be drawn between the time of the Raja's minority, when the British Government was the guarantee of the conduct of the minister, and the time when he himself assumed the Government. The interference exercised in the former case, could not be justified in the latter. It was noticed with regret that the Resident did not appreciate this distinction. The public disapproval of the Raja's proceedings and "the tacit though perhaps unintentional encouragement given to the subjects to appeal to the protection and the redress of the Resident, accompanied by public reproof and advice relative to the affairs of his government, could produce no other effect on the mind of a prince, of any independence of spirit, than aversion to the advice so conveyed, and dissatisfaction to the person from whom it proceeded." Following the spirit of this policy the Resident was also told not to force on the Raja a minister of the Resident's choice, but to leave him free to select one for himself. Even if Bakir was to be appointed, "the proposition must come from the Rajah." And lastly, the suggestion of the Resident, to let Ram Rao, the minister in office, continue in name, and to vest the real power in Bakir's hands, was disapproved.[83]

The Resident, who did not relish these instructions, followed them in a halting spirit.[84] Affairs continued in this manner, without any particular improvement either in general administration or in the personal relations between the Raja and the Resident. The Government of Madras were disposed to reduce the Raja's condition to that of the Nawab of the Karnatic.[85] This Government considered that the rendering of deference and attention to a ruler like the Maharaja of Mysore, was accompanied by the danger of exciting overweening notions of self-importance, quite inconsistent with his dependent position, which he must be made to feel as much as possible. Hastings did not subscribe to that view, but adopted a different attitude. He particularly considered the very zealous and efficient assistance rendered by the Raja to the British during the Pindari operations, and desired to apply a liberal policy to Mysore. He also recommended to the Secret Committee that the Mysore Resident should be placed directly under the Supreme Government.[86]

Travancore and Cochin

Two other States in the far south, Travancore and Cochin, were also in subsidiary alliance with the Company. A subsidiary force had been introduced into Travancore in 1795.[87] The Treaty of 1805, concluded in Wellesley's time, further increased the strength of the force[88] and in general imposed on this State almost the same conditions as were embodied in the Mysore Treaty of 1799, particularly in reserving to the Company the powers of assuming the Government of the country if the subsidy should not be regularly paid.[89]

British control was resented by the State, and in 1809, the Diwans of Travancore and Cochin combined to offer armed resistance to the British. A military force was despatched by the Madras Government and the rising was quelled with excessive severity.[90] The Raja of Travancore died in 1810, being succeeded by Lakshmi Bai, who became the ruler of the State. During her time, the British Resident, Colonel Munro, discharged the duties of the Diwan.[91] The Rani died in 1814, and was succeeded by her infant son. Her sister became Regent during the Raja's minority. The advice of the British Resident continued to guide the administration. Travancore became thereafter pacified and subjected to British supremacy.

After the military action of 1809, a fresh treaty was concluded with Cochin. The annual subsidy payable by that State to the Company was raised from one lakh to Rs. 2,76,037. The protection of the State and the distribution of the subsidiary force rested entirely with the Company.[92] Both these States were so completely reduced in 1809 that no spirit of freedom remained in them to give any further political embarrassment to the British Power.

The Gaekwar

Another important State, a former member of the Maratha Empire, which was brought under subsidiary relations by Wellesley, was that of the Gaekwar of Baroda. The reigning Prince, Anand Rao succeeded to his father's throne in 1800, but his half-brother Kanoji disputed the succession with him. Raoji Appaji, Anand Rao's minister, sought British help, and a Convention was signed on the 15th March, 1802.[93] The Bombay Government sent a force which drove out Kanoji and his supporter, Malhar Rao. The Convention was confirmed by a formal Treaty. A secret Article of the former was incorporated in the Treaty to provide for the permanent stationing of a British subsidiary force consisting of two thousand sepoys and one company of European artillery to be paid for by the Gaekwar.[94] By this instrument, the British offered a loan of money to reduce the Arab soldiery of the Gaekwar. The method of repayment was also provided for. As a security the British were authorised to collect the revenues of certain districts yielding Rs. 11,75,000 a year. The Company undertook to protect the Gaekwar against his enemies.[95] Along with this engagement, which was ratified by Anand Rao personally in a separate document,[96] Governor Duncan of Bombay made a private engagement with Rajoji Appaji, the Gaekwar's shrewd minister, guaranteeing to him the permanent Diwanship of Baroda State, and promising similar support and protection to his son and relatives against the possible encroachment on their rights and privileges by the Gaekwar or anybody else.[97] This was a step similar to the one later taken by Hastings in the case of Raj Rana Zalim Singh of Kota. As was natural, it also became a cause of serious embarrassment to the Resident at Baroda, when Sita Ram, the adopted son of Raoji,[98] claimed the benefit of the guarantee given by the Governor of Bombay. Unfortunately, its fulfilment became very inconvenient by the change of circumstances.[99]

The engagements contracted in 1802 between the Governments of Bombay and Baroda were all consolidated in 1805 by another Treaty, which further increased the strength of the subsidiary force to the thousand Sepoys, one company of European artillery and their proportionate equipment: the functions of the force were to be the protection of the Gaekwar's person and country, the chastisement of rebels and inciters of disturbances, and the correction of his defaulting subjects and dependents. Cessions of territory made by the former Treaty were confirmed and the Provinces of Chourasi, Chikli and Khera were added, along with the Chouth of Surat. The Gaekwar was to submit to British arbitration all his disputes with other Powers, including his unsettled accounts with the Peshwa.[100]

The internal difficulties of the Gaekwar's Government afforded to the British Power a great opportunity of extending their influence over his country. The ground gained in 1802 and later, by the establishment of a military ascendancy, and by financial transactions, was maintained, and the British position became increasingly strong during the years preceding Lord Hastings' arrival.

Anand Rao was a weak ruler, himself incapable of carrying on his government. He had as his able minister, Raoji Appaji.[101] The British defeated, pursued and put to flight his energetic rival Kanoji,[102] whilst Malhar Rao was defeated by Withal Rao (Raoji's relative, and brave general.)[103] After Raoji's death, his adopted son become the minister, and later, Fateh Singh, Anand Rao's brother, was selected as the Regent of the State.[104]

The first British Resident, Major Alexander Walker, was a person of uncommon tact and great ability. During his seven years' stay at Baroda (1802-1809), he rendered invaluable service to the country. Not only did he gain great advantages for the Company, but by his industry and prudence he was successful in settling the Gaekwar's country as well. Although he was the real power behind the administration, he did not assume a tone of open authority in the country, a temptation which very few Residents could resist in that situation. He preserved the prestige of the Gaekwar over his subjects. Although as he himself wrote, "Certain causes of a delicate nature called for and demanded an active interference in, and vigilant control over, every part of internal management, without which the subjects of the Honourable Company's Government could scarcely have been obtained, and the Government of the Gaekwar saved from the state of anarchy and confusion with which it was threatened."[105]

His great service to the two governments and a remarkable personal achievement consisted in the discontinuance of the practice of *Mulkgiri* expeditions; which were annually undertaken by the Gaekwar's army into Kathiawar for the purpose of collecting his tribute from the numerous feudatory Chiefs of that region. The exactions and oppressions of these predatory incursions were indeed ruinous to peaceful life and industry. Walker invited the Chiefs to fix the amount of their tribute to the Gaekwar and agree to remit it voluntarily and regularly without the movement of the *Mulkgiri* force. His appeal met with a favourable response, and accordingly, bonds were executed between the Gaekwar and over a hundred and twenty Chiefs of Kathiawar. These were countersigned by Walker in the name of the British Government.[106] It was the accomplishment of a great object for both the Governments, and for the peace and tranquillity of the land.[107]

Walker was succeeded in the Resident's office by his assistant, Captain J. Carnac.[108] The latter could not maintain the standard set by his able predecessor, and always found reasons to continue the supervision of the affairs of the Gaekwar.[109] When the pecuniary claims of the Company over that State had been liquidated,[110] the chief justification for that minute interference ceased to exist. But, like many other Residents, he also could not resist the temptation of reforming the administration by means of the power and influence possessed by the British Government. Not only was the external policy of the Gaekwar controlled by him, but, as Wallace, a later Resident at Baroda, declared, "the constant well-meaning dictation in domestic affairs under the guise of advice of the Resident, and still worse, the ever-prying intermeddling action of his native agent, must have been galling in the extreme to any Chief of spirit, and the candid compiler must admit that gradually, almost imperceptibly, the habituate of advice had induced a tone more lordly, an impatience more impatient, and an assumption more aggressive than in the days of Governor Duncan and Colonel Walker.[111]

The negotiations which were opened at Poona for the settlement of the mutual claims between the Peshwa and the Gaekwar, which ended in the murder, on the 14th July, 1815, of the Baroda envoy, Gangadhar Shastri, have been already recapitulated.[112] As previously noticed, the plot, which culminated in that crime, had accomplices at Baroda also.[113] When it was discovered that Sita Ram had been engaged in that conspiracy, and that he showed secret hostility to the British influence at Baroda,[114] the Resident demanded the surrender of the ex-minister to the British Government, who proposed to send him to Surat. Although the Regent, Fateh Singh, had no hostile intentions against the British,[115] he strongly resisted that demand, expressing his readiness to punish Sita Ram if he were found to be connected with the murder of the Shastri. The surrender of his subject to another Government was, he said, a great humiliation for his State. Whether it was this pride, or his fear of the faction which sympathised with Sita Ram, the Regent assumed a spirited attitude in the matter.[116] However, he was obliged, though not without a great deal of pressure, to surrender Sita Ram to the Government of Bombay.[117]

By the Treaty of Poona (June 1817) the Peshwa was forced to give up all his claims on the Gaekwar in return for a fixed annual payment of four lakhs of Rupees, and to farm in perpetuity to the Gaekwar his (the Peshwa's) share of the City and District of Ahmedabad for a sum of four lakhs and a half a year.[118] This led to the conclusion of another Treaty between the British and the Gaekwar, by which the strength of the subsidiary force was further augmented by one battalion of infantry and two regiments of cavalry. The farm of the Peshwa's territories, which the Gaekwar had obtained by virtue of the Poona Treaty, was transferred him to the Company to meet the increased expense of the subsidiary force. The Gaekwar agreed to an exchange of territory, ceding to the Company his own share of Ahmedabad (net value Rs. 12,61,969 a year) and certain other districts, obtaining in return some paraganas belonging to the Company. The usual provision of the treaties of Hastings' time was also inserted, by which the Gaekwar engaged "in case of war, to bring forward the whole of his military resources for the prosecution of the war." He further agreed to maintain a body of 3000 horse to be placed under the command of the officer of the subsidiary force. The British were to have a controlling voice in matters of pay, efficiency and muster of this contingent. On the other hand the Company agreed "to take into consideration and determine partition of territory acquired in foreign wars." (Article 8.)[119]

This Treaty, which was concluded on the eve of the war, secured, for the Company considerable political, military and territorial gains in Western India, and strengthened its influence over the Gaekwar's Government. The attempt to persuade the Gaekwar to cede his share of the Kathiawar tribute to the British, failed because the former attached a great importance to his suzerainty over that region. But this disappointment was considerably compensated for by the cession of the rich city of Ahmedabad which, by its central position, historical association and commercial importance, was a valued and coveted acquisition for the Company.[120]

Fateh Singh, the real head of the Geakwar Government, died in 1818. His younger brother, Siyaji Rao, was recognised as Regent in Fateh Singh's place. In the following year, on the 2nd October, the nominal ruler, Anand Rao, also died, after an inefficient rule extending over a period of nineteen years. Siyaji Rao then became the full ruler, both in title and reality.[121] The young Prince was a different mettle from his feeble brother, whom he succeeded, and, although he was inexperienced, possessed ambition, talent and energy of character.[122]

During the war the Baroda subsidiary force was accompanied by the Gaekwar's contingent and both rendered very useful service in the operations in Malwa in 1817-1818. The Gaekwar's heavy debts (amounting to over a crore of rupees in 1820)[123] were in part due to the amounts that were borrowed for the upkeep of the expeditionary force.[124] Siyaji Rao, relying on the provision made in Article Eight of the Treaty of 1817, claimed a share of the conquered territory. Although his help was warmly recognised, his claim was not admitted.[125]

The relations between the Company and the Gaekwar were defined in 1820, when Elphinstone personally repaired to Baroda for that purpose.

The British Government decided to withdraw from the minute control exercised by the Resident and his agent in the details of civil administration during Anand Rao's time. The conditions for that withdrawal were that the Gaekwar would observe the agreements made by him with the bankers, the tributaries, and the ministers about their salaries, since all these three cases had been settled under British guarantees. The British would control exclusively all foreign intercourse, but in internal matter, the Resident would occasionally offer advice, and acquaint himself with the yearly budget and accounts of the State. Siyaji Rao was particularly anxious that all representations be made to him in private, and that all acts of Government should emanate directly from himself. He complained against the fraud and rapacity of Dhakji Dadaji, and he was determined not to have that person as his minister.[126] Siyaji Rao desired to have Sita

Ram back in that situation. Elphinstone would not permit Sita Ram's return under any circumstances, but left him free to choose his own minister, though he was to consult the British Government before appointing him. The principles of the agreement were, at the particular request of Siyaji Rao, given to him in writing by Elphinstone, and a proclamation was issued, announcing the restoration of the Gaekwar's authority in his internal administration.[127]

Before leaving Baroda, Elphinstone settled another matter of pressing importance. That part of Kathiawar, which had formerly been an integral part of the Gaekwar's dominions, had for many a year groaned under oppression and misery. The people had suffered, not only from famikne and plague, but from the extortion of the Gaekwar's agents many of whom were introduced by his commander Withal Rao Diwanji as the managers of the various chiefships.[128] The force kept in that region by the Gaekwar disturbed the peace on the British frontier for a hundred miles. Moreover, Walker's arrangement in Kathiwar, and later on in Mahi Kantha, were made for ten years only.

Elphinstone proposed to Siyaji Rao that the British should collect his tribute in Kathiwar and Mahi Kantha, and that he should engage to have no concern whatever with the tributaries unless the British called for his aid. The Gaekwar naturally did not like the suggestion, fearing that the British would eventually absorb his authority over his own tributaries. However, the proposal was agreed to, and a memorandum was drawn up and executed by Siyaji Rao, engaging not to send any troops, nor to make any direct demands on the Zamindars of Kathiawar and Mahi Kantha. The British Government undertook to collect the tribute on his account.[129]

All these arrangements were approved in their entirety by Hastings,[130] and Elphinstone was satisfied with their working. He found that Siyaji Rao's conduct was more satisfactory than he had expected it would be.[131]

The Nizam of Hyderabad

One of the oldest, and by the position and extent of its territories, the most important of the Company's allies, was the State of Hyderabad. It was also one of the earliest of the Indian Powers with which the British had contracted treaty relations. These relations were, in all essentials, similar to those of the other subsidiary States. The British Government furnished a subsidiary force[132] and undertook to defend the State against all enemies. The Nizam had no dealings with any other Power, except with the consent of the British, and engaged to submit all his external disputes to their arbitration, and to accept their award. He was also pledged to furnish, in time of war, a contingent of 6,000 infantry and 9,000 horse to serve with the subsidiary force in the field.[133] These were the general features of the subsidiary alliance which applied to all States of that class. However, speaking very roughly the position of Hyderabad resembled that of Baroda more than that of Oudh or Mysore. The case of Hyderabad differed from the two latter in-as-much as the Company was precluded, of the Nizam.[134]

The reigning sovereign, Sikandar Jah, had succeeded to the *Masnad* in 1803. He possessed neither the ability nor the character to make an efficient ruler.[135] The British maintained their influence on his Government by insisting on the appointment of a minister of their choice.[136] On this principle. Mir Alam, who was always loyal to the British alliance, was made Premier in 1804, to the exclusion of Raja Mahipat Ram, whom the Nizam favoured.[137] On the death of Mir Alam, in December 1808, the same controversy was renewed between the British Government and the Nizam. Minto wished to appoint Shamsul Umra, but the Nizam favoured Munir-ul-Mulk. After protracted negotiations, an arrangement was arrived at in June 1809, by which the latter became the ostensible minister, whilst it was understood that the administration would be carried on by Chandulal, the deputy (Peshkar) of Mir Alam, who was attached, to and trusted by, the British.[138]

On the appointment of Henry Russell to the Residence in 1810, Munir-ul-Mulk attempted in vain to obtain power for himself, little realising that the change in the personnel of the Residency did not mean any change in British policy. He had nothing to do with public administration, which was left entirely in the hands of Chandulal. The Nizam also retired from the administration in disgust, leading a life of gloomy retirement and sullen discontent, as later recorded by Metcalfe.[139]

It is indeed curious to see that the character of the minister who, with British support, ruled the State of Hyderabad like a despot for nearly thirty-five years, should have made quite a different impression on two such able and distinguished Englishmen as Russell and Metcalfe.

In the former's opinion, Raja Chandulal was "mild, intelligent, thoughtful, unaffected, humble . . . incredibly hard-working." Experienced in every mode of business. "Naturally humane and benevolent," and "with our support he is qualified to make a better minister than any other that could be chosen." Lack of political courage and firmness was his "great and perhaps his only defect."[140] Metcalfe, on the other hand, thought the Raja to be insincere, intriguing, vicious, unreliable, having "the plausibility ascribed to Satan," addicted to the vices of bribery and corruption, faithless and unscrupulous to his master, oppressive and extortionate to the people, subservient to the Residency staff.[141]

After allowing for the exaggeration resulting from strong opinions, the two estimates will be found more complementary than contradictory to each other. Russell's own remark, "his virtues belong to his private and his faults to his public character" goes some way to explain Metcalfe's later tirade against this man around whom the affairs of Hyderabad centred for so many years.[142]

In any case, there appears to be no doubt that the Raja was a very able and experienced administrator, who enjoyed the support of the British Power against all his enemies, even against the Nizam himself. It would only be natural that such a man should give his first attention to maintaining himself secure in power and counteracting the jealous intrigues of his opponents. Consequently public affairs could not be attended to with that disinterested thoroughness which the wretched state of the country badly required.[143] The poor people suffered the evils of mal-administration in the form of insecurity, extortion and tyranny.[5] Whenever the Resident exerted his influence to remedy these evils, Chandulal, who was only too anxious to keep the British envoy pleased, allowed his readiness to co-operate in the measures proposed by the Resident.[145]

Before mentioning these attempts at the reform of the Nizam's administration, notice must be taken of an incident which, though an unconnected and internal event, was yet serious enough to induce the Resident to take a decided attitude. Incidentally, it serves to reveal the state of the country at the time.

The Nizam had three illegitimate sons, Nazir-ud-dowla, Shams-ud-dowla and Mubariz-ud-dowla. The two latter had for some time been behaving in a most violent manner. They were supported and encouraged in their high-handed deeds by their cousin Imtiaz-ud-dowla. These young Princes (aged between twenty and thirty) resorted to acts of open defiance of the constituted government, as though compensating with a vengeance for the utter disregard of their father towards his administration. They set up a sort of tribunal, tried cases, inflicted sentences, and executed money demands. Life and property were not safe from the rapacity of the Princes. High and low alike suffered insults and injuries at their hands. Matters were steadily becoming intolerable. At one time, a servant of the Residency was arrested by the orders of the Princes. This brought matters to a head. Measures had been taken in 1814, a year before this incident, to restrain the violent activities of the young Princes, but they had proved unavailing. The resident complained of the indignity which he had received, whereupon the Nizam authorised the

Resident and Chandulal to adopt severe measures. Captain Hare was ordered to proceed with a force and mount guard over the Princes' Place. On the 20th August, 1815, Hare marched out with seven hundred men, and after reconnoitring the position, moved with three hundred of them to the house itself. While he was about half a mile from the Princes' palace, firing was opened on the force by men concealed in the upper stories of the houses on either side of the street. The captain advanced, blew open the gates of the house, and attempted to set fire to it, but he was repulsed by the Princes' men and forced to retire. The Resident Dispatched Major Macdowell, at the head of all the available forces (which then consisted only of 316 Europeans and 412 Sepoys), with some cannon.[146]

There was a great commotion in the town. Insecurity and fear of insurrection prevailed. Both the nobles and the common people, even the Nizam himself, felt alarmed. There was a vague fear in the popular mind that the English would destroy the town. On the other hand, the Resident realised the weakness of his situation, since at that time he had at his disposal only an insignificant number of troops as compared with the armed population of the discontented Pathans (about 10,000, in the two villages very near the city walls, and within three miles of the Residency). Russell thought it too hazardous to let Macdowell's force remain in the city, and withdrew it.[147] At the same time, he requested the commanding officer at Bellary to send five companies of Europeans and one battalion of sepoys to his support, and asked Doveton to proceed from Akola to Hyderabad with the whole of the subsidiary force, or at least the horse artillery of the 25th. Dragoons, five companies of Europeans and three battalions of sepoys.[148] These two or three days were a time of suspense and acute anxiety. At this very time, news came from Poona of the Peshwa's uncertain attitude in the surrender of his favourite Trimbakji. This further strengthened the Resident's resolve to settle the trouble quickly, before it had any time to spread.

During this period of disturbance, Chandulal shut himself up in his own house, too nervous to move out. The Nizam, fearing that the British might avenge Captain Hare's defeat, effected the removal of his two sons Shams-ud-dowla and Mubazir-ud-dowla, and also their cousin, Imtiaz-ud-dowla, to his palace on the 23rd August.

The Resident called upon the Nizam and his ministers to confine the Princes in the fortress of Golkunda, and demanded that their violent adherents should be punished, adding that he had sent for reinforcements from Bellary and Akola. Although he showed a readiness to comply with these demands of the Resident, the Nizam argued that it was not necessary to intern the Princes. Besides his own feelings as a father, he was being pressed by the ladies of the family, his wife and mother, not to be too severe on the youthful Princes. By the 28th August, the talk of sending them away to Golkunda had died out. Therefore, Russell wrote a strong note to Chandulal, sending him the draft of a letter which he was required to address to the Nizam. This produced the desired effect on the latter. The Princes were removed to Golkunda and lodged there under a strong guard on the 30th August. The Begums raised a great cry over this treatment of the Princes, and went with them to the place of confinement. But the Nizam remained unmoved by their threats. The city was quiet, and good order prevailed.[149] The lawless adherents of the Princes were punished with varying terms of imprisonment.[150]

In a study of the relations of the British and Hyderabad Governments, the reorganisation and reform of the Nizam's contingents forms indeed an integral part. A brief reference to this subject here is proper for the additional reason of its connection with the financial affairs of the Nizam's Government, which later became the cause of an acute controversy.

In 1798, the British had succeeded in ousting the French battalions in the Nizam's service, trained by Raymond, and later commanded by Perron. In 1800, after the Mysore war, in which the Nizam sent a contingent to aid the English, Colonel Kirkpatrick, the able English Resident at Hyderabad, concluded the treaty by which the Nizam was bound to furnish a contingent of 6,000 foot and 9,000 horse. This force co-operated with the British against the Marathas in 1803. The Nizam's forces, cavalry (of two kinds, *Sarkari* and *Jagirdari*) and infantry, were in a very defective condition. Excepting the troops of Salabat Khan the Nizam's army was "incomplete in numbers, loose in discipline, badly armed and irregularly paid."[151]

Although the employment of British officers in all arms of the State forces began quite early, the contingent was not properly organised unit 1618, when the "Russell Brigade" (named after the Resident) consisting of two battalions was taken under his supervision in the matter of pay and discipline. In 1814, Lieutenant Hare was appointed to its command. All through the years 1814-1817 the Brigade received particular attention from Russell, and consequently rose to a high pitch of efficiency. In 1815 it was used against the Princes, and in 1817-18 it rendered valiant services on the British side against Holkar's army at Mahidpur, and in the operations against the Pindaris.[152]

In the same way the plan of reforming the Nizam's cavalry was undertaken. This was a task full of difficulties. The Nizam himself was silently obstructive, the interested nobles naturally hostile, and even the minister's opposition was feared. But the scheme was carried out and Captain Davis was appointed commander on the strong recommendation of the Resident. This reformed cavalry under Davis was 4,0000 strong, and was stationed in different parts of Berar. After its reorganisation in 1817, it became another very efficient section of the contingent.[153]

The Russell Brigade, as already noticed, consisted of only two out of the six battalions of the infantry. The other four in Berar had not been so thoroughly organised as the two favoured ones at the capital. In January 1819, the whole force was reorganised. Two field officers from the Company's army, Majors Pitman and Doveton (the latter in suppression of Major Hare of the Russell Brigade) were in command of the two sections of the contingent on either side of the Godavari.[154] In order to ensure regular payment to the troops, the minister came to an arrangement with the firm of Messrs. William Palmer & Company, by which the latter furnished two lakhs of Rupees a month, required for the payment of the regular battalions and the reformed horse at Aurungabad. For that purpose, the firm was assigned the revenue of certain districts amounting to thirty lakhs of Rupees a year to meet the principal, interest, and contingent charges.[155]

The Ellichpur Brigade, which was Salabat Khan's contingent, was also brought under British control, with the appointment by the Governor-General of Major James Grant, of the Madras Army, as its commander. Both Grant, and still more, his successor in office, Captain Sever, carried the reform of that force into complete effect.[156]

This reform of the Nizam's contingent was brought about at the Resident's initiative, and in course of time, the reformed forces came, for all practical purposes, under the control of the British Resident. As Hastings wrote in one of his Minutes:—"It is perfectly true that these troops are, in fact, more ours than those of the sovereign by whom they are maintained.[157]

The efficiency of the contingent was greatly raised, but this was brought about at an enormous expense. The annual expenditure on the contingent about the year 1820 amounted to thirty-six lakhs. This figure excluded Salabat Khan's Brigade, which was maintained by a separate Jagir valued at fourteen lakhs of Rupees.[158] The emoluments and conditions were so attractive that "employment in the Nizam's service was generally coveted by the officers both of the King's and the Company's army."[159] When one appointment followed another, it became a proverbial expression, according to the able writer in the Calcutta Review, to say: "Poor Nizzy! Nizzy pays for all."[160]

While these improvements were being effected in the regular forces of the Nizam, his Government was steadily becoming oppressive and demoralised. The cost of the contingent alone was a heavy demand on the public treasury. "Extraordinary expenses, therefore, must be met by extraordinary exactions," wrote Russell.[161] In order to meet the demands of the Government the revenue collectors extracted from the cultivators more than they could afford to pay. Whilst the country was becoming reduced to a wretched state, the Nizam, himself, was every day growing more indifferent to its affairs. He took no interest, either in the disturbances that went on in the Peshwa's country in the spring of 1817, or in the wars and treaties that followed them. This indifference was due more to the weakness and helplessness of his position than to fidelity towards his allies. Chandulal was kept fully informed by the Resident, of all the events, and he returned that confidence with an unfailing devotion to the Birtish cause. He fully realised that if the Maratha influence prevailed on the Nizam, the first consequence would be his own dismissal as a traitor. But the Nizam, he said, was too fickle and timid for any decisive action. As the head of the executive Government, the minister provided a force of 13,425 men (7,425 infantry and 6,000 cavalry) to fight for the British support of Chandulal.

After the close of the war, Russell drew the Governor-General's attention to the oppressive administration of Hyderabad, and recommended speedy action. The disorders and weakness of that Government were, in a great measure, due to the political alliance of a subsidiary nature. They had now reached such a stage, that Russell considered, that the remedy could be applied only by the British Government. The plan of reform must be "general and comprehensive." In the existing circumstances, he favoured increased interference in order to support the executive authority of the minister, Chandulal. Although "nothing short of a close, vigilant and decided control over the internal administration" would be desirable, yet it was to "be exercised through the medium of advice and influence, and not by direct exertion of authority." He thus summed up the desired policy: "I would rather enlarge the sphere than increase the degree of interference."

The reforms would consist in the retrenchment of public expenditure, chiefly by the reduction or useless and unnecessary troops. In the selection (through the Resident's recommendation) as Talukdars, of men of reputation and integrity, and in the appointment to the districts of collectors instead of farmers (system of *Inami* rather than *Ijara*.) The Nizam's opposition was to be avoided by the pleasing offer to release his sons, whose confinement he regarded as a great disgrace.[163]

These suggestions were entirely approved. Russell was authorised to "interpose your advice and influence for those purposes." The instructions said"—"A salutary control over the internal administration of the country, accurate accounts of all establishments, receipts and expenditure, the correction of abuses, a proper distribution of justice, the reduction of expense, the amelioration of the revenue system, including the customs and duties levied on commerce, the improvement of resources, the extinction of debt, the efficiency of troops retained, and the discharge of such as are useless are objects to which your attention will naturally be directed." Chandulal, as the fittest instrument for carrying out these reforms, was to be assured of the protection and support of the British Government. And the release of the Princes from Golkunda was sanctioned.[164]

The reforms met with much opposition from interested nobles. But the Nizam was appeased by British consent to release his sons.[165] On the 1st September, Russell reported his great satisfaction at the improvement effected in the administration, and commanded the co-operation of the minister in establishing a purer system of rule. The districts had, in almost all cases, been given in *Inami* instead of *Ijara*, hereditary police officials were restored, the *Nazarana* charged from the Talukdars on their appointment abolished, and the administration of justice attended to by the appointment of a tribunal of a Hindu Pandit and a Musalman Kazi. Russell himself exercised a personal supervision on the administration by receiving petitions. In the course of eight months, he had sent 1042 such petitions to the minister.[166]

These glowing accounts, which brought forth the "highest approbation" of Hastings[167] must have aroused in the mind of Metealfe, then Political Secretary at Calcutta, the hopes of having a time of case and leisure at Hyderabad, whither he proceeded at the end of 1820, to succeed Russell.[168] His stay at the Nizam's Court, however, proved to be a time of considerable grief, bitterness, and strenuous anxiety, including a temporary estrangement from his chief, the Governor-General. The unhappy discussions which generated those feelings centred round the firm of Messrs. William Palmer and Company, to which a short reference is now necessary.

William Palmer, son of General Palmer by his Muslim wife, was in the military service of the Nizam. About 1810 or 1811, he retired from that office, and opened a banking and commercial firm at Hyderabad. In 1814, the partnership was reconstituted, with the following members: Hastings, Palmer, Bankati Das, a Hindu millionaire, Samuel Russell and William Currie. The last named was the Residency surgeon at Hyderabad. The firm carried on business with the countenance of the British Resident, in fact, the its offices were in one of the Residency bungalows. A number of European servants of the Company invested money with the firm, which paid them 12 per cent interest, while the firm itself transacted business with the Nizam's Government and his nobles, charging 24 and 25 per cent. per annuam.[169]

As the firm's dealings with the Hyderabad State were growing, it began to be feared that their activity might be declared illegal, since the partnership included British subjects.[170] Therefore, on application to the Bengal Government, William Palmer and Company obtained, in 1816, under the dispensing powers of tl 'aw, a licence to carry on their banking transactions with the Nizam's Government.[171]

The position of the Palmer Company, which was locally regarded as belong more or less identified with the British government, was thus completely strengthened. This impression was further confirmed by the addition to the partnership, in 1815, of Sir William Rumbold. He had gone out to India in the Governor-General's suite to make his fortune, and had married Hastings' ward, whom the latter treated as his own daughter.[172]

The powerful influence which the firm began to exercise in Hyderabad was further increased by an agreement (already referred to in passing) by which, at the suggestion of the Resident, and with the concurrence of the ministers, they established their branch at Aurungabad in 1819, to disburse the pay of the regular forces.[173] For this service, they received interest at the rate of 25 per cent from the Government, by the assignment of the revenues of certain districts in Berar. This arrangement was sanctioned by the Governor-General in Council.[174]

In 1820, the Minister and the firm negotiated another loan of sixty lakhs of Rupees. Chandulal represented that with that sum he would be able to pay off certain old debts, and also make *taccavi* advances to cultivators for improving their agricultural holdings. The Raja also announced that he would make reduction of unnecessary establishment, to the extent of twenty-five lakhs of Rupees annually.[175] The Palmer Company wished to have the transaction guaranteed by the British Government. Russell regarded Chandulal's proposal as sound and genuine, and recommended it for sanction.[176] The details of the transaction were with held from the British Government. It was arranged to pay the firm a bonus of eight lakhs of Rupees,[177] and the rate of interest was not revealed to the Calcutta Government.[178] The consideration of the question involved a spirited discussion at Calcutta, in which the Council was equally divided, and finally the loan was sanctioned with the casting vote of the Governor-General.[179] The sum of sixty lakhs was to be repaid in six years by annual instalments of sixteen lakhs of Rupees.[180]

In the meantime, information regarding Messrs. William Palmer and Company and the sanction given to their dealings, reached England. The Directors strongly censured the action of their Indian Government in granting the licence to the Company. It was a misuse of an extraordinary power, amounting to the protection of an otherwise illegal traffic. They issued positive and peremptory orders to the Government at Calcutta, to revoke the licence. After the experience of the abuses in the Karnatic and Oudh, of similar dealings, the Directors in England could not approve of the indulgence shown to Messrs. William Palmer and Company.[181] These orders arrived in India in November 1820. Since prompt compliance with them was emphatically demanded, the Resident was at once directed to refuse all further pecuniary arrangements between the Nizam and the firm.[183] When the news of the sixty lakh loan was received by the Directors they refused to ratify it, and further instructed Hastings' Government to discontinue the plan of paying the troops through the firm.[183]

Metcalfe took over charge from Russell on the 1st December 1820. With his characteristic energy, he soon began to acquaint himself with the real state of affairs in the country. His investigations showed that his predecessor's mild measures had been hardly effective. The new Resident found the Nizam's subjects groaning under oppression. The Government was thoroughly disorganised, and in many parts the frequent cases of dacoity and robbery made life and property insecure.[184] He found that public interests were neglected by the self-seeking minister, who spent lavish sums to strengthen his own position.[185] He had bought the support of William Palmer and Company, with enormous sacrifices of public money.[186] Besides the pecuniary transaction which with their high rate of interest and obscure accounts, were extremely profitable to the firm, William Palmer, his brother and two sons (at school in England) drew separate personal allowances front the State treasury.[187] The Nizam's government had become involved in serious financial difficulties. The last loan of sixty lakhs which Metcalfe characterised as " a fiction,[188]" had been grossly misapplied, with the result that, instead of its being a relief to the State, the public indebtedness to the firm had increased by Rs. 18,22,000 between August 1820 and January 1822.[189] Metcalfe saw how the accounts of the debts, new and old, with interest, boonuses and allowances, were every day leading the State into deeper distress.[190]

The alliance of an unscrupulous and all powerful minister with adventurous moneylenders, was not merely a financial evil. The Palmer Company wielded a considerable political influence in the county. The character of the house and "the British name became involved in detestable acts of oppression, extortion, and atrocity."[191] Their badged peons went about the country making exactions from the ryots. The common people closely associated the bankers with the British Power.[192] As Metcalfe put it, armed with the double authority of the British and the Hyderabad Governments, they were making rapid strides towards the entire possession of the revenues of the country.[193]

These political and financial entanglements of the Nizam grieved metcalfe intensely. He witnessed "the plunder of the Nizam by William Palmer & Co., in league with an unprincipled minister,"[194] and was indeed anxious to stop it.[195]

The measures which appeared to him to be most essential in the circumstances were, the reduction of public expenditure, land revenue settlements with the village communities for a term of five years, and, thirdly, the prevention of oppression through the agency of European superintendents of districts.[196]

Metcalfe lost no time in putting into operation his scheme of village settlements. He anticipated that the cultivators would obtain from them security of tenure and freedom from exaction. These hopes were fulfilled, and he felt gratified by the excellent results produced by the revenue settlements made in various divisions by his assistant, Wells, and other

European officers, Captain Sutherland, Seyer, Hollis, Clark, Hislop and Lieutenant Sutherland.[197]

These measures were distasteful to Chandulal. At first, he pretended to like them, and promised the Resident his hearty co-operation in their execution. He undertook to settle some parts himself. But in a short time it became clear to Metcalfe that the minister was counteracting the reforms by indirect yet effective means. He either did not carry out the settlements of the parts which he had taken upon himself, or nullified the true benefit of it by turning the district collector into a farmer.[198] Notwithstanding all this obstruction, Metcalfe was able to report his profound satisfaction at the happy results which his plan had produced.[199]

He received encouragement and tacit support from Hastings, in the reforms of the land revenue system.[200] This attitude of the Governor-General soon changed. In August 1822, Chandulal addressed a private letter to Hastings which was transmitted through the irregular channel of William Palmer. In it he complained of the Resident's unfriendly attitude towards him.[201] And since Metcalfe's measures undoubtedly involved direct interference in the internal affairs of the Nizam—a matter on which Hastings had always held strong opinions the Governor-General addressed him an emphatic official communication sharply condemning his action in asserting and enforcing such a degree of encroachment on the Nizam's authority, as was wholly unjustifiable.[202] There was a general agreement in principle (in which Metcalfe himself always joined) that direct interference in the internal concerns of rulers such as the Nizam was objectionable, and to be deprecated. However, the other members of the Council (and the Resident) argued that in the special circumstances of Hyderabad, the general principle of non-interference could not be applied. Since the British Government supported the minister in power, they would be responsible for his oppression, if they did not step in, to protect the people's interests.[203] Hastings' advocacy of non-interference (in the despatch of the 25th October and also in his Minute of the 19th December, 1822),[204] lacked consistency. He, himself, had authorised Russell to exercise "a salutary control over the internal administration of the country," by interposing his "advice and influence."[205] Secondly, it was but a meaningless and mischievous policy which prohibited the British Agent from meddling with the Nizam's affairs, and at the same time urged him to support Chandulal (even if the Nizam wished to remove him).[206] Thirdly, as pointed out by the Court of Directors, where was the consistency in objecting to interference in the Nizam's civil Government, whilst at the same time authorising and sanctioning measures for the payment, organisation and discipline of his army—measures which were extensively adopted in Hyderabad States.[207]

Metcalfe met with similar displeasure from Hastings in another attempt to serve the true interests of the Nizam. When he saw that in its monetary transactions with the Palmer Company, the state was becoming involved in increasing distress, he desired to rescue it from the firm's clutches. In the spring of 1821, he proposed that the debts of the house should be paid off by the Nizam's Government by raising a loan on British guarantee at six per cent in the Calcutta money market.[208] The firm naturally could not relish a proposal of this kind.[209] On Rumbold's representation, Hastings reproached Metcalfe for officially proposing that embarrassing plan, without taking his consent, and for injuring the interests of the firm by his unfriendly attitude towards it. [210] The subject engaged the attention of the Calcutta Government for more than a year, during which time correspondence both public and private, involving much acrimony and acute differences, passed between Calcutta and Hyderabad. For a time Metcalfe's detractors triumphed over him and his scheme was rejected.[211] But eventually Metcalfe emerged successful. Under the instruction of the Directors, the Calcutta Government informed the Resident that the British Government was prepared to advance to the Nizam from their own treasury, up to a crore of rupees, to pay off his debts to the Palmer House. The annual tribute of seven lakhs (*Pesh Kush* for northern Circars) was to be considered a security for the proposed loan.[212] Eventually a sum of nearly eighty lakhs was accordingly advanced to relieve the Nizam's Government from its debtors,[213] and an acute and troublesome problem was thus solved. Yet, so far as the Palmer firm was concerned, this did not end matters. Even after its liquidation, it continued its agitation for redress.[214] In 1824 (February and March) the matters relating to this concern and Hyderabad in general, furnished the occasion for most heated and bitter debates at the India House. The public acts of Hastings (also Metcalfe and others were reviewed in a critical and animated atmosphere where the spirit of partisanship prevailed.[215]

In any case, it was extremely unfortunate that at that time serious and pronounced differences should have divided those two friends. In ranging his influential support behind Rumbold, Plamer and Chandu Lal, against his tried and trusted agent, Hastings no doubt displayed a deplorable partiality. He was unduly credulous in thinking that William Palmer and Company, although reaping enormous profits were yet rendering beneficial service to the Nizam's Government. He failed to realise that his private feelings for friends might possibly injure public interests.[216] So that while there is no reason to question Hastings' motives, his acts certainly proceeded from an erroneous judgment, which caused Metcalfe avoidable grief, and hindered his public work. It must, however, be said to the credit of both Hastings and Metcalfe, that they were reconciled before the former left India.[217]

On the eve of Hastings' departure, almost his last public act of a political nature was to ratify a Treaty concluded with the Nizam on the 12th December 1822, by which the latter was formally released from all claims of *chouth,* past and future, which the Peshwa had asserted over him, and which, with the Peshwa's disappearance, descended to the Company as his successors. This was the chief object of the Treaty, which also provided for the exchange of territory.[218]

Although it certainly destroyed a vexatious demand against the Nizam for all time.[219] It must be admitted that the Company had previously agreed to arbitrate for its abolition. For by a separate and secret Article to the Treaty of 1800, the British Government had given a sort of undertaking to the Nizam that they would use their influence to obtain for him total exemption from the Peshwa's claim of *chouth*.[220]

Whilst negotiations for this treaty had been proceeding, Hastings desired that the Nizam should be asked to make a gift to the Company of sixteen lakhs of rupees for building a cathedral and an episcopal palace at Calcutta. The Resident had been instructed to make it appear a voluntary offer for public purposes on the part of the Nizam.[221] Chandulal was not at all difficult to persuade in a matter of this description, and he readily assured Metcalfe that the Nizam's consent could be taken for granted. And he was right; the Nizam gave his assent to it.[222] But the Board of Control rejected the suggestion, strongly disapproving a demand for such a big sum from a Prince whose public finances were then in a ruinous state of indebtedness.[223] Consequently, the offer was declined. Hastings keenly resented this reprimand, and this incident caused a lasting breach between him and George Canning, who was then at the head of the Board of Control. Hastings wrote Canning an indignant letter, accusing the latter of an anxiety to get rid of him. The letter concluded with these words:—"Adieu, my dear Sir, our public relations will soon terminate."[225]

Conclusion

This survey of the situation of the Subsidiary States reveals a number of features common to them. They all suffered from more or less the same ills, and experienced similar advantages by the suppression of the disorderly elements in society by the agency of an outside Power. Their rulers were losing alike their self-reliance and their self-respect. There appears to be a resemblance between the sullen retirement of Nizam Sikander Jah and the imbecility of

Anand Rao Gaekwar, between the demoralisation of the Wazir of Oudh and the incompetence of the Maharaja of Mysore. Since the time when their predecessors had wielded great authority was not very remote, they were naturally all discontented with their severely controlled position. In all the four major States mentioned in this chapter, there were minister ruling at one time or another, whom the reigning Princes distrusted as agents of the foreign Power.[226] But these Princes were conscious of their utter weakness. So that while their fidelity to the British was not (and could not be) sincere, at the same time, they had not hostile designs against them whatsoever.[227]

In this connection one must further observe that whatever the condition of the Subsidiary States was in the time of Hastings, it was certainly not the result of his policy, but the natural sequel of the measures adopted earlier than his own day. In fairness to Hastings, it must be readily granted that against this class of States, he had no ambitions of an aggressive nature. On the contrary, from the beginning to the end of his term of office,[228] he raised his voice in favour of these allies of the Company and advocated the restoration of them of complete independence in their internal concerns. He claimed with pardonable pride that he had rescued the Wazir of Oudh from the thraldom in which he had been held.[229] He refrained from applying drastic measures to the Maharaja of Mysore, thus deferring by many years that ruler's evil day.[230] In his time, Siyaji Rao Gaekwar was restored to the sovereignty of his domestic affairs after seventeen years of British control of his State. And lastly, he severely condemned.[231] Metcalfe's action in reducing the authority of the Nizam's Government by his minute interference and the employment of European Superintendents in the domination of Hyderabad.[232] It appears that his earlier ideal of a confederation of States, internally autonomous and free, had not altogether disappeared from his vision although it was undoubtedly dimmer than before.

But, with regard to these States, as with others, the other and more important part of his ideal had been fully realised; "we should have thus complete control over the politics of the whole confederacy,"[233] in order to establish a more "operative ascendancy."[234]

REFERENCES

1. Chapters III and V.
2. Signed 10th November, 1801, Aitchison (1909). Vol. I. pp. 123-7.
3. In the form of propositions of the Nawab and answers of the Governor-General, *Loc. Cit.*, (1909), pp. 127-35.
4. This double title meant the Nawab (Ruler) of Oudh and Wazir (Minister) of the Mughal Empire. The latter title became hereditary from the great Nawab Safdar Jung, who was the powerful Minister of the Emperor of Delhi.
5. Articles 3 & 5 of the Treaty of 1801. *Op. Cit.*
6. Bishop Heber's *Narrative,* (1829), Vol. II, pp. 7-8. Irwin's "*Garden of India." chapters on Oudh History and affairs* (1880), pp. 108-10, Prinsep. *Transactions,* etc., Vol. 1, pp. 217-8.
7. Baillie to Nawab Wazir, 2nd July, 1883. p. 533, *Oude Papers, Home Misc.,* Vol. 518. In this letter he emphatically told the Nawab that "the grant of a district in farm, the establishment of a court of Adaulat, the reform or alteration of any branch of the police of your Excellency's dominions, however frequently these measures have occurred. Without my previous knowledge or concurrence, are measures that unquestionably required your previous consultations with our government, and your conformity to our advice in the execution of them."
8. For instance, both the Resident and the Governor-General repeatedly urged the Nawab to grant pensions and restore their property to Ali Naki Khan and Hussain Ali Khan. (Minto to Nawab Wazir, 8th May, 1812, pp. 283-5, Baillie to Nawab Wazir, 29th Apr., 1813, p. 103, Baillie to Minto reporting his conferences with the Nawab about the two cases, 29th Sept., 1813 pp. 534-9, etc., *Oude Papers Op. Cit.*) The disposal of Tehsin Ali Khan's personal property, also became a subject of similar interference, (Baillie to Adam, 24th Aug. 1813, pp. 520-1, and Adam to Baillie, 3rd Sept. 1813, pp. 524-5, *Loc. Cit.*) Again the settlement of the younger Begum's claims was brought about through the Resident's intervention (Baillie to Adam, 16th July, 1813, Baillie

to the Begum, 10th July, 1813 and Adam to Baillie, 30th July, 1813, *Loc. Cit.*, pp. 516-20).

9. In his discussions with the Wazir, Baillie assumed an intimidating tone which forced the former into an outward acquiescence, (Baillie to Minto, 30th Aug., 1813, pp. 527-30 and 29th Sept., 1813, pp. 534-40) but which was regarded by the Wazir as coercion. (Baillie to Adam, 13th Dec. 1813, p. 551). The Nawab complained of the disrespectful tone of the Resident's addressed (Nawab Wazir to Baillie, 7th Jan. 1813, pp. 340-2). His distress at Baillie's interference, and the consequent loss of his own dignity became painful to him. (Capt. McLeod' statement, pp. 902-4.) Baillie himself speaks of "my immediate control through the operation of fear on his (i.e., the Nawab Wazir's) mind." (Baillie to Minto, 30th Aug. 1813. *Loc. cit.*, p. 527).
10. This was very frequent. For example, the case of the Zamindars of Dariabad. Baillie to Edmonstone, 27th Feb., 1812, pp. 263-4, and Baillie to the Nawab Wazir, 15th Jan. 1812, pp. 264-4, *Loc. Cit.*
11. Minto's letter to Nawab Wazir, 28th Dec. 1810, contained these final proposals, *Oude Papers,* pp. 131-3, *Op. Cit.*
12. Both Minto and Baillie united in maintaining that demand right up to the closing days of the former's term of office. (For example, Minto's strong note to Sadat Ali, 8th May, 1812, pp. 283, Baillie's conferences with Sadat Ali. pp. 497-99, 501, 527-8, Minto to Sadat Ali, 2nd July, 1813, p. 507, etc., etc., *Oude Papers.)*
13. The Nawab would hear subserviently what the Resident said, and would agree with it (e.g.p. 536). He would promise to act (pp. 540, 544) but in the end, evasions and excuses would follow, (pp. 551-2, etc.) *Loc. Cit.*
14. Summary of operations, etc., *Parliamentary Papers* 1831-32, Vol. VIII, *Political Appendix* p. 95.
15. Baillie to Adam, 28th Aug., p. 525. *Oude Papers Op. Cit.*
16. Baillie to Adam, 24th Aug., pp. 520-1, *Loc. Cit.*
17. Adam to Baillie, 3rd Sept. 1813, pp. 551-54, *Loc. Cit.*
18. Baillie to Adam, 23rd Nov., 1813, pp. 51-54, *Loc. Cit.*
19. Hastings to Nawab Wazir, 31st Dec. 1813, p. 564, *Loc. Cit.*
20. Adam to Baillie, 31st Dec. 1813, pp. 564-7, *Loc. Cit.*
21. Political letter to Bengal, 8th May, 1815, p. 844, *Loc. Cit.*
22. Hastings to Nawab Wazir, 7th Jan. 1814, pp. 579-81, *Loc. Cit.*, stating the position in a frank and friendly spirit.

23. Baillie to Adam, 8th Mar., 1814, pp. 604-5, *Loc. Cit.*
24. According to the provision of the Treaty of 1801, Art. 6, *Loc. Cit.*
25. Adam to Baillie, 25th Mar. 1814, pp. 608-10, *Oude Papers.*
26. Political letter to Bengal, 22nd Mar. 1816, p. 857, *Loc. Cit.*
27. Viz.: "always advise with, and act in conformity to, the counsel of the officers of the said Honourable Company," Art. 6.
28. Baillie to Wazir, 2nd July, 113, p. 5833, and also the conditions laid down for the Nawab's acceptance before he could be allowed to proceed on his long-contemplated journey. (Baillie to Minto, 5th June, 1813, p. 502) *Oude Papers.*
29. "In urging the adoption of that most necessary reform. I exercised a right derived from the specific provisions of the existing engagements, nay, I fulfilled a positive obligation imposed upon this Government, by an express article of the treaty of 1801". Minto to Nawab Wazir, 8th May, 1812, p. 283, and another of 2nd July, 1813, remonstrating with the Wazir for not complying with his demands about reforms, p. 507, *Loc. Cit.*
30. Edmonstone to Baillie, 6th July, 1811, contains the best vindication of that interpretation on the part of the Nawab Wazir, p. 235, *Loc. Cit.*
31. Baillie repudiated this emphatically in his letter to the Wazir, 2nd July 1813, p. 533, *Loc. Cit.*
32. The Bengal Government (in Minto's absence) interpreted it in a liberal manner and instructed the Resident not to use compulsion on the Nawab in the matter of reforms. It was held that the British Government would not be right in withholding the aid of troops from the Nawab. Edmonstone to Baillie, 6th July, 1811, *Oude Papers,* pp. 284-7.
33. Adam to Baillie, 12th Nov. 1814 (this decision was given by Hastings after he had seen the working of the relations for a year, and when matters approached a crisis in the time of the successor of Sadat Ali). p. 919, *Loc. Cit.*
34. His *Private Journal,* Vol. I, 200-31.
35. Baillie to Nugent, 11th July, *Oude Papers,* p. 614, *Loc. Cit.*
36. Calculated by Baillie to be about 13 millions sterling (his evidence before the Parliamentary Committee, *Loc. Cit.,* Vol. XIV, p. 60, 1831-32). Although Bishop Heber in his *Narrative* put it over 2 millions sterling (*Loc. Cit.* 4th Edition, Vol. II, p. 78). But obviously Baillie's estimate should be regarded as more reliable.

37. Nawab Shamsudaula to Hastings, 11th Oct. 1814, *Oude Papers, Loc. Cit.*, pp. 869-70.

38. Baillie was very satisfied at the cordial way in which the new Wazir behaved to him (Baillie to Moira, 15th July 1814, *Loc. Cit.*, p. 618.)

39. Adam to Brooke (Agent to the Governor-General at Benares) 11th Nov. 1814, *Loc. Cit.*, p. 868.

40. Heber, *Loc. Cit.*, p. 78, and Baillie to Adam, 5th Aug. 1815, *Oude Papers,* p. 695.

41. Baillie to Adam, 2nd Sept. 1814, *Loc. Cit.*, p. 621.

42. *Ibid,* and Baillie to Lieut.-Col. Burrell, 27th Aug. 1814, pp. 622-23, Col. Frith to Baillie, 5th Sept. 1814, p. 627, and 8th Sept., p. 628, Baillie to Adam, 20th Sept., pp. 629-30, and 25th Oct. 636, Lieut.-Col. Burrell to Baillie, 4th Nov. 639-40, and again pp. 642-52, etc., etc. *Loc. Cit.*

43. He saw in the new arrangements the loss of his authority and the reduction in his revenue because of the payment of 10% commission to the revenue collectors introduced on the lines adopted in the ceded provinces. (Nawab Wazir to Hastings, received on the 23rd June, 1815, p. 686, and McLeod's statement, p. 901, *Loc. Cit.*)

44. Clarke and McLeod interviewed Thompson, the Governor-General's secretary, and later both saw Hastings himself, *Private Journal,* pp. 178-81, Governor-General's Minute of 30th Nov. 1814, particularly Gibert's interview with the Nawab Wazir, *Oude Papers,* pp. 920-3. He complained specifically how the Resient forced on him a physician (Wilson) whom he did not want, in preference to his father's (Law) whom he liked, also that the Resident and disallowed the time-honoured practice of beating the *Nobat* (Big Drum) at the Gateway. *Private Journal* Vol. I, pp. 204-6.

45. Ricketts' conference with the Nawab Wazir, on 1st Nov., pp. 875-6, Agha Mir's message, pp. 880-1, conference between the Wazir and Adam and Swinton on 2nd Nov., pp. 881-2, and another conference between him and Adam, Swinton and Ricketts on 4th Nov., pp. 885-9, *Oude Papers*.

46. McLeod's to Adam, 9th Nov. 1814, p. 891. They were all declared innocent. Adam to McLeod and others, 12th Nov. 1814, pp. 905-6, *Loc. Cit. Private Journal,* Vol. I, pp. 210-13.

47. Hastings wrote:—"The issue of the intrigue was none of my business. I had only to accept the Nawab Wazir's own statements

and to concur in what he chose to say was his wish." His Minute, 30th Nov. 1814, *Oude Papers,* p. 926.

48. His Minute of 30th Nov. *Op. Cit.,* p. 924, *Oude Papers.*

49. Hastings' Minute, 30th Nov. 1814, p. 923, Baillie though him to be a man of noble birth, talent and education (Baillie to Adam, 29th Apr. 1815, p. 950). In an anonymous letter received by Hastings, Agha Mir's parentage was described as low and even doubtful. (p. 1,000), *Loc. Cit.*

50. The Nawab made that request to Hastings (Minute of 30th Nov. 1814, p. 923). Irwin, *Op. Cit.* p. III.

51. The Resident defended them in his reports. (Baillie to Adam, 29th May, 1815, p. 681-3. It was arranged to have the investiture of the ministers preformed by the Governor-General in open Durbar. *Private Jornal,* Vol. I, pp. 227-8.

52. Baillie to Adam, 18th July, pp. 688-93, 5th Aug. 1815, pp. 694-5; and 4th Sept., p.697, *Oude Papers.* Irwin writes:—"Agha Mir plundered his master in almost every possible way," and that he had appropriated half a million sterling out of public works fund. *Op Cit.,* p. 111. His violence and selfish aggrandisement described by Heber, *Narrative, Op. Cit.,* Vol. II, pp. SC-1.

53. Adam to Baillie, 12th Nov. 1814, p. 919, *Oude Papers. Op. Cit.*

54. Nawab's papers of requests, 9th Nov., and Governor-General's reply, 12th Nov. 1814, *Oude Papers,* pp. 909-15.

55. His Minute emphatically upholding the character of an ally for the Nawab of Oudh, and the preservation of his independence within his territory. (15th May, No. 6, Bengal Secret Consultations, 21st June, 1814.)

56. He was gratified to hear later how his action was remembered by he Wazir in a tone of affectionate energy, *Private Journal,* 18th Sept., 1817, Vol. II, p. 213.

57. Governor-General's letter to the Secret Committee, (31st Aug. 1815, p. 515 onwards, paras 12-15, *Bengal Secret Letters*). Hastings to Nugent, 29th Oct. 1814, p. 711, *Oude Papers,* Baillie wrote " I was instructed by his Lordship's secretary. Mr. Ricketts, to open a negotiation with the Wazier, for the loan of a crore of rupees to the Honourable Company, to appear as a voluntary offer," to Adam. 29th Apr., but forwarded on 20th Sept. 1815, *Oude Papers,* p. 952.

58. Baillie to Adam, 16th Mar. 1815 *Oude Papers,* pp, 722-3.

59. *Private Journal, Op. Cit.,* Vol. II. pp. 54-5.

60. Treaty signed 1st May 1816, Aitchison Vol. I, pp. 155-6, (1909).

61. As he himself wrote in his *Journal.* "This agreement enables me to assert that the Gurkha war has not cost the Company one single shilling." *Op. Cit.,* Vol. II, p. 121.

62. In his long letter to Adam, 29th Apr., though despatched on 20th Sept. 1813, *Oude Papers,* pp. 936-62.

63. Hastings' Minute, 3rd Feb. 1816, pp. 966-94.

64. The Council unanimously concurred in that decision. The Minutes of the Governor-General and Councillors, 31st Oct. 1815, *Oude Papers,* p. 963.

65. Correspondence between the Resident and the British military Officers in 1815, pp. 621-52, and 710, etc. *Oude Papers.* Wilson (1854) Bk. II, p. 503, Heber's *Narrative,* Vol. II, (1829) pp. 83-4.

66. His new designation was:— "Abu Muzzaffar, Moizuddin, Shah-i-Zaman Ghaziud-din-Hyder, Shah, Padsha-i-Avadh" (Wilson, Bk. II, p. 504).

67. Hastings observed at Lucknow, that the Royal Princes, although residing there, as the Nawab's pensioners, received, from the latter, marks of ceremonial courtesy due to their regal blood.

68. Hastings' *Summary of Operations,* etc. *Op. Cit.,* p. 110.

69. *Loc. Cit.,* p. 112.

70. Irwin, *Op. Cit.,* p. 112.

71. Book II, *Op. Cit.,* pp. 505-6.

72. Art. 14 of the Treaty of Mysore, 1799, is fairly comprehensive on this point (Aitchison, *Op. Cit.,* Vol. IX, p. 224, (1909 Ed.) and resembles the similar provisions of Art. 6 of the Oudh Treaty of 1801 (already referred to).

73. Partition Treaty of 22nd June, 1799, by which the Company's net share was territory yielding 5,37,170 pagodas, and the Nizam's 5,37,332 pagodas (pp. 57-8). The Peshwa's share, worth 2,63,957 pagodas was further divided between the allies, since the former declined to accept it, (p. 60). The territory retained for the Maharaja for Mysore was estimated to yield 13,74,076 pagodas (pp.63-5). In addition to this, the English kept the town of Seringapatam (p. 59), Aitchison, Vol. IX, *Op. Cit.,* (1909).

74. Treaty of 8th July, 1799, particularly Arts, 4 & 5, (pp. 221-2) Aitchison, *Op. Cit.,* Vol. IX, (1909).

75. When Purniya was first made prime minister, the Resident, Colonel clouds exercised a close check over him, but later he

released that control. (Cole's dispatch of Madras Government, 10 Feb., No. 3, Bengal Secret Consultations, 1 Mar., 1814.)

76. *Mysore and Coorg Gazetteer,* by L. Rice, (1877), Vol. I, p. 297.

77. *Ibid,* also Major E. Bell, *"The Mysore Reversion"* (1965), p. 12.

78. *Ibid.* (Bell).

79. Cole, the Resident, to the Chief Secretary, Fort St. George, 18th Dec. 1813, Bengal Secret Consultations, No. 1, 21st Jan. 1814. Also from Coles Madras Government, 10th Feb., No. 3, Bengal Secret Consultations, 18th March 1814.

80. Rice, *Op. Cit.*, p. 298, Bell, *Op. Cit.*, p. 14.

81. "Not a day has passed of late in which the Rajah has not secretly pressed upon Bakir Sahib the situation of Prime Minister, but he always declined it, replying 'I shall obey the wishes of the Resident and whatever situation he gives me I will act in it.'" Cole to Madras Government, 10th Feb. 1814, No. 3, Bengal Secret Consultations, 18th Mar. 1814. And later, he reported to the same authority that the Raja's mind was poisoned to the greatest possible extent against Bakir. (Letter 8th Dec., No. 49, Bengal Secret Consultations, 29th Dec. 1814.)

82. Cole's Despatches to the Fort St. George Government, 10 Feb., No. 3, Bengal Secret Consultations, 18th Mar. 1814, 22nd June, No. 45, 4th Aug. No. 47, and 8th Dec., No. 49, Bengal Secret Consultations, 29th Dec. 1814, and 17th Jan., No. 68, Bengal Secret Consultations, 30th May, 1815.

83. Despatch from the Bengal Govt. to Madras Govt., 25th Mar., No. 2, Bengal Secret Consultations, 25th Mar. 1814.

84. Cole to Chief Secretary Madras, 22nd June, No. 45, 4th Aug., No. 47, and 8th Dec., No. 49, Bengal Secret Consultations, 29th Dec., 1814.

85. Cole to Adam, 1st May, 1818, *enclosures to secret letters from Bengal* (accompanying Governor-General's letter to Secret Committee, 11th July, 1818, Vol. 18, *Secret letters from Bengal*).

86. Hastings to the Secret Committee, 11th July, 1818, Bengal Secret Letters, Vol. 18.

87. Treaty of that year, Art. 3, Aitchison, Vol. X, p. 130, (1909).

88. Art. 5 of the Treaty, *Loc. Cit.* p. 136.

89. Art. 5 of the Treaty, *Ibid.*

90. The Diwan fled when beaten, and killed himself. His body was gibbeted at Trivandrum. His brother was seized and executed for his cruel conduct. Wilson, *Op. Cit.* pp. 265-7.

91. Col Munro's evidence before the Select Committee on 27th March, 1832. *(Parliamentary Papers.* 1831-32, Vol. XIV, pp. 20 and 22.

92. Aitcheson, *Op. Cit.*, Vol. X, pp. 101-11.

93. Aitchison, *Op. Cit.*, Vol. VIII, pp. 32-33.

94. Signed 6th June, 1802. Aitchison, Vol. VIII, pp. 33-5.

95. *Ibid.* Articles 4 and 5.

96. Dated 29th July, 1802, Aitchison (1909). Vol. VIII, pp. 36-39.

97. This was dated 8th June, 1802. Aitchison, Vol. VIII. p. 46. The Governor also gave to this minister the valuable village of Bhatta near Surat in Jagir, for his services to the British government. (Grant dated 6th June, 1802, *Ibid.*)

98. Adopted on the 23rd May, 1803. R. Wallace, *The Guicovar and His Relation with the British Government.* (1863) p. 90.

99. Wallace, *On. Cit.*, p. 79, pp. 90-91 and pp. 141-4.

100. Treaty of 21st April, 1805 (Aitchison (1909), Vol. VIII, pp. 61-66). As the revenues of the territory formerly assigned to the Company fell short of the expected amount, a further cession was made by a memorandum of 12th July, 1808, to the value of Rs. 1,76,168 a year. (*Loc. Cit.*, pp. 69-71.)

101. Raoji died on 18th July, 1803. His services to the British Government are thus described by Wallace, "that he placed in its hands the virtual sovereignty of a magnificent province" and those to his own master. " that he released him from perils far too great to have been surmounted by his feeble energies." Wallace, *Op, Cit.*, p. 90.

102. *Loc. Cit.*, p. 85. Kanoji was of independent and enterprising nature. His great ambition was to free his own country from British subjection, to reconquer Kathiawar and expel the traitor Raoji Appaji, Wallace, *Op. Cit.*, pp. 93-2.

103. *Loc. Cit.*, p. 87.

104. *Loc. Cit.*, p. 104.

105. His last letter to the Bombay Government. Wallace, *Op. Cit.*, p. 155.

106. *Loc. Cit.*, pp. 105-7, and pp. 128-133.

107. *Loc. Cit.*, pp. 123-4.

108. *Loc. Cit.*, pp. 157-8.

109. *Loc. Cit.*, p. 159.

110. As Carnac reported on 22nd Mar. 1812, Wallace, *Op. Cit.*, p. 187.

111. *Loc. Cit.*, p. 207.
112. Chapter III, ante.
113. Elphinstone to Adam, 23rd Aug., No. 85, with an enclosure (an intercepted letter) No. 86, Bengal Secret Consultations, 7th Oct. 1815.
114. It was further reported that through Sita Ram's intrigues the forces of Dhar, under Bapu Raghunath were assembling on the frontier of Gujarat. The Resident had to take military measures against that possible danger. (Carnac to Warden, 29th Aug., No. 2) Bengal Secret Consultations, 13th Oct., 1815, again, 21st. Aug., No. 16 and 23rd Aug., No. 17, Bengal Secret Consultations, 20th Oct. 1815.
115. Carnac to Warden, 9th Sept., No. 23, Bengal Secret Consultations, 20th Oct. 1815.
116. Warden to Adam (enclosing a copy of Carnac's Despatch) 20th Sept., No. 2, Bengal Secret Consultations, 3rd Nov. 1815; also Wilson, *Op. Cit.*, Vol. II, p. 105 and Prinsep *Op. Cit.*, Vol. I. p. 323.
117. The Bombay Government also took a decided view in the matter and insisted on Sita Ram's removal from Baroda. Warden to Carnac, 18th Oct., No. 3, (in which the Supreme government concurred) Adam to Warden, 25th Nov., No. 4, (Bengal Secret Consultations, 25th Nov. 1815). Also Prinsep, *Op. Cit.*, Vol. 1, p. 323, wilson, II, p. 105.
118. Articles 5 and 15 of the Treaty. Aitchison (1909), Vol. VI, pp. 64-70.
119. The Treaty was signed on 6th November 1817, and ratified by the Governor-General on 12th March 1818, Aitchison, (1909), Vol. VIII, p. 75.
120. Hastings to the governor of Bombay, 26th September, No. 18. Warden to Adam. 10th September, No. 19, and Carnac to Warden, 26th August, No. 2C, Bengal Secret Consultations, 17th October 1817.
121. Wallace, *Op. Cit.*, pp. 226-7 and 235.
122. Elphinstone's minute of 18th April, 1820, Wallace, *Op. Cit.*, p. 278, and also pp. 233-4.
123. Appendix to Elphinstone's minute of 18th April. Wallace, *Op. Cit.*, pp. 288-9.
124. Resident Baroda (to Chief Secretary Bombay, 24th June, 1819) calculated that amount at Rs. 39,63,956. Wallace *Op. Cit.*, p. 232.

125. Wallace, *Op. Cit.*, pp. 229-30.
126. Dhakji was drawn from Bombay, and forced on Fateh Singh by Carnac, who compelled him to send away his own favourite, Manik Das. (Wallace, *Op. Cit.* pp. 208 and 209-11.) Siyaji complained to Elphinstone that Dhakji misused his influence over Carnac to his own selfish ends. *Loc. Cit.*
127. Elphinstone, on his return to Bombay, recorded the whole transaction in a Minute, 18th Apr. 1820. Wallace, *Op. Cit.*, pp. 251-78, proclamation issued 7th Apr. 1820, Wallace *Op. Cit.*, pp. 308-9. The instructions embodying the principles of the agreement sent to Resident Williams per Warden, 3rd May, 1820. Wallace, *Op. Cit.*, pp. 309-15. And written paper given by Elphinstone to Siyaji Rao 3rd Apr. 1820, Apr. 1820, Aitchison, (1909) *Op. Cit.*, Vol. VIII, p. 80.)
128. Wilson, *Op. Cit.*, Vol. II, p. 471 and Elphinstone's Minute (Wallace, *Op. Cit.*, pp. 273-4).
129. Elphinstone's Minute (Wallace, pp. 275-6) the Memorandum, Wallace, pp. 306-7.
130. Metcalfe to Warden, 17th June, 1820 (Wallace, *Op. Cit.*, p. 317).
131. His Minute, 16th Apr. 1821 (Wallace, *Op. Cit.*, pp. 319-324).
132. Its strength was increased in 1800 by two battalions of infantry and one regiment of cavalry, making the total 8 battalions of infantry of 1,000 Sepoys each, and tow regiments of cavalry of 500 horse each. For the upkeep of the additional force, the Nizam ceded to the Company all the territory which had fallen to his share by the two partition treatise with Mysore, in 1792 and 1799. (Arts. 3 and 5 of the treaty with the Nizam, 1800, Aitchison, (1909) Vol. IX, pp. 68-69.)
133. Treaty of 12th Oct. 1800, *Loc. Cit.*, pp. 68-72.
134. Art. 15 of the Treaty, *Loc. Cit.*, pp. 71-72.
135. Russell to Hastings 24th Nov., 1819, No. 13, Bengal Secret Consultations, 22nd Jan. 1820.
136. Barlow's Minute of 2nd Oct. 1806 (Wilsoon, B,. I, p. 31).
137. Sydenham to Edmonstone, 8th Sept., 1806 (Kaye's *Life of Metcalfe* (1854), Vol. II, p. 5.).
138. Sydenham's private letters to Edmonstone (Kaye's *Metacalfe, Op. Cit.* Vol. II, p. 7), Metaclfe's Minute of 13th May, 1829 (Kaye's *Selections from the Papers of Lord Metcalfe*, p. 223).

139. Kaye's *Metcalfe papers*, pp. 222-3, Kaye's *Life of Metcalfe, Op. Cit.*, Vol. II, pp. 8-9. The British protected Chandulal "against the jealousy of the Nizam ad the intrigues of Mooner-ool-Moolk." Russell to Hastings, 24th Nov. 1819, No. 13, Bengal Secret Consultations, 22nd Jan. 1820. The Nizam's indifference to public affairs can be judged from the fact that when in 1815 the Resident conveyed to him the news of the Bhopal negotiations, he took no interest, one way or the other. He merely enquired whether Bhopal was on the North or on the South side of the Narbada. (Russell to Moira, 22nd Jan., No. 93, Bengal Secret Consultations, 25th Feb. 1815)

140. Russell's estimate of Chandulal's character quoted by Syed Hoossain Bilgrami and Willmott; *Historical and Descriptive Sketch of H. H. the Nizam's Dominions.* (1803), Vol. I, pp. 136-8, and also Russell to Hastings 24th Nov. 1819, No. 13, Bengal Secret Consultations, 22nd Jan. 1820.

141. Kaye's *Metcalfe papers, Op. Cit.*, pp. 98, 115, 225.

142. In Metcalfe's words, written in 1829, "the subsequent history of the Nizam's country and our further interference therein, turns entirely on the character of this minister, Chandoolali." Kaye's *Metcalfe Papers, Op. Cit.*, p. 224.

143. Sutherland: *Sketches of the Relations Subsisting Between the British Government in India and the Different Native States, pp. 54.5.*

144. Russell to Hastings, 24th November, 1819, No. 13, Bengal Secret Consultations, 22nd January 1820. Metcalfe to Swinton, 31st August 1822, paras, 9, 14, and 15, No. 1, Bengal Secret Consultations, 20th December 1822.

145. Swinton to Metcalfe, 25th October, No. 4, Bengal Secret Consultations, 20th December 1829, para. 8.

146. Russell to Hastings (then Moira), 23rd August, No. 124. To Adam, 21st August, No. 116, Bengal Secret Consultations, 20th September 1815.

147. Russell to Hastings, 23rd August. *Loc. Cit.*

148. Russell to Officer in Command, at Bellary, 21st Aug., No. 118, to Doveton. No. 119, Bengal Secret Consultations, 20th September, 1815.

149. Russell to Hastings, 5th Sept. No. 33, Bengal Secret Consultations, 27th Sept. 31st Aug., No. 55, Bengal Secret Consultations, 7th Oct., to Adam 30th Aug., No. 127, Bengal Secret Consultations, 20th Sept., 1815.

150. Chandulal to Russell, 1st Sept., No. 34, Bengal Secret Consultations, 27th Sept. Russell to Hastings, 30th Nov., 1815, No. 11, Bengal Secret Consultations, 6th January 1816.

151. *The Calcutta Review,* Vol. XI., 1849, an article on the Nizam's contingent, p. 156.

152. *Loc. Cit.*, pp. 156, 159, 170-2.

153. *Loc. Cit.*, pp. 162-4.

154. *Loc. Cit.*, pp. 174-5.

155. *Hyderabad Papers,* printed by the order of the Court of Directors, *Home Misc.*, Vol. 517, p. 9.

156. *Calcutta Review, Op. Cit.*, p. 176.

157. 10th Nov. 1819, *Hyderabad Papers, Op. Cit.*, p. 31.

158. The *Calcutta Review, Op. Cit.*, p. 183. Metcalfe's estimate was above forty lakhs. (Kaye's *Metaclfe papers, Op. Cit.*, p. 224).

159. Kaye's *Life of Metcalfe,* Vol. II, pp. 15-16.

160. Vol. XI, p. 175. He writes "Major Doveton's appointment was thought superfluous; as it cost the Nizam's Government some sixty thousand rupees a year, it might have been dispensed with." *Ibid.* He gives the amount of the table allowances drawn by officers, p. 183, *Loc. Cit.*

161. Russell to Hastings, 24th Nov. 1819, No. 13. Bengal Secret Consultations, 22nd Jan. 1820. The ruinous condition of the country described by Hastings (in his letter to Russell of 26th Oct., 1819 *Hyderabad Papers,* p. 88).

162. Russell to Hastings. 11th June, No. 5, Bengal Secret Consultations, 5th July, 1817, and 8th Dec. 1817 No. 71, Bengal Secret Consultations, 30th Jan. 1818.

163. These proposals were embodied in Russell's Despatch to Hastings, 24th Nov. 1819, No. 13, Bengal Secret Consultations, 22nd Jan. 1820.

164. Metcalfe to Russell, 22nd Jan. 1820, No. 14, Bengal Secret Consultations, of date.

165. Russell to Hastings, 30th April, No. 1, Bengal Secret Consultations, 30th September 1820.

166. Russell to Hastings, 1st Sept., No. 8, Bengal Secret Consultations, 30th September 1820.

167. Metcalfe to Russell, 23rd Sept., No. 10, Bengal Secret Consultations, 30th September 1820.

168. Kaye's *Life of Metcalfe,* Vol. II, pp. 30-31. He was pressed by Russell to accept the Hyderabad Residency on those very hopes. (His letter to Metcalfe in April and May 1820, *Loc. Cit.,* Vol. I, pp. 492-96.)

169. William Palmer's Memorial to Lord Amherst, 12th May, 1824, *Home misc.,* Vol. 158, pp. 1-2. Adam to Russell, 22nd Apr. 1814, instructing the Resident to afford all facilities to the firm, *Loc. Cit.,* MS. pp. 35-6, and Briggs *The Nizam* (1861) Vol. II, pp. 165-9.

170. According to Act 37, George III, Cap. 142, Section 28, of 1797 by which British subjects were prohibited under pain of penalty from having any kind of dealings with the Indian Princes or States. (Section reproduced in *Hyderabad Papers, Op. Cit.,* p. 8)

171. The Instrument of Lincence issued on 23rd July. *Hyderabad Papers. Op. Cit.,* Vol. 517, pp. 5-6.

172. The Instrument of Lincence issued on 23rd July. *Hyderabad Papers, Op. Cit.* Vol. 517, pp. 5-6. Russell's letter to the Court of Directors, 21st Sept. 1824. *Home Misc.* Vol. 758, MS., pp. and 113, Hastings' Minute, 17th June 1820, *Hyderabad Papers.* p. 44 and Metcalfe's Minute, of 11th Dec. 1828, (Kaye's *Life of Metcalfe,* Vol. II. pp. 45-6).

173. Palmer's Memorial, Vol. 758, *Op. Cit.,* p.3.

174. Political letter from Bengal (*Hyderabad Papers,* Vol. 517, pp. 9-10). One member, Stuart, dissented, and recommended further enquiry before sanctioning the arrangement (His Minute *Loc. Cit.,* pp. 22-4). The Governor-General thought any further enquiry unnecessary, being satisfied by the oral statement of Sir William Rumbold before the Council. (His Minute *Loc. Cit.,* pp. 31-4.)

175. Chandu Lal to Russell (Hyderabad Paper, p. 39).

176. Russell to Metcalfe, 19th May, 1820, *Loc. Cit.,* p. 38.

177. Palmer's Memorial, Vol. 758, *Op. Cit.,* p. 4.

178. Stuart's Minute, 10th June, 1820,. *Hyderabad Papers,* p. 43. The nominal rate was 18%, but with the bonus it amounted to about 25%, p.a.

179. Hastings had the support of Fendall. But Adam and Stuart strongly opposed the sanctioning of the loan. Hastings, since he was personally interested in one of the partners, did not at first wish to take a share in the decision. (His Minute, 17th June, pp. 44-6). But when the Council was found to be opposed to the measure, he had to change his mind and voted in its favour. (Minute of 14th July, p. 55.) Other Minutes of the Councillors, Fendall, Adam, Stuart, pp. 43-54, *Hyderabad Papers, Op. Cit.*

180. Metcalfe of Russell, July 11th 1820, *Loc. Cit.*, p. 55.
181. Letter to Bengal, 24th May, 1820 *Hyderabad Papers*, pp. 7-8.
182. Swinton to Russell, 16th Dec. 1820, *Loc. Cit.*, p. 70.
183. Letter to Bengal 28th Nov. 1821. *Loc. Cit.*, pp. 70-84.
184. Kaye's *Life of Metcalfe*, Vol. II, pp. 26-7, Sutherland, *Op. Cit.*, p. 55. Metcalfe to Swinton, paras. 11, 12, & 15, 31st Aug., No. 1 Bengal Secret Consultations, 20th Dec. 1822.
185. Munir-ul-Mulk told Metcalfe how Chandulal brided the servants and members of the (Minur's) and the Nizam's household, (*Hyderabad Papers, Op. Cit.*, p. 185). Also Kaye's *Metcalfe Papers*, pp. 100 and 225.
186. Sutherland, *Op. Cit.*, p. 66.
187. Amounting to Rs. 64,800 per annum. (Wm. Palmer Rs. 2,000, his sons Rs. 12,00 each, Hasting Palmer Rs. 1,000 per mensum.) Metcalfe to Swinton, 1st Aug. 1822, *Hyderabad Papers*, pp. 181-2.
188. Because of the renewal of the old debts and the payment in cash of far less than the amount stipulated. Kaye's *Life of Metcalfe*, Vol. II, p. 42, also Metcalfe to Swinton, 1st Aug. 1822. *Hyderabad Papers*, p. 181.
189. *Loc. Cit.*, pp. 181 and 184.
190. Even Chandulal complained to the Resident of "the interest upon interest, interest upon interest" (*Sood dur Sood dur Sood*") charged by the Palmer Company. (Metcalfe to Swonton, 3rd Sept., No. 2, Bengal Secret Consultations, 20th Dec. 1822.)
191. Metcalfe to Hastings, Kaye's *Life of Metcalfe*, Vol. II, p. 59.
192 Metcalfe to Swinton, 30th Sept. 1822, *Hyderabad Papers*, pp. 244-5.
193. Kaye's *Life of Metcalfe*, Vol. II p. 45.
194. As he wrote to John Palmer, *Loc. Cit.*, p. 94.
195. He made detailed enquiries into the Revenue management of the State. He desired the ministers to discontinue the clandestine allowances to the Residency servants, and the presentation of fruits, dinners, etc. (Kaye's *Life of Metcalfe*, Vol. II, p. 28.)
196. *Loc. Cit.*, pp. 30 & 32.
197. Kaye's *Life of Metcalfe*, Vol. II, p. 35, Sutherland *Op. Cit.*, pp. 57-9. Metcalfe to Swinton, 7th Nov. 1821. *Hyderabad papers*, pp. 155-7.
198. Metcalfe to Swinton, 31st Aug., No. 1, Bengal Secret Consultations, 20th Dec. 1822, paras. 18-22.

199. *Loc. Cit.*, prra 28.

200. Kaye's *Life of Metcalfe*, Vol. II, p. 37. (Hastings' most encouraging letter to him in April 1821), also Swinton to Metcalfe, 7th Apr. 1821, in which Metcalfe's plans of settlement are called "highly judicious." Although it must be said in fairness to Hastings that he had written a Minute on the 27th May 1821, which was not officially recorded until Sept. 1822, in which he disapproved of the minute interference which Metcalfe exercised. (*Hyderabad Papers*, p. 207.)

201. Chandulal to Hastings, (no date received 16th Aug. 1822) *Hyderabad papers*, pp. 173-4. He feared that the Nizam might dismiss him, and that Metcalfe would not support him. These imaginary fears led him into that intrigue. (Metcalfe to Swinton, 3rd Sept., No. 2, Bengal Secret Consultations, 20th Dec. 1822, paras, 4, 5, 9, 10 and 11).

202. Swinton to Metcalfe, 25th Oct., No. 4, Bengal Secret Consultations, 20th Dec. 1822, paras, 2, 3 & 4. From this view, although officially expressed in the name of the Governor-General-in-Council, all his colleagues Adam, Fendall and Bayley, expressed their dissent. (Minutes respectively, 1st Nov., No. 5, 19th Nov. No. 6, 25th Nov., No. 7, Bengal Secret Consultations, 20th Dec. 1822.)

203. *Ibid*.

204. No. 8, Bengal Secret Consultations, 20th Dec. 1822.

205. Metcalfe to Russell, 22nd 1820, No. 14, Bengal Secret Consultations of date.

206. These self-contradictory instructions were issued by Hastings in the same despatch of 25th Oct. 1822. He directed Metcalfe to let the Nizam understand by intelligent hints that the removal of Chandulal would cause a material change in the connection between the two Governments, and that the British Government would "claim for itself as standing in the Paishwah's position all those rights over the Hyderabad Dominions which that prince had possessed." etc., para, 9, p. 227. *Hyderabad Papers, Op. Cit.*

207. Court of Directors to the Governor-General in Council, 21st June, 1824, *Hyderabad Papers, Op. Cit.*, p. 388.

208. Metcalfe to Swinton, 5th Apr. 1821 (*Hyderabad Papers*, p. 194).

209. Although, perhaps, to mark time, they showed outward willingness to cooperate with the Resident in the matter. (Their letter to Metcalfe, *Home Misc.* Vol. 758, MS. p. 45.)

210. Hastings to Metcalfe, 27th Aug. 1821. Kaye's *Life of Metcalfe*, Vol. II, pp. 54-5.

211. Hastings had the support of Fendall in voting against the loan, either from the Company's treasury, or as guaranteed loan in the open market. (Hastings' minute, 3rd May, 1821, pp. 198-200.) Fendall's minute, (21st May, 1821, pp. 203-4). Adam supported Metcalfe's plan (Minute, 4th June, pp. 207-8). *Hyderabad Papers, Op. Cit.*

212. Swinton to Metcalfe, 23rd Nov., 1822, *Hyderabad Papers,* p. 288.

213. Kaye's *Life of Metcalfe,* Vol. II, p. 87.

214. Its memorial to Lord Amherst. *Home Misc.* Vol. 758.

215. Extracts from speeches, Kaye's *Life of Metcalfe,* Vol. II, pp. 88-92. Russell's speech is reproduced in Briggs' *The Nizam,* Vol. II, pp. 178-215.

216. However, when the real state of the accounts was revealed to him, the Governor-General joined with his Council in expressing extreme displeasure at the "highly repressible" conduct of the firm and the "unworthy deception" practised by the minister in grossly misapplying the funds. Even Russell's "blameable neglect of duty" was noticed. But it is curious that even in this despatch the Resident was instructed not only not to withdraw any assurances of support of Chandulal, but to renew them. (Swinton to Metcalfe, 13th Sept. 1822. *Hyderabad Papers,* pp. 186-9.)

217. Hastings to Metcalfe, 27th Sept., 1822, Kaye's *Life of Metcalfe,* Vol. II pp. 82-4. Perhaps it would be more accurate to say that they were only "outwardly reconciled". *Loc. Cit.,* p. 87.

218. As a share of the conquests of the war, the Nizam was given territory out of the parts acquired by the Company from the Peshwa (Estimated value Rs. 5,69,275) the Raja of Nagpur (worth Rs. 3,13,743) and Holkar (worth Rs. 1,89,373). The Nizam ceded to the Company territory worth Rs. 4,31,785, and engaged to pay Rs. 1,20,000 annually as due of the assignment of chouth on the Nizam's territory to Appa Desai and the Patwardhans. Treaty ratified on 31st Dec. 1822. Aitchison (1909) *Op., Cit.,* Vol. IV, pp. 86-9.

219. Art. 2, *Ibid.*

220. Separate and Secret Article, Aitchison, Vol. IX, p. 74.

221. Hastings to Russell, 26th Oct. 1819, *Hyderabad Papers, Op. Cit.,* p. 88. Metcalfe had gone out with instructions on his point (Kaye's *Life of Metcalfe,* Vol. II. p. 24) The offer was to take the form of an additional article to the treaty. (Metcalfe to Swinton, 21st Dec., 1820, Nos. 15 & 16, Bengal Secret Consultations, 27th Jan., 1821)

222. Kaye's *Life of Metcalfe,* Vol. II, p. 25.
223 Secret Despatch, 22nd June, 1820, *Board's Drafts,* Vol. IV, pp. 116 and 118.
224. Chasteney to Metcalfe, 27th Jan. No. 17, Bengal Secret Consultations. 27th Jan. 1821.
225. "Private" letter to Canning, 2nd Feb. 1821, additional MSS. (*Liverpool Papers*) 38,411 fo. 29, (British Museum), to this Canning wrote an equally spirited reply, 20th Aug. 1821, *Loc. Cit.,* fo. 54.
226. Agha Mir at Lucknow, Mir Alam and Chandulal at Hyderabad, Gangadhar Shastri and Dhakji Dadaji at Baroda and Purniya and Ram Rao in Mysore.
227. For example, in one of his otherwise very unfavourable reports about the Maharaja of Mysore, Cole says: 'It is but fair to the Rajah to observe, that in every instance connected with the British Government, he is liberal and accommodating, and as far as he can show favour, he does on this particular." (10th Feb., No. 3, Bengal Secret Consultations, 18th Mar. 1814.) Carnac wrote similarly about Fateh Singh Gaekawar, 9th Sept., No. 23, Bengal Secret Consultations, 20th Oct. 1815.
228. From 1814 (when within a few months of his arrival in India, he recorded his Minute of 3rd Apr., No. 4, Bengal Secret Consultations, 21st June, 1814) to 1822, less than a forthnight before his departure, (His Minute of 19th Dec., No. 8, Bengal Secret Consultations, 20th Dec. 1822).
229. Hastings to Russell, 26th Oct. 1814, *Hyderabad Papers,* p. 89.
230. Lord William Bentinck assumed the Government of Mysore in 1831.
231. In this he had the support of the authorities in England (their letter 21st Jan. 1824, *Hyderabad Papers, Op. Cit.,* p. 388.
232. Although the effect of this attitude was greatly nullified by his insisting on supporting Chandu Lal even against the Nizam.
233. Minute of 1st Dec. 1815, *Op. Cit.,* para. 149.
234. *Loc. Cit.,* para. 72.

9

Financial Problems

Financial difficulties—demands on the Bengal revenues—land problems—salt and opium—public works and education—Metcalfe as Machiavelli—the Company has recourse to an old and tried fried—His Majesty of Oudh.

Lord Hastings on arrival had found the Bengal Government in one of its periodic states

'of great pecuniary embarrassment. The Directors were so urgent with me to send home treasure that I overcame the reluctance of my colleagues, and we remitted gold pagodas to the amount estimated by ordinary exchange of £300,000. Should the price of gold in England be still what is was when I left Europe, this bullion will be sold by the Directors for not less than £450,000. We have, however, in consequence been on the brink of great distress.'

'The Embassy in Persia, though wholly appointed by the Crown, is entirely supported by the Government of Bengal; such being the arrangement made by ministers with the Directors, or rather imposed on the latter. Without any means of curbing the prodigality of the ambassador, or of determining the property of expenditures quite unconnected with the interests of

> India, we are bound to answer the bills drawn upon us by Sir Gore Ouscley. Of course they come both heavily and unexpectedly. The Governor of the Isle of France and the Governor of Ceylon have both had the privilege granted to them of drawing upon us, furnishing us in return with bills on the English Treasury, which we often cannot negotiate. Java is a still worse drain than the others. Instead of the surplus revenue which, for the purpose of giving importance to the conquest, was asserted to be forthcoming from that possession, it could to be maintained without the treasury as well as the troops of Bengal. Just now, in the height of our exigencies we receive an intimation from the Lieut.-Governor that the cannot pay his provincial crops unless we allow him 50,000 Spanish dollars monthly in addition to the prodigious sum which we already contribute to his establishment.'[1]

The China tea investment also had to be financed from Bengal.

This crisis makes a convenient pause, to consider the principles of East India Company finance, a subject to intricate that only a cursory survey can be attempted. Until the Charter Act of 1813 on attempt was made to separate political and commercial accounts, and further complications arose from repeated additions of new territory, from military operations which were partly debited to the British Exchequer, from continual changes in the method of keeping accounts for the three presidencies, and from the lack of a uniform currency.[2] This last problem was a continual embarrassment to the earliest settlers, for in Mogul times each prince had his own coinage and none of these circulated throughout the peninsula. There were three mints in Bengal in 1765. These the Company abolished, and began issuing rupees from a mid in Calcutta, and after 1773 produced a 'sicca' rupee of standard weight but bearing the name of the Mogul Emperor Shah Alam, and the date 1779.[3] Their rupees gradually ousted other rupees from Bengal, and replaced the copper coinage which was equally complicate, and was further confused by the recognition of such gold coins as the Madras *pagoda* and Bombay *mohur*. It was not until 1835 that a uniform silver currency was established throughout India.

Until 1833 the Governor-General had to serve, financially, two masters. He was responsible to the Directors of a large trading company carrying on business under difficult circumstances. He was also a colonial administrator in charge of mixed forces, the King's and the Company's always liable to be involved in wars with neighbouring princes, or with representatives of some European Power. The latter character predominated from the time of Cornwallis. Each successive Governor-General had financial disputes with the Directors, and in 1805 these were so acute that, a part from questions of general police, they must have led to Wellesley's resignation. The Company's insistence that a part of the revenue should be expended on goods for export is an example of this conflict of interests. The matter has also some theoretic importance because it raises the question of 'tribute' and the 'financial drain', which were the subject of later controversies.

On taking over the *zemindari* rights of Bengal the Company had incurred certain financial responsibilities to the British Exchequer. Parliament insisted that territorial acquisitions belonged to the Crown, and the yearly payment of £400,000 demanded from the Company represented a form of rent. At the time the acquisition of land was considered certain source of revenue, an idea which has led to confusion of thought even up till today. A government is not a landlord, and in extending its territory it increases the cost of its administration and its liability to be drawn into a war. These items may easily convert an apparently prosperous area into a 'deficit province'. The eighteenth century English had not learnt that lesson. When taking over the reputedly fertile area of Bengal it was felt that the revenues should supply a surplus which could be remitted home. The Company arranged that this should take the form of goods to be sold in order to meet interest charges on home debts and the Exchequer demands. Each Governor-General was expected to devote a portion of his revenue to the purchase of commodities, which would be sent to England as part of the 'Investment', the early name for the cargoes which were exported to be sold of the benefit of the Company. About twelve million pounds were expended in this way between 1766 and 1780, and as part of the money realised by the sale of these commodities was paid to the British Exchequer it formed a kind of 'tribute', though only indirect. The demands of the Exchequer ceased in 1773, but the system of investing part of the surplus revenue in commodities for export was revised, after the lapse of some years as a purely commercial transaction. Between 1793 and 1813 some twenty-five million pounds worth of goods were sent to England in this way and the money was used to meet the interest on the growing 'home debts' of the Company.[4] Wellesley and his successors protested against the system and it was finally abandoned in 1813.

This is the only time when anything which could be correctly described as 'tribute' was taken from India by the British Treasury and it is important to differentiate two periods. Until 1780 the need for surplus cargoes was partly due to the demands of the Exchequer, but during the second period, from the nineties onwards, the extra commodities went to defray the interest on debts incurred during the France war. The Directors were not yet reconciled to the modern idea of raising loans to meet war-time expenditure and the complicated system described above was really due to this hesitation. Almost exactly the same result would have been obtained it the home debt had been reckoned as an Indian debt, bearing interest at about eight per cent. The surplus cargoes would have represented interest charges. Force of circumstances brought about this change, against the wishes of the Directors. The period from 1793 to 1813 covered the Mysore and Maratha wars of Cornwallis and Wellesley, and deficits piled up until the government debts in India had risen to over thirty millions in 1814, an increase roughly equivalent to the Indian revenue spent on buying extra goods for export. From 1813 onwards trade relations between British India and England began to assume a more modern form. The balance of trade was no longer strongly in India's favour, and this checked the steady flow of bullion from Europe eastwards which had characterised the sixteenth, seventeenth, and eighteenth centuries. An important factor in this change was the raising of Indian loans for war expenses and then for productive purposes, such as railways and canals. At first these were taken up almost entirely in England though by the time of the Mutiny Indian investors had begun to purchase them. Other home charges steadily increased during the first half of the nineteenth century, as the British administration spread over the whole peninsula, and became more complicated and expensive. In the time of Cornwallis this process was only just beginning, and it will be convenient to study the financial system while there was still only the bare frame-work of an administration, and before the series of internal wars which we connect with the names of Wellesley and Lord Hastings.

A rough budged worked out for British India is, say, 1790 will made it easier to appreciate the interaction of financial policy and adminsitration.[5] Cornwallis had four busy years, but the war with Tipu was still to come. The revenue was made up of four main items. The land revenue was by far the most important, bringing in some four million pounds, of which over three-quarters came from Bengal. The salt monopoly produced about half a million, the opium trade £80,000, and customs perhaps half that amount. A police tax was collected and employed locally, and the beginnings of the Excise department appear in the *abkari* regulations laid down by Cornwallis for a taxing the sale of liquors. The complete dependence of the Government upon the land revenue remained a feature of British India for many years. It was recognised as an evil, but it is difficult to see what alternative was possible, and it is worthy of note that the two other practical sources of income—salt and opium—have been the subject of bitter attack up to the present day. Apart from customs, the chief resources of a modern government are income tax and death duties, both of which present special difficulties in India because of the Hindu joint family system. In the eighteenth century there was little ascertainable income apart from land, and another fifty years were to pass before Peel, in 1842, tentatively and experimentally introduced an income tax into England. The first Indian income tax was to follow still later, in 1860, but even under for more settled conditions it has been found very difficult to bring the moneylender and trader within its meshes. Death duties have never been imposed.[6] In 1857, the last year of the Company's rule, land revenue made up half of the Government's receipts and salt, opium, and customs brought in more than two-thirds of the remainder.[7]

The incidence and collection of land revenue are bound up with peasant life, and import duties with the prosperity of the craftsmen. They will be discussed in a later chapter. The salt and opium monopolies have had long and controversial histories, with certain points of resemblance. Both commodities had been taxed under Muslim rule, and these taxes were retained by the British when other inland duties were abolished. The method of direct collection proving unsatisfactory. Warren Hastings in each case assumed the monopoly, and farmed out the right of manufacture. This led to the abuses usually connected with the farming system. Large profits were made by speculators, the actual salt-makers and poppy cultivators were oppressed. In 1780 Hastings instituted a salt office, with agents who arranged for the manufacture of salt, and sold it to wholesale dealers at prices fixed from year to year. In 1799 Wellesley abandoned the contract system for opium, and substituted a single agency under a covenanted civil servant. Both monopolies became part of the permanent revenue system.

Much nineteenth-century criticism of the salt and opium policies was based on the idea that any State enterprise which makes a profit is tyrannous, and was especially objectionable in the case of a 'foreign' Government. There is to-day less belief in the virtue of free competition, especially in the production of articles in which purity is of great importance. The real charge against the government's salt policy was that too much profit was taken on supplying an essential to life, and against the opium policy that the government was engaging in an immoral business. At the end of the eighteenth century neither criticism had very much force. The salt monopoly ensured a plentiful supply of good quality, and the profit up to 1788 was under Rs. 1 as 8 for 80 lb.[8] As the average yearly consumption per head was under 12 lb., the charge was not a vary heavy burden, and there is not reason to believe that salt would have been retailed cheaper under a system of open competition. Subsequently the salt trade became more complicated. From 1817 there was a small import from England, the salt being loaded as ballast, and private manufacture was allowed under licence. Later governments were tempted by the elasticity of this source of revenue to raise their charges to meet unexpected calls, and the duty was as high as three rupees per 80 lb. during the first Afghan War. After the mutiny the salt duties were open to far greater objection. The imposition of income tax in 1860 had shown the possibility of differentiating taxation so as to fall chiefly on the rich, and thus provided a strong argument against continuing a taxed on an essential food. Opium was on different footing. It was at best a luxury, and was intended chiefly for export to China. The government made very large profits on the trade, but the high price was mostly paid by Chinese, and was virtually a luxury tax upon them. The moral aspect was hardly considered. It was not an age much given to interfering with other people's domestic habits, and opium-eating—as contrasted with the exotic indulgence in opiumsmoking—has never been considered in India as dangerous vice. Both Indians and English would probably hold it less beneful than alcoholism.

The expenditure side of the 1790 budget would have been under two main heads, military and civil. Attempts were made to keep the expenses of the army, then about 70,000 strong, to a million and a half pounds, but the struggle with

Tipu Sultan upset these plans, and by 1793 the army had risen to nearly ninety thousand men, and the cost to three million. During Wellesley's time expenses rose immediately, and by 1813 the army had a strength of about two hundred thousand.[9] A considerable part of these military expenses were not paid out of revenue, but in peace or war the army must have absorbed about two thirds of the total receipts. Civil expenditure came under very few heads, for it was only about the middle of the nineteenth century that governments, even in Europe, began to develop the 'social services'. The main item was salaries for officials, but the expenses of revenue collection were usually deducted before remittance, and it is almost impossible to estimate the amount of this charge. It is certain that the immediate effect of Lord Cornwallis's judicial and other reforms was a heavy increase in these expenses. The old system, whereby the Company had paid its servants small salaries, but had connived at irregularities, had at least been cheap. With a very inelastic revenue each successive Governor-General was continually hampered by financial difficulties, even before the Mysore War, and the police system was rendered ineffective by the very small amounts available for salaries.

The other branches of Government activities were still in an embryonic state at the end of the eighteenth century. The first public works were military, but Lord Cornwallis was interested in the repair of the many minor irrigation works of Bengal, most of which had been allowed to degenerate during the anarchy of the past century. Local committees were appointed, and pressure put upon *Zemindars* to undertake this work. The Marquess of Hastings was one of the first statesmen to emphasise the importance of better communications, and from about 1820 there was considerable activity in the *maramal* department while the trunk roads were put in hand after the Charter Act of 1833. There was at that time little knowledge of hydraulic engineering and the effort made under Lord Amherst to revive the old Mogul Jumna canal only proved that the original alignment had been wrong.

Mass eduction was at that time not considered the duty of a government. In England it was entirely in the hands of the Churches, and it was not until 1833 that the first Government grant of £20,000 was given to the two leading societies engaged in this work. 'Free and compulsory' education did not, of course follow till after 1870. A few Europeans countries were earlier in recognising governmental responsibility, but most were later. It is an anachronism to imagine that in 1790 any Indian Englishman would have thought it to be the Government's duty to undertake or even assist the work of the little temple and mosque schools which existed in many of the villages. Higher education was considered in a different light. Government interference was justified by the need of men trained for Government service. The Calcutta Madrasa was founded in 1781, and a Sanskrit College was founded in Banaras in 1792, but little more was done until after 1813. Under the Charter Act of this year the sum of £10,000 was appropriated yearly for the 'revival and improvement of literature and the improvement of the sciences' the wording of which shows clearly that it was intended to assist in higher education. The amount remained unappropriately for some years, though in 1816 the Hindu College was founded in Calcutta, chiefly through the energies of David Hare and the Chief Justice, Sir, Hyde East. The grant was, however the basis of the struggle which took place under Bentinck between the 'Orientalists' and the English school, and which finally settled the future of higher education in British India.

The Nepal campaign heavily deepened the Government's financial distress, to which we return. The Directors noted (October, 1815),

> 'with extreme concern that the effects of the Nepaulese war are so strongly felt in your financial department as to induce the apprehension that the advances to be issued to our European investment will be reduced to a very small sum indeed. If the advances for the investment are to be withheld, the sales at this House for Indian goods will soon be brought to a stand.'

The Company's administration therefore had recourse to the Nawab of Oudh, their old and (in every sense of the phrase) much-tried ally. His government 'since the forced cessions of 1801, had been conducted systematically on a principle of selfish avarice, which aimed to draw as much as possible from the country, at the smallest possible charge'.[10] It is perhaps not easy to explain how his aim differed from the Company's; but Anglo-Indian writers are so sure that there *was* an immense difference, that we may take it that there must have been, and that the passage of time has blurred our chances of perception of it. Possibly part of the difference lay in his wasteful expenditure of what he wrested from his people, whereas the Company built up an admirable military machine; Metcalfe, whose mind was clear as the Governor-General's own, and whose advice was very congenial to Hastings, wrote that they ought:

> 'Ist. To make it the main object of all the acts of our Government to have the most efficient army that we can possible maintain, not merely for internal control or the defence of our frontier, but also for those services in the field which our army is perpetually called on to perform on emergencies when we have not time to increase it to sufficient strength.
>
> '2nd. If our resources should, at any time, be unequal to the maintenance of an ample force, not to cripple our strength by attempts to reduce our force within the limits of fixed resources at the imminent peril of our dominion; but to endeavour to raise our resources to meet the demands on us for force.'

If the revenues of British India proved inadequate,

> 'we ought to draw forth new resources; and if these of impracticable within our own dominions, we must look to increase of territory by conquest over our enemies in the interior of India. There is no doubt that opportunities will arise for effecting such conquests, for with the utmost moderation and justice upon our part,

misunderstandings and wars in the course of time will be occasionally unavoidable.'

'4th. To apply the net revenues of conquered countries to the maintenance of additional force, and the acquisition of additional force to the achievement of new conquests, on just occasions—thus growing in size and increasing in strength as we proceed, until we can with safety determine to confine ourselves within fixed limits, and abjure all further conquests....'

No one in any country at this date considered that the revenues of conquered countries belonged to those who paid them.[11] They were at the conqueror's free disposal, to spend—as Metcalfe urged—on bigger and better armies, which were to conquer bigger and better lands, which in turn were to pay for bigger and better armies again—or else to put into the annual investments (as the Directors urged), and send home thus as a disguised tribute. And the Nawab himself, whatever we may think about his subjects' case, was undoubtedly deeply beholden to the Company, as without outside support Oudh could never have gone on and on being scandalously misgoverned for decade after decade and by Nawab after Nawab. He had won additional security by removal of the menace of the Gurkhas at his doors, and it was not unjust (as justice went in the India of those days) that he should pay towards that war.

His administration, moreover, needed improvement, even as seen from the distance of Calcutta. As far back as 1810, he had been urged to,

> 'assimilate the administration of Oudh to that of the British provinces . . . dividing the territory into districts, with revenue and judicial officers, acting under separate controlling authorities at the capital.'[12]

He betrayed as his chief characteristics 'extreme folly and timidity', which were heightened by his Resident, Major Baillie, who interfered high-handedly and continually. In 1814, while Lord Hastings was on his way to a personal meeting, the Nawab died; when the Governor-General reached Lucknow, he found that Baillie had zealously forced on the new Nawab the reforms desired, and that 'all the most lucrative appointments . . . were filled by the Resident's own moonshees and dependents'[13]. Full conviction of what had been happening did not come to Hastings till a year later, when he immediately removed Baillie. Meanwhile, in October, 1814, His Excellency of Oudh was privileged to contribute a large loan to equip the Company's armies against Nepal. In the Governor-General's absence from Calcutta, his Council used part of this in an unauthorised fashion, which led to a second application to the Nawab, 'the financial officers being unable to devise any other remedy'.[14] His Excellency was slack in response, offering only fifty lakhs, which was refused, his offer being 'assumed to be made from an imperfect acquaintance with the extent of the embarrassment for which we sought relief'. The gaps in his knowledge were repaired, and an additional crore collected from him. In recognition of his helpfulness the Nawab was allowed to take the title of King, thereby outraging Muslim Mogul dynasty:

"His Majesty" of Oude makes me sick. If the King of Delhi was in fact an absurdity or a mockery (I do not admit it was either), it had its root in a wise conformance to usage, in a generous consideration of the feelings of fallen greatness. It was the veneration of a great power that had passed away; and the superstition that continued to give homage to the shrine which we had a addressed to propitiate our rise, was sanctioned by the example of the wisest among nations. There was little except goodness in it. The expenditure was duly repaid in the return of impression ...'[15]

REFERENCES

1. *The Private Journal of the Marquess of Hastings* (February 1, 1814), i. 40-41.
2. For further information see P. Banerjea's *Indian Finance in the Days of the Company*.

3. Del Mar, *History of Money in Ancient Countries,* III. It is difficult to understand why this date was chosen, and retained over a long period.

4. By 1786 the Company had a nominal capital of £3,200,00 and debts in Europe of £11,800,000, besides an Indian debt of over eight millions.

5. No such budget was, of course, prepared. The three provinces kept separate accounts, and their form was not that of a modern budget.

6. Probate duties are now charged, but these are estate duties. They are really a court fee, and only applicable when there is a will, which is exceptional amongst Hindus. Muslims are not liable. The charge is about 3 per cent.

7. Land revenue, £15,317,337; customs, £2,148,834; salt, £2,131,346 (against charges of £605,880); opium, £8,864,209 (against charges of £629,480). Total receipts, £31,706,776.

8. Pramathanath Banerjea, *History of Indian Taxation,* 253.

9. Martin, ii. 101 ff., letter of the Right Hon. Henry Dundas so the Earl of Mornington, March 18, 1799. The whole letter deserves careful study and fuller quotation than we can find space for.

10. Prinsep, i. 217.

11. See Appendix a.

12. Prinsep, i. 218.

13. *Op. cit.* i. 222.

14. *Op. cit.* i. 227.

15. John Malcolm to Gerald Wellesley (Kaye, *Life of Malcolm,* ii. 378).

10

The Pindari and Maratha Wars

The Governor-General's dealings with the Maratha States—influence of Metcalfe—three types of native State—destruction of the Pindaris—murder of Gangadhar Sastri and imprisonment and escape of Trimbakji—the Peshwa's attack—battles of Kirki, Yeraoda, Koregaon, Sitabaldi—war with Holkar—battles of Mahidpur and Ashti—settlement of Central India—changing racial relations—administrative changes—the Palmer scandal—suttee.

The Maratha States deserved the eclipse about to overtake them. Their original revolt against Mogul tyranny and bigotry was so successful that even to-day its victories are written on the map, in great Maratha principalities far outside the Deccan, which is ethnically Maratha territory. But these principalities, so valued an element in modern India, could not be established as we known them, expect on the ruins of the system which preceded them and was their beginning. That system in 1817 was solely rapacious, except for the Gaekwar's dominions (which had settled into an administration more or less of the kind we known now as an Indian State). Holkar's and Sindhia's 'States' were merely the range within which they normally pillaged; their boundaries were liable to sudden extension or retraction according as the pillagers' armed power waxed or waned.

For exemption from their attentions, these chieftains claimed tribute from many princes who had moved into the British sphere. Sindhia had claims on Bhopal, whose Nawab had assisted Goddard's march in Warren Hastings' time and thereby set up connections with the Company. By Maratha political notions, the claims were good ones; Sindhia,

> 'having been in the habit of . . . levying contributions on this territory as his peculiar and exclusive prey, he conceived no one else had any right to interpose. This is the meaning he attached to the word dependency.[1]

The Nepal War and the Burmese threat seemed to provide a good occasion for reasserting rights of pillage. But, warned by Lord Hastings, he withdrew (December, 1814); and the Nawab, whose conduct had been marked by double-dealing, was effectively protected.

It became increasingly clear that a new Maratha war was pending. Relations became strained in 1815, when, following on its interference for Bhopal, the paramount Power took charge of differences between the Nizam and Peshwa, the latter having claimed *chauth* as due under an agreement concluded after the Nizam's defeat at Kardla. Two sets of circumstances brought about the final break. The first was the continual application of the miserable Rajput kingdoms to be taken under Company protection. The granting of this request was precluded by the unnecessary treaty of 1805, whereby Sir George Barlow had pledged the British not to come between Sindhia and his prey in this quarter. The second precipitating factor was the inroads of the Pindaris, a name loosely applied to those banditti-cavalry which reinforced all Indian armies. Hordes of these swarmed in Central India, and their numbers had been augmented by the successive annexations of the Company, driving into the continually contracting region of native India those who had found employment as soldiers of Tipu or the Nizam. The Pindaris, Malcolm noted, were now 'what the Mahratta power was in the decline of the Mogul Empire of India. Let us take warning, and save the a British Empire from the downfall which its predecessor sustained, chiefly from the hands of the predecessors of the Pindarees'. As those words show, the political possibilities were remarkably well understood. Such Pindari leaders as Amir Khan were themselves almost established as independent princes inside the territory of Holkar or Sindhia, and seemed at the start of a career very like that of these chieftains themselves, not so long ago. There was, however, much obscurity as to their relationship with the leading Maratha States. They certainly appeared in the field with Sindhia and Holkar, and in varying degrees obtained protection from them; yet Sindhia and Holkar exercised little, if any, authority over them.

From contemporary documents, and the tradition perceived by men who, like Kaye, had talked with officers who passed through this last great Maratha war, we can recover the intense excitement with which the British anticipated the hoped-for conflict. But the immediate move was against the Pindaris only, whose depredates into Bengal, and still more, into the Northern Sarkars, were increasing, and were accompanied with terrible cruelty. They forced bags of hot ashes over the faces of those they suspected of concealing riches, and carried off young girls, tied on horseback 'like calves.[2] Three or four together. Whole villages committed suicide to escape them. At last Hastings, in defiance of the Directors' veto (while urging them to remove it, which in consideration of his horrible evidence, they did), prepared his wide net to sweep this curse out of being. He gathered two armies amounting to 120,000 men, the northern under himself, the southern under Sir Thomas Hislop, with Malcoln as the letter's principal political officer. The Gwalior Resident was told to make Sindhia 'sensible to the benefits' he would 'derive from frank co-operation', and the territories were ordered to allow free movement through their territories and to assist in every say this drive against general nuisances. Sindhia's Minister 'shrugged' up his shoulders and said, "The weakest must obey the stronger" which the Governor-General thought 'a curious avowal of incapacity for effectual resistance'[3] Hastings with justice (he was not a man to cherish illusions) noted that the Maratha leaders were in correspondence together, and 'We must not look to the security of honourable pledges from them, but be satisfied with carrying point by point through gentle intimidation.[4] Sindhia was made to yield up or temporary occupation two forts. Hastings was not a Wellesley, and he felt compunctions over the humiliation he felt bound to impose.[5]

> 'He subscribes to all the conditions which I dictated, and has swallowed a bitter drench in so doing. I should have thought myself oppressive had be not been so thoroughly false a fellow. The engaging to co-operate in the Eurpean of the Pindarries, whom he has fostered—to whom he has plighted, and who really have hitherto constituted a material part of his strength, must be deeply mortifying. But he hardened his heart, determined to 'rivet such shackles upon Scindiah and Holkar as that all the treachery they are at this moment meditating will be impotent. In fact, the downfall of the Mahrattas is achieved'. A fact so patent as that last was not lost on the Marathas themselves. Nor on anyone else.'
>
> 'Let the reader place before him any map of India, and contemplate the expanse of country lying between the Kistnah and the Ganges rivers. Let him glance from Poonah in the south-west to Cawnpore in the north-east; mark the positions of the principal Native Courts, and think of the magnificent armies—the very flower of the three Presidencies—which were spreading themselves over that spacious territory, closing in upon Hindustan and the Deccan, and compassing alike the Pindaree hordes and the substantives States in their toils. The sportsmen of the day, indeed, regarded it as a grant *battue* of the princes and chiefs of India; and we cannot be surprised if those princes and chiefs looked upon the matter in the same light, and thought that the Feringhees, after a long season of rest, were now again bracing themselves up for vigorous action, and were putting forth all their immense military resources in one

comprehensive effort to sweep the native principalities from the face of the earth.'

'The Maratta was roused. He had been uneasy. He was now alarmed. The whole history of our connexion with India shows that for a native prince to apprehend danger is to precipitate it by his own conduct. He is more often ruined by his fear than by anything else ... He commits himself to hostility before he is aware of it; and when all is over—when, prostrate and helpess at the feet of his conqueror, he declares that he had no intention to provoke the war which has destroyed him, there is often more truth in the words than we are wont to admit. It is said in such cases, that our diplomatists are duped and over-reached, because they have not perceived hostile designs before they were formed, and known more about the future movements of our enemies than was known, at the time, to themselves. It is not a want of good faith, so much as want of consistent counsel and steadtest action, that brought so many of the princes of India to the dust.'

'So it was, it appears to me, with the Peshwa and the Rajah of Berar. They were alarmed by the gathering and the advance of our armies. They did not believe that these immense military preparations had been made simply for the suppression of the Pindaris. They thought that whatever the primary and ostensible object of the campaign might be—a campaign conducted by the Governor-General himself in person, at the head of the Grant Army—it would eventually be directed against the substantive Maharatta states. And this was no baseless suspicion. The probability of another Mahratta war, as the squeal of the Pindari campaign, was the subject of elaborate State papers and the small gossip of our camps. Statesmen solemnly discussed it at the council-board, and soldiers joyously predicted it at the mess-table. Had the whole scope of our policy been fully understood at the Mahratta Courts . . . they would not have suffered their fears to hurry them into aggression. But they only knew that we were putting our armies in motion from all points, and that in every cantonment of India the talk was about the probability of another was with the Mahrattas....'[6]

When Mr. P.E. Roberts remarks of Lord Hasting's dealings with native Powers,[7] 'Full justice has not perhaps always been done to the moderation of British policy throughout this epoch. Seldom have forbearance and firmness been more happily combined. Those bad rulers, the Peshwa and Appa Sahib, were again and again given chances to reform', we must wonder that so judicious a historian should write with what appears unconscious irony. The Peshwa, it may be said in passing, was where he was at all only because we had seen to it that he was there, whether his own people wanted him or not. Lord Hastings's treatment of native princes looks moderate and courteous, because we remember Wellesley's extreme of high-handed contemptuousness. For what he did, there was justification in the facts of the Indian situation—which were that all Central India was in anarchy, and the rulers with whom he dealt so rigorously were silly or wicked (the Peshwa was both). But this does not alter the fact that the princes near enough to feel the weight of British might were rounded up like wild beasts—that rebellion (if it was rebellion) was made humanly certain, and then punished. Malcolm thought the Maratha chiefs,

> 'had at least as good a right to prepare for contingencies as we had. If, when the British Government first took arms, and calculated the scale on which it would be expedient to conduct its military operations, the contingency of a Mahratta war was duly provided for, and that provision is to be considered demonstrative only of wisdom and forethought, we must surely be blinded by or national self-love, if we would denounce as treachery, or as folly, a like provision on the part of the Mahrattas, who were in much greater danger than ourselves. We surely expect all the world to dismount

their guns whilst our own are loaded and primed, and the portfire is burning in our hands.'[8]

It is often said that Britain acquired her World Empire in a fit of absent-mindedness; the epigram has served to support our useful reputation with foreigners for stupid stolidity, but has been overworked. From Clives' time onwards, British India never lacked minds seeing and planning far ahead. There was no trace, even momentary, of absent-mindedness in such rulers as Warren Hastings. Wellesley, Lord Hastings, or Dalhousie.

Metcalfe had the Governor-General's ear to an exceptional degree and his influence, so inadequately noted by historians, outweighed the representations of men who desired to see the native States given more, not less independence. As Resident in Delhi, he saw only the abundant seamy side[9] of these country regalities, beginning with the dilapidated Mogul 'Empire' at his door; his increasing scorn of them worked with Hasting's own desire to sweep away the whole system of outdated pretence. They had discussed Central India together during the Governor-General's original tour up-country; and in a memorandum Metcalfe divided existing States into three classes:

> 'Substantive states, ardently desiring our overthrow, and ambitious to aggrandise themselves....
>
> 'military powers not substantive states... living by plunder and devastation—the enemies of all regular governments, more especially hostile in spirit to us...
> 'petty states . . . subject to the continual plunder and oppression of the two former classes, who in consequence look up to us for protection, and are, therefore, well disposed towards us.'

The division, though admirable, presented difficulties. Holkar and the Nagpur *raj*, both ranking with Sindhia as 'substantive states', were so reduced that they were in danger of splitting into predatory fragments; Amir Khan and others were partly of the free booting class, partly dependents of Sindhia or

Holkar, partly on the point of themselves emerging as 'substantive states'.

The preliminaries of the Pindari campaign were pushed forward. The petty States, mostly Rajput, whose protection was desirable both for their own sake and for the revenues they would afford to prosecute the war which was bound to come against the Marathas, were taken into the British system. Hastings announcing to Sindhia and Holkar that the treaty of 1805 was abrogated. The Maratha Powers were told again that no neutrality in the drive would be permitted. If they hung back to the extent of themselves becoming enemies, so much the better,

> 'The war in this case would require greater exertions, but would also be attended with better prospects of solid advantage. The territories of Scindiah, Holkar, or the Rajah of Berar, would afford a recompense of the expenses of the war, and an increase of resources of the payment of additional force.'

So Metcalfe to the Governor-General; and Metcalfe's biographer surmises that 'perhaps the expectation entertained that some previous reluctance or some subsequent infidelity would embroil us with the substantive states in such a manner as to enable us to make certain new distributions of their territory was not, in some quarters, much unlike a hope.[10]

The Pindaris' most vigorous leader, Chitu, routed by a surprise attack, was chased into jungle where he was, appropriately enough, eaten by a tiger. Other leaders surrendered. The worst, Amir Khan, who had been a fiend for twenty years, made his peace before operations commenced, and became an orthodox chieftain. As admitted at Poona reasons to believe that war was inevitable. To have sent to the cantonments at that hour would have occasioned considerable stir; and in the meantime, by the report of the Peshwa was evidently deliberating the din in the city was far away; the night was passing; and the motives which had hitherto be determined Mr. Elphinstone to defer it some hours latter and the command of the European regiment on its march that had been made acquainted with the critical state of affairs, and was hasten'n forward.'

If any one wonders why the British passed to the supreme control of India, this scene, happily preserved by the vivid memory of one of its two participants, should remove his difficulty—Elphinstone listening from his veranda to the mud tumult of the city close to which his handful of troops slept onward, risking their lives and his deliberately on the chances of peace and lest he should mar the train of action which his Governor-General was laying elsewhere.

Next day, after ascertaining that attack was a matter of hours. Elphinstone stationed 250 men at the Residency, and moved out the rest of his tiny army to Kirki, four miles away. His sepoys stood fast against seduction and threats; and after further fruitless negotiations, on November 5 the Company's troops, which had been reinforced, were invested. Again the scene is preserved by an eyewitness:[11]

> 'Those only who have witnessed the Bore in the Gulf of Cambay, and have seen in perfection the approach of that roaring tide, can form the exact idea presented to the author at sight of the Peshwa's Army. It was towards the afternoon of a very sultry day: there was a dead calm, and no sound was heard, except the rushing, the trampling and neighing of the horses, and the rumbling of the gun wheels. The effect was heightened, by seeing the peaceful peasantry flying from their work in the fields, the bullocks breaking from their yokes, the wild antelopes startled from sleep, bounding off, and then turning for a moment to gaze on his tremendous inundation, which swept all before it, levelled the hedges and standing corn, and completely overwhelmed every ordinary barrier as it moved'.

The Peshwa's heart failed him, seeing the enemy standing firm in the floods that swept around them. The attack, launched by his gallant general Gokla, failed miserably; 2800 men, of whom 800 were Europeans, with a loss of 86 killed and wounded, repulsed 18,000 horse and 8000 foot, with a loss of 500. The Peshwa vented his rage and disappointment on the Residency, which was gutted, not one stone being left upon another. He had shot his bolt; after Kirki he 'never rose above the character of a heartless and desperate fugitive.'[12]

A relief force advanced swiftly on Poona, and routed the Peshwa on the 16th at Yeraoda, since famous as the site of Mahatma Gandhi's periodic 'retreats' in jail. Poona fell, and the chase of the Peshwa began. He caught Captain Staunton's 800 at Koregaon 'the Indian Thermopylae',[13] where for eight hours, frantic with thirst, they held out against attack after attack by thirty times their number. 'Their situation towards evening was very hopeless'[14] But the Peshwa withdrew, and in the darkness Staunton evacuated the shaltered mud hovels, carrying off as many of his wounded as the could. The Marathas, a magnanimous people, lost heavily, but 'have the generosity, on all occasions, to do justice to the heroic defenders of Korygaum'.

Meanwhile, the Peshwa's secret ally, the Raja of Nagpur, had attacked his own Resident, Jenkins, in the first of a series of events that were almost exact repetition of those at Poona. In fightings which began on the evening of November 26, 1817, and lasted for eighteen hours, the Marathas were repulsed from Sitabaldi, two hills near Nagpur, with a ridge yoking them. The victory cost the defenders 333 killed and wounded, more than a quarter of their number. On December 16, a battle took place in front of the capital, which presently surrendered.

Holkar's durbar had continued in 'everlasting turmoil', the normal condition of that turbulent court. Its real ruler was Tulsi Bai, who had been a concubine of Jeswant Rao Holkar—a woman profligate but intelligent and educated of exceptional beauty and endowed with the vigorous qualities that have so often showed in the women of her blood. She offered secretly to place herself and the young Holkar, a minor, under British protection. Her own people discovering this put her to death; and presently Indore, in the indeterminate causal manner of most of its wars, found itself in hostilities with the British southern army. On December 20 Sir Thomas Hislop forded the Sipra, and defeated the Marathas at Mahidpur. Again, Holkar's troops showed themselves the most dangerous of all Maratha adversaries. The victory cost 778 men, including 38 British officers; and though Holkar lost 3000 men, mainly in the pursuit, many of his infantry managed to retreat in good order, despite the enemy's cavalry strength. Mahidpur,

> 'is the only action in the third Maratha was in which there was any considerable European element in the British forces engaged. Other battles, such as Kirkee, Sitabaldi, and Koregaon, were won almost entirely by native troops under the command of trusted British officers'.[15]

The war was now nearly over. Gokla's aware that all was lost, died fighting in the last battle, the cavalry skirmish of Ashti (February 20, 1818). A number of fortresses remained to be captured, the last, Asirgarh, surrendering in April, 1819.

The Governor-General's comprehensive settlement left Holkar and Dindhia with approximately the territories they have to-day, but now definitely and finally part of the British system, with powers and limits plainly indicated. The Bhonsla Raja was deposed, and lost his lands north of the Narmada; he fled to the Sikh, and a minor took his place, with the British in real control. The Peshwaship was abolished; Baji Rao, by Malcolm's precipitate generosity, was given a large pension, the refusal to continue which was the action which gave mortal offence to his son, 'the Nana Sahib'. At Ashti, the Raja of Satara was among the captives, rescued from the Peshwa's control, he was re-established in his kingdom, with additional sanction from the all-powerful Kompani Bahadur. Elphinstone as Commissioner, seated him on his throne 'with great pomp' (April, 1818); and the Raja 'published two proclamations, the one announcing his connexion with the British Government, the other making over entire powers for the arrangement and government of his country's to Captain Grant (Grant Duff), the future historian of his people. In 1817 the Rajput States, in quick succession, were formally made protectorates. In 1819 the Rao of Kachchh (Cutch) who had also 'been caught in the wide sweep of the net of treaties',[16] kicked against the meshes, and after a brief war was deposed for an infant. The Company thus reached the Indus mouth, and only the Punjab remained independent.

Hastings encouraged Stamford Raffles in founding Singapore, 1819. The Dutch were exceedingly vexed, but were placated, a few years later, when the Company exchanged its Sumatran settlements for the Dutch possessions still left in India.

Probably peace has never descended any where more gratefully than on the wasted regions of Central India. Sir John Malcolm, who played so prominent a part in the ending of tumults, wrote shortly afterwards;[17]

'With the means we had at our command, the work of force was comparatively easy; the liberality of our Government gave grace to conquest and men were for the moment satisfied to be at the feet of generous and humane conquerors. Wearied with a state of continued warfare and anarchy, the loss even of power was hardly regretted; haleyon days were anticipated, and men postrated themselves in hopes of elevation. All these impressions, made by the combined effects of power, humanity, and fortune, were improved to the utmost by the character of measures. The agents of Government were generally individuals who had acquired a name in the scene where they were employed: they were infettered by rules and their acts were adapted to soothe the passions, and accord with the habits and a prejudicious of those whom they had to conciliate or to reduce to obedience. But there are many causes which operate to make a period like this, one of short duration; and the change to a colder system of policy, and the introduction of our laws and regulations into countries immediately dependent upon us, naturally excite agitation and alarm. Its the hour in which men awake from a dream. Disgust and discontent succeed to terror and admiration; and the princes, the chiefs, and all who had enjoyed rank or influence, see nothing but a system dooming them to immediate decline and ultimate annihilation.

'The same classes of men do not fill the same places in society, under our governments, as they did under a native prince; nor are men actuated by similar motives. Our administration, though just, is cold and rigid. If it creates no alarm, it inspires little, if any emulation. The people are protected, but not animated or attached. It is rare that any native of India living under it can suffer injury or wrong; but still more rare that he can be encouraged or elevated by favour or distinction. Our rules and regulations constitute a despotic power, which is alike imperative upon the governors and the governed. Its character impels it to generalize, and its forms as well as principles, are unyielding.'

The Governor-General's own observations in Bengal and his enlightening tour through the up-country corroborated Malcolm's testimony from Central India. 'Our people', he wrote, 'are too dry with the natives, who give us high credit for justice, but I far they regard us in genral as very repulsive'[18] When Munro from Madras pleaded passionately[19] with him against the now settled policy of granting no employment but the most mechanical and trivial to even the ablest Indians, we seem to be listening down a prolonged lapse of time, to Henry Lawrence's criticism, on the eve of the Mutiny, of the absurdity of expecting men endowed with feelings and ambitions to rest content with a clerkship in administration or a corporal's authority in the field; or to the complaint of Rabindranath Tagore[20] in our own day, that his country's Government and become like patent foods, something 'untouched by hand'. But the generation whose memory went back to an era when British and Indians met on terms of equality and often of friendship was passing fast. Munro's course was nearly run; he and others like him were growing into survivals, venerated as having been fine men in their prime but recognised as now not quite up-to-date.

We come to the one really perplexing and distressing part of Lord Hastings's career. We have seen how heartily historians reprobate the misgovernment of 'those bad rulers, the Peshwa and Appa Sahib'. Unfortunately, the countries of princes meritorious enough to retain the paramount Power's support were no happier than theirs. Haidarabad was,

> 'a great congeries of disease. Nothing seemed to flourish there except corruption. . . the wretched people were dragooned into submission, and the required payments extorted from them at the bayonet's point or the sabre's edge'.[21]

Monotonous iniquity, unchecked, unmitigated, reigned. Outside the swing of the sword was mere banditry. The 'State' was as little of an ordered system as any Maratha one, the only difference being that it was more steadily and pitilessly pillaged, and for the benefit of aliens. The Nizam's contingent were so highly paid that employment in his service, civil or military, was eagerly sought 'by the officers both of the King's and the Company's army. The Resident was importuned with applications for these comfortable staff appointments, and large sums passed annually into the pockets of our own people'. The joyous catchword was, 'Nizzy pays for all'. At last a firm of money-lenders, William Palmer & Co., came to the distracted ruler's help. They lent him, mainly to pay his costly troops. £20,000 a month, in return for assignments of £300,000 a year on his revenues, that is, at 25 per cent interest. The system as that used with the nawab of the Carnatic; and the Nizam dealt with rascals even more impudent.

Throught these transactions the Governor-General showed 'strong domestic attachment and excessive vanity.'[22] 'Influenced by the fact that one of the partners was married to a ward of his, a young lady whom he regarded as his daughter',[23] he sanctioned without enquiry all that the Palmer combination (a firm 'without office or establishment' did, and displayed a ferocity and tenacity of rage at opposition, which are exemptible only on the supposition that Indian and age had worn down his principles and mental soundness. In saying this, we give due weight to the possibility that he may at first have thought the arrangement justified as making the contingent's pay secure; no administration was ever so incubus-ridden as the Company's, with black financial care seated behind the horseman, while on every wind that blew from England the clamorous voices of Directors and shareholders cried out that dividends, whatever happened, must be safe.

Sir William Rumbold, husband of the Governor-General's ward, was adventurer pure and simple, and 'had accompanied his Lordship to India with the not very rare or unintelligible design of making as much money as he could.'[24] Too old to make it by soldering or in administrative service, he had toured native Indian in quest of a centre for operations; had looked longingly at Oudh, but it was oversupplied already with people like himself—at Delhi, but with Metcalfe there he decided it was no good—at Mysore, but it was too close to the recently purged Carnatic. Haidarabad therefore secured the advantages of his presence. His firm soon had a stranglehold on the State, when a piece of cruel ill-luck befell it, in Metcalfe's arrival as Resident (1820).

Metcalfe came at a time when all of even his valour and honesty were to be hardly strained. Lord Hastings, entirely cynical where Nizzy's plucking was in proposal, forced the Resident to insert in a revised treaty imposed on the Nizam the following article, which he brought in the Governor-General's own handwriting:

> 'His Highness the Nizam, contemplating the great benefits which he has reaped from the late military operations, in the security of his dominions, and in the advantages accruing to his revenue, is anxious to manifest his sense of such a boon by a gratuitous contribution. In this view his Highness desires that he may be allowed to furnish sixteen lakhs of rupees (payable at the rate of four lakhs yearly till the amount be completed) for public purposes connected with the city of Calcutta or its vicinity. . . the sum shall be applied in such portions and for such objects as the Governor-General in Council may direct.'

The European quarters of the British capital were to obtain from the gratitude of the Company's one Faithful Ally lights, water and roads. A graceful gesture, but the Directors disallowed it—Lord Hastings thought, because they paid undue attention to what seemed to them 'the inconsistency of exacting from the resources of the State such a sum when we represent it is finances to be embarrassed in such a degree as to require the aid of a British house of agency'. It may have been so.

Metcalfe succinctly summarised Sir William Rumbold's ambition as 'to make a large and rapid fortune in the style of the old time, by other means than his own personal labour'. It is an ambition which society everywhere considers entirely respectable, if achieved along accepted lines and within the law. The Plamers' only misjudgement was in underestimating Metcalfe's courage. He was appalled to discover everywhere 'decay and depopulation', and to find foreign financiers exercising control superior not only to the Nizam's, but to the paramount Power's. He quickly came to suspect that he was understood to be bribed into complicity; 'fruits, dinners, &c., &c., were sent to the Residency, he reported, in such quantities as to give them the appearance of regular supplies, instead of being merely complimentary'. His predecessor's entire household had been in collusion with the Palmers and the Nizam's officers, and his own servants, of whatever race, expected Metcalfe to continue the arrangement. Recusancy was assumed to be unthinkable with the Governor-General's son-in-law by adoption at the head of the enterprise; and Metealfe's duty was excessively hard, to one who had been in such intimate friendship with Lord Hastings. Moreover, he had close relations with the Palmers themselves. William Palmer was brother of one of his dearest friends, and son of General Plamer; Sir William Rumbold had been his guest in Delhi, and nursed by him through serious illness. Nevertheless, when in 1820 the firm proposed to the Nizam a sixty lakhs loan, he pointed out that the loan would be 'a mere fiction', made up by a transference of the existing debt, with eight lakhs commission to the lenders for their kindness added to it. It was true that interest on this swollen sum was being reduced to 18 per cent. But as to further accommodation, the Palmers 'went on with confidence leading afresh at their usual rate of interest, above 25 per cent'.[25] Sir William instructed him to keep quiet, and to use his influence to keep the Governor-General Council quiet. As he very reasonably asked.

> 'What can the Government care whether the arrangement be more or less beneficial to us, provided it bestows upon the Nizam's Government the great advantages that have been held out?'

The firm represented that the Resident was backing the proposal, and Lord Hastings was fooled (it must be admitted, fooled very easily) into what looked like Government guaranteeing. "The accumulation of wealth' in the firm' books, 'from the immense interest which they charged, seemed to be boundless'. European officers eagerly put their money into so splendid a ramp, and these resources, combined with the Nizam's payments for his mainly mythical loan, 'was such as to supply the most wasteful expenditure on the part of the members of the firm, and was nevertheless overflowing'. Happy days had come again in Haidarabad.

But Metcalfe was miserable and indignant. In 1821 he proposed to open in Calcutta a loan at 6 per cent, to liberate the Nizam, though at enormous cost, from meshes that meant ruin. He was deeply concerned also for what always was close to his heart, the credit and dignity of his own people and Government. The Palmers replied with effrontery on a scale that moves into the region of musical comedy. They pretended to acquiesce, but claimed 6 lakhs 'compensation' for being paid: 'the sudden liquidation of the loan to the Nizam would inflict a very serious injury on the firm'.[26] Racked with unhappiness—he repeatedly said that if he had suspected what was happening, nothing would have induced him to come to Haidarabad—and anxious to close a business to humiliating, Metcalfe agreed to this. Rumbold nevertheless wrote the Governor-General an urgent private representation (or rather, misrepresentation) of the Residents' hostility. The Governor-General's wrath was hot and implacable. But

Metcalfe stuck to his guns. Few letters so stiff and unyielding, while perfectly respectful, have every been written to a Governor-General; and the writer's integrity throughout this intensely painful episode coast him Lord Hastings's friendship, and furnished him with a host of unscrupulous foes at home as well as in India. It probably kept him out of the Governor-Generalship later on. We may excerpt a few of his 'laments'. As to the Palmers, he says,

> 'I lament their connexion with some of the most profligate and rapacious of the governors of districts, through whom their character, and what is of more consequence, the British name become involved in detestable acts of oppression, extortion and atrocity. I lament the power which they exercise in the country, ... enforcing payment of debts, due to them either originally or by transfer, in an authoritative manner not becoming their mercantile character; acting with the double force of the Nizam's Government and the British name ... I lament the monopoly established in their favour by the sanction and virtual guarantee of the British Government, because it deprives the Nizam's Government of the power of going into the European money-market, where, with the same sanction, it might borrow money at less than half the rate of interest which it pays to Messrs. Palmer and Co. I lament the political influence acquired by the House through the supposed countenance of your Lordship to Sir Wm. Rumbold, because it tends to the perversion of political influence for the purposes of private gain.'

He scouted the accusation that his opposition was due to personal spite. But Lord Hastings, whose administration in his last years went all to pieces, took the side of the Palmers.

Metcalfe became an object of ridicule in Haidarabad. But he was not the man to accept such a position. The Resident, he means to be recognised as such; and to protect the people and British reputation. He found a cautious but convinced sympathiser in John Adam, the senior member of the Governor-General's Council; Adam was particularly shocked by Metcalfe's proof that the officers of the Residency, in his predecessor's time, had been in the gang, even if the Resident was not (and he probably was). Hastings himself, having incurred the Directors' censure for the affair, resigned, 1821, lingering listlessly in India until the end of 1822. Though a reconciliation was patched up between him and his brilliant and too fearless servant, after his return to England he kindled enmity against Metcalfe.

The Palmer controversy rose to heights of scurrilous partisanship unequalled since the time of Warren Hastings's trial; 'Sir William Rumbold's levie,[27] beating up all the prejudice they could. John Adam, who acted as Governor-General for seven months, until Lord Amherst arrived in August, 1823, disallowed the more flagrantly dishonest items of the Palmer claims. The firm were paid to the extent of eighty lakhs, a sufficient tax of Indian resources; and withdrew, a year later, by the simple process of going bankrupt,

> 'not from any run ... but merely from want of funds to meet ordinary demands' (Minute in Council, C. T. Metcalfe, December 11, 1828).

But their affairs haunted India for long enough, and Sir William Rumbold remained active and dissatisfied.

The episode lowered Metcalfe's opinion of human nature, as he sorrowfully recorded, but give him that contemptuous assessment of the worth of popularity (of which no man won more, and by entirely worthy means) which accompanied his courage to the end. The uncomplaining gallantry with which he supported through years the cancer which killed him in a story too deep for tears; but his stand against his own countrymen, and his friend the Governor-General in particular, called for no less of character, and should be gratefully remembered by all who love the memory of brave men.

Lord Hastings's attitude is almost inexplicable, unless we take into account the influence exercised by a woman loved as a daughter and roused to hard anger and greed. Even so, it remains difficult to understand, for the himself was incorruptible to almost a prudish degree. Indeed, if anyone doubts that there was justice as well urbanity in Lord Minto's partial recantation of his earlier severity of judgment:

> 'The loose principles which formerly prevailed amongst the Company's servants. . . deserved. . . a little more indulgence perhaps than, as one of its sworn enemies and persecutors, I was disposed to show it. Peculation and abuse were not merely tolerated: they were in a manner established and authorised by the parsimony of the Company in the regular remuneration of its servants'—

and, we may add, established and made almost inevitable by the pestilential sycophancy of the country—let him read Lord Hastings's *Private Journal* with its reiterated narration of the way enormously valuable fights were pressed upon him, despite his firm, courteous, and continued refusal. He and lady Loudoun never took a thing; and it was almost superhuman to stand out when the donors were so unwearyingly silly in their determination to put the all-powerful British in their debt.

Lord Hastings refused to abolish suttee, and made the mistake, in 1813, of ordering that police officer must be present at a widow-burning. This regulation was interpreted as giving official sanction to the cowardly and detestable rite; and Hastings Himself finally admitted that it had increased 'these sacrifices'. As against 378 suttees officially reported in Bengal in 1815, 839 were reported in 1818. It was about this time that British notice was widely and often drawn to the seamy side of Hinduism, which in practice had become thoroughly decadent and degraded. The contempt engendered was an increasingly powerful factor making for ruthlessness in the attitude of the stronger towards the weaker people. The impartial historian, whatever his race, must admit that much of the scorn entertained for the practices and thought of the people of India at this time was deserved. The Governor-General brought out with him the European mind, jaded from experience of world-shaking revolutions followed by the dragging Napoleonic wars and from the Prince Regent's disillusioning friendship. He was perhaps unfortunate in having his closest contact with Bengal, whose inhabitants, sunk in centuries of oppression, had not yet begun their striking mental recovery. He regarded them with pity, but also with contempt; and there are periods in the history of every nation when both are merited:

> 'Every day more and more satisfies me that I formed a just estimate of those who inhabit Bengal at least. They are infantine in everything. Neat and dexterous in making any toy or ornament for which they have a pattern, they do not show a particle of invention; and their work, unless they follow some European model, is flimsy and inadequate. Their religious processions constantly remind me of the imitation of some public ceremony which English children would make. One sees seven or eight persons gravely following a fellow who is tapping on a kind of drum that sounds like a cracked tin kettle, and though nobody looks at them they have the air of being persuaded that they are doing something wonderfully interesting. The temples they build are just such as would be constructed by schoolboys in Europe, had they the habit of dealing in brick and mortar. The edifices are rarely above four feet high, exclusive of two or three steps on which they are raised, and contain some rude and shabby carving or delineation of their gods. If this be the rate of the men, one may easily conceive what that of the women must be. Never enjoying even female society, their lives are passed in the extreme of listlessness. It is this which produces so many instances of women burning themselves.'[28]

As for suttee, though the Government of Bengal dared not suppress it, Metcalfe in Delhi, following the discountenancing of it by its Muslim rulers, prohibited the rite. The Marathas also, who exercised—this is one of the paradoxes attaching to these freebooters—a genuine of capricious humanity, were in advance of the British administration:

> 'The Mahomedan rulers endeavoured, as much as they could without off ending their Hindu subjects, to prevent it; and the Maharattas, since they acquired paramount power in this country, have by a wise neglect and indifference, which neither encouraged by approval, nor provoked by prohibition, rendered this practice very rare. In the whole of Central India there have not been, as far as can be learnt, above 3 or 4 Sutties annually for the last 20 years'.[29]

Only in Rajasthan and Bengal did this cruelty persist on a large scale within the British sphere of influence; and in both countries the men had lost their natural heritage of independence, and were at the mercy of oppressors.

REFERENCES

1. Prinsep, i. 243.
2. Hastings, *Private Journal, April* 15, 1816.
3. *Private Journal*, October 11,1817.
4. *Op. Cit*. 30, 817.
5. *Op. cit*. November 7, 1817.
6. J.W. Kaye, *Life of Sir John Malcolm,* ii. 187-9.
7. *History of British India*, 288.
8. *Life of Sir John Malcolm,* ii. 189-090.
9. He was much pestered by this or that prince begging to be allowed to make war on some neighbour.
10. *Life of Metcalfe,* i. 456-7.

    That this surmise was soundly based, no one at the time would have bothered to deny. When Sindhia accepted the terms dictated to him, the Governor-General thought it necessary to apologise to the army for their disappointment: 'His Higness engages to afford every faciliatation to the British troops in their pursuit of the Pindaris through his dominions, and to co-operate actively towards the extermination of those brutal freebooters. In consequence, the troops and country of His Higness are to be regarded as those of an ally. The generous confidence and animated zeal of the army may experience a shade of disappointment in the diminished prospect of serious exertion; but the Governor-General is convinced that the reflection of every officer and soldier in the army will satisfy him that the carrying every point by equity and moderation is the product triumph of the British character'.

Cf. also: 'These threatening appearances at the Native Courts were regarded fearlessly by all—hopefully by many'. *Life of Malcolm*, ii. 187).

11. *Op. cit.* ii, 47.
12. Prinsep, ii. 82.
13. Colonel Tod's phrase.
14. Grant Duff, 486.
15. *Op. cit.* ii. 503 (editor's comment, in Oxford University Press reissue).
16. *Oxford History of India*, 639.
17. *A Memoir of Central India*, ii. 264-8.
18. *Private Journal*, i. 338.
19. See Appendix B, Opinions of Sir Thomas Munro and Bishop Heber'.
20. In his *Nationalism*.
21. *Life of Metcalfe*, ii. 10 ff.
22. M. Martin, *The Indian Empire*, iii. 42
23. *Oxford History of India*, 639.
24. Kaye, *Life of Metcalfe*, ii. 45.
25. *Op. cit.* ii. 44.
26. *Op. cit.* ii. 51.
27. *Op. cit.* ii. 90.
28. *Private Journal*, June 23, 1814.
29. Malcolm, *Central India*, ii. 207.

11

The New Ideology

The three schools of thought—Benthamite Radical, Evangelical and the Traditionalist—sought each in its own say to fulfil this necessary task.

The Radicals

The Radicals were secular in their outlook and for them the justification for British conquest and rule lay in securing peace and order in a country which was torn by dissensions and fratricidal wars and was groaning under the misrule of Nawabs and Rajas. They believed in the rule of law which would replace anarchy and create conditions in which people would live happily. For, what they needed most was not liberty or self-government but peace and welfare. Only an omnicompetent State, working through an auhoritarian executive endowed with all powers, could maintain order, give the necessary laws which define and protect rights, introduce inexpensive and expeditious judicial processes to uphold them, and establish a political and economic system which would ensure to the individual opportunities of self-realisation as a member of a capitalist society.

The Radicals had no patience with the collectivistic, static Indian civilisation which was cluttered up with mediaeval customs and bound inexorably in the iron chains of caste, a society in which the masses were oppressed by the landlord and the priest. Their remedy was a root and branch transformation through Europeanisation which alone could improve social conditions and prevent political revolution.

In economic matters they were followers of Malthus and Ricardo. They put their faith in the doctrine of *laissez faire,* in individual enterprise and free trade, and they condemned aid or intervention by the state. In matters of land-revenue administration, they opposed the introduction or extension of the British type of landlordism in India and supported direct dealings on the part of the government with the peasants. James Mill was a strong supporter of the Recardian theory of rent, and urged upon the Government to stand forth as the landlord and absorb the whole of the economic rent of land, which the economists of the time defined as the difference between the total produce and the wages of labour plus profit no stock.

The Evangelicals

The Evangelicals' point of view was religious. For them temporal welfare and eternal salvation could be attained only through the acceptance of Christianity. They looked upon the British conquest of India as a divine dispensation, a punishment for the sins of the people, for "the abysmal depths of Indian paganism", and as a promise of redemption from "the most depraved and cruel system of superstition which ever enslaved a people."[1] Naturally they aimed at the conversion of the Indian people, and their assimilation to the Christian ways of Europe. But they were not interested merely in saving the souls of the heathens; they wisely reckoned that Anglicisation would stimulate the desire for English goods. The spread of Christian ways was bound to promote the flow of Christian-made commodities. For the achievement of these laudable objects it was necessary that restrictions upon the free entry of English settlers and missionaries and upon the free admission of English merchants and goods, should be removed.

In order to propagate Christianity, it was necessary for the Christian Government to continue and to maintain peace and order so that necessary conditions for the fulfilment of the mission's objective might be created. But they laid great emphasis upon education, for the conquest of the mind was the key to success in every other enterprise.

The Traditionalists

So far as aims were concerned, there was little difference between the Traditionalists and the other two schools. The object of all of them was to strengthen the foundations of British rule. Some of them might entertain the vision of a far-off day when India might be free, and a Macaulay might look upon that day as the most glorious in the history of England, but they had no illusions that this adorable vision could be realised in any forsecable future. Looking at Indian affairs from a practical point of view, they thought that a paternalistic government was the best suited to India. Their theory that power was a trust from Providence supported the view that the British official—the Collector, the Governor, the governor General—was an Olympian god and should be regarded by the subjects as a manifestation of the divine attributes of Preserver, Sustainer and Destroyer, for such a government would be in accord with the Indian tradition. They were opposed to Anglicisation which they regarded as impracticable and undersirable. Like Burke they were suspicious of abstract principles. They believed in the continuity of history and culture and deprecated catastrophic changes. Mount-stuart Elphinstone, admonishing the Governor General, said, "it is, however, to be remembered that even just government will not be a blessing if at variance with the habits and character to the people".[2] He defended the dispensation of justice by the village Panchayat in these words: The intimate acquaintance of the members with the subject in dispute, and in many cases with the characters of the parties, must have made their decisions frequently correct; and it was an advantage of incalculable value in that mode of trial that the judges, being drawn from the body of the people, could act on no principles that were not generally understood, a circumstances which, by preventing uncertainty and obscurity in law, struck at the very root of litigation."[3]

Malcolm in his Instructions to Assistants and Officers, notes: "our power in India rests on the general opinion of the Natives of our comparative superiority in good faith, wisdom, and strength, to their own rulers. This important impression will be improved by the considerations we shew to their habits, institutions and religion, by the moderation, temper, and kindness with which we conduct ourselves towards them; and injured by every act that offends their belief or superstition, that shews disregard or neglect of individuals or communities, or that evinces our having, with the arrogance of conquerors, forgotten those maxims by which this great empire has been established, and by which alone it can be preserved."[4]

Their conception of paternal government involved the union of executive and judicial powers, the substitution of individual agency for collective boards, and a ryotwari system of land settlement.

The History of Administrative Development

It is not necessary to discuss the details of the proposals put forward by the different protagonists, or the interesting debates in all these matters that took place. But it is desirable to review briefly the outcome of the discussions and describe the shape of the administration as it developed from Cornwallis to Canning.

Act of 1813: Investigation into the affairs of the Company began in 1808, when an enquiry committee of the House of Commons was appointed. It submitted its report after four years, and he Act of 1813, which renewed the Charter of the Company, was based upon it. The main features of the change were that: (i) the monopoly of trade of the company was abolished except in tea and in trade with China, (ii) the Church establishment was placed under a bishop maintained from the Indian revenues, and (iii) provision was made for granting permission to Englishmen to settle and hold land in India, to the missionaries for introducing useful knowledge and propagating religious and moral improvement, and to traders for their lawful purposes, under a system of linceses.

Act of 1833: Twenty years later, in 1833, the constitution was changed again. The Company's monopoly of tea trade and China trade was taken away and it was required to wind up its commercial business. But it administrative and political powers were continued, as also it patronage over India appointments.

So far as the Indian Government was concerned, a fourth member was added to the Council of the Governor General for legislative purposes. This was a significant step. It inaugurated a separation between the legislative and executive functions of the Central Government. It put an end to the variety of law-making authorities and judicatures whose spheres of activity were ill-defined. Among these authorities were the Governor General in Council and the Governors in Council of the presidencies of Bombay and Madras, whose regulations—frequently conflicting—were enforceable only in the company's courts.

Besides, there were the Hindu and Muslim laws with their variety of texts and interpretations, and lastly the English statutes, common law and equity, applied by the King's courts—the Supreme Courts and the Mayor's courts. The Act of 1833 vested the legislative power exclusively in the Governor General in Council and deprived the governments of the Presidencies of their legislative function. The Governor General was empowered to make laws and regulations for all persons whether British or Indian, foreigners or others, for all courts of justice whether established by charter or otherwise, and for the whole of the territory under British rule. Of course, the permanent right of Parliament to legislate for India was not affected.

The Governor General was directed to appoint an 'Indian Law Commission' to enquire into the administration of justice and into the nature and operation of all laws. Macaulay was appointed the fourth member of the Council and the chairman of the commission. The deliberations of the commission led to the formation of the Indian Penal Code, the Codes of Civil and Criminal Procedure and other codes of substantive and adjectival laws. The emergence of unified system of laws, a uniform judicial procedure and a uniform judicature, gave a powerful stimulus to the growth of unity in India.

Act of 1853: In 1853 the Charter of the East India Company was renewed for the last time. The Council of the Governor General was enlarged for legislation to twelve members who were all salaried officials. They included besides the governor General and the four Councillors, the commander-in-Chief, the Chief Justice of Bengal, a puisne judge and four members to represent Bengal, Madras, Bombay and the North West Provinces (Utter Pradesh). The meeting of the Legislative Council were made public and its proceedings were published officially.

The Company had ceased to be a commercial concern after 1833 and was merely an instrument of the British crown to carry on the government of India. This indirect method of governing a vast empire was so logical that it is a wonder that it lasted three quarters of a century. The Revolt of 1857, however, gave it a death blow, and in 1858 the British crown assumed directly the government of India.

Effects of Administrative changes

During the last fifty years of the Company's rule, the edified of administration was completed. The Regulations for Bengal which Cornwallis had promulgated, served as the foundation. But under the stress of new ideas and circumstances, and in the light of experience, modifications were inevitable when new governments were set up in the different provinces.

The problems that the British administrators had to face were extremely complicated. Their first concern naturally was to safeguard the interests of their own people, and to secure the permanency of their empire. Issues involving the relations between the rulers and the subject race had to be settled. The most important among them were how far Indian traditions were to be approved or rejected, what part should be assigned to the Indians in administration, and what should be the limits social intercourse between the rulers and the ruled.

The Cornwallis system had sought to final a solution to these. The settlement of land had guaranteed revenue adequate for the dual purpose of administration and investment. The Indians had been deprived of all opportunities of acquiring influence that might threaten authority. But the Permanent Settlement had created new problems. It had created a alcss of men of property who might prove a potential danger to British rule and the policy of separation of functions tended to weaken the authority of the executive officers and lower the prestige of the Government.

Change in the English Attitude After 1793

Insofar as cultural and social contracts were concerned, the early Englishmen were merchants and ambassadors who recognised the differences between themselves and Indians, but did not suffer from racial arrogance. Many of them learnt Indian languages, adopted Indian ways and manners, and practised friendly intercourse with them. Warren Hastings knew Persian and Bengali well, and Sir William Jones was an eminent Sanskrit scholar who translated Kalidasa's *Shakuntale* into English. They participated freely in the entertainments arranged by wealthy Indians, nawabs and rajas. "On both sides there was much give-and-take", says Spear. "The English had long acquired a taste for nautches, and developed new ones for elephant fights and hookah smoking; the Nawabs on their part experimented with

English food drink."[5] Musalmans acquired a liking for harm which they ate under the designation of "Vilayati Hiran" or English venison. Friendship also grew. The Hastings circle included Beneram, his brother Bishambar Pandit, Ganga Gobind Singh, and Ali Ibrahim Khan.

But the Cornwallis regime had marked a change. Reciprocal entertainments had decreased, formation of friendships had ceased, and higher posts had been reserved for Englishmen. Government' designs "became more imperial and its attitude more haughty and aloof."[6] With the spread of Radical and Evongelical opinions, the English attitude changed altogether. Tolerance was replaced by contempt and aversion. "A superiority complex was forming which regarded India not only as a country whose institutions were bad and people corrupted, but one which was by its nature incapable of ever becoming any better."[7] It stamped the Indian people individually and collectively, with the mark of inferiority.

The New Land Settlements

Changes in the methods of administration took place in the new climate of opinion. The extension of the empire necessitate a new type of administrative organisation based on a different system of land-revenue settlement. The permanent Settlement of Bengal had been decided upon after a protracted debate over its various aspects, but one thing was never in doubt, viz. that the settlement must be made with the zamindars. When, however, the wars in the south brought an accession of territories where the zamindari tenure was not in general use, but was confined to isolated tracts and to local chiefs, the advisability of settling the lands on the model of Bengal was seriously questioned. The defeat of the Marathas and the expansion of the British dominion over the Deccan raised the same problem in this region.

The expectations from the zamindari system, moreover, had not been justified. It had been argued that the landlords would prove a bulwark of order and stability, and would entertain a warm and zealous attachment to the Government founded on the solid basis of their own interests.[8] In actual practice the contrary proved to be true. Immediately after the Permanent Settlement both in Bengal and the Northern Sarkars, a struggle commenced between the local governments and the zamindars, which was "not always confined to chicanery, falsehood and flight on the one side, nor to the utmost exercise of civil rigours on the other." The collectors' bailiffs supported by their armed force and sometimes the regular troops, and the zamindars with their own courts, police and means of private defence, faced each other. Instead of cooperating in the matter of administration, the zamindars were not averse to embarrassing the Government. They resented enquiry into their relations with the cultivators, filed attempts to determine their rights, and prevented the ryots from seeking justice outside their courts. They promoted bribery and corruptions and connived at crime. The zamindari areas were infested with gangas of robbers and dacoits. In the Northern Sarkars there were frequent rebellions of the zamindars.

The system was conducive to a looseness of ties between the government and the people. So long as the zamindar continued to pay the fixed revenue, the Government left him to do what he liked, and the collector just "loomed like Fate in the background and was as little heeded in every day life." The lack of knowledge of the interior and of real contact with the masses affected the Government's capacity to control the country and weakened its authority.[9]

Other disadvantages soon began to be realised. The Permanent Settlement deprived the State of a share in the increase of rent which resulted from the general improvement of the economic conditions, and handed over the entire undarned increment to the zamindar. In the second place, while the settlement favoured a handful of landholders, it completely ignored the interests of the vast mass of the oppressed cultivators whose resentment and dissaftisfaction seemed to evoke no sympathy. Munro wrote, "It seems extraordinary that it should ever have been conceived that a country could be as much benefited by giving up a share of the public rent to a small class of zamindars or mootadars as ...by giving it to ryots, from whom all rent is derived."[10]

Read and Munro led the attack on the Permanent Settlement, and gradually convinced the home authorities of the unwisdom of extending it to other parts of India. The Select Committee of the House of Commons which reviewed the affairs of the East India Company preceding the renewal of their Charter in 1813, decided in favour of the ryotwari settlement.

Munro pressed that "when the settlement of a great province is in view, the prosperity of the body of the people should be the grand object to which everything else should be made to yield."[11] This object, Munro thought, would be best achieved under a ryotwari settlement. To the objection that under the ryotwari system there was no person between the cultivator and the revenue officer, Munro replied: "This objection is made from not understanding the condition of the Indian husbandman; for in this country, the landlord and cultivator can never be permanently separated as in England. The minute division of property will always render them the same person with very few exceptions. The landlord must always cultivate his own fields; and hence the collections must always be made directly from the cultivator in his quality of landlord, and there can be no person between the cultivator and the revenue officer, without a creation of Zemindars, who must themselves, in time become, either petty princes, or cultivators."[12] There was not need, therefore, of creating a class of contractors, the zamindars—"who undertake to get a greater fixed rent for government from the ryots, than can be done, in any other way".[13]

The ryotwari settlement of the Deccan was supposed to perpetuate the agrarian relations which had existed for centuries in the past. It proposed to confirm the cultivator's proprietary rights in the land that the cultivated, subject to the payment of the government demands, and thus to combine in him the characters of the labourer, the farmer and the landlord. The system was advantageous both to the Government and to the cultivator. To the former, it ensured the benefit of all future increases of revenue resulting from the extension of cultivation and the rise of prices of agricultural produce. A further advantage was that it helped to win over the mass of the cultivating population to the support of British rule, and free it from dependence upon the support of a few big zamindars. The strength of British rule, it came to be realised, would lie more in the contentment of the masses than in the loyalty of the few who lived by the exploitation of the peasants. Even for the future progress of cultivation, the ryotwari system offered greater promise than the rival zamindari system. Once the peasant was confirmed in his hereditary rights in land, it was argued, he would apply his energy and resources to the improvement and extension of cultivation. The magic of property would concourage enterprise and help to raise the standard of farming.

Munro summed up the case of the ryotwari system in the following words: "It may be also said, that it is better calculated to promote industry, and to argument the produce of the country; because it makes more proprietors and farmers and fewer common labourers, than the Zamindary and mootadary scheme; because the ryot would be more likely to improve his land as a proprietor than as the tenant of a zamindar; and as he would enjoy the whole remission instead of a small part or perhaps none, he would be more able to do it; and because the small proprietor, being the better manager and farmer, and more immediately interested than the great one in the cultivation of his land, would bestow more pains upon it, and make it yield a more abundant crop: that supposing the amount of the property to be the same, it would be better that it should be in the hands of forty or fifty thousand small proprietors than of four for five hundred great ones; that by the remission going at once to the ryots, it would improve the circumstances of the class of men from whom the revenue is principally drawn, and would enable them to raise a greater quantity of food, and thus to favour the increase of population; that by allowing the revenue to increase or diminish, according to the extent of land in cultivation; it eases the farmer, without occasioning on an average of years, any loss to Government; that this fluctuation would lessen every day as the ryots become more wealthy, and would at last be confined to tank lands; and that the ryotwari system by retaining in the hands of the Government all unoccupied land, gives it the power of gradually augmenting the revenue, without imposing any fresh burdens upon the ryots, as long as there is an acre of waste on the country".[14]

Ryotwari tenure was the only land system that was possible under the circumstances outside Bengal. To quote Munro again, 'it is the system which has always prevailed in India—that no other can be permanent; and that however different any new one may be, it must resolve itself into it at last because the duration of great property in any family is opposed by early and universal marriage, by the equal division among all the sons, and by adoption where there are none; that it is more simple than the mootadary plan, because it requires no artificial restraints contrary to customs and the laws of inheritance to prevent the division of estates, because it admits of all gradations of large and small farms."[15]

What distinguished the ryotwari system from the zamindari, was that it substitute for the multiplicity of landholders one zamindar, namely, the Government. It brought the cultivators into direct relations with the Government which functioned as the sole landlord. It interposed no intermediate agency between the workers on the soil and the rulers of the county. It recognised, however, the proprietary rights of the cultivator in the land which he cultivated.

The ryotwari system established the closest relations between the people and the government; for the system required the realisation of rents by the officials directly from each holding. It was necessary that each field should be measured and surveyed, and its boundaries determined, and boundary marks set up. It involved the preparation of field maps, village maps, and taluq maps, and a whole department of the Surveyor General to carry out these duties.

The survey is preliminary to the assessment of the rent of each holding. But the fixation of the amount due is dependent on the calculation of the produce. A classification of soils—wet or dry, agricultural or horticultural—and an enumeration of the particulars concerning the areas occupied by houses, trees, tanks, rivers, nullahs, hills, roads, barren land, wells, gravers, etc., is necessary before the amount of produce can be estimated. On the basis of this estimate a settlement has to be made and the agreement (*patta*) drawn up between the Government and the ryot.

The collection of the stipulated amount from each cultivator is another elaborate proceeding which brings the officials and the peasants into close contact. Considering that the survey and the settlements have to be annually scrutinised and revised, the intimate and detailed character of the administration becomes evident.

The ryotwari tenure, which was introduced in the Madras and Bombay Presidencies, was supposed to be a close approximation to the old Indian system prevailent in these regions. But the fact is that in fundamentals it departed as much from the ancient usages and customs of the country as the zamindari system of Bengal. It created private property in land, destroyed the unity and cohesion of village life, and exposed the cultivator to the ruthless oppression of the revenue authorities who demanded and enforced payment of the land-revenue even in years of drought when land grew no crops and the cultivator had no resources to pay the Government dues.

Marquis Hastings' victories in the last Maratha war brought the Gangetic valley under British rule, and subsequently the annexation of the Punjab, Oudh and Nagpur completed the British dominion in India.

The settlement of these regions naturally followed. Here new systems were tried which borrowed some features from the zamindari system of Bengal and some from the ryotwari system of the Deccan, but embodied some original elements of their own.

In the Gangetic valley, then named the North-West Provinces (now Uttar Pradesh), the Government entered into agreements for payment of revenue with the villages as units. Under the advice of Holt Mackenzie, the Regulation of 1822 was issued, which established the village system. The essential feature of the system was that the Government made the settlement not with the individual cultivator but with the village community as a whole. Each village was assessed as such as was made responsible for the payment through a responsible person. The individual owners paid their shares for their portions of the estate (mahal) by mutual arrangements to the representative. The assessment was periodically revised, usually after every, thirty years. The Muqaddam was the village representative who dealt with the Government. He was assisted by the Patwari who kept the registers and accounts. The collector and the Tahsildar carried but the work of periodical settlements and acted on the information supplied by the Qanungo, the Patwari, and villagers.

The periodic settlements brought the people into contact with Government officials, but as the settlement was made with the village, and not with the individual, the community's organisation was not disrupted.

In the Punjab a modified Mahalwari system was introduced. In the words of John Lawrence, "The proprietors did not engage individually with the Government but by villages. The brotherhood of the village, through its headman or representative, undertake to pay so much for so many years and then having done so, they divide the amount themselves assigning to each one his quota. Primarily each may cultivates and pays for himself; but ultimately he is responsible for his companions and they for him and they are bound together by a joint liability."[16]

The Civil Administration and Judiciary

The successors of Cornwailis shifted the emphasis from the adjudication of rights to the preservation of order, from the administration of impersonal law to the exercise of personal discretion, from civilian to military rule. The result was a concentration of authority, which bordered on military discipline.

Cornwallis had vested the magisterial and police control of a district in the judge-magistrate, and the collection of revenue in the collector, under the supervision of the Board of Revenue at Calcutta. The first breach in this system was made in 1829 when the post of commissioner was created and wide powers were entrusted to him. Each commissioner was placed in charge of a division to supervise the work of the collectors and to superintend the administration of judges, magistrates and the police. He became a judicial officer, too, for the duties of the sessions judge and the Provincial Courts of Appeal, were transferred to him. The Provincial Boards of Revenue and the Provincial Courts of Appeal were abolished.

Two years later, on finding that the charge of a commissioner had become too heavy, charges were effected. The commissioner's criminal juridiction was transferred to the district judge, and the magisterial duties of the judge were handed over the collector. Thus by 1831, although the judiciary was formed into a separate branch of the administration, the executive "was welded into a single charm of command". The collector came to combine in himself the functions of magistracy, police and judiciary in rent and revenue cases. A hierarchy of subordinate staff was established to assist the collector.

In this way the paternalistic principles of union of powers and of individual and personal responsibility, replaced the ideas of separation of powers and collective responsibility exercised through boards. "The double institution of the divisional commissioner and district officer permanently modified the Cornwallis structure and supplied the orthodox model for future British colonial administration."[17]

So far as the judiciary was concerned, although its importance was maintained, its pre-eminence was reduced. The main changes after 1793 affected the system in all its grades. In 1801, the Sadr Diwani Adalat and Sadr Nizamat Adalat became separated from the Governor General in Council. In 1811, the Sadr Diwani Adalat was constituted of a Chief Justice and there puisne judges selected from the covenanted servants of the Company. In 1831, the provincial courts of appeal were abolished, and the powers of the district courts were enhanced. They could try original suits of the value of more than Rs. 5,000 and hear appeals from the courts of Sadr Amins. From their judgments appeal lay to the Aadr Diwani Adalat.

On the criminal side, the Sadr Nizamat Adalat was reconstituted. The Governor General in Council ceased to function as a court, and its place was taken by four judges who were assisted by the chief Qazi and two Muftis. In the reforms of 1831, the circuit courts were wound up. At first the commissioners and them the district judges were required to undertake the sessions work and hold goal deliveries.

On both sides the jurisdiction of Indian judicial officers was extended. On the civil side was instituted a principal Sadr Amin, who could hear cases of Rs. 5,000 valuation, and appeals from the lower courts. On the criminal side, the principal Sadr Amin, Munsifs and Sadr Amins, magistrates and their assistants, were authorised to sentences persons convicted of crimes.

After 1832, permission was given to obtain the assistance of Indian Panchs, assessors or jurors, in the trials of civil and criminal suits. Quazis and Muftis were now not considered necessary and their services could be dispensed with, especially in view of the fact that non-Muslims were exempted from trial under the Muslim law.

There were some changes in the police organisation. The village chaukidars, who were dependent upon the zamindars for their maintenance and were responsible to Daroghas of the *thana* for their duties, did not prove equal to the task.

They failed to suppress crime and gang robbery continued to plague the countryside. An attempt was made to appoint respectable persons as Amins to help the Daroghas, but they were not paid any remundration and soon faded out. The zamindars had been relieved of their authority and were unwilling to resume the duties of crime detection and prevention, which was a thankless task. The office of the Provincial Superintendent of Police was created in 1808, but determinated in 1829. Then the commissioners were entrusted with this work. Two years later the collector-magistrates of the districts obtained the supervision of police arrangements while the actual duties of crime prevention remained in charge of the district superintendents of police who were assisted by the Daroghas.

The Army

The expansion of dominion and the relative paucity of Englishmen were responsible for the strengthening of the executive and the employment of Indians in subordinate posts on a large scale. The same needs led to the enlargement of the army. The Marquis of Hastings enumerated the functions of the army as follow:

(1) to guard against the ebullitions among the people, and to increase of the striking power of the army depended essentially on good communications.

The help of the army was also sought in matters of health and sanitation, utilisation of forests, development of irrigation, and execution of public works. Even in land-revenue administration, the services of military officers were utilised. Warren Hastings had often deputed a number of them as farmers of revenue. Read and Munro were the authors of the ryotwari system; Robertson, Briggs, Pottinger, Wingate, Barwell and Sykes made settlements in the Deccan, and Jacob in Sind. Although their employment was discouraged, they still constituted the bulk of officers in charge of collecting land-revenue in the Punjab, Sindh and the Central provinces (Madhya Pradesh).

The semi-military character of the British Government is clearly revealed in these administrative arrangements. The Duke of Wellington testified: "The system of government in India, the foundation of authority, and the modes of supporting it and of carrying on the operations of government are entirely different from the systems and modes adopted in Europe for the same purpose. . . The foundation and the instrument of all power there is the sword."[18]

It is demonstrated in the appointment of the Governors General. Cornwallis was a soldier with extensive military experience. He had served in the War of American Independence, and, although defeated, had not lost honour. The Marquis of Hastings also had fought in the war of American Independence and in the revolutionary wars in Flanders. Bentinck saw service in the Netherlands, and in Italy with the Austrian forces, and in Spain in the Peninsular War. Hardinge was a verteran of many battles in the struggle against Napoleon, and actually served under the command of Hugh Gough, the Commander-in-Chief of the Indian Army in the Sikh war. Wellesley, Auckland and Ellenborough were more military-minded than even the professional soldiers. They were not only protagonists of the imperialist forward policy, but showered such great favours upon army men that Henry Torrens in doggerel verse, full of sarcasm, remonstrates:

> "All but B.C.S. Collectors for their offices sufficient are!
> All Moonsiffs are immaculate, all Judges inefficient are!
> No military favourite (whatever his condition) errs!
> And Colonels of Artillery are heaven-born Commissioners!"[19]

The Civil Service

The civilian services, however were the main pillars of the administration. In the beginning, when the Company was purely a mercantile concern, its servants were recruited from the middle and humbler classes. Later 'gentlemen'—peers, knights and squires—became members of the Company and by the beginning of the eighteenth century men of good birth came to be recruited in its service. They entered as apprentice at an early age with hardly any qualification, and after seven years's service were eligible for promotion to the writer's grade. Next to the writers were the grades of the junior factor (later junior merchant) and senior factor (later senior merchant). Their salaries were low. The apprentice received £5, the writer £ 10, the junior factor £20, and the senior factor £30 to £40 annually. They were, however, permitted to supplement their incomes by investment in the stock and private trading.

Between 1744 and 1765, the Company of merchants became transformed into rulers of provinces as a result of the wars in the Deccan Bengal. The acquisition of the Diwani of Bengal, Bihar and Orissa added and governmental functions to its trading activities. The task fell on the writers, factors, and merchants of the Company who were quite unqualified for such duties. The thirty years after Plassey were a period of confusion, in which the worst instincts of self-aggrandisement had full sway. The results were terrible. The province of Bengal was devastated, and although the servants enriched themselves, the Company suffered great losses. What is worse, its future interests were jeopardised.

From Clive onwards efforts were made to set matters right. In order to mitigate the evils of bribery, corruption and illicit trade it was necessary to raise the salaries, and to resist the pressure of influential people in making appointments. Clive's scheme of creating a fund out of the monopoly of salt to increase the salaries was turned down by the Directors. But they themselves increased the salaries of the senior servants. The remunerations fixed in 1772-73 raised the emoluments of the Governor of Bengal to £23,000 per year, and those of the members of the Council from £1,5000 to £3,000 according to their rank.

In 1793, the question was permanently decided. The junior grades of assistants were given Rs. 300, 400 and 500 a month, and the collector drew Rs. 1,500 with a commission of about one per cent on his collection of revenue, up to a maximum of Rs. 27,500 a year.

Cornwallis made great efforts to purify the services, and firmly put his foot down on the vicious practice of awarding posts to unworthy favourities of eminent and influential men. Wellesley desired to improve the quality of the young civil servants and he opened the Fort William College at Calcutta. The intention was to arrange a three-year comprehensive course in subjects which were regarded necessary for the cadets. Unfortunately, Wellesley had offended the Directors and the plan had to be modified so that the College became a school of oriental languages. But the Directors realised the importance of army as

(1) to maintain military stations throughout the country to give timely aid to the civil authority;

(2) to assist the Indian protected princes from the danger of the uprisings of their subjects;

(3) to keep roads free from robbers and dacoits, and to protect traders;

(4) to offer a career to the numerous disbanded Indian soldiers; and

(5) to counterbalance the armies of independent rulers like the King of Oudh, and the Maharajahs of the Punjab and Gawalior.

It was obviously impossible to bring an adequate number of European troops from the King's army to India, not only because enough could not be spared from their duties in the other parts of the world—especially as the Napolenoic wars were not over and Europe was in a state of ferment—but mainly because European troops were far too expensive and the Company was constantly complaining against the dumping of such troops at its expense in India.

From the point of view of recruitment, the situation in India was most favourable. Indian possessed an inexhaustible reservoir of soldiers of good quality; among them were many castes and tribes whose occupation was fighting and numerous disbanded soldiers from the establishments of the conquered Indian princes. These men were brave fighters; they possessed endurance and were amenable to discipline and training. Their traditions of loyalty of the salt created no conflicts in their devotion to duty and willing obedience to their officers' orders. They were cheap too.

At the departure of Cornwallis, the Company's troops numbered 70,000 of whom the British were only 13,500. By 1826, the number had increased to about 2,81,000 men, of whom 10,541 were Europeans of the Company's army and about 22,000 belonged to the King's forces. On the eve of the Revolt of 1857, the army comprised 3,11,374 men, of whom 45,522 were Europeans.[20] The cheapness of the Indian soldier may be gauged by the fact that the sepoy received a salary of Rs. 7 every month, and his non-commissioned Indian officers Rs. 25 and Rs. 67 per month. In 1856, in the Indian army which was 2,75,000 strong, there were only three Indian officers receiving a salary of Rs. 300 per month.

The anti-Indian policy of Cornwallis found its fullest scope in the army. After 1784, European subalterns were attached to the command of Indian companies. Between 1790 and 1796 a reorganisation was effected in which the European element was increased and each sepoy battalion was given nine European officers. In 1848, a sepoy infantry regiment of 750 or 800 men had a complement of twenty-four European officers, and a regiment of cavalry twenty European officers. By 1826, no Indian could rise to a military command. An Indian risaldar was heard by Sir Henry Lawrence to exclaim, "we live and not without hope". The displacement of Indian officers was deplored by no less a person than Colonel Wellesley (later the Duke of Wellington).

Semi-Military Character of British Rule

It was in accord with the general character of British rule that he army played not an ostentatious, but a substantial role in the governance of India. The immediate control and administration of newly-acquired territories was entrusted to the military officers as could be expected in the circumstances, and it is not surprising that the Punjab, Sind and earlier, the ceded districts in the north, the south and in central India were placed in charge of military officers. What is peculiarly interesting is that a number of civil departments were run by the army officers. The political department which dealt with the Indian states was almost wholly monopolised by them. The residencies and agencies were their sole preserve.

Another department which leaned heavily upon the army was that of the Police. In spite of the circulars of the Government condemning the calling up of the military to put down civilian troubles, the magistrates continued to call them up. Their police duties became so numerous that not even half a battalion could remain permanently at the headquarters. The cantonments multiplied and even the dependent stations were occupied. The army personnel accompanied the transit of treasure from one place to another and escorted the transport of stores from Calcutta to other cities. They had to keep prisoners in their custody. In Bengal 'provincial battalions' used to be attached to the police, till the practice was discontinued by Bentinck. In the Bombay Presidency, military guards were posted in northern and southern Khandesh. In the Punjab, 8,100 troops, among whom two-thirds were infantry and one-third cavalry, did the police duties. In Sind also there was policing by the military.

Apart from these essential departments, the army was in charge of many other important functions. They built up the survey department and taught surveying to land revenue officers. They built roads; and railways for communications were primarily a military concern. Thus the Punjab road system was first laid out to watch the Sikh, and Dalhousie extended the Grand Trunk Road from Lahore to Peshwar in the interests of defence. The construction of the East Indian Railway was given to a company and its profits guaranteed on condition that the carriage of troops and military stores would be given priority. The North-Western Railway was regarded as the most important line in India from the military and political points of view. It is not necessary to stress the obvious—that the consolidation of the empire and the and found the Haileybury College, which gave a two years' course. At first the age of entrance was fifteen, but in 1833 it was raised to seventeen. The maximum age was fixed at twenty-one. The object of the College was to turn out officers who realised that "there were certain traditions to be kept up and handed over, ... a political faith to be cherished, and a code of public and private honour to be rigidly maintained."[21] Blunt adds, "so long as the I.C.S. continues in the Haileybury tradition, it cannot go far wrong."[22] But in 1853, on Macaulay's proposal, appointment to the civil service was taken away from the Directors, and it was decided that selection should be made through competitive examinations alone. The first examination was held in 1855. The College was closed in 1857.

The reforms created the steel frame which sustained the British empire in India for over a hundred and fifty years. The service was indeed a wonderful invention of the practical genius of the British race. It was costly, as it was the highest paid permanent service in the world. But is was imbued with pride; its powers and responsibilities were great and its demands on the versatility of its members truly astonishing. It had the sense of a mission, for it believed to be divinely ordained to spread the blessings of *Pax Britannica* over vast lands and innumerable human beings. It gave to India a system of government which was 'miracle of organisation.'

The Consequences of British Rule

The immediate consequences of the new system of administration were dismal in the extreme. The complete elimination of Indians from the higher services and their total exclusion from any share in government had the most untoward effects both immediately and in the long run. Of the unfairness and unwisdom of such arrangements some of the high officials of the Company were conscious. Wellesley wrote to the Court of Directors: "It is a radial imperfection in the constitution of our establishments in India, that no system appears to have been adopted with a view either to conciliate the goodwill or to control the disaffection of this description of our subjects, whom we found in possession of the Government, and whole we have excluded from all share of emolument, honour, and authority, without providing any adequate corrective of those passions incident to the loss of dignity, wealth and power."[23]

Munro, in his minute dated August 12, 1817, to Lord Hasting says: "The strength of the British Government enables it to put down every rebellion to repel every invasion, and to give its subjects a degree of protection which those of no Native power enjoy. Its laws and institutions also afford them a security from domestic oppression, unknown in those states; but these advantages are dearly bought. They are purchased by the sacrifice of independence of national character, and of whatever renders a people respectable. The Natives of the British provinces may, without fear, pursue their different occupations . . . and enjoy the fruits of their labour in transquility; but none of them can aspire to anything beyond this mere animal state of thriving in peace—none of them can look forward to any share in the legislation or civil or military government of their country. It is from men who either hold, or are eligible to public office, that Natives take their character; where no such men exist, there can be no energy in any other class of the community. The effect of this state of things is observable in all the British provinces, whose inhabitants are certainly the most abject race in India. No elevation of character can be expected among men who, in the military line, cannot attain to any rank above that of subahdar, where they are as much below an ensign as an ensign is below the Commander-in-Chief, and who, in the civil line, can hope for nothing beyond some petty judicial or revenue office, in which they may, by corrupt means, make up their slender salary". He adds, "The consequence, therefore, of the conquest of Indian by the British arms would be, in place of raising, to debase the whole people. There is perhaps no example of any conquest in which the Natives have been so completely excluded from all shares of the Government of their country as in British India."

Then again on November 12, 1818, he wrote, "Foreign conquerors have treated the Natives with violence, and often with great cruelty, but bone has treated them with so much scorn as we; none have stigmatised the whole people as unworthy of trust, as incapable of honesty, and as fit to be employed only where we cannot do without them. It seems to be not only ungenerous, but impolitic, to debase the character of a people fallen under our dominion." He concludes, "The exclusion from offices of trust and emoluments has become of part of our system of government, and has been productive of no good."[24]

A few years later, Minro reflected on the probable condition of Britain if subjected to such a rule as that of which the himself had been an instrument in India in these words: "Let Britain he subjugated by a foreign power to-morrow, left the people be excluded from all share in the Government, from public honours, from every office of high trust or emolument, and let them in every situation be considered as unworthy of trust, and all their knowledge and all their literature, sacred and profane, would not save them from becoming in another generation or two, a low-minded, deceitful, and dishonest race."[25]

Elphinstone stated, "It may be alleged with more justice that we dried up the fountains of native talent, and that from the nature of our conquest not only all encouragement to the advancement of knowledge is withdrawn, but even the actual learning of the nation is likely to be lost and the productions of former genius to be forgotten"[26].

Malcolm, at the close of the Maratha wars, remarked: "Our present condition is one of apparent response, but full of danger." Then he added, "There are many causes which operate to make a period like this one of short duration; and the change to a colder system of policy, and the introduction of our laws and regulations into countries immediately dependent upon us, naturally excite agitation and alarm. It is the hour in which men awake from a dream. Disgust and discontent succeed to terror and admiration and the princes, the chefs, and all who had enjoyed rank or influence, see nothing but a system dooming them to immediate decline and ultimate annihilation.

"The establishment of the British authority over Central India, though recognised at first by almost all classes as a real blessing because it relieved them from intolerable evils, begins already to be regarded by the princes, the chiefs and the military portion of the community, with very mixed sentiments, among which serious apprehensions as to the permanence of their present condition are predominant.

"The same classes of men do not fill the same places in society under our governments, as they did under a Native prince; nor are men actuated be similar motives. Our administration, though just, is cold and rigid. It is creates no alarm, it inspires little, if any, emulation. The people are protected, but not animated or attached. It is rare that any native of India living under it can suffer injury or wrong; but still more rare that he can be encouraged or elevated by favour or distinction."[27]

All avenues to fame, wealth or power were closed to Indians; no opportunities were left for public service, or the performance of the citizen's duties, to defend the country or to advance its prosperity. Munro had forecast that such exclusion would foment a spirit of discontent or opposition, and if it did not do so, then the people "would sink in character. . . and would degenerate into an indolent and abject race, incapable of any higher pursuit than the mere gratification of their appetites."[28]

He rightly observed that "he who loses his liberty loses half his virtue. . . The enslaved nation loses the privileges of a nation as the slave does those of a freeman; it loses the privilege of taxing itself, of making its own laws, of having any share in their administration, or in the general government of the country. British India has none of these privileges."[29]

A deadly pall hung over India, under which the classes were smothered and the masses breathed with difficulty. The Muslim and Hindu ruling princes were disarmed and isolated; the Muslim and Hindu families, tribes and castes which had provided soldiers, administrators and leaders, were ostracised from offices of responsibility, and condemned to serve as helots; the Muslim and Hindu learned classes were deprived of patronage and slowly squeezed out of their avocations. So far as the masses were concerned, excessively heavy assessments, severity of realisation, growth of population, and the pressure upon land, depressed the miserable standards of living of the peasants, while the economic policies of the rulers brought ruin upon Indian artisans and craftsmen, so that many of them sank of the position of landless labourers, while the obstacles placed in the way of industrial development prevented the creation of fresh avenues of employment. Writing in 1837, about the commercial policy of England, Montogomery Martin said, "We have done everything possible to impoverish still further the miserable beings subject to the cruel selfishness of English commerce."[59]

It was perhaps necessary that in order the new might be born, the old should suffer an agonising and violent death.

REFERENCES

1. Coupland, R., *Wilberforce*, p. 317.
2. Forrest, G. W., *Selections from the Minutes and other Official Writings of the Hon. Mountstuart Elphinstone* (London, 1884), p. 57.
3. *Ibid.*, p. 355.
4. Malcolm, J., *A Memoir of Central India*, Vol. II (1880 edition), p. 358.
5. Spear, T.G.P., *The Nobobs*, p. 131.
6. *Ibid.*, p. 136.

7. *Ibid.*
8. H. Colebrooke's Minute, Para 37, vide *Selection of Papers from Records at East India Horse,* Vol. I (1820), p. 50.
9. Sec Carstairs, R., *The Little World of an Indian District Officer* (Macmillan, 1912), Books I, II and IV.
10. Firminger, *Fifth Report,* Vol. III, p. 504.
11. *Ibid.*
12. *Ibid.* p. 505.
13. *Ibid.*, p. 504.
14. Firminger, *Fifth Report,* Vol. III, p. 503.
15. *Ibid.*, p. 503.
16. See *Report on the Administration of the Punjab Territories,* 1854-55 to 1855-56, para 39.
17. Stokes Eric, *The English Utiliarians and India,* p. 164.
18. The Duke of Wellington, *The Marquess Wellesley's Government of India,* quoted by Ramsay Muir, *The Making of British India,* p. 209.
19. O'Malley, L.S.S., *The Indian Civil Service,* p. 51.
20. Ruthnaswamy, M., *some Influences that made the British Administrative System in India, op. citl,* pp. 127, etc.
21. Blunt, Sir E., *The I.C.S.* (London, 1937), pp. 35-36.
22. *Ibid.*, p. 36.
23. Wellesley to the Court of Directors, April 22, 1799, see Thompson and Garratt, *The Riss and Fulfilment of British Rule in India* (1958 edition), p. 207.
24. Thompson, Edward, *The Making of the Indian Princes,* p. 273.
25. Quoted by Reginald Reynolds, *The White Sahibs in India,* p. 65; also Romesh Dutt, *The Economic History of India under Early British Rule* (sixth edition), p. 163.
26. Forrest, G.W., *Selections from the Minutes and other Official Writings of Elphinstone,* p. 102.
27. Thompson, Edward, *The Making of the Indian Princes,* p. 272.
28. Quoted by Romesh Dutt, *The Economic History of India under Early British Rule,* p. 10.
29. *Ibid.*

12

The Peshwa and Pindari War (1816-1818)

In the meantime the freebooting bands of central India were increasing in numbers and audacity. The Pindaris, who were openly disowned and secretly encouraged by the Maratha chiefs, had made an inroad into certain districts of the Madras Presidency, carrying off great booty; they had also plundered on the frontier of Bengal. Amir Khan, the Pathan leader, was besieging Jaipur, whose Raja applied for succour to the English. After much negotiation Lord Hastings succeeded not only in bringing the Rajput State of Jaipur within the English protectorate, but also in concluding a subsidiary treaty with the Bhonsla Raja of Nagpore, whereby an important member was detached from the Maratha confederation. But this Raja soon repented an engagement which affected is complete independence; and under the influence of a party at his capital hostile to the English, he began to correspond secretly with the Peshwa at Poona, who had become restless, disaffected, and exceedingly impatient of British mediation in his dealings with feudatories or neighbouring States. The war in Nepal, which seemed likely to be long and troublesome, encouraged among the Marathas an inclination to try conclusions agian with the English. The Peshwa began to assemble his troops and collect military stores; the British Resident replied by calling in the subsidiary force; and a kind of sporadic insurrection, privily fomented by the Poona authorities, was breaking but in the country. All these threatening symptoms reached a crisis when the Gaekwar's envoy, who had been sent to Poona on a special missing under British Guarantee, was assassinated, with the Peshwa's connivance, by one of his confidential favourites. The murderer's surrender was exorted from the Peshwa, with the greatest difficulty, by the British Resident; but he escaped from prison, and the Peshwa, who seemed about to take up arms in his defence, only lost courage and made terms just when an open rupture was becoming imminent. He signed, in 1817, a treaty making cessions of territory in exchange for an increased subsidiary force, and renouncing virtually all pretensions to supremacy in the Maratha confederation.

Lord Hastings now decided that the time had come when he could begin his combined operations for the suppression of the freebooting rhodes, and for such a general reformation of the condition of central India as might eradicate the predatory system. The policy of isolation had, he found, completely failed; its effect was not only to foster the spread of confusion and disorder outside our frontiers, but also to endanger the main position of the British government. The number of the Pindaris was reckoned at 40,000 horsemen; there were also two Mahommedan adventurers in command of large bodies of infantry, with artillery, quite independent of any regular government; while to these may be added a horde of loose mercenaries nominally in the service of the Marathas. Beyond the ring fence of British territory the whole country was exposed to depredation; and the lesser States held the British responsible for the anarchy that prevailed. So Lord Hastings at last resolved to step forward as arbitrator and authoritative peacemaker, to dissolve the plundering bands, and to mark out the whole of the vast inland region into recognized the jurisdiction of some responsible authority. He relied on/the supreme influence and paramount power of the British government in arms to insist, when this had been done, upon the pacification of the whole country through the chiefs to whom it should have been in severally assigned. He projected, in short, the consummation of the work that had been begun by Lord Cornwallis, and carried very far by Lord Wellesley—the extension of our supremacy and protectorate over every native State in the interior of India.

In such a cause, however, the hearty co-operation of the Maratha princes could not reasonably be expected. Amir Khan, the Pathan leader, was persuaded or intimidated into disbanding his army and settling down on the lands guaranteed to him. But Sindhia agreed reluctantly to associate himself with the campaign against the Pindaris: he delayed the departure of his troops with the manifest purpose of watching events, and was only overawed into signing a treaty of co-operation by the display of force. The Peshwa, galled by the yoke which the treaty had fixed upon him, collected his forces and broke out into open hostility, attacking the British troops at Poona[1]; while at Nagpore the Raja declared from him as the head of the Maratha nation, and sent his own troops against the British Residency. On both occasions the Marathas were repulsed, though not without stout fighting at Nagpore; and as Holkar's army, which attempted to join the Peshwa, had been defeated at Mehidpore[2], the opposition of the Maratah powers to the Governor-General's policy of pacification soon came to an end. The Peshwa, pursued by the British flying columns, fought one or two sharp actions; but his troops were at last scattered, his forts were taken, and hehimself was pursued until he finally surrendered upon an assurance of suitable provision.[3] Lord Hastings had determined to exclude him and his family from any further share of influence or dominion in the Dekhan; and the greater part of his territories passed under the British sovereignty. The State of Satara was reconstituted out of the Peshwa's domains, and placed under the descendant of Shivaji, the original founder of the Maratha empire, whose dynasty had been supplanted by the Peshwas, a line of hereditary prime ministers. The Nagpore State had also to cede several important districts; and its military establishments passed under British control. The group of ancient Rajput chiefships which had been spoiled and ransomed for years by the Marathas and Amir Khan, with a number of minor principalities, were placed under the immediate protection and guarantee of the British government. The tributes claimed from the lesser States by the Maratha rulers were fixed and confirmed, upon the condition that payment should be made through the British treasury.

By these measures the Maratha rulership of the Peshwa was now finally extinguished, and the three leading families that had so often opposed us—Sindhia, Holkar, and the Bhonsla of Nágpore—were definitely bound over to keep the peace of India. The Pindaris, who were merely the remnants of the once flourishing predatory system, the dregs of the roving bands that had harried India during a century of anarchy, were dispersed or exterminated. These formidable bands melted away with wounderful rapidity. Lord Hastings notes in his diary that the actual campaign lasted only three months; and five years later Sir John Malcolm, to whom much of the credit for its success was due, reported from Central India that the Pindaris had been so effectually destroyed that their name was almost forgotten; and that hundreds of villages which had been deserted and roofless were now re-peopled. All this wide region had been so exhausted by nearly a century of intolerable disorder and political dislocation, that for the vast majority of the population a strong government was above all other things the prime necessity. The Maratha States were now shut up within carefully demarcated limits; the trades of marauding conquest and of mere brigandage on a large scale were abolished; the whole species vanished with the change of those conditions of government and society by which it had been engendered. The result was to secure for our own provinces unbroken immunity from the hostile attacks or plundering inroads to which they were always exposed so long as rapine and violence thrived in the centre of India.

But it would have been useless to put down these enormous evils unless precautions had been also taken against their revival. Henceforward it became the universal principle of public policy that every State in India (outside the Punjab and Sindh) should make over the control of its foreign relations to the British government, should submit all external disputes to British arbitration, and should defer to British advice regarding internal management so far as might be necessary to cure disorders or scandalous misrule. A British Resident was appointed to the courts of all the greater princes as the agency for the exercise of these high functions; while the subsidiary forces and the contingents furnished by the States, placed the supreme military command everywhere under British direction.

This great political settlement of central India—the disarmament and pacification of the military chiefships, and the adjustment of distinct relations of supremacy and subordination—established universal recognition of the cardinal principle upon which the fabric of British dominion in India has been built up. It completed and consolidated the policy of Lord Wellesley. The last shadow of interference by any European rival had now for the time faded away. The contest with the native States for ascendancy was finally decided, and not only the right but the duty of intervention for the security and tranquillity of the Indian people was now everywhere acknowledged, from the two seas northward upto Sindh and the Sutlej river. From the Sindh frontier at the mouths of the Indus river, down the west coast of the peninsula to Cape Comorin, and thence north-eastward again along the Bay of Bengal to the frontier of Burmah, the whole sea-line of India was under our authority. On the north we held a long belt of the Himalayan highlands, and our political jurisdiction extended to the western edge of the deserts bordering on upper Sindh and the Punjab. The largest, most important, and by far the most valuable portion of this region was now under our direct administration; the rest was under our sovereign influence. Taking the natural boundaries of India to be the ocean and the mountains, it may be said that our empire now commanded the whole circuit of its sea frontier, that it was securely settled upon a base in the

Himalayas, and that its western flank was to a great extent covered by the cis-Indus desert. On two sections, and two only, the frontier was still unstable and liable to disturbance—on the north-east, where the Burmese were advancing into Assam, and on the north-west, where the Sikh kingdom beyond the Sutlej had acquired formidable fighting strength under Ranjit Singh.

REFERENCES

1. November, 1817. See picturesque description, by an eye-witness, of this action in Grant Duff's *History of the Marathas*, vol. iii, ch. 18.
2. December, 1816.
3. June, 1818.

13

Peasantry and the Middle Class

The British conquest of India was different in character from all the provisions conquests of the country. In the past the change of rulers implied merely a change of the dynasty that exercised political authority over the people, but it did not affect the social fabric, the productive organisation, the property relations or the system of administration. Under British rule all this was altered, and a socio-economic revolution was started which culminated in the destruction of the old institutions and in the emergence of new social classes and forces.

Land Tenures

Now in countries where the economy is predominantly agricultural, the main source of the people's income is land, and the people pay a portion of their produce to their rulers for the services of law and order, defence and protection. In the pre-capitalist conditions of Indian society this payment acquired the character of sharing of the produce between the village and the government. The village stood for a co-operative group in which functions were fixed by tradition and custom and the individual was merged in the collectivity. But the ruler and the villager were interested principally in the use of the land and neither was worried about its ownership, for uncultivated waste land was as free as water and air. Under the circumstances the problem of individual rights scarcely emerged, rent and revenue were regarded as customary dues and the idea of taxation was absent. The relations based upon the exploitation of land and the distribution of its products determined the activity of the people and their economic and social relations. Therefore the structure of society and the form and functions of the State were determined by them.

The social framework of an agrarian economy and the production and distribution of wealth are conditioned by land tenures. The British introduced new forms of land tenures in India when they made their early settlements, and these brought in their wake a revolution in the economic and social relations in the countryside.

When the Diwani or the land-revenue administration of the lower provinces was transferred to the East India Company in 1765, the merchants of the Company were absolutely unprepared for the exercise of any administrative functions of this nature. Clive was obliged to continue the old arrangements for collecting revenue and he left the task to the Deputy Diwan of the Nawab unsatisfactory and Warren Hastings on assuming the governorship of the Presidency divested the Deputy of his functions in 1772. Then began a period of trial and error, involving a satisfactory system of land-revenue and fixing the responsibility for its payment. In the course of discussion many abstract questions were raised, for instance, who was the owner of agricultural land in India; who was ultimately responsible for the payment of revenue to the State; what was the share of the State in the produce of land; and were the zamindars or revenue farmers of Mughal times the proprietors owning land or merely intermediatries between the cultivator and the State?

Warren Hastings proceeded on the assumption that all land belonged to the sovereign, and that the intermediaries were merely agents who entitled only to a commission for collecting the rents from the cultivators. It followed that the existing zamindars could be allowed to continue only if they undertook to pay the amount of land-revenue that the bidders in the open market offered for it. In the auctions the old zamindars were treated on par with the fresh bidders so as to realise the maximum possible amount of land-revenue. The result was that most of the lands in Bengal were farmed out to the new bidders. Thus many of the old zamindar families were ousted, "an old-established link between government and the cultivator of the soil" was severed, and the old relationship between the zamindars and their tenants was seriously impaired.

The discomfiture of the zamindars was further aggravated by the excessiveness of the demand and the Harsh methods of realisation employed by the collectors under government orders. Not did the cultivators escape, for they were the final victims of over-assessment and of the greed of the new farmers. The effect was the wholesale ejectment and oppression of the ryots by the farmers— "defaulting zamindars, absconding farmers, and deserting ryots". This was the first breach in the rural organisation of India.

The deplorable conditions created by Hastings' measures brought into open discussion the assumptions regarding the ownership of land. Philip Francis propounded the view that the zamindar and not the sovereign was the real proprietor of land. He was opposed by Warren Hastings. The effect of these discussions was that from 1777 to 1783 new schemes were formulated which increased the importance of the zamindar at the expense of the cultivator. Then in 1793 Cornwallis decided to proclaim the Permanent Settlement of Bengal.

Under the Permanent Settlement of 1793 the zamindar was declared the absolute owner and proprietor of his estate. He was permitted to appropriate the whole of the rental to himself after defraying the dues of the government. In the beginning his demand was fixed, the rent realised by the landlord from the cultivator was left unsettled and unspecified. This provided the zamindar with the opportunity to squeeze the cultivator to the limit of the latter's capacity. In this way the immediate aim of the government to receive the economic rent from the soil was realised.

But eventually the Permanent Settlement benefited the zamindar more than the government. For, with the growth of population, the extension of cultivation, the rise of prices, and the growing scarcity of land, the zamindar's position improved. His title to the succession of an estate did not now require the execution of any deed of investiture or the payment of any *peshkash* or *nazrana* for its ratification, as had been the case in the past. He could transfer or alienate his landed property by sale, mortgage or gift without requiring the permission of any superior authority. He was relieved from the vexatious regulations of the Mughal administration, which very much limited his authority and obliged him to collect cesses over and above the land-revenge demand, and to furnish accounts of receipts and disbursements. But the British-created zamindar was divested of all political and public duties. He ceased to be the feudal aristocrat of the Mughals, and was transformed into a petty capitalist, "a mushroom gentleman."

The erstwhile revenue farmers became the proprietors of estates or landlords in the English sense of the term, possessing the same rights in land in India that the landowners did in Britain. For instance, while the State and the revenue farmers in India did have a claim to a part of the produce, they did not enjoy the right of dispossessing the cultivator of his holdings or raising the rent of the land arbitrarily. In fact, before the British conquest, the distinction between the rent paid to the landlords and the land-revenue collected by the State hardly existed in any part of the country. The Permanent Settlement destroyed the old relationship and invested the zamindars with proprietary rights.

The change in the status and functions of the zamindar or land-holder also affected the socio-political organisation of the Indian village, destroying eventually its isolation and self-sufficiency. Two principal results of the change were: (i) the creation of absolute property in land and its transfer into the hands of the new moneyed class which had no interest in land other than that of getting the maximum return on the investments, and (ii) the sub-infeudation of estates and holdings so that, as the competition for land increased, there emerged a chain of middlemen and intermediary rent-receiving interests between the original land lord and the cultivator.

The changes had begun with Murshid Quli Khan, who had replaced many old jagirdars and taluqadars with new farmers—largely Hindus. Thus at the time of the British conquest of the province, most of the zamindar families of Bengal could trace their origin only to the early days of his rule, although there were a few who could claim continued possession for more than a century or a century and a half. Warren Hastings caused a further revolution in the composition of this class by his land-revenue settlements. He introduced the method of assessment by auctioning the zamindaris. The severity of such assessments and the rigidity of collection worsened the situation. The enactment of the Permanent Settlement in 1793 completed their process. What ensued during the period of twenty-two years following the Settlement was that half of the landed property of Bengal changed hands by sale and most of the transferred lands went to new purchasers—the merchants and moneyed classes of Calcutta.

In this manner the first generation of zamindars created by the Permanent Settlement had a short shrift. The heaviness of assessment and the rigid law of sales proved most devastating for them. The following facts throw some light on the incidence of land-revenue in Bengal during the early British period:

			Land-revenue assessment
Todarmal's	assessment	(1596)	Rs. 107 lakhs
Murshid Quli Khan's	assessment	(1722)	Rs. 145 lakhs
Allahwardi Khan's	assessment	(1755)	Rs. 186 lakhs
Mir Qasim's	assessment	(1763)	Rs. 256 lakhs
Cornwallis'	assessment	(1793)	Rs. 286 lakhs

In interpreting this table it has to be remembered that the actual realisation under the Nawabs rarely came upto the assessed amount, for large arrears were left from year to year. On the other hand, the Company's arrears were never more than 2½ per cent. Thus "the land-revenge collected by the Mughal's agents in Bengal in 1764-65 amounted in value to £818,000; in 1765-66, the first year of East India Company's financial administration, it rose to £ 1,470,000. By the year 1790-91 it had been forced upto £2,860,000, and it was on the basis of that year's collection that the Permanent-Settlements were made."

In 1793, the Company's share of the total rental collected by the zamindars came to 89 per cent while in England, at the same time, the government demand amounted to between 5 to 10 per cent of the net rental. The share of the Indian zamindar was, in fact, the barest minimum to compensate him for the troubles of collection, for discharging obligations towards the government and for defraying his personal expenses.

The worst feature of the system of realisation was that the government revenue had to be deposited by the zamindar with rigid punctuality before sunset of the appointed day. If the payment was not made at the stroke of the hour, the zamindar was dispossessed, and a part or the whole of the estate was seized and sold by public auction. No excuse was entertained, no allowance was made for any difficulties. But while the government realised its dues at the point of bayonet, the zamindar had no power to constrain the cultivator to pay the rent in time. According to the Collector of Midnapur, "they all (the zamindars) say, that such a harsh and oppressive system was never before resorted to in this country; . . . The system of sales and attachments . . . has in the course of a very few years reduced most of the great zamindars in Bengal to distress and beggary; and produced greater change in the landed property of Bengal, than has, perhaps, ever happened in the same space of time, in any age or country, by the mere effect of internal regulations."[1]

The alienation of estates by the existing zamindars assumed assumed alarming proportions during the first few years of the Permanent Settlement. In 1796, lands carrying a rental of Rs. 28,70,061 on the roll and representing one-tenth of the three provinces were sold in one year.[2]

According to Baden-Powell, in the two years between 1796-7 and 1797-8, the sale of estates yielding 14 lakhs and 22.7 lakhs respectively was effected, and "by the end of the century the greater portion of the estates of the Nadiya, Rajshahi, Bishanpur and Dinajpur Rajas had been alienated. The Burdwan estate was seriously crippled and Birbhum zamindars completely ruined. A host of smaller zamindaris shared the same fate. In fact, it is scarely too much to say that, within the ten years that immediately followed the Permanent Settlement, a complete revolution took place in the constitution and ownership of the estates which formed the subject of that Settlement."[3]

The distress of the zamindars led the Government to help them by passing the notorious Regulations of 1799. The new law invested the zamindar with arbitrary powers to eject the cultivator, attach his agricultural stock and implements for non-payment of arrears, and start other proceedings against him with a view to pressing him to his utmost capacity. The law of 1799, on the one hand, opened the floodgates of exploitation of the helpless peasantry, and on the other, confirmed the revenue farmer as absolute proprietor of the estate.

The second effect of the changes wrought by the Permanent Settlement was the sub-infeudation of zamindari rights. The process was rapid. In thirty-nine districts of Bengal and Bihar, the number of estates multiplied in twenty years to the high figure of 1,10,456. Of these estates .4 per cent were large (over 20,000 acres each), 11 per cent of medium size (between 500 and 20,000 acres) and 88 per cent small (less than 500 acres). In England, on the countrary, 2.4 per cent of the estates were of the average area of 13 acres, 12 per cent of 180 acres, and 85.6 per cent of 4,260 acres.[4] In twenty years, the number of estates had doubled in the Patna division and trebled in the Tirhut division.

The tendency to subdivision was accentuated by the Regulations. Under the Mughals the head of the family was chosen as the zamindar. The British gave up the practice, and admitted the existence of private property in land, to which the Indian laws of inheritance applied. This soon led to the division of property among coparceners. The danger of the holdings becoming smaller in size and uneconomical to cultivate was realised as early as 1808 by the Court of Directors, but then no remedy was applied. As there was no alternative avenue of employment for the younger children of the zamindars, primogeniture could not be introduced in India, and the partition of property could not be prevented.

Not only the units of cultivation but the rent-collecting rights also came to be subdivided. The new zamindari rights proved valuable property and only twenty years after the Permanent Settlement, the zamindar's interest which amounted to no more than eleven per cent of the revenue assessment, were being sold for nearly twenty-eight years' purchase. "It follows, therefore," the Court of Directors wrote, "that the Zamindars' allowance must, from the beginning, have greatly exceeded their nominal amount, or that their emoluments must have subsequently been increased by arbitrary exaction, or that, in the interval, the agricultural prosperity of the country and the value of the landed property must have advanced with a rapidity, perhaps beyond example."[5] Be that as it may, the fact is that rent-receiving rights came to have a value which they did not possess before and became a commodity to be freely bought and sold in the market. Instead of the land being a source of production and livelihood for the cultivator, it became an object of speculative investment and a source of profit to the moneyed class. The zamindar farmed out his revenue to a middleman (*patnidar*) who, in turn, contracted with a sub-farmer (*dar patnidar*), and the latter, too, entered into dealings with a number of underlings (*seh patnidars*), and so on. A chain of rent-receiving interests was, thus, created and the evil assumed such ugly proportions that some holdings in Bengal are said to have got at the time of the abolition of zamindari as many as one hundred and fifty intermediary interests between the original landlord and the actual cultivator. Each sub-agent tried to squeeze the next man in the chain to the utmost and the burden of all exactions ultimately fell on the cultivator.

This revolution property relations was a fact of great consequence to the country. It led to the emergence of new social classes—(i) the rich landlrods who looked upon the land as their private property to be used for the a maximum monetary return, and (ii) the dispossessed cultivators who were left with nothing but their labour to sell to earn their livelihood.

The intermediaries were, of course, not all rich. The interest of each was small and their economic position, so far as income was concerned, was only slightly better than that of the cultivator. The process of sub-infeudation thus levelled the zamindar, the intermediary and the cultivator. Sir H. Strachey, commenting on the situation, remarked, "By us all is silently changed. The ryot, and the Zemindar, and the *gomashtah,* are by the levelling power of the Regulations very much reduced to an equality."[6]

There was consequently a clash of interests between the two classes; and what is more, there was nothing in common between them. The new landlords, in most cases, were businessmen who purchased land in search for profitable investment of surplus funds. They were unfamiliar with the affairs of cultiviation and were uninterested in the work of agricultural improvement, which was left to the cultivator who had neither the means, nor the knowledge, nor the will to carry it out.

In Europe, the agricultural revolution was brought about by investments and improvements in land made by enterprising landlords; in India, the landlords were mere rent-receiving absentee businessmen who cared more for their rents than for the improvement of agriculture. Instead of being natural leaders of the rural population, the landlords in India in the days of the Company played the role of agents to the foreign political power. Against a guarantee of regular payment of a fixed amount of land-revenue to the government, they purchased the right of exacting whatever they could from the politically defenceless and economically weak peasantry.[7] In the past the ryot in India had united in his own person the characters of labourer, frame and landlord; the British land-revenue system separated the characters of labourer and farmer from that of landlord, and thus created the two classes of the exploiters and the exploited.

Exploitation of the Peasantry and the Backwardness of Agriculture

One of the worst consequences of the new Regulations was the subjection of the cultivator to untold misery. The new landlords were unlike the old zamindars. They had no roots in the village. They were a class of rentiers who were only interested in the realisation of the profits on their investments. They were unjust to their ryots. At one stroke they wiped out the traditional rights of occupancy of the cultivators, reduced them to the position of tenants-at-will and subjected them to rack-renting and ejectment. They appropriated the whole surplus of the land, leaving just enough for the subsistence of the tenants.

In short, the system established by Cornwallis led to the creation of property in land in the Western sense. The frequent sales of the estates converted the ancient divided land rights into a marketable commodity, consolidated and exclusively owned by individuals. But the new proprietors of the estates were no longer and order bound to the interests of their villages and their ryots. Many purchasers of the estates were absent landlords living in cities, who never visited their estates and whose agents did not share the life of the tenants.

The Money-lender and the Ryotwari Settlements

The consequences which followed the introduction of the ryotwari system in Madras and Bombay were equally revolutionary. Only, instead of the zamindar, the peasant became the proprietor. The recognition of private property in land gave him the rights of lease, mortgage and sale rights which he had either not possessed in the past, or which were strictly circumscribed. Unfortunately, the acquisition of these valuable rights failed to improve his condition. For the government loaded him with such heavy demand as to leave property was reduced to a point where its purchase in the market became unprofitable.

The Government, however, soon realised the folly of exorbitant assessments, and undertook a process of downward revision, so that eventually the holder of land came to enjoy a surplus of rent over the revenue paid to the Government. Immediately land values registered an increase; property began to yield profit, and attract the investor. In Bengal, the moneyed class made outright purchases of zamindari rights; in Bombay and Madras it was in expedient to oust the cultivator, so the money-lender brought the lands and crops under control by loans. This became possible because the rigid revenue collection forced the cultivator to pay the Government demand even in a year when the crop had failed. His ignorance and improvidence were exploited by the money-lender who offered the facilities of credit on terms which enmeshed him in perpetual debt.

Once the farmer was in the money-lender's clutches, the latter used all the chicanery and cunning that he had at his command, to keep his victim in bondage. Interest rates were fixed so high that the cultivator was at best able to pay only the interest on the loan; the repayment of the principal with fluctuating and low levels of income was generally beyond his capacity. Even if a debtor by extraordinary industry and prudence tried to repay the loan and free himself, he was not allowed to do so, for the accounts were manipulated and the documents forged so that the arrears of interest accumulated more rapidly than their repayment by the debtor. The cultivator found himself helpless, for he could turn nowhere for protection. The courts were, of course, open to him, but under the judicial system introduced by the British, he had hardly any chance of success against his creditor. He did not possess the resources to fight a protracted law suit. And even when he ventured upon that course, he found himself confronted with documents, bearing his thumb impressions, about the contents of which he was generally ignorant. The courts, steeped in the British system of justice, accepted the documents and account books of the money-lender as valid proof of the debt and awarded decrees on such false evidence as the creditor produced in the court. If the cultivator did not go to the court, the money-lender kept his lien on the produce of the land which he purchased from the debtor at less than the market prices. But if the cultivator went to the court, he usually found himself deprived of his holding in discharge of his obligations to the money-lenders. The zamindari system had revolutionised the relations between landlords (revenue farmers) and tenants; the ryotwari system revolutionised the relations between creditor and debtor and thus introduced another grasping and exploiting element into the rural society.

Henceforth there began a perpetual struggle between the two classes, money-lenders and cultivators, the former trying to obtain the larger proportion of the annual produce of the industry of the latter. The money-lender helped by British rulers and British laws[8] easily succeeded in achieving his object. As Captain Wingate remarked in 1852, "this miserable struggle between creditor and debtor is thoroughly debasing to both . . . It is disheartening to contemplate, and yet it would be weakness to conceal the fact that this antagonism of classes and degration of the people, which is fast spreading over the land, is the work of our laws and our rule. The corruption and impoverishment of the mass of the people for the enriching of a few has already made a lamentable advance in some districts, and is in progress in all, and the evil is clearly traceable, in my opinion, to the enormous power which the law places in the hands of the creditor." As to the class of money-lenders, Captain Wingate went onto testify that "a set of low usurers is fast springing up, by whom small sums are lent for short period at enormous rates of interest to the very lowest of the population who have not credit enough to obtain advances from the more respectable of village bankers."[9]

In some districts in the Deccan and in northern India, the earlier settlement officers made a mahalwari or joint-village settlement. This type of settlement was in conformity with the ancient practice of the country. But, from the very beginning, the intention with regard to this form of settlement was to treat it as a transitional measure and establish ultimately the ryotwari system instead. As the Madras Board of Revenue observed in 1818: "The village settlement, however, though it commenced by fixing the assessment on each village and making over the lands to the people collectively or to the head of the village, expressly contemplated its gradual subdivision and distribution, not indeed upon each field but upon the entire lands of each Ryot, and consequently the gradual conversion of the collective into an individual settlement wherever the interests of the village community would admit of this change. One of the chief advantages of the ryotwari system was thus engrafted on the village settlement, but the measure was not to be universally or immediately introduced. The people were not to be constrained to adopt an arrangement, which, however abstractedly expedient, was in a great number of cases at variance with the landed tenures, the ancient institutions, and the circumstances of the inhabitants. It was hoped that as their means improved, the obstacles to this arrangement would be overcome, and accordingly it was to be rather promoted than introduced by the collectors."[10]

The Emergence of the Indian Middle Class

The intended political result of the ryotwari system may best be stated in the words of Thackeray. In defending the system he observed: "As we generally see Indian affairs with English, eyes, and carry European notions into Indian practice, it may be necessary to say a little respecting the gradation of ranks, or in other words, the inequality of conditions which is supposed by some to be necessary in a well ordered society....

"This equality of conditions in respect to wealth in land; this general distribution of the soil among the yeomanry, therefore, if it be not most adapted to agricultural improvement, is best adapted to attain improvement in the state of property, manners and institutions, which prevail in India; and it will be found still more adapted to the situation of the country, governed buy a few strangers, where pride, high ideas, and ambitious thoughts must be stifled. It is very proper that in England, a good share of the produce of earth should be appropriated to support certain families in affluence, to produce senators, sages and heroes, for the service and defence of the state, or, in other words, that great part of the rent should go to an opulent nobility and gentry who are to serve their country in parliament, in the army and navy, in the departments of science and liberal professions. The leisure, independence, and high ideas which the enjoyment of this rent affords, has enabled them to raise Britain to the pinnacle of glory. Long may they enjoy it;—but in India the haughty spirit, independence, and deeply thought, which the possession of great wealth sometimes gives, ought to be suppressed. They are directly adverse to our power and interest. The nature of things, past experience of all governments, renders it unnecessary to enlarge on this subject. We do not want generals, statesmen and legislators;

we want industrious husbandmen . . . Considered politically, therefore, the general distribution of land among a number of small proprietors, who can not easily combine against Government, is an object of importance."[11]

As Mr. Thackeray wrote, it was not part of the British intentions to create and promote a class which provides "senators, sages and heroes for the defence of the State." But laws do not always work in accordance with the wishes of their makers. The British rule by adopting the new land and civil laws produced a social class which ultimately destroyed the very power which had created it.

The land laws introduced by the British were thus responsible for the disruption of the old agrarian structure and the creation of a new social order. The new rent-receiving landlords, money-lenders and businessmen came to form the nucleus of the new middle class that emerged in the country in the nineteenth century. They, together with the traditional castes whose occupation was study and teaching or government service, were the first to avail themselves of the benefits of English education. It was to the educated of this heterogeneous group that the lawyer, the teacher, the civil servant, the merchant and the industrialist of the nineteenth century belonged. They constituted the country's intelligentsia which formed the link between the East and the West, and provided political leadership to the Indians. Their aspirations and desires became the aspirations and desires of India.

On the other and, the dispossessed cultivation, the village artisans and the village menials, who had lost their customary ties with the agricultural population on the decay of the village communities and on the introduction of competition instead of custom in the determination of the relations between the classes, came to constitute the landless wage-earning class—the country's proletariat. According to Karl Marx, "the forms or conditions of production are the fundamental determinant of social structure which in turn breed attitudes, actions, and civilisations."[12] In India, however, it was the change in the property relations which caused the "social revolution."[13]

The Indian middle class historically had, therefore, a different origin from that of its counterpart in the West. There the middle class was mainly composed of merchants and industrialists together with the intellectuals and the people belonging to the learned professions: these classes did not depend upon agriculture for their livelihood, but some of them might purchase estates for the sake of prestige and profit. The middle class in India, on the other hand, had its roots in the agrarian system of the country and it largely lived on the fruits of agricultural industry. So far as the exploitation of the peasantry was concerned, the new class gave support to the ruling power and was content to serve as its subordinate agency.

The earlier years of British rule—the period upto the middle of the nineteenth century—were marked by a spirit of cooperation between the British rulers and the neo-rich—landlords, traders and money-leaders. But this cooperation could not last long. The natural instinct of this class was to seek openings in commerce, industry, and the civil service; but here it found itself faced with stiff opposition from the middle classes of Britain that constituted the main power behind British rule in India. The national movement in India was an expression of the conflict between the middle classes of the two countries, one aspiring for wealth and influence, the other already in possession of them.

The new class was imbued with the profit motive like its counterpart in Europe but in the pursuit of that aim it was balked by the British monopoly in trade and business, and by the lack of means and conditions of industrial development. It was largely an urban class with urban interests. It developed a thrist for Western education, a hankering for government service and a keenness for the learned professions. It imitated blindly the Western ways, customs and manners of their rulers. But it was neither respected by the rulers, nor loved by the rural masses for whose welfare and improvement it did nothing. Yet this class supplied the force which cracked the cake of custom. It provided the corps of the intelligentsia who became the spearhead of the movement for India's emancipation. But this was a totally unforseen consequence of the land-laws introduced by the British.

Disintegration of Village Communities

The land-revenue system established by the British in India and the assumption of all judicial and administrative functions by government officials destroyed the powers of the old intermediaries—zamindars and farmers, and of the village Panchayats. This led to the break-up of that ancient social frame-work within which the agricultural population had lived for centuries. Later administrators looked upon this result with disfavour and a strong plea for the preservation of village communities in northern India was made by Sir Charles Metcalfe in his famous minute. He wrote, "The village communities are little Republics, having nearly everything that they want within themselves, and almost independent of any foreign relations, . . . they seem to last where nothing else lasts." He added: "the union of the village communities each one contributed more than any other to the preservation of the people of India through all revolutions and changes which the have suffered, and it is in a high degree conducive to their happiness and to the enjoyment of a great portion of freedom and independence. I wish, therefore, that the village constitutions may never be disturbed, and I dread everything that has a tendency to break them up."[14] An attempt was made to translate this into action by Robert Bird in his settlement operations in northern India. But the mahalwari settlement, in this pat of the country, failed to check the process of destruction of the village communities, for although the assessment was fixed on the village as a whole, individual rights in the land were recognised and guaranteed by the State. The growing pressure of population on agriculture made land valuable property and its price steadily increased. The opening of the market for agricultural produce and the growth of cash crops by the farmer also produced similar effects. These developments imposed a heavy strain on the rural organisation and the "village Republics" which, to Metcalfe, had appeared "to last where nothing else lasts", faded out of existence in the mahalwari areas of the north in the same way as they had done under the zamindari system in Bengal and the ryotwari system in the south.

With the disintegration of the old village organisation, the social bonds that had held different elements of the rural society together were snapped. The joint family system and the Panchayats received shattering blows. Cooperation was replaced by competition. Prices, rents and wages, all came to be determined by contrast between the buyers and the sellers. The collective life of the village gave way to individualism.

The modes of production and the structure of the rural economy also underwent fundamental changes. Agricultural production, instead of catering to the needs of the village population, came to be adapted to the requirements of the external market. The farmer's need for money increased and to procure it he began to produce cash crops. In the past he had suffered from fluctuations in his income from climatic causes only; he was now exposed to all the vicissitudes of fortune caused by market fluctuations. A fall in the price of agricultural produce in any art of the world became, for him, as much a matter of grave concern as a failure of his crops caused by drought. The exigencies of the payment of revenue demand at the fixed time, as well as his other annual needs for cash, forced him to part with his produce immediately after the harvest. The agriculturist was thus drawn into the vortex of the money economy, but partly because of his small holdings, partly because of the heavy assessments and partly due to the rack-renting by the landlord and the usurious charges of the money-lender, he failed to benefit from the change. The advantage was mainly reaped by the village grain dealer and by the commission agent in the produce market.

Nor was the agriculturist alone in suffering the ill effects of the changes wrought in the rural economy of the country. The opening of the village to foreign imports gave a deadly blow to the village crafts and industries. The village artisan lost his custom and the market for his wares. From an industrial worker he was transformed into a landless labourer seeking work in agriculture, sometime as a tenant and at other times as a wage-labourer. Next to the uprooted peasantry, the weavers and other village artisans came to constitute the most important part of the rural proletariat in the first half of the nineteenth century.

Heavy Assessment and the Backwardness of Agriculture

While the land tenures introduced by the British broke up the old rural organisation, the heavy assessments held up agricultural progress and reduced the cultivating classes to a state of abject poverty and resourcelessness.

The theory of the early British rulers was that, unlike Europe, agricultural land in India belonged to the ruler, that by the right of conquest the ownership of all land in India had come to vest in the East India Company, and that, as the overload, the government was entitled to the whole of the economic rent—the Ricardian surplus—which, for any piece of land, was found by deducting the cost of production from the value of crops raised.

At the time of the Permanent Settlement in Bengal, the Government demand was fixed at 89 per cent of the estimated economic rent. The remaining eleven per cent was left to the landlords as compensation for the labour of collecting land-revenue. In northern India, under the provisions of Regulation VII of 1822, the revenue demand was pitched at 80 per cent of the net assets of land.[15]

In the Bombay Presidency, under the experimental settlements prior to the first regular settlement of 1824-28, the demand had been fixed so high that even the Governor was constrained to write in respect of Broach, that "the assessment . . . on the plan here adopted is utterly impossible.

An increase of four lakhs and a half has taken place this last year: a circumstance that I can not contemplate with pleasure, while the sources of the revenue and the principles of the increase are so completely in the dark."[16] In the Ahmadabad district the granting of villages to the highest bidders had the "tendency to strain the revenue to the highest pitch."[17] The districts of the Deccan and Khandesh had a similar story to tell about the burden of land-revenue. Systematic surveys and settlement operations were commenced by Pingle in 1824. The work was abandoned in 1828. In fixing the land-revenue demand, the principle of limiting the government share of fifty-five per cent of the net produce was accepted. But this was only on paper. In actual practice, the demand worked out at a much higher proportion of the net assets. This was because the measurement of land was "grossly faulty", and "the estimates of produce" on which the demand was based were highly exaggerated.[18] In the re-survey that was started in 1835 by Messrs. Goldsmid and Wingate, the very basis of assessment was changed: the State instead of demanding a share in the produce of land came to levy a tax on the estimated value of the land.

In Madras, in the earlier settlements, the government demand was fixed at 45 to 55 per cent of the gross produce of the land. Assuming the cost of production to work out at half the gross produce, the assessment in the Presidency took away the whole of the economic rent. This was found oppressive and the Madras Government recommended to the Court of Directors to limit the assessment to one-third of the gross produce. The Court, however, expressed "a doubt whether a third, or any other proportion of the produce, can be assumed as an invariable standard of assessment."[19] The principle of limiting the land-tax to one-third of the gross produce, was however, ultimately accepted for this Presidency. But, on the assumption that the cost of production is about one-half of the gross produce, the rate of tax works out at $66\frac{2}{3}$ per cent of the economic rent of the land. In smaller farms where the cost of production is comparatively high, it would amount to much more; sometimes almost the whole of the net assets of the farmer were claimed.

With such high rates of taxation, it was impossible for capital to accumulate in agriculture or any incentive to be left for the land-owner to make improvements in land. In the permanently settled areas, the zamindar considered his function to be limited to the collection of his rent which was unrelated to the produce of land. The rent, in these areas, depended on the bargain that could be struck with the tenants, rather than on the increase in the produce of the land. The landlord rack-rented the tenants and appropriated to himself the whole of the economic surplus, thereby leaving little for meeting the vicissitudes of seasons and fortunes. In the ryotwari areas, the Government played the role of the rack-renting landlord. The land-revenue demand in Madras and Bombay Presidencies, as also in the temporarily settled mahawlari tracts of northern India, was so excessive as to devour the whole of the surplus production of land.[20] Agriclutural progress was consequently held up for want of capital in the hands of the cultivating population.

It is not difficult to explain the reasons for the adoption of an oppressive land-revenue policy. They lay in the anxiety of the East India Company to meet the cost of their conquests and to support the expensive system of their administration. The gross expenditure of the East India Company was £10 million in 1799-1800 and £12.4 million in 1801-2. It showed almost continuous increase thereafter, reaching the high figure of £24.2 millions in 1825-26. With the arrival of Lord William Bentinck in India in 1828, a policy of retrenchment and economy in expenditure was carried through over the next six years and the annual expenditure was brought down to £16 million in 1835-36. But it again showed an upward trend and by the time of the Revolt of 1857 it had reached the high figure of £32 million.

India was called upon to bear this heavy cost of administration with her declining resources. With her trade and industry ruined by the foreign conqueror[21] the burden of taxation had to be borne by the none too-prosperous agriculturist. In 1792-93 the land-revenue demand for the Bengal Presidency amounted to £3.1 million; in 1835-36 it had risen to £3.3 million. Since the province was permanently settled, the increase was due mainly to the extension of cultivation. In Madras, Bombay and the North-West Provinces, however, it was mostly the higher assessments that caused the increase. In 1810-11, for instance, the revenue receipts in Madras amounted to just a little over £1 million; in 1825-26 the figure had risen to a little under £4 million—a fourfold increase in a period of fifteen years. The Bombay Presidency tells the same tale. The land-revenue receipts in the Presidency rose from £800,000 in 1817 to £1,150,000 in 1818 and to £1.86 million in 1837-38.[22] The land-revenue was the backbone of Indian finance in the days of the East India Company and its rate was determined more with an eye on the requirements of the government than by considerations of what the peasantry cold pay. It is little wonder that under such an in equitous system of taxation the peasantry was ruined and agriculture declined to a state of extreme backwardness.

"Agrarian troubles generally spring from a conflict between a vitiated land system and the passion for land from which the most thriftless classes of an agricultural society are not free."[23] The Indian cultivator, even under such adverse circumstances, stuck to the soil and toiled and sweated for his subsistence in his unremunerative occupation, not so much because of his "passion for land" as for the perfectly understandable reason that he had no alternative opening for emloyment. A growing population was condemned to subsist on a declining agriculture. The misery of the masses, the increase in the incidence of famine and disease, and the chronic unemployment in the country were the inevitable results of the system.

The British fiscal policy and land system destroyed the ancient institutions and the rural organisation under which the Indian cultivator had lived for centuries. The shell which had protected the social organisation from all external influence was thus broken and the way was opened for the establishment of a society organised on the bases of private property, individual enterprise, accumulation of capital, and technological progress.

REFERENCES

1. Letter dated February 12, 1802, vide *Fifth Report* (Firminger, Vol. I), p. 108.
2. Mill, *History of British India,* Vol. V, p. 367.
3. Macneile, J., *Memorandum on the Revenue Administration of the Lower Provinces of Bengal* (Calcutta 1873), p. 9.
4. Phillips, H.A.D., *Our Administration of India* (1886), p. 5, footnote, table (percentages workd out by the author).
5. Revenue Letter to . . .
6. Mill, *History of British India,* Vol. V, pp. 371-72.
7. That private property in land and a new landowning class were created in India with a view to securing the government revenue, may be seen from the following statement of Thomas Munro, Principal Collector of Ceded Districts (vide para 2 of the letter dated August 15, 1807: Extract Proceedings, Board of Revenue at Fort St. George, February 4, 1808 (*Selection of Papers from Records at East India House,* Vol. I, 1820, pp. 94-95)

   "There is some difficulty in ascertaining what proportion of the gross or net produce of the soil ought to be left to the landholder, in order to render the land private property and saleable, so as to be security for the rent of the Government. Had the public revenue in India ever been paid by the private landowners, the share of the produce which was then received by the sovereign might now have served as a standard to regulate the demand. *But nothing can be plainer than that private landed property has never existed inIndia, excepting onthe Malabar coast."*
8. Captain Wingate, Revenue Survey Commissioner, Bomaby, showed remarkable insight into the problem of the deterioration of the relations between creditor and debtor when he explained how debts of the agriculturists had increased in the Deccan under British Rule (vide letter No. 319 of September 24, 1852, from Captain G. Wingate to the Registar of the Courts of Sadar Diwani Adalat, Bombay). "It may then be affirmed that for all practical purposes, the relations between debtor and creditor were

determined under the Mahratas without reference to any legal means of enforcing payment of debts. The creditor trusted chiefly to the honesty and good faith of his debtor, and it followed as a matter of necessity that loans were sparingly granted unless upon the security of property, such as jewels left in pawn, or a mortgage on land or houses or standing crops. In agricultural villages, the relations between the money-lender and the cultivators were those of mutual interest and confidence. The *Bania* advanced the cultivator as much as he felt satisfied that he could and would pay, but no more, and at no higher rate of interest than was sanctioned by usage and public opinion. If the *Bania* had insisted on a higher rate than was deemed equitable, it is not probable that his debtors would have paid up their instalments with usual regularity, and he had no means of compulsion at his command. Under these arrangements, the village money-lender and the ryot worked in harmony, and both alike shared prosperity and adversity together.

"Under our system this happy and mutually advantageous state of affairs has been completely overtuned. The prosperity of the ryot is no longer necessary to the prosperity of the village money-lender. The latter has no longer occasion to trust to the good faith or honesty of the former. Mutual confidence and goodwill have been succeeded by mutual distrust and dislike. The money-lender has the ever-ready expedient of a suit at law to obtain complete command over the person and property of his debtor. It becomes the interest of the former to reduce the latter to state of hopeless indebtedness in order that he may be able to appropriate the whole fruits of his industry beyond what is indispensable to a mere existence. This he enabled without difficulty to do. So long as a ryot is not much involved the money-lender is ready to afford him the means of indulging in any extravagance and without troubling him at all about future repayment. The debt may lie over and he may choose his own time for repayment. The simple and thoughtless ryot is easily inveigled into the snare, and only becomes aware of his folly when the coils are fairly around him and escape is impossible. From that day forward, he becomes the bondsman of his creditor. The latter takes care that he shall seldom do more than reduce the interest of his debt. Do what he will, the poor ryot can never get rid of the principal. He toils that another may rest, and sows that another may reap." (Vide *Deccan Riots Commission Report,* Vol. II, pp. 87-88)

9. Letter No. 319, dated September, 24, 1852, to the Registrar, Sadar-Diwani Adalat, Bombay, vide *Deccan Riot: Commission Report*, Vol. II, pp. 88-89.

10. Minute dated January 5, 1818, para 286, vide *Selection of Papers from the Records at East India House* (1820), Vol. I, p. 946.
11. Report of Mr. Thackeray on Malabar, Canara and Ceded Districts, dated August 4, 1807, vide Firminger, *Fifth Report,* Vol. III, pp. 575-576.
12. See Schumpeter, *Capitalism, Socialism and Democracy* (second edition, 1947), p. 12.
13. Karl Marx, 'British Rule in India', article in the *New York Daily Tribune,* June 10, 1853: Marx Engels, *Selected Works,* Vol. I (Moscow edition), p. 317.
14. Minute dated November 7, 1830 (Quoted in R. C. Dutt Economic History under Early British Rule).
15. Letter from the Governor-General to the Court of Directors, dated April 7, 1831, para 107, see R. C. Dutt, *Economic History under Early Britiish Rule,* pp. 384-85.
16. Minute dated April 25, 1821, *Selection of Papers from Records at East India House,* Vol. III (1826), p. 662.
17. Minute of the Governor of Bombay (Elphinstone) dated April 6, 1821, para 45, vide *Selection of Papers, op. cit.,* p. 686.
18. *Bombay Administration Report,* 1872-73, p. 41.
19. Revenue letter from the Court of Directors to Madras, dated December 12, 1821, Para 34, *Selection of papers from the Records at East India House,* Vol. III (1826) p. 523.
20. "With the introduction of the ryotwari system middlemen, the chief stay of indigent cultivators, have disappeared with their capital: . . . But the government owns and appropriates the only surplus production of the land, while the ryotwari cultivators are destinated to the misery which cannot be avoided in the absence of capital." —*Calcutta Review,* Vol. LXXV (1863), p. 119.
21. For a detailed account of the decline of trade and industry, see Chapter X, *infra.*
22. Dutt, R. C., *Economic History of India,* etc., p. 357.
23. *Calcutta Review,* Vol. XXXVIII (1863), The Land System of India, p. 111.

Index

Index

G

H

I

J

K

L

□□□